# The Hymns of St. Louis Marie de Montfort

# God alone II

# God alone II

## The Hymns of St. Louis Marie de Montfort

Montfort Publications Bay Shore, NY 11706

First Printing

Printed in Canada
ISBN 0-910984-63-8

Design: Ken Sell

# Foreword

**Father Gerald J. Fitzsimmons, SMM**

Louis De Montfort is called many things: Saint, Apostle of Mary, Founder, Author, Ascetic, Mystic and rightly so, he was all these. But first and foremost he was a working missionary, an itinerant preacher, spending his life ministering to God's People. Everything he did, in his life, was about serving God's People, so that they might know who they are, as loved and redeemed in Christ's blood. St Louis writes, "Is it possible for persons to love that which they do not know? Can they ardently love that which they know imperfectly? Why then is the adorable Jesus, Eternal and Incarnate Wisdom loved so little? Because He is not known, or known but little" (LEW 8). Montfort spent his entire life; every breath he drew was directed to serving the people so that they might know the adorable Jesus. Because, "TO KNOW JESUS CHRIST, ETERNAL AND INCARNATE WISDOM, IS TO KNOW ENOUGH; TO KNOW EVERYTHING AND NOT TO KNOW HIM, IS TO KNOW NOTHING" (LEW 11).

Montfort wanted the knowledge of Jesus, Eternal and Incarnate Wisdom not just to inform but also to take root in the hearts of the people. These Hymns are the tools of the missionary Montfort, going about his pastoral ministry. Pope John Paul II, in his Letter to the three Congregations founded by St Louis, refers to the whole body of Montfort's Works, including the Hymns and says, "What we are dealing with is a *lived tradition*, of remarkable ascetical and mystical depth, expressed in a lively and ardent style, which often appeals to images and symbols. Since the days of St Louis Marie, Marian theology has nevertheless developed a great deal, thanks above all to the decisive approach taken by the Second Vatican Council. Montfort's teaching, therefore, must be re-read and interpreted today in the light of the Council while retaining substantially the same value" (JP II Letter #1) This volume of **God Alone II: The Hymns of St Louis De Montfort** makes available, for the first time, in English, all the hymns of Montfort, so that we can, as the Holy Father asks, re-read and interpret for today this lived tradition, and drink more deeply of the ascetical and mystical depth of Montfort's teachings. So that Jesus, Eternal and Incarnate Wisdom might take deeper root in our hearts.

O Jesus alive in Mary,
Come dwell in us and reign

Pour out your life in us,
No more to live but for you (Hymn 111)

*There are many people to thank but I want to especially thank Fr. Patrick Gaffney, SMM and Sr. Rosemary Gaffney, DW whose work and dedication produced this volume. They are not only blood siblings but also spiritual son and daughter of St Louis De Montfort, as a Montfort Missionary and a Daughter of Wisdom; it's all in the family.*

Father Gerald J. Fitzsimmons, SMM
Provincial Superior
U.S. Province - Montfort Missionaries

# Introduction

**Father Patrick Gaffney, S.M.M.**
**Sister Rosemary Gaffney, D.W.**

Thanks especially to Pope John Paul II's repeated praise for Saint Louis Marie Grignion de Montfort (1673-1716),[1] the fame of this Breton preacher of parish missions has spread throughout the Church. The solid teaching of this "excellent theologian" (as the Holy Father names him) has prompted a growing number of the hierarchy and of the faithful to request that he be named a "Doctor of the Church."

## A. The Works Of St Louis De Montfort

For most Catholics, the name Louis de Montfort is strongly connected to Marian devotion, more specifically to his well-known masterpiece, *True Devotion to the Blessed Virgin Mary.* And rightly so. However, in order to grasp the full depth of his spirituality, his other works cannot be ignored. The 1987 volume, *God Alone: The Collected Writings of St. Louis-Marie de Montfort* [2] (GA) brought together most of his works:

*The True Devotion to the Blessed Virgin Mary.* (TD)
*The Love of the Eternal Wisdom.* (LEW)
*The Secret of Mary.* (SM)
*Letter to the Friends of the Cross.* (FC)
*The Admirable Secret of the Most Holy Rosary.* (SR)
*Letters.* (L)
*Prayer for Missionaries.* (PM)
*Rule of the Missionary Priests of the Company of Mary.* (RM)
*Letter to the Members of the Company of Mary.* (LCM)
*Rule of the Daughters of Wisdom.* (RW)
*Letter to the People of Montbernage.* (LPM)
*The Rules* [of the Forty-four Virgins (RV). Of the White Penitents (RP), of the Penitents' pilgrimage to Our Lady of Saumur (PS)].
*Short Excerpt from the Book of Hymns.* (H)
*St. Louis de Montfort's Last Will and Testament.* (W)

---

[1] There is a need of additional English biographies of St Louis de Montfort. Benedetta Papàsogli's life of the saint, originally written in Italian, has been well-received in its English translation: *Montfort A Prophet for our Times*, Edizioni Monfortane, Roma 1991. A popular account of Montfort's life is Eddie Doherty's *Wisdom's Fool*, Montfort Publications, Bay Shore, N.Y. 1998 (4th printing).
[2] Montfort Publications, Bay Shore, N.Y. 11706

*Morning and Night Prayers.*[3] (MP; NP)
*Excerpts from the Book of Sermons.*[4] (S)
*Rules on Voluntary Poverty in the Early Church.*[5] (RVP)
*Four Short Meditations on the Religious Life.*[6] (MRL)
*Dispositions for a Happy Death.*[7] (HD)

The entire book, *God Alone*, contains only a half of all his actual text. This present publication remedies the situation by offering to the English-speaking world the full 24,000 lines of his hymns or songs.

**B. The Utility of St Louis-Marie's Hymns in English**

Although some of the *Cantiques* were published by Father de Montfort in 1711 as biographies attest,[8] it is only lately that the

---

[3] Although the original manuscript has been lost, the 1859 General Chapter of the Company of Mary spoke of these prayers as "a faithful copy of the author's own manuscript." The text is followed by the words: "Conformed to the manuscript of the Venerable Montfort which has recently been printed." The *Little Crown* (part of *Morning Prayer*) is a form of prayer used in the 17th century. The final prayer of the *Little Crown* evokes ideas and expressions of the Middle Ages. *Night Prayer* 's structure was commonly used at the time of St Louis de Montfort. Cf. *GA* pp. 509-510. Each of the works found in *GA* are preceded by an important informative introduction.

[4] Although an important excerpt of *The Book of Sermons* is found in *GA*, it is published in its entirety: *Le Livre des Sermons du Père de Montfort, Documents et Recherches VI*, Centre International Montfortain, Rome 1983. The saint's *Notebook*, (as such not found in *GA*) compiled for the most part when he was the seminarian-librarian at St. Sulpice, is made up of references to works which treat principally of Jesus and Mary. The manuscript has been mimeographed with explanatory introduction by Peter H. Eyckeler, s.m.m., in 1952. In 2000 the Postulator General of the Company of Mary issued a new presentation of the volume based on Eyckeler's work. Only a relatively few copies were made of both the 1952 and also of the 2000 "editions" of the *Notebook*.

[5] These rules are found in the saint's *Notebook* and were copied from some unknown author.

[6] Appended to a copy of the *Secret of Mary* and is doubtfully a work of Montfort.

[7] When the dying Father de Montfort dictated his last will and testament, Father René Mulot transcribed it on a few blank pages of a printed pamphlet, *Dispositions for a Happy Death*. This short work has five sections, three of which are from J. Nouet who died in 1680, and another section is obviously not Montfort's. The one section left – the first one – is doubtfully from the pen of St Louis-Marie.

[8] Cf. M l'abbé Pauvert, *La vie du Vénérable Louis-Marie Grignion de Montfort, Missionnaire Apostolique, Instituteur des Missionnaires de Saint-Esprit et des Filles de la Sagesse*, Henri Oudin, Paris-Poitiers 1875, p. 620. No copies of this first edition of the hymns has been found. There have been many editions of Montfort's *cantiques* in French.

*Book of Hymns* has been published in other languages.[9] Probably because of the growing influence of St Louis Marie, there is a increasing interest in his songs.

**General Purpose**: The overarching purpose of this work is to render faithfully into English each line of these 164 French *cantiques*. More than half of these poems contain 100 or more verses and some even go beyond 400 verses; hymn 127, a stage production, stretches out to 630 verses. Among the shortest, only 23 have less than 50 verses. Of course not all the hymns are of equal worth, few of them are easy reading, not all of them can even be understood at one sitting. Montfort's stanzas often require some meditative digging before gold is struck.

Translators are traitors, as the Italian proverb goes. Nonetheless, the task has been accomplished not only joyfully but with, we hope, enough success to let the reader experience the great beauty and depth of Father de Montfort's authentic spirit.

Although there are a number of these translated stanzas which – with a little tweaking - fell into some type of rhyme or beat, the texts here presented are not, as is evident, poetically polished. That needed task will be founded on this faithful rendition of these three hundred year old songs, originally destined for the simple and earthy folk of northwestern France during the *Grand Siècle* of King Louis XIV.

In this volume, authentic fidelity to Montfort's text extends not only to each stanza but also, for the most part, to each line. The *Oeuvres Complètes de saint Louis-Marie Grignion de Montfort* (*OC*)[10] was used as the source. The critical study of the *cantiques* by F. Fradet[11] plus the additional study by M. Gendrot in *OC* make it clear that these hymns have been authored by the Father from Montfort.[12] The basic difference between Fradet's edition and Gendrot's is that the former arranges the hymns by themes, the latter by their order in the four manuscripts of *cantiques* preserved at the Generalate of the Montfort

---

[9] S. Luigi Maria da Montfort, *Opere Volume II, Cantici,* Edizioni Monfortane, Roma 2002; San Luis Maria Grignion de Montfort, *Obras Completas*, Ediciones Montfortianas, Centro Mariana Monfortiano, Bogota, Colombia 2003

[10] Editions du Seuil, Paris 1966.

[11] *Les Oeuvres du Bx de Montfort: Ses Cantiques,* Librairie Mariale, Pontchateau 1929.

[12] Concerning the authenticity of the hymns, cf. Dorio M. Huot, "Il *Corpus* Degli Scritti di San Luigi Maria di Montfort" in *Spiritualità Monfortana 2,* Centre International Montfortain, Roma 2003, pp 59-95.

Missionaries in Rome. Gendrot's arrangement is now the *editio typica* and has been followed in this English version as it has in other translations.

This volume is part of a trilogy: 1. *God Alone: The Collected Writings of St Louis-Marie de Montfort (GA).* 2. This volume, *God Alone II: The Hymns of St Louis-Marie de Montfort (H).* 3. *Jesus Living in Mary: Handbook of the Spirituality of St. Louis-Marie de Montfort* (*JLM*).[13] All three are indispensable for anyone interested in plumbing the spiritual way of the Breton missionary. The first two contain the works of the saint; the *Handbook* quite thoroughly examines 89 themes of montfort spirituality, from *Adoration* to *Zeal.*

**The Montfort Congregations**. This translation of the Hymnal of Father de Montfort is needed for the formation of the novices and the professed members of the congregations founded by the saint: The Missionaries of the Company of Mary (Montfort Missionaries), The Daughters of Wisdom, and the teaching Brothers of Saint Gabriel. English is the *lingua franca* of international affairs with the consequence that it is the second language in many non-anglophone countries. A number of those territories are blessed with vocations to the Montfort family and they, along with native English speaking confreres, will undoubtedly benefit from this translation of the founder's verses.

**The Larger Montfort Family**. However, the purpose of publishing the hymnal extends far beyond the core Montfort family. It includes the thousands upon thousands who have made their consecration to Jesus living in Mary, as taught by the saint. Also, Frank Duff's Legion of Mary is founded on the teachings of Louis de Montfort. The French School of Spirituality (also called "Spirituality of the 17th Century," or "the Berullian School of Spirituality") into which the young Louis Grignion was immersed during his eight years of study with the Sulpicians, counts among its followers not only the sons of Jean-Jacques Olier but also the Eudists, the Oratorians, the Religious of the Good Shepherd, the Little Sisters of the Poor, the Christian Brothers of St. John-Baptist de la Salle, and many other religious orders, both old and new. The songs of Louis de Montfort, "the last of the great Berullians,"[14] opens a new depth of the incarnational vision of the French School.

---

[13] Montfort Publications, Bay Shore N.Y. 1994.

[14] This expression of H. Bremond is examined by R. Deville in *L'Ecole Française de Spiritualité*, Desclée, Paris 1987, p. 139 ff, and in his article "The French School of Spirituality" in *JLM*, pp. 437-457. Cf. P. Cochois, *Bérulle et l'Ecole*

**All Catholics**. It is also our hope that priests, religious and all Catholics will find these *cantiques* a goldmine for meditation. St. Louis de Montfort himself declares (cf. H 2:41, 43):

> *Read them [the hymns] then, and sing them,*
> *Weigh them well and mull them over,*
> *Seek not here some lofty wit*
> *But the truth that I declare.*
>
> *Here are topics for meditation*
> *I believe I rightly claim,*
> *For often a verse, a line,*
> *Can communicate a truth.*

This compilation of songs can rightly be called the Montfort Hymnal. But even more so, it is a prayerbook, a catechism, a book of meditations, and perhaps a source for homilies. This practical missionary never wrote to produce a literary piece. Rather, these poems are noteworthy only for their content which is always centered on Jesus, the Son of God and the Son of Mary. (cf. Hymn 2).

**C. The Context**

The readers of these hymns will encounter a candid view of the situation in northwest France at the end of the 17th century and the beginning of the 18th century. The general context of the age has been studied elsewhere;[15] there are, however, a few points to be underlined before meditating on these hymns.

**Benefices.** These songs are an insight into the custom of "commendatory abbés"; hymn 136 speaks directly of the often sorry spinoffs of benefices which a cleric acquired as part of his livelihood, e.g., property, pastor of a parish or bishop of a diocese with the right to revenue from their possessions. There were absent pastors – and bishops and abbots - who were often interested in the prestige and profits involved and not in responsibilities. The saint describes in burning satire the state

---

*Française*, Seuil, Paris 1963, pp. 164-166 where the author judges Montfort to be the best representative of the most pure, most mystical bérullian thought.

[15] For an overall view of the milieu of St. Louis Marie, cf. P. Pénisson, "Milieu" in *JLM*, pp. 725-741. Also important is J. Saward's insights into Montfort and Ecumenism (*JLM* pp. 323 ff.), especially since the Father from Montfort used the extravagant and intemperate words of the age: "*Every heretic I abhor/ The Jew, the Turk the pagan,/ The schismatic and the apostate,/ The Catholic alone belongs to me.* (H 6:32).

of affairs when the hireling actual pastor – who may not even have been in ecclesiastical orders – runs a parish in the name of the one who owns the benefice. St. Louis Marie did not make friends when he encouraged his fellow secular priests to embrace voluntary poverty as he had (H 22:21-25).

**Jansenism**. The songs reveal a roving missionary's view of the Church in northwestern France in the baroque age when Jansenism and Gallicanism were flourishing in varying degrees. The hymns on the Blessed Sacrament, the Noels, the Sacred Heart, Divine Wisdom, Our Lady, all disclose the religious mindset of the age and are, then, an insight into the development of spirituality at the end of the baroque era. It is inspiring that Father de Montfort, an itinerant parish preacher, called his simple country folk to the heights of sanctity.

True, at that time Gallicanism and Jansenism were ravaging some areas of the Church in France. However, as a preacher of parish missions in northwestern France, Jansenism as a grace/freewill theological dispute was not a subject of Montfort's sermons. A parish mission is not the arena for debates on conflicting opinions concerning such a complicated topic. Moreover, theological Jansenism was not a critical issue in Montfort's corner of France until the last few years of his life.[16] In hymn 139:55, probably written or revamped around 1711, the saint sings:

*Far from me the heretics condemned by the Church*
*With their fancy practices and their crafty books.*
*Far from me Calvinism, far from me Jansenism.*

The latter heresy had the nickname, "the novelty." St Louis Marie is probably referring to it when he sings:

*Flee novel teachings and the latest heretics* (H 6:47; cf. H 22:17, 30).

However, "the type of piety that developed out of Jansenism was inflexibly rigorist and was characterized by the tension experienced by souls weighed down by the thought of

[16] In 1711 the Bishops of Luçon and La Rochelle issued a joint pastoral condemning the heresy as represented by Quesnel, for which they received a public reprimand from Cardinal de Noailles of Paris, an ardent supporter of Quesnel and a determined combatant against the Bull *Unigenitus* which listed and condemned 101 errors of Quesnel's writings.

damnation."[17] It can be said that Jansenists despised the Father from Montfort, for he preached on the tenderness of God, the love of Mary our Mother, the constant and loving call of God to the greatest sinners:

*Sinner, God urges and is waiting;*
*Be then converted to Him,*
*Prolong not His grief,*
*For He is full of tenderness.* (H 13:20)

Small wonder that some attempts were made – at times probably by the Jansenists - to murder St. Louis de Montfort. They did succeed in seriously weakening his health by poisoning his soup. Nonetheless, he continued to steer clear of pessimistic Jansenistic rigorism as he proclaimed the radical demands of the Gospel.

**Gallicanism**. At the time of Father de Montfort, Gallicanism was rife among the hierarchy and the abbés of France. It can be considered a mindset more or less defiant of papal authority and strongly jealous of its own independence. It came close to imitating England's Henry VIII who sparked the split with the successor of Peter and thus formed his own rebellious national church. It is then understandable that during an audience with Pope Clement XI in 1706, the obedient and faithful Father from Montfort was told not to go to the foreign missions but to remain a missionary in France.

The very fact that St. Louis Marie made a long and arduous pilgrimage to Rome in order to seek the Pope's advice, made him suspect in the eyes of many bishops and priests. Yet he would not in any way lessen his allegiance to the one who is ordered by the Lord to confirm the brethren in the faith (cf. Lk 22:32). He had his people sing their obedience to the *Bishop of Rome* (H 142:2):

*The Vicar of Jesus Christ,*
*An organ of the Holy Spirit* (H 147:3).

He then draws conclusions:

*Believe Jesus in His Vicar*
*In all that touches on faith,*
*And take what he says from the throne*

---

[17] B. Matteucci "Jansenistic Piety" in *The New Catholic Encyclopedia Vol VII,* McGraw-Hill, New York 1967, p. 825.

*As an oracle and certain law (H 6:50).*
*I believe what the Holy Father says,*
*Hell's keen henchman notwithstanding;*
*He is my leader and my light,*
*For I see naught, and he most clearly.* (H 6:57).

**Respect for the King**. Although St Louis Marie's allegiance is above all to Christ and his Church, he has respect for the King as we see in his hymn "The Good Soldier" (H 95:1):

*Under the cross and the fleur de lis*
*I battle all my foes;*
*Everywhere I am both*
*Good Christian and French soldier.*

Even more so, the saint lets his people know that authority exists in Paris as in Rome:

*In Paris as in Rome,*
*In the lawmaker*
*I no longer see man*
*But God alone, my Creator* (H 91:30 cf. H 138:2; H 148:9; H 154:5)

These plainspoken songs open a large window on the religious and secular landscape of northwestern France at the time of the *Roi-Soleil*, Louis XIV.

**D. Characteristics Of The Hymns**

**Forceful Language**. What strikes the reader even in the introductory poems (H 1-4) is the earthy and vigorous language employed by this preacher of parish missions. For example, in the first song, he condemns the lyrics of drunkards, rakes, who are really *the voices of satan* (1:30). Those who sing bawdy tunes, are called nothing more than *cesspool of filth* (1:33). The Breton missionary from Montfort never hedges.

From the beginning to the end of *To the Poets of the Day* (H 2) we hear Montfort the satirist at his best. His biting verses, joined with a light-hearted flair, give us for example, verse 4 addressed to *the awkward tribe of great poets*:

*I might well, on a thousand grounds*
*Dismiss you to a place of ease...*
*[where] rhymesters scrawl their own [poems].*

Louis de Montfort is assigning to the outhouse the stars of French literature, comparing their elegant work to the scrawling on its walls.[18]

Montfort mentions no names; he gives the reason why in a caustic yet comic way:

*Come now, I dare not name you*
*Not for fear of shaming you*
*But lest I sully these pages*
*With such baleful luminaries* (v. 25)

The great poets of the time would easily fit under his very broad umbrella of condemnation since they fail to tell people, in some way or another, about Our Lord and His Mother:

*Do your poems preach of virtue?*
*Proclaim good Jesus' name?*
*Nowhere at all but only empty praise,*
*Lewdness and vile idol-worship* (v. 22).

Another instance of direct, strong language is his Hymn 12 on virginity. This earthy hymn's context – at least in its final form - is probably a country parish mission. Virginity is personified; she herself is the speaker throughout the hymn. Her audience would be laywomen, perhaps members of the confraternity of virgins which Louis Marie established at various parishes. Lady Virginity makes it clear that she is speaking to laywomen (avoiding fancy hair-do's, dancing, dating, etc.) except for a reference to nuns in the final verses (cf. v.49 ff.).

Preaching virginity – Kingdom virginity, lived for the glory of God and neighbor, as a possible state of life for some of the not very well-off laywomen of a little village, would be challenging indeed. Lady Virginity presumes that everyone knows the benefits of marriage: marital love, stability, husband, children. It is not surprising then, that when she extols herself, she takes the opportunity of informing her hearers that marriage even with its splendor, is not all that rosy.

Virginity therefore boldly sings in extravagant, flowery language that marriage puts the woman in slavery and some in the

---

[18] The seventeenth century produced the masterpieces of Molière (well-known for his ribald double entendre), Racine (like so many baroque poets, portrayed pagan mythology), Corneille, the author of *Le Cid* and other tragedies which involved some lurid love stories.

audience probably nodded their head. The married woman is a "slave" to her jealous husband, to the children, and to all the household chores (vv. 25-28). And even more explicitly, she mentions that marital love itself is not all that great either (v. 26). Even after these remarks, Lady Virginity herself has to conclude (v. 29) that she never intended to say that marriage is bad (for Montfort's view on the sacredness of marriage, see H 146:9,10 written on the occasion of a wedding).

Examples of this idiomatic, strong language are interlaced throughout the *Book of Hymns*.

**Baroque**

Pope John Paul II who has repeatedly praised and recommended St. Louis de Montfort's spirituality,[19] found that the saint's baroque language and florid phrases at first turned him away from the *True Devotion..* It was only after re-reading it that he recognized the solid theology wound up in the baroque terms. Montfort is a child of his times. And yet he is far more concise, far less florid than many of the spiritual authors of the age, e.g., St John Eudes, J.J. Olier.

So often when this missionary composes his thoughts on spiritual matters, he himself is ravished by their beautiful truths and his writing becomes a cry of praise and exaltation (cf. especially the hymns on *Wisdom*, the *Eucharist*, the *Sacred Heart*). These prayers from the heart's depth, the French School terms *elevations*, and some of the saint's writings, like the hymns, are chock-full of them. The *Oh!*"s and the *O!'*s found in a number of his hymns are all part of the culture of the baroque age.

**Melodies**

For most of his hymns, the Father from Montfort indicates the name of the tune or melodies to which the song may be sung. "Some may find it surprising that Saint Louis Marie used popular secular tunes for his sacred hymns and even for the most solemn of them. If he found a good one that caught the

---

[19] Cf. *Crossing the Threshold of Hope*, Knopf, New York 1994 pp. 212-213; of great import is the Holy Father's *Letter on the Spiritual Doctrine of Saint Louis Marie de Montfort* addressed to the Men and Women Religious of the Montfort Family, L'Osservatore Romano, January 14, 2004, pp. 4-5. An English translation may be found in the review *Queen of All Hearts*, Montfort Publications, Bay Shore, N.Y. May-June 2004, pp. 4-8.

people's fancy, he would not hesitate to use it for one or more of his hymns."[20]

In his "medieval mystery play," *The Abandoned Soul Freed From Purgatory By The Prayers Of The Poor And Of Children* (H 127), the saint used eighteen different airs.[21] He also drew a diagram indicating the stage position for the eighteen actors and its various choruses.

Fradet has discovered a few of the original melodies to which the hymns were sung.[22] The Father from Montfort must have known all the airs of his day, including at least three tunes of drinking songs.

Indicating the names of very old and long-forgotten French songs was not considered necessary in this English edition.

**E. Themes**

St Louis de Montfort was not the first parish missionary to compose hymns for retreats and missions. Rather, he was following in the footsteps of Maunoir (1642, the date of his edition of hymns), Surin (1657), Crasset (1684), de la Colombière (1692), and many others. Each hymn writer chose the themes of his songs to fit the topics to be covered during the several weeks of a parish mission.

These *Cantiques* are, therefore, a view into some of the great themes of St. Louis de Montfort's preaching.[23] Although a number of his hymns date from his seminary days at St. Sulpice[24] (probably the scholastic style didactic hymns with outlines in the margins, cf. H 5-28), he continued to compose his

---

[20] O. Demers, "Hymns" in *JLM*, p. 521.
[21] He also drew a diagram indicating the stage positions for the eighteen actors and its various choruses; cf. H 127 in this volume.
[22] Fradet, *Les Cantiques*, 93-95.
[23] But not all of the themes. For example, there is no specific hymn on Baptism.
[24] Jean-Baptist Blain, *Summary of the Life of L-M Grignion de Montfort*, Documents & Research III, Montfortian International Centre, Rome 1977, pp. 71-72. Note 41, p. 71 states: "When Mr. [Rev.] Blain mentions the warmth and popular meaning of these hymns, he refers to the journey he made to St Laurent-sur-Sèvre (1724), where he heard them sung by the parishioners." St Laurent is the village where Father de Montfort preached his last sermon and where he died on April 28, 1716.

songs right up to his last mission in 1716 at St. Laurent-sur-Sèvre.[25]

The principal themes of these hymns would include: Glory to God Alone (H 50-52, 114, 135, 153);[26] H 5 on Charity (understood as our love of God) which seems to overflow into the hymn on faith (H 6) and on hope (H 7); love toward our neighbor (H 14, 148); the presence of God (H 24); abandonment to divine providence (H 28; cf. also his autobiographical hymns, 22, 91, 144); the Cross (H 19 and 102, probably one hymn originally, also H 61-73, 123-126, 137, 138, 164); Jesus Christ and His great love for humanity (H 47-49, 57-66 and throughout the hymnal), Eternal Wisdom (H 78, 103, 124-126), the Eucharist (H 112, 128-134, 136, 158); Christmas carols (H 57-66); Sacred Heart (H 40-44, 47, 48); Our Blessed Mother (e.g., H 49, 74 – 90, 104, 111, 134, 145, 151, 155, 159 and throughout the hymnal); The Word and its Snares (H 29-39, 106, 107, 150, 156).

There are also hymns written for groups or individuals, for example: a wedding gift to friends (H 146); to the Daughters of Wisdom (H 149), on Poverty of Spirit (H 144), probably composed in view of his hoped-for Missionaries of the Company of Mary (Montfort Missionaries); to the Visitation Nuns (H 48); his lyrical and spontaneous hymn 143 in honor of Benigne Pagé's entrance into the Poor Clares;[27] in gratitude for permission to enter their

---

[25] For a likely chronology of the hymns, cf. Alberto Rum, "Introduzione ai Cantici di San Luigi Maria di Montfort" in *Spritualià Monfortana 3*, Centre International Montfortain, Roma 2004, pp. 125-148.

[26] *God Alone* is the battle-cry of Louis de Montfort. God Alone is the source of all, God Alone is the goal of all. He often writes these words at the end of a hymn. It can be called not only his motto but also his written logo. All of his songs, all of his works are for *God Alone!* It is found about 135 times in the *Book of Hymns.*

[27] Around 1713, Saint Louis de Montfort was preaching in the area around La Rochelle. A young, well-known socialite, Benigne Pagé, decided among her friends that she would crash the evening service by prancing up to the first row in her fancy, worldly gown, sitting right under the preacher's nose and by gestures and laughter, so upset and anger the famous Father from Montfort that he would lose his line of thought. She was sure she could do it, for she had already succeeded with other preachers. It is said that Father de Montfort spotted her quickly (as did the rest of the congregation). As was his custom, he knelt for a few moments before the Tabernacle, then mounted the pulpit to begin his sermon. The word of God shook her. The congregation seemed to be caught up in the Spirit, weeping openly and Miss Pagé could not help from crying. After the service, she stayed in church for a while and then asked to see the missionary. That very evening, they talked together for two hours. Saint Louis-Marie spoke to her with such kindness yet firmness that the decision was reached: Benigne had to definitively break with her way of life. She spent the night arranging her affairs and in the morning knocked at the door of the

Third Order, he sent the Dominicans a hymn in honor of the Canonization of the Dominican, Pope Pius V (H 147).

### F. The Theology Of The Hymns

The general theology and spirituality of St Louis Marie de Montfort are quite thoroughly examined in *JLM*, the 1380 page handbook of the saint's thought. There are, however, some theological issues found so predominantly in the *Book of Hymns* that they deserve a few words in this introduction.

#### The World

The term "world" does not have a univocal connotation. Among its various meanings would be the cosmos itself, or only planet earth, or the people on earth with all their thoughts and actions, etc.

St Louis de Montfort describes for us the meaning he gives to "world" especially when he sings of *Contempt for the World* :

> *What is this deceiving world?*
> *It is the global gathering*
> *Of sinners waging war,*
> *Atrocious and cruel, against the Lord;*
> *Sometimes very openly*
> *But more often secretly.*
> *The Holy Spirit called the world*
> *The chair of pestilence itself,*
> *The great church of the wicked,*
> *The infamous, great Babylon,*
> *Where the devils, as the lords,*
> *Are so cleverly enthroned,*
> *Where all good is opposed*
> *And all the sins are taught.* (H 29:5-7)

This troubadour missionary has then a rather clear understanding of "world." Everything, everyone not turned to the Lord is therefore turned against Him. "No man can serve two masters," says Our Lord. Those things or persons who are not passing through the narrow gate which leads to life (cf Mt 7:13-14) constitute the "world."

---

monastery of the cloistered Poor Clares, and remained there as a professed religious for the rest of her life. She died, said the nuns, in the "odor of sanctity."

Satan, of course, although fully under the rule of God, is the leader of "the world." Those who are on the "wide road" to perdition are Satan's followers. Their thoughts, words and actions demonstrate their allegiance is not to God but to Satan.

The first act of human freedom is a radical "no" to God and has tainted and weakened this universe, although never destroying human freedom or the innate goodness of creation. There is, however, a tendency to create idols of our own: pride, money, prestige, etc. Anything created is capable of being molded into a golden calf, as Montfort the parish reformer, clearly knows.

St Louis de Montfort powerfully condemns the idols of his time, most especially in his songs on the snares of the world. Some today may believe that this preacher goes too far in his list of "worldly snares." But that is difficult, if not impossible, to judge since we cannot reconstruct the culture of northwestern France of 300 years ago. In his day, dancing, galas, balls, games of chance, wealthy lifestyles were, so he ardently believed, fraught with serious temptations even though in themselves, as he notes, they are not evil.

**The Angry God**

All the writings of Saint Louis Marie are qualified by his itinerant preaching. He is not a pastor of a parish but a missionary sent by Jesus (cf. H 163:13) and the Holy Father[28] to proclaim the Good News of Jesus Christ. His vocation was to offer his life for the reform of the Church and the renewal of the face of the earth (cf. H 22:13).

It is not surprising then, that Father de Montfort is highly sensitive to sin which can destroy the loving relationship of man to God. Also, he apparently was a man who lived in a deep mystical union with the Trinity. He then sees serious sin in its true light: it is horrendous, an abomination which, if not repented, casts a soul to hell.

Montfort considered the parish mission as an outpouring of the Spirit. The ceremonies, processions, dramas, the preaching, raised the consciousness of sin and joyful repentance, thereby convincing the parishioners of the horror of offending our loving

[28] When in Rome during his pilgrimage in 1706, the Father from Montfort was granted an audience with Pope Clement XI. Although the Pope refused to grant him permission to go to the foreign missions, the Holy Father did name him an "Apostolic Missionary" to his own countrymen.

God. Within this context, St Louis de Montfort is not reluctant to underline the biblical anger of God when His infinite Love is rejected. Terms like *wrath, anger, avenger,* are used to describe God's response to sin. Yet God continues to call even the most hardened sinner. It is the sinner who by willingly turning against God, must accept the consequences of an eternity turned against infinite Love. St Louis Marie's missions proclaimed the words of Paul: "Beloved, never avenge yourselves but leave it to the wrath of God; for it is written 'Vengeance is mine, I will repay, says the Lord' " (Rom 12:19).

But the Breton missionary also insisted on another text, Rom 13: 12, 13: "Let us cast off the works of darkness and put on the armor of light ... put on Jesus Christ and make no provision for the flesh, to gratify its desires" (cf. H 139). Montfort, the legate of Jesus and of his vicar, always strove to lead people out of the darkness of sin into the light of God's glory.[29] If holiness brings with it a sensitivity to sin, it even more so brings the deep experience of God's loving mercy:

*Far from me austere zealots,*
*Filled with harshness and anger*
*Used as pretexts of charity.*
*Little vinegar, much oil,*
*Converts the greatest sinners,*
*And wins both mind and heart*
*As we see, we see in the Gospel* (H 22:17).

This "tell it as it is" missionary rejoices in the proclamation of the radical demands of the Gospel, for only they bring true joy.[30]

**Our Lady**

It is almost impossible to give all the references to the Mother of God in the hymns. It is even difficult to name the precise hymns dedicated to her for she is found throughout the book. As A. Rum points out, "In the spiritual doctrine of Montfort, the Marian note – much more than a devotional "coloring" – is a *dimension* of his spirituality, a *focal point* for contemplating the

---

[29] Seven Hymns bear titles of "Conversion" or "Converted," H 45, 79, 98, 139, 140, 142, 143.
[30] Cf. J. Morinay. "Beatitudes" in *JLM*, pp. 57-66.

entire Christian mystery."[31] It is not surprising then that Our Lady is understood in the same way in his hymns.[32]

The Marian hymns and references reflect the *True Devotion* and *The Secret of Mary*. As in the *TD* (numbers 14, 39), Montfort's hymns underline Mary's hypothetically necessary consent to the Incarnation, and in the name of the whole world:

*Offering no resistance,*
*You have achieved by your consent*
*What the whole world*
*So ardently desired.*
*May we glorify, honor and praise your faith!*
*The Savior came to us*
*Only because you believed*
*The word of the angel.* (H:63:4 cf. 27:9)

Imitating St. John Eudes, Montfort not only speaks of the heart of Mary (H 47:27; 40:33, etc.) but that Jesus and Mary form "one heart" (H 40:36, 37; H 134:8), so intense their union.

There are also songs which poetically replicate well-known prayers to Our Lady: the *Memorare* (H 83), *Jesus Living in Mary* (H 111), the *Magnificat* (H 85), the *Regina Coeli* (H 84), the *Little Crown* (H 88), the *Ave Maria* (H 89), and above all, the *Rosary* (H 90) with 63 stanzas.

The itinerant preacher also was inspired to compose Marian hymns when visiting a small shrine of Our Lady, e.g., at La Séguinière (probably): *Our Lady of Patience* (H 145); at Saint Savior of Nuaillé: *Our Lady of Gifts* (H 151); at La Chevrolière: *Our Lady of Shadows* (H 155); at Vouvant: *Our Lady of Consolation* (H 159).

Father de Montfort's Mariology and his Marian spirituality founded upon it is, above all, Christocentric. Like everything "montfort," the central stress is on God Alone, God Alone Who is Love, the Alpha and the Omega of the entire cosmos. "Laurentin demonstrates that Montfort rectified the Mary-centered language that had been established by Los Rios, Rojas, Fenicki, Van der Zandt, Boudon, etc."[33]

---

[31] A. Rum (article cited above), pp. 142-143.
[32] For an overall study of Our Lady in Montfort Spirituality, cf. P. Gaffney, "Mary" in *JLM*, pp. 687 724.
[33] A. Amato, "Jesus Christ" in *JLM*, p. 571

*It is you alone whom I adore,*
*Heart of my God, glorious Heart,*
*But, adoring you, I also honor*
*The Heart of heaven's Queen* (H 40:34).

*The cross is adorable,*
*Mary is not* (H 102:23).

There is a deep mysticism in many of St Louis Marie's stanzas on Our Lady. The "presence of Mary" which he experiences, is mentioned "as something hard to grasp." It is, however, not the presence of Mary alone but as Montfort the mystic clarifies it,

*I have Jesus and Mary*
*Etched in my heart;*
*My friend, could I have*
*More perfect joy?* (H 99:18).

*Here is something hard to grasp:*
*In my heart's center I carry her*
*Etched with strokes of glory,*
*Yet in faith's darkness still* (H 77:15).

When someone speaks about Mary, although she is unique because the Mother of God, he is ultimately clarifying himself and all the people of God: what it means to be redeemed, the joyful experience of freedom from sin, centering on Jesus, the firm hope of eternal life. She is our model of total, loving surrender to the Trinity:

*Hail Mary,*
*In your divine communion*
*Throughout your life.*
*Your actions*
*Are a model*
*Pure and faithful.*
*We fashion ourselves on you.* (H 90:29).

And if we model ourselves on Our Lady, through her and in her we will

*Gaze only upon Jesus Christ,*
*[For]He is our perfect model* (H 35:55).

**The Trinity and Jesus**

The culminating point of the theology found in the hymns is its Trinitarian-Christocentric foundation and goal. This is the very fabric of Montfort spirituality. Since it is treated elsewhere, especially in *JLM*,[34] only a few of the references in the hymns will be touched on.

In one of his catechetical *cantiques*, Montfort sings:

*There are three persons in God:*
*Father, Son and Holy Spirit.*
*Three infinitely perfect,*
*I believe it, God has said it.*
*The three are only one God, for the three have only one essence:*
*The Father is God, the Son is God,*
*And the Holy Spirit is God,*
*All equal in substance* (H 109:2).

However, St Louis Marie is not primarily interested in the abstract complexities of Trinitarian theology. He wants his people to experience God as Father, as Son, as Holy Spirit.

The Father is infinitely good (H 27:1), *loving to excess* as the saint so often repeats not only of the Father but of Eternal Wisdom as well (H 128:6; H 158:5). The primary characteristic of God the Father, our *ABBA, Father* (H 7:31) is his goodness (H 27:1), his tenderness (H 13:20; H 28:24; H 52:11).

The Son is the Divine Wisdom from all eternity who becomes enfleshed in the bosom of Mary, the Lady of the Eternal and Incarnate Wisdom. The hymns on Jesus Wisdom are the gems of Montfort's poems.

It is somewhat surprising that only one hymn is explicitly dedicated to the Holy Spirit (H 141) since other writings, especially the *True Devotion*, emphasize the Spirit's role in Our Lady. However, many other hymns contain references to the Third Person of the Trinity.[35]

---

[34] Cf. *JLM* especially entries on "Mary," "Jesus Christ," "Consecration," "Noels," "Trinity."
[35] Cf. R. Laurentin, "Holy Spirit" in *JLM*, 493-405; the article also contains important references. Cf. S. De Fiores, "Montfort, un home disponible à l'Esprit" in *Dieu Seul: A la rencontre de Dieu avec Montfort*, Centre International Montfortain, Rome 1981.

The ten noels are excellent references to the saint's faith-insight into the Incarnate Wisdom, Jesus Christ (cf. H 57-66). There can be no doubt that Montfort, representing the thought of the age, stresses a Christology from above (i.e., God the Word comes down into the human family), with its emphasis on the divinity of Jesus, the awesome Son of God. It is for this reason that he uses the imagery of an *eclipse* to explain the incarnation. The Eternal Wisdom's Divine Light is so blinding that we can only see and gaze upon the Second Person of the Trinity when the Son, in his humanity, is "eclipsed."

*Proud creature,*
*Come meet your pitfall*
*In the loving eclipse*
*Of the divine Sun* (H 62:4).

*Behold greatness in miniature,*
*A sun in darkness,*
*Whose eclipse invites us*
*To approach Him confidently* (H 66:5; cf. H 101:42).

This eclipse of God indicates that as incarnate, the Word is clothed with true humanity and can, therefore, be seen, looked upon, touched (cf. 1 Jn 1-4). Montfort's noels are replete with an emphasis that the Child is both God and man. The incarnation, therefore, validates the exchange of predicates (*communicatio idiomatum*), i.e., both human and divine terms can be applied to Jesus:

*All power*
*In powerlessness,*
*Brilliance*
*In obscurity* (H 65:10).

*In order to save man, God*
*Decided on a marvelous mystery:*
*He becomes what we are,*
*Making us become what He is* (64:1).

*Do you see this dear infant*
*Lying in the manger?*
*He is the almighty Lord*
*And the true God.*
*Of all crowned heads*
*He rules as sovereign Master,*
*His hands cup the universe,*
*He is the God of armies* (H 61:1).

**A final point** on Jesus and the sacraments. In Montfort's beautiful poem on Our Lady and the Eucharist (H 134), this minstrel-missionary tells us that Jesus instituted the Eucharist because he could not bear being away from her:

*Jesus could not leave Mary,*
*So strong the love which bound them;*
*That is why, just before his death,*
*He established the Eucharist,*
*So that after the Ascension,*
*He could be her consolation here below* (H 134:1).

So too for us. Mary epitomizes the Christian community so loved by God. The stanza speaks of her in a unique way, yet it can also be applied in a true manner to every follower of Jesus. The Eucharist, and all the sacraments, were instituted for us, undoubtedly. But Montfort surfaces another truth: Jesus instituted the sacramental mystery for himself so that he could rejoice in giving himself to us.

It is of the very being of Jesus that he is our servant (cf. Mk 10:45; Lk 12:37; Lk 22:27; Jn 13:2-5). He rejoices then in the fulfillment of his incarnation when a lost sheep is found, when the prodigal son comes home and when the sinner is forgiven. We confess our sins so that Jesus may have the joy of embracing us in his redemptive love, we are baptized so that Jesus may have the joy of taking us into his life and so on for all the sacraments.

Montfort often stresses the joy of Jesus in forgiving us (e.g., H 51:9) his happiness in dying for us (e.g., H 41:30). The parish missionary apparently used this dimension of the sacraments – Jesus infinitely loves us and yearns for us – to draw people to a deeper sacramental life.

We pray that all who meditate on these hymns may experience the joy we had in bringing them – at last – to the English speaking world.

Father Patrick Gaffney, S.M.M., S.T.D.
Sister Rosemary Gaffney, D.W., Ph..D.
General Translators and Editors

Feast of the Presentation of the Lord
February 2, 2005

We would like to thank those who have assisted us in the translations, the editing, and in many other ways, especially the members of the Montfort Family: the Montfort Missionaries and in particular, Fathers Gerald Fitzsimmons (Provincial), Francis Allen, Theodore Murphy, Paul Allerton; the Daughters of Wisdom, particularly: Sisters Eileen Berton, Marie Immaculata Vane, Ann Gray; also, Rev. Charles Underhill Quinn (+), Mr. H. McDonald, Richard and Stephen Payne of Arcadia Publications and the many people who have accompanied our work with their prayers.

A special thanks to Ken Sell who kindly accepted and brought to excellent completion the laborious task of designing and preparing the entire document for publication.

We also wish to express our gratitude to Dorothy Anderson for her assistance in publishing this volume. Her gift was given in memory of her husband, Matt Anderson. Both Dorothy and Matt have been long time associates in our Montfort ministry.

## *Table of Contents*

## *Table of Contents*

## *Table of Contents*

## *Table of Contents*

## *Table of Contents*

Procession at La Rochelle, August 16, 1711

**Translation of the captions that accompany the drawing of the procession at La Rochelle**

A. Banner of the Jacobin Fathers (Dominicans), and a large number of men and women who marched behind it.
B. A group of daughters of the common people, barefoot and dressed in white.
C. A white banner for the same.
D. A group of the daughters of merchants, most of whom were barefoot, carrying a cross, a candle, a rosary and a picture on which was written: contract of renewal of baptismal promises.
E. A blue banner for the daughters of the townsfolk.
F. Brother Mathurin, the missionary's assistant, keeping the marchers in order and leading the singing of the different songs.
G. The clergy also controlling and keeping the marchers in order while leading the singing of hymns.
H. A red banner for the married women, a few of whom were barefoot.
I. Another banner for the young ladies of the town.
K. Two ladies carrying torches.
L. Two gunners' oboes that were played at the close of each of the verses sung by the women.
M. The banner of Our Lady of the Seven Sorrows.
N. The black and white banner of the Third Order Jacobin Sisters.
O. Navy men to maintain order and keep back the crowds present at various places.
P. The Jacobin Fathers' Cross encircled with a rosary.
Q. The chief dance masters and violinists of the town whom the missionary railed against in his sermons. They were paid with a good supper, like the sergeants and soldiers.
R. M Chauvet, the hospital chaplain and dispenser in reserved cases.
S. M. (Gabriel) Grignion, the missionary's brother who held a few procession rehearsals inside and outside the town to familiarize the women with its rubrics. He almost always carried the book of the Gospels.
T. M. de Montfort, Missionary, secular priest of the province of Brittany. He has given several missions, always having the rosary as a theme.
V. Rev. Fr. Collusson, Jesuit, seminary professor who followed part of the procession.
X. Rev. Fr. Doiteau, Jacobin, who always accompanied the missionary in his processions.
Y. Sergeants and soldiers from the regiments of Angles and La Lande, then garrisoned at La Rochelle, who controlled the crowds.

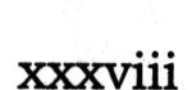

# 1
# USEFULNESS OF HYMNS

1. Sing out, dear soul, sing out,
Let us make our song resound
With a most hallowed melody,
Heaven and all that is call out to us.

1st point.
*Hymns give glory to God.*

2. Our great and ever joyous God
From highest heaven hears us,
Hymns he loves eternally,
They are the concert of his angels.

Motives
1st Motive.
God loves singing.

3. Listen to the angels singing
And let us sing in imitation,
By their praises they are angels,
By song shall we be angels too.

2nd Motive.
Angels sing.

4. Aflame with holy fire, day and night
They sing of God and his glory,
And God himself listens.
Like them let us sing of his wonders.

3rd motive.
In singing we become like them.

5. In singing they are ablaze with love,
Let us sing, let us too be afire,
Through song they fan their flame,
Let us sing and so kindle our souls.

4th motive.
Singing lights love's fire.

6. With their melodies the heavens ring out,
Let us be their wondrous echo,
Let everyone sing and be glad,
Let earth become one with heaven.

5th motive.
Earth must answer heaven.

7. Let us sing, but sing properly,
So we may sing in highest heaven;
Sing, predestined soul,
Sing for our blessed crown.

6th motive.
It is proper to the predestined to sing good hymns.

8. My song is not acclaimed
By the worldly nor the outcast.
No matter! They want not to believe;
To them shall I sing victory!

9. God wills that his good servants
Sing his glory day and night.
When his whole Church sings
His triumph is in her winning voice.

7th motive.
God wants his servants to sing and be happy.

10. Since he is in eternal bliss
He wants his servants happy.
Discord turns him from a soul away
And gloom snuffs out its flame.

11. God makes the song of priest and monk
Everywhere ring out,
As they chant his mysteries
Throughout each day and night.

8th motive.
The whole Church sings

12. In their most heartfelt songs
He finds a flawless tribute.
In the gloomiest service he desires
Our song in sacrifice.

9th motive.
Even in the office of the dead.

13. The Christian saints of yore
In their chanting came to life.
By singing heavenly hymns
They became like the seraphim.

10th motive
Example of first christians

14. The Holy Spirit guided them.
To them Saint Paul so often said:
Be joyful! Sing, you faithful,
Psalms and spiritual songs.

11th motive.
Words of Saint Paul

15. Hymns the saints so often make,
It is a secret of their holiness.
Mary sang her own fair song.
Let us sing in imitation.

12th motive.
The example of the saints and the Blessed Virgin.

16. Sing then, but with passion;
Sing and we shall gladden the Lord;
Sing and we shall give him glory;
Sing and we shall sing of triumph.

2nd point.
*Hymns are useful for the soul.*

## *USEFULNESS OF HYMNS*

17. Know that a sacred hymn
Illuminates and clears the mind,
Chases all black humor from the heart
And sets God firmly in remembrance.

1st motive.
They enlighten the mind.
2nd motive.
They pacify the heart.
3rd motive.
They refresh the memory.

18. When the heart is sapped of strength
A hymn restores its vigor.
O sing - your sorrow notwithstanding -
And you shall be filled with jubilation.

4th motive.
They restore courage.
5th motive.
They fill with joy.

19. Song, as Scripture tells,
Opens the heart to the Holy Spirit;
God comes down to a singing heart
And gives it grace abounding.

6th motive.
Opens the heart to the Holy Spirit and his grace.

20. Hymns charm away our ills
And enliven us in what we do;
When we sing we are prepared
To work for greater things.

7th motive.
Charm away our ills.
8th motive.
They renew our works.
9th motive.
They ready us for great tasks.

21. Song is a godly secret
For chasing all demons away;
The holy song we sing
Makes our tempters flee.

3rd Point.
*It frightens the devil and the world.*
1st motive.
It chases the troubling evil spirit away.

22. The world has blended sin
With the tunes it has designed;
Its music is the training school
For refining its depravity.

2nd motive.
It enlightens the world.
1. Which has composed scandalous tunes and songs.
2. Learns its evil-doing through singing.

23. Let us sing and restore the honor
Of which its songs have robbed the Lord;
With new tunes of righteousness
Let us destroy its wicked airs.

3. Dishonors God

24. Sing on, you drunkard, in your cups;
Drink up this bane and then
Shed tears and so with fury crazed
Chase after the Dragon's brew.

4. Drunkards sing their songs and enchant

25. You rake, what will it cost you
For this wicked song of yours!
Vile Satan thought it up,
And your singing serves his whim.

5. Libertines sing and arouse their passions.

26. Gulp down, gulp down the toxin
Of your bawdy melodies,
One day these unchaste delights
Will be your most fell torment.

6. These songs are poisonous.

27. The devil, with his ribald jest,
May make you laugh, but to your loss;
He blows your tune and kindles you
With a fresh but wicked pleasure.

7. They damn souls.

28. You take a hellish poison
And claim no harm is in it,
Yet what you say both hides
And brings about your doom.

29. You say we are too scrupulous
And we say woe to you,
For at your lay so pleasing
They wail in heaven and croon in hell.

30. Away, you Bacchic minstrels!
Away, you minstrels of Venus!
Away, shrewd henchmen of the devil!
So wretched is your ill fortune.

31. You sing out your reeking melody
Distinctly that all may hear;
You teach them its rhythm
And thus demean their virtue.

8. They scandalize the neighbor.

32. Be damned if you will, O worldly soul,
    But do not condemn your neighbor;
    He listens and learns of the sin,
    He commits it and falls to his ruin.

33. Away, you cesspool of filth,
    Spew forth no foulness here
    No flowery songs of desire,
    No sweet words of bewitchment.

Flight from the world.

34. You friends of my God, hold fast
    Against the world and the demon,
    They look fair and speak sweetly,
    But let us keep from listening.

Resolution

35. Let us sing in honor of Jesus,
    The eminence of his virtues
    To fix them in our memories
    And practice them with glory.

36. Let us make the universe resound
    With our songs and our rhymes,
    That God may be glorified
    And our neighbors be uplifted.

## 2
## TO THE POETS OF THE DAY

1. I write you not to beguile;[36]
   You think only of verses and rhymes,
   Great poets, you awkward tribe,
   Your methods I consign to others.

2. I know well that you prize only
   Modish rhymes and meters,
   Double-storied lines and quatrains
   That produce no wise man but a fool.

[36] For a short explanation of this hymn, see the Introduction on page xiv

3. You go round and round again
   Just to make an irksome poem,
   Uttering balderdash and twaddle,
   A futile spat in a passing dalliance.

4. I might well, on a thousand grounds,
   Dismiss you to a place of ease.
   How so? There you belong,
   There the rhymesters scrawl their own.

5. Your verses are refined with skill
   But often it is merely rouge,
   Your mind is in torment,
   As, I vow, are all your lines.

6. Your great poems are not dull,
   I agree, but they are troublesome,
   You rush from pole to pole
   To utter barren words.

7. If your poems were truly noble,
   A child could grasp their gist;
   They are so lofty, they are so rare,
   That they have become grotesque.

8. August poets, I hear you:
   You spurn the simple folk,
   Your lines are for the brilliant,
   Teeming like you with madness;

9. Unless the famed minds of the day
   Find in them their comfort,
   Even were they most majestic lines,
   You make of them great crimes.

10. A sermonizer, up to date;
    A subtle rhymester, up to date;
    Unless a man is up to date,
    He is a ninny or a bumpkin.

11. Your conceit and lofty style
    Show well your shameless taste.
    The only pay your poor sick men
    Desire is tiresome praise.

12. You look in myriad by-roads
    To find the latest fool
    Thoughtlessly to tell you,
    "What fair verses, what fine rhymes!"

13. Poor sirs, you make me laugh,
    For you almost all write verses only
    To have your brainstorms cheered.
    But your efforts cost too dear.

14. Yet too many buy your rhymes,
    Since they abound but in useless fancies
    And a hundred sorts of fleeting romances
    So unseemly for flawless souls.

15. For beneath your rhymes and thinking,
    You conceal a deadly poison,
    A cruel snare so enticing
    We can scarce resist it.

16. Your poems are good, there's no denying;
    Nothing so fine, so well expressed,
    With rhyme so rich and cadence fair.
    True, but what loathsome wickedness!

17. Were your verses rich with God,
    I should esteem them highly,
    But in virtue poor, and rich in vice,
    I loathe even their resplendency.

18. You peddle vanity
    As if it were the truth,
    And you pass off a fable
    As true history.

19. You can do anything, they say;
    We take you for the enemy
    Of truths most certain,
    And friend to earthly follies.

20. Like the pagan poets
    You take ill for good,
    I could call you ungodly,
    Or, to be more candid, asinine.

21. O imitators most wicked,
    Of no account you deem your poems
    Unless you borrow some graceful phrase
    From those of Virgil or Homer.

22. Do your poems preach of virtue?
    Proclaim good Jesus' name?
    Nowhere at all, but only empty praise,
    Lewdness and vile idol-worship.

23. Do you tell of those predestined?
    You praise only the hell-bound,
    Men who thirst for blood
    And foolhardy, reckless lovers.

24. You spiteful poets of false gods,
    You call me scrupulous or else,
    Out of stupidity, you think
    That now I merely want to shock.

25. Come now, I dare not name you,
    Not for fear of shaming you,
    But lest I sully these pages
    With such baleful luminaries.

26. Baleful yes! I do not lie
    For perhaps you are indeed below;
    Be what may, your books abide,
    Those cunning toxins that infect us.

27. In them we hardly find a thing
    That does not cause us harm,
    A lewdness most enticing
    That for them seems without blame.

28. Your rhymes are fair, they bring acclaim,
    They are verses gleaming in the night,
    The wise man spurns their affectation,
    While they hoodwink the hapless fool.

29. Your verses, so skillfully conceived,
    Burn incense to Bacchus and Venus,
    And everywhere they toil and strive

To enrapture with their excesses.

30. Hell is filled with people doomed
By your books so widely sold.
The Holy Bible is cast aside;
By your verses only are they moved.

31. Oh! They doom people every day!
Their onrush cannot be thwarted;
Almost everyone sings their praises,
As they are presented on the stage.

32. Yes, this wise and worldly book
You may have in your hand
May have condemned more souls
Than the wretched words it holds.

33. You will tell me, "I see nothing
That is not good, that is not choice."
Dear brother, don't be fooled:
Sooner or later their poison works.

34. Their sparkle hides the toxin,
Their charms conceal the hook;
Among myriad witty words is one
That makes you fancy, fall and yield.

35. Play not the Holy Spirit,
You author of such nasty prose;
It is forged by the unclean spirit
To lead the people of the world astray.

36. Should you keep it, then will the devil
Always claim that it is safe,
No sin in reading it,
For laughing God does not forbid.

37. Throw all these romances in the fire,
Do so for the love of God,
Without looking at the cover,
The printing, nor their gilded edges.

38. To the flames, these shameless tales,
To the flames, these romantic jests,

To the flames, these tender tragedies,
And these loathsome comedies.

39. These are my poems and my songs:
If they are not elegant, they are pure,
If they flatter not the ear,
They tell of great wonders.

40. If they are but for children,
They are not for a lesser price;
If they are but ordinary verse,
They are no less beneficial.

41. Read them then, and sing them,
Weigh them well and mull them over,
Seek not here some lofty wit
But the truth that I declare.

42. You, preacher, in my songs
Can find your homilies,
I have digested their substance
For your guidance and delight.

43. Here are topics for meditation
I believe I rightly claim,
For often a verse, a line
Can communicate a truth.

44. Each word of a verse must be such
That you can ponder its intent,
And keep it in remembrance
For its fragrance and its worth.

45. Ailing heart, sing out, sing out,
In singing healing comes;
Hymns are a potent remedy,
Bringing and grace and rapture.

46. Sing with tongue and heart,
With voice fervent with devotion
To cast out sadness from the soul
And fill it with jubilation.

47. Be on the watch for vanity,

The singer wishes to be heard;
If your voice is flawless,
Let your soul be blameless.

48. Let us then all sing, and properly,
Let us sing of the glories of the Most High,
In song let us wipe out depravity
And make righteousness beloved.

GOD ALONE.

## 3
## TO MEN PREDESTINED

This is the road most joyful
That leads straight to heaven;
If you wish to learn it,
Then sing with mighty faith,
I shall say nothing of me,
I cannot surprise you.
O predestined one, sing my songs,
You will keep clear of hell.
God, God, God, I sing for God,
Let all come and hear me.

## 4
## RESPECT AND DESIRE FOR VIRTUE

1. One day I saw in the Lord
Someone who ravished my heart:
A charming Princess.
Smitten with her great beauty,
I ask who she is.
Heaven is silent; I persist.
I say it is out of love,
They answer, "Mortal man,
It is the Virtue of God,
Take her as your mistress!

1st Point.
*The excellence of virtue.*

2. Virtue comes from the Creator,
She is the divine breath
Of his glory everlasting;
He wants her in all his friends,
As enemies he condemns
All those who forsake her.
In heaven he crowns only
Her faithful lovers.
God, God, God, Virtue of my God,
How beautiful I find you!

Motives
1st motive.
She is eternal in God
2nd motive.
She makes his favorites.
3rd motive.
Without her we are his enemy.
4th motive.
Heaven he gives only to those who have virtue.

3. God himself has come forth
To show this reality divine
To every creature;
To reveal it tangibly
He became a mortal man,
He took on his nature,
In his manhood
He laid bare his utter holiness.
God, God, God, Virtue of my God,
How pure I find you!

5th motive.
God became man to show virtue and to practice it in its truth.

4. In the midst of poverty,
Jesus is rich in truth,
He has all abundance
Since he is full and clothed
With Virtue's great treasures
And her innocence.
Oh! How rich we are in her embrace!
Oh! How poor we are when we let her go!
God, God, God, Virtue of my God,
O my treasure immeasurable!

6th motive.
Jesus, though poor, is rich in virtue, for virtue is wealth.

5. If God takes from us so many cares,
If he provides for all our needs,
It is for Virtue herself;
Day and night he smites our heart
To take us to her love.
It is his paramount desire,
It is his chief purpose,
And all that he expects of us.
God, God, God, Virtue of my God,
Suffer me to love you.

7th motive.
Virtue is the purpose of nature, grace and God's blessings.

6. To her the Holy Spirit leads,
Be perfect, Jesus said,
Like God your father. (Mt 5,48)
Why, Martha, are you troubled?
As for everyone Virtue
Is all you need;
It is truly the better part
That we always too late embrace.
God, God, God, Virtue of my God,
In you is my hope.

8th motive
It's the intention
of the Holy Spirit

9th motive.
It is the only thing
necessary and the
better part.

7. Virtue alone is a treasure
Before which all gold and silver
Are but mud and sand;
Without her all is vanity,
Sin, lies, infirmity,
Dreadful woe;
With her all is of value,
Be it pain or scorn.
God, God, God, Virtue of my God,
O my true blessing!

10th motive.
Virtue is more
precious than any
gold or silver.

11th motive.
Without virtue
everything is
nothing.

12th motive.
With her the
smallest is the
greatest.

8. Saints aflame with passion seek her
As their substantial dignity
And their beatitude;
Woe to them who do not possess her,
Or do not make her here below
The center of their meditation!
Since she is our chief possession,
Our purpose, our wherewithal.
God, God, God, Virtue of my God,
Your yoke is not harsh.

13th motive.
The example of
the saints.

9. So powerful is her appeal
That we can never resist her,
The profligate admire her;
Even the most barbarous of heathens
Find how great a blessing she is,
They love her and they long for her.
O Virtue, there is nothing like you,
Nothing so staunch, nothing so sweet.
God, God, God, Virtue of my God,
For you my heart is yearning.

14th motive.
Nothing is so
strong or sweet.

15th motive.
She is loved by
the
wicked and the
heathen.

10. Each man is made for Virtue,
Without her he is weak and downcast,
Without pleasure, without victory.
Had Virtue not charmed him,
His heart would ever hunger;
Man of the world, I want to believe you;
Ah, if you opened up your heart to us
We would see what is your woe.
God, God, God, Virtue of my God,
O my peerless glory.

16th motive. Without her man's heart is never happy or content.

11. She is the secret most certain
For edifying our neighbor,
For converting his soul.
She is a sweet-smelling balm
That gently fills his heart
With a divine flame;
She speaks to him with eloquence,
And sends him into rapture.
God, God, God, Virtue of my God,
It is you I beg for.

17th motive. She wins our neighbor for God.

12. Without her a fine preacher
Merely stuns his listener,
Without converting him,
He does not fail to cause division,
And never makes his central point;
The point of righteousness.
Can he give what he does not have?
Make people walk without taking a step?
God, God, God, Virtue of my God,
Let me be your sanctuary.

18th motive. Without her the preacher preaches in vain.

13. A truly virtuous man,
Be he the lowliest of beggars,
Is far more respectable
Than all the kings and doctors,
Have they not Virtue in their hearts,
A virtue that is true.
Without her the finest talents
Sparkle falsely and in vain.
God, God, God, Virtue of my God,
O my transcendent glory!

19th motive. Virtue makes the small greater than monarchs and doctors.

14. What good for all those tradesmen,
For all those famous conquerors,
Who fill up history's pages,
To gain this whole universe,
And doom themselves to hell?
Dear God, what foolishness!
Without Virtue all is lost,
But no one understands this word.
God, God, God, Virtue of my God,
O treasure of my life!

20th motive.
Without her what good is it to gain the whole world?

15. When the Lord judges us,
What will he ask of us:
A great nobility,
A great capacity,
A sublime ability?
No, no, but wisdom only,
Virtue in her purity,
Genuine holiness.
God, God, God, Virtue of my God,
O my great wealth!

21st motive.
God will demand an account only of virtue at the judgment.

16. You friends of holy Zion,
Let us desire perfection,
Since God commands it.
But let us desire it purely
And seek it passionately,
Its reward it great;
Let us strive hard to obtain it,
Let us labor until death.
God, God, God, Virtue of my God,
It is you I ask for.

2nd Point.
*The practice of virtue.*

1st motive.
Desire it.

2nd motive.
Desire it purely for its own sake.

17. But we must strive to excel:
Not to push forward is to fall back.
Let us never stop pushing forward,
And spare nothing to achieve it.
To do better in the future
Charity urges us on.
Let us not think of our past as worthy,
Or that we have done something good.
God, God, God, Virtue of my God,
Toward you my heart hastens.

3rd motive.
Fervently without lukewarmness.
4th motive.
By working hard.

5th motive.
Always advancing in virtue.
6th motive.
Think that you have done nothing.

18. Let us pile coin upon coin,
As they do in every trade:
No measly little virtue.
Aim always for the most excellent,
For thus did the saints
To attain their reward;
Whoever grows in virtue
Receives the rest as well.
God, God, God, Virtue of my God,
I follow in your footsteps.

7th motive.
Do not neglect the little things.
8th motive.
Aim for the most perfect.
9th motive.
Seek first the law of virtue and the rest will be given to you.

19. Let us confound our cowardice
By pondering the holiness
Of all the saints our brethren.
Against these mighty giants
We are but shiftless manikins,
Full of every wretchedness;
They were made of iron and fire,
And we for God are naught but ice.
God, God, God, Virtue of my God,
O Virtue of my fathers!

10th motive.
Consider the piety of the saints and our cowardice.

20. We attain pure virtue
Only after a noble fight,
A lawful combat;
Let us fast then unceasingly and pray,
Let us subdue our passions,
The root of every sin;
And practice earnestly
The great virtues of the Savior.
God, God, God, Virtue of my God,
O my sublime glory!

11th motive.
Fight, fast, pray.

21. Forgive me, God of goodness,
In truth my virtue is
But mere posturing;
I wish to follow you step by step.
Lord do not forsake me.
Grant me your grace;
Not gold, nor silver, nor renown,
But only the virtues of your heart.
God, God, God, Virtue of my God.
Yes, it is you I embrace.

Prayer.

22. O worthy Mother of Jesus,
O great Queen of virtues
And their perfect model!
If I am your servant,
Let me be your imitator!
O Virgin most faithful,
Let your virtues enter into me,
Wisdom and Faith above all.
God, God, God, virtue of my God,
My Bride everlasting.

23. Away with you, false world,
Your fancied bliss
Sullies and starves me both;
By your pompous glamor you want
To make me forever woeful.
Begone, accursed, loathsome one,
And spread your poison elsewhere,
Virtue is my only song.
God, God, God, Virtue of my God,
I sing of your radiance.

GOD ALONE.

## 5
## EXCELLENCE OF CHARITY FIRST HYMN

1. I am a royal virtue
Or rather divinity,
The first theological virtue
Called charity.

The essence of charity and its definition.

2. I alone cause you to love
God first above all else,
And your neighbor as yourself
Solely for the love of God.

1st Point. The excellence of charity.

## *EXCELLENCE OF CHARITY FIRST HYMN*

3. I am hard to understand,
I am from all time,
In his bosom the Lord begot me,
Over him I have command.

Motives.
1st Motive.
It comes from the bosom of God.

4. Alone I conquered, but without war,
This formidable king of heaven,
I made him man on earth
To save the hapless there.

2nd Motive.
It caused God to become man.

5. Among the virtues I am queen,
They all walk in my wake,
All blessings have I in my domain,
My law God himself obeys.

3rd motive.
She is the queen of the other virtues.

6. Law receives its life from me,
Its success it finds in me,
Without me nothing is made holy,
Without me all virtue flags.

4th motive.
She is the law's fulfillment and the life and truth of every virtue.

7. I make virtue easy,
Its loving goad am I;
Ablaze with strength,
The weightiest burden flies off to heaven.

5th motive.
It is virtue's sweetness and good.

8. I make the wise man
All abandon, and all-suffering,
Hazard all with courage,
Setting his joy on dying.

6th motive.
It makes us leave, suffer and do everything for God.

9. With my powerful charms
I exchange the bitter for the sweet,
And from the hands of the fearsome foe
Make weapons fall.

7th motive.
It charms or disarms.

10. The faithful soul I send up
To God in a chariot of fire;
I marry God himself to her
And remake her wholly into God.

8th motive.
Charity unites and transforms into God.

11. I am that very mark
That sets all the elect apart;
I am the glory, the light, the bond
That links all their virtues together.

9th motive.
She is the character of the elect and the bond of their virtues.

12. Gold is but clay without me,
And even virtue is but sin;
But all is great, all is useful
When once joined to me.

10th motive.
Without charity
nothing is great.

13. I mark off and measure
The point of honor of the blessed;
Charity great and pure
Transports a soul to highest heaven.

11th motive.
She measures
glory in
heaven.

14. Love this God who wants our love,
It is his greatest charge;
Love, or be condemned
And cursed forever more.

12th motive.
God commands
us to love him.

15. God loves you, he is true,
Love him then in turn;
He is all good, all lovable,
On him all your love bestow.

13th motive.
God loves us.

16. Need we for love be sound
Or rich or strong or powerful?
Have we a heart? It is simple,
For love is gentle and fair.

14th motive.
Love is easy to
attain.

17. Whoever loves works wonders,
And will achieve all he wants.
Without great toil, without long watches,
Despite everything, he will be saved.

15th motive.
With love we do
great things.

18. Without me life is pointless,
Without grace or virtue.
You believe in the Gospel but to no avail;
Forlorn is the noblest heart.

16th motive.
Without love we
do nothing.

19. Grace and all of nature,
Earth, water, fire and air,
Indeed, all of creation,
Shouts of love, the love of God.

17th motive.
All creatures are
motives of the
love of God.

20. But self-esteem cloaks me
With finer subtleties.
Allow me then to tell you
Of my true qualities.

2nd point.
The qualities of
divine love.

21. I am never idle;
Should I rest it is in God;
My character is venturesome,
I am lissome like the fire.

1st quality.
She is active like a fire.

22. I am the unyielding warrior,
I am powerful like death;
Nothing is so strong, so stubborn
That my striving cannot vanquish.

2nd quality.
She is strong like death.

23. I make every burden light,
I smooth the way to heaven;
I make the bitterest cross
Sweeter than a drop of honey,

3rd quality.
Sweet as honey.

24. With blameless cunning,
Like a magnet, I beguile the heart;
In an instant, I make it a peerless victim
Of the very heart of God.

4th quality.
She attracts like a magnet.

25. There is nothing like me,
Without me all is vanity;
All things die out, but I abide
Like God in eternity.

5th quality.
Durable like eternity.

26. I lack boundaries or borders,
No end and no beginning,
For loving God as he deserves,
Means loving him without end.

6th quality.
Infinite like God.

27. Pure as gold and even purer am I,
Without self-interest, I love God alone,
Without regard for creatures,
Nothing pleases me save God alone.

7th quality.
Pure as gold.

28. Of my own nature am I
The fulfillment of the law;
But once it is betrayed,
Men are led astray, it is I no more.

8th quality.
In short she is faithful to God's law.

29. These five things oppose me:
The flesh, self-will,
Love of worldly things,

Five obstacles of divine love.

Sloth and wickedness.

3rd Point.
*The means for having divine love.*

30. Since self-will is quite averse
To the holy fire of divine love
We must endure all and do everything
To drive this subtle poison out.

1. Renounce all self-love.

31. To burn with my own flame,
To savor my holy unction,
We must even hate our souls
Through self-denial.

2. Mortify oneself.

32. Men quench my saving fire
With the waters of venial sin;
Whoever does not commit any willfully
Attains the pure love of heaven.

3. Avoid venial sin.

33. Where can I be found in fullness
But in the Most Blessed Sacrament?
I am hidden there in solitude,
It is my true element.

34. Blest is he who takes Communion
With humble heart, faithful and pure,
Without lukewarmness or hypocrisy;
My flame he shall possess, for he is pure.

4. Communicate often and fervently.

35. Do you wish me to enliven you?
Apply yourself to prayer;
There my victim you become
And I your soul's perfection.

5. Pray.

36. Flee the world for solitude
To pray there to God in peace;
There in secret the saints relished
My fires and acquired my traits.

6. Love solitude.

37. Toward all be charitable,
Love even your enemies;
Without this love most genuine,
It is not allowed to possess me.

7. Love one's neighbor.

38. To love Jesus night and day,
The secret is to love Mary,
For she is the mother and the glow
Of fair and perfect love.

8. To be devoted to the Blessed Virgin.

39. Speaking of God and what he does,
Suffering for him, keeping his law,
Loving the Cross and prayer,
Are sure signs of my presence.

Five marks of divine love.

40. A thousand times my heart desires you,
Love divine, come to me:
To be without you is a martyrdom,
Come then, impart to me your law.

Prayer.

41. Here is my body, here is my soul:
All is yours, O Queen of heaven,
In every place your flame enkindle,
Sacrifice all things to your ardor.

42. To make room for the Creator
Spare not the creature;
Make him, my nature notwithstanding,
The master of my heart and king.

43. Forgive, O charity divine,
My defiance and my coolness.
That is past, I open my breast
To your charm and your ardor.

44. By Mary's womb,
By the merits of Jesus,
Come to me, I beg you,
No more shall I rebuff you.

45. Divine Jesus, love supreme,
You alone I love on earth;
I love you and call accursed
Those who love you not.

46. Yes, dear love, I love you,
Not for fear of punishment,
Nor even for the reward,
But only for you alone.

47. Dear Bridegroom, I embrace you.
All I am I give to you,
It is right for me to do so,
For you were first to embrace me.

GOD ALONE.

## 6
## LIGHTS OF FAITH

1. I am pure light
And make all believe with certainty,
As long as God ensures it
With the Church in concert.

2. I am altogether supernatural,
Through the senses, no one can learn of me;
Dark I am but fairer still,
For all my splendor is within.

The essence and definition of faith.

3. I am the root unshakable
Of all we hope for here on earth,
I am the wonderful proof
For all we cannot see.

4. That glowing lamp am I
That glimmers in the gloom,
I am the column of fire
That by night leads to heaven.

1st Point.
Her necessity and her motives.

5. I am in truth most necessary,
For by faith alone do we see God,
Without faith no one can please him,
Not even the foremost king.

1st motive.
She is necessary to know God and to please him.

6. Senses shape the fleshly beast,
While reason forms the worthy man;
But I make the faithful man,
The man of God, the upright Christian.

2nd motive.
To be a Christian.

7. Life's light am I
Who guide men to the truth;
I must be followed
Else men abide in darkness.

3rd motive.
To be saved.

8. It is I who make poor children
Sing of triumph,
It is I who earn their glory
For all faithful believers.

4th motive.
She creates and brings victory to all, children as well.

9. It is I who bring down and overwhelm
The demon, that haughty prince;
It is I who confront him to his face
It is I who plunge him into his pyre.

5th motive.
Victory over the devil.

10. I am the victory over the world
Which wields such authority.
Men must be grounded all in me
So as to know its wickedness.

6th motive.
Over the world.

11. I captivate and I mortify
The flesh and its carnal desires,
By showing it in the next life
The sweetness of eternal bliss.

Over the flesh.

12. I make man pure without malice
In his body, heart and spirit;
Then of them all make a sacrifice
Pleasing to the eyes of the Lord.

7th motive.
Over the whole man.

13. I make the soul to grace compliant
And the flesh yielding to the spirit,
And I make men see that what appears
Deceives, sullies, dooms and damns.

8th motive.
Over his senses and powers.

14. Vices I extinguish and destroy
By my flawlessness divine.
Over virtue and righteousness
Have I title and full sway.

9th motive.
Over virtues and vices.

2nd point.
Her marvelous effects.

15. All powerful am I in God,
I obtain from him all I want;
Through my might an innocent soul
Works marvelous wonders.

1st motive. She gets and does every-thing.

16. I created all those great figures
Who commanded the elements,
I made all the greatest works
Of every place and every time.

2nd motive. The example of the prophets and other great figures.

17. Samuel brought forth thunder,
Elijah set fire to the air,
Moses opened up land and sea
By the faith they had in God.

18. One drew water from a stone,
Another stopped the sun,
All won warless victories;
My power has no peer.

19. It is I who brought elation
To the persecuted apostles,
Who made them race unceasingly,
All hardships notwithstanding.

The apostles.

20. Amidst most bitter torment
I made the martyrs laugh,
I gave them more delights
Than their hearts could have desires.

The martyrs.

21. I made them see the crown,
The blessings and joys of heaven,
Which the Lord bestows
Only on the victorious faithful.

22. We hail the Blessed Virgin
For her faith in the Lord alone.
It is faith that hallowed her
The mother of her creator.

The Blessed Virgin.

23. Give ear, give ear, O creature:
God himself has used me
In grace and nature.
I was his arm, I was his law.

Jesus Christ.

24. Often was he wont to ask:
"You will be healed, you do believe?
Without faith I will do nothing,
In answer to faith I help all men."

25. To the faithful soul I will reveal
The whole universe in an instant,
Death and everlasting life,
Heaven, earth and hell.

26. I am the key that grants entry
To the mysteries of Jesus Christ,
To the wonders of the empyrean,
To the august secrets of the Holy Spirit.

3rd motive.
She is the key of
the predestined.

27. I am that divine armor
That arms true Christians,
In whom, as God assures us,
The flame of strife is quenched.

4th motive.
She is the weapon
of the Christian
soldier.

28. The ineffable treasure am I
Of the poor man here below,
I am the wretched miser,
Jointly we destroy ourselves.

5th motive.
The treasure of
the poor.

29. Much more I do than people think!
It is I who form the blessed,
I create their merit on earth
And their degree of heaven's glory.

6th motive.
The merit and the
degree of glory of
the blessed.

30. I am, in the visible Church,
The staunch buttress of truth,
Most holy, infallible, invincible,
Despite hell in agitation.

7th motive.
The Catholic
Church is
faith's sole abode.

31. Universal is my Church,
In all things subject to Jesus Christ;
Outside her there is no salvation
And doomed is he who withstands her.

32. All heretics I abhor,
The Jew, the Turk, the pagan,
The apostate and the schismatic,

The Catholic alone belongs to me.

33. Here are motives you may call
Motives of credibility,
That more faithful you may be to me
As to the absolute truth.

34. My truths are very believable:
In holy prophecy,
In miracles uncountable,
In fairest conversions,

8th motive.
The motives of
credibility.

35. In the harmony of all mysteries,
In the purity of the law,
In the wondrous ways
Faith came to the world,

36. In the solidness of the Church,
In the impact of her enemies.
Believe then with compliant faith,
And all blessings are your pledge.

37. In the Gospel look for me
Where I hide in every word.
A humble, docile heart you need
To find me there in quiet.

38. To possess me in my purity
Learn how I behave,
Believe all I say; a heretic alone
Denies a truth.

3rd Point.
The qualities of
faith.

39. Believe the practical truths
And those that are not as well.
Alas, how many Catholics
On this point are heretics.

1.
She must be
universal.

40. Faith that is simple is fine and good,
Of exceeding merit and great price:
I desire that people not quibble
About the truths I tell.

2.
Simple.

41. You must believe with great courage
Despite the flesh, despite the senses

3.
Courageous.

Despite the demon and his wrath
Despite the world and its tyrants.

42. Whether threatened or caressed,
Or even if it comes to conflict,
Profess the faith with boldness
Before the greatest profligates.

43. I am a soulless carcass
When I am idle;
I am as nimble as a flame,
But without charity I die.

44. Beware a sterile faith,
All believing and doing naught,
Live rather in the Gospel's light,
Believing it all and living it well.

4.
Lively and effective.

45. Beware of a deception
That believes from moment to moment.
You believe the Gospel only in part,
Then you will live it imperfectly.

5.
Evangelical and not worldly.

46. Among the millions of nonbelievers
Doomed by unbelief,
Give undying thanks
That you have known the truth.

*Faith in practice.*
1. Giving thanks.

47. Flee novel teachings
And the latest heretics:
They sow the keenest errors
That everywhere bring great harm.

2. Fleeing heretics.

48. Put no trust in fables,
In tales without foundation;
For those stories that are true
Believe them, but with devotion.

3. Do not believe unfounded things.

49. Be content with my light,
And search not for visions.
Welcome the decisions
Of the Church your mother.

4. Do not seek visions.

50. Believe Jesus in his vicar,
In all that touches on faith,
And take what he says from the throne
As an oracle and certain law.

5. Submit to the Church and the pope.

51. Your own mind is diabolical,
Be wary of its luster;
For such creates the heretic,
Apostate and schismatic.

6. Not to follow one's own mind.

52. You will give me much glory
If you teach children
All they must do and believe
In order to win Paradise.

7. Teach Cathechism to children

53. Say often this prayer:
Increase my faith, Lord,
That it may pass utterly
From my mind to my heart.

8. Ask God to increase our faith.

54. Grant me a faith simple and pure
Believing all without seeing or feeling,
The senses and nature notwithstanding
As it gainsays their significance.

55. O faithful Virgin, pray for me,
Only increase my faith,
That in life everlasting
I may clearly see you in God.

Prayer

56. With most compliant faith do I believe
With all my heart, and without question,
Everything taught by Holy Church
For God himself has said it.

57. I believe what the Holy Father says,
Hell's keen henchmen notwithstanding;
He is my leader and my light,
For I see naught, and he most clearly.

58. In all things, O God, I want to believe you.
Keep broadening my faith,
That I may see in glory
More clearly what I believe.

59. Make your Gospel's sweet thunder
Rumble far and wide,
That the faith through all the earth
May glorify your name.

GOD ALONE.

# 7
# SOLIDITY OF HOPE

Her essence and her definition.

1. The virtue of Hope I am,
I make you expect from the Lord
Grace and its reward
Through the merits of the Savior.

2. I am that anchor firm and stable
That steadies instability,
That unshakable pillar
That supports all holiness.

3. I draw all my riches
From a God so full with truth,
Faithful to all his promises
Both now and in eternity.

1st Point. God's will is that we hope in him.

4. Here is why I am so mighty:
God wills that man hope in him,
He warns, he repeats, he requires:
O mortal, in me place your reliance.

Motives.

1st motive. God is our Creator.

5. I love you as my handiwork,
I am your God, I am your King;
Hope in me. This is the homage
You should render to me alone.

6. I do not want you to perish,
I am your friend, I am all good,
I want you to change heart
And beseech for forgiveness.

2nd motive.
God is our friend.

7. O Christian, God himself is your father,
Hope in his charity.
A great fool is he who despairs
Of his father's kindness.

3rd motive.
God is our father.

8. Jesus is your faithful friend,
Your savior and your bridegroom.
It is I, he said, I am calling you,
Fear nothing and have confidence.

4th motive.
Jesus is our Savior.

9. Mary is your mother fair
And the sinner's haven.
Hope everything from her prayer,
Expect all things from her favor.

5th motive.
Mary is our mother.

10. The many priceless blessings
God showers upon you every day
Are certain motives
For trusting in his help.

6th motive.
God showers all kinds of blessings on us.

11. Can hope ever be flighty
In what God himself has promised?
His word he keeps,
He is the best of friends.

7th motive.
God's promises.

12. Whoever has put his trust in God
Has never been confounded,
God has given overplenty,
And man has always more obtained.

8th motive.
The examples of those who have hoped in God.

2nd Point.
*The happiness of those who hope in God.*

13. I make a soul unshakable
Like a tower, like a rock;
The most fearsome foe
Cannot make it budge.

1st motive.
Hope makes a soul strong as a rock.

14. We drop anchor in a storm
So as not to founder;
The wise man's anchor am I
In the midst of direst peril.

2nd motive.
Sturdy as the anchor that holds it fast.

15. With me all grows easy;
You are happy, you are joyful,
You are an eagle, you are agile,
You have wings to fly.

3rd motive.
Agile as an eagle.

16. Through me man exchanges his strength
For that of the Almighty;
He breaks out from himself,
And thus becomes alive.

4th motive.
Hope changes one's strength.

17. All the martyrs in my presence
Laughed in their grimmest anguish;
For I showed them their reward,
And they toppled every tyrant.

5th motive.
With the martyrs' examples Hope gives joy in suffering.

18. Grace only do I seek
And the blessings of eternity
And I scorn the passing show
As the purest vanity.

6th motive.
Hope detaches the soul from earth.

3rd Point.
*The woes of those who trust in creatures.*

19. Woe to the man, God said himself,
Who puts his trust in the flesh;
In life he is accursed,
At death he tumbles into hell.

1st motive.
God curses them.

20. It is foolhardy and absurd
To trust the waters to hold you up.
Creatures are fickle
Like the water and the reeds.

2nd motive.
Relying on creatures is ineffectual like the water and the reeds.

21. Man lasts but an instant,
Like a breeze we cannot grasp,
He is like comely foam,
Only fools trust in its support.

3rd motive.
Ephemeral like wind and froth.

22. All things beguile man here below,<br>
And often he himself deceives.<br>
He is an impostor, a phantom,<br>
If he hopes not in the Lord.

4th motive.<br>
Deceptive like a phantom.

23. If God does not take part<br>
In consoling the afflicted,<br>
In vain we trust in man,<br>
He cannot soothe our ills.

5th motive.<br>
Often useless.

4th Point.<br>
*The qualities of hope.*

24. In God alone I place my trust<br>
And not on human succor;<br>
Should man help and soothe me<br>
His hands are merely borrowed.

1. Supernatural without human support.

25. Rely not on your misfortunes:<br>
With you nothing has strength or power,<br>
But rather on the Father of Lights<br>
From whom all perfect gifts descend.

2. Humble without relying on the self.

26. Count on all things from his charity,<br>
Both here on earth and in eternity,<br>
Since with his Providence<br>
He has for you a father's care.

3. Universal and without exception.

27. No graver insult can you give him<br>
Than despairing of his help;<br>
For since he is by nature good,<br>
When he forgives, he abounds with joy.

4. Firm without despair.

*Means for increasing hope.*

28. Work in fear for your salvation,<br>
Without yielding to despair,<br>
Join holy hope to your striving,<br>
Without too much presuming.

1. Work for salvation with fear and hope.

29. Without delay renounce the world,<br>
So artful, fickle and shrewd,<br>
And base your hope on God alone<br>
Who holds you in his hand.

2. Renounce the world.

30. To gain this reliance<br>
And this leaning on the Lord,

3. Keep purity of heart.

Keep fast your innocence,
Have purity of heart.

31. Say: God himself is my dear Father,
And I cry out to him: Abba Pater.
Mary is my most gracious Mother,
Never shall I go to hell.

4. Prayer.

32. When out of weakness or of guile,
You fall sadly into sin,
Pray God to show you favor
And do not despair.

5. Hope after falling.

33. Cling tightly to his mercy,
In his blood drown your sins.
Always good, he grants pardon
To hearts that are stirred.

Penance.

34. Imitate the faithful Virgin,
Take care to serve her,
Put your hope in her,
And you cannot perish.

35. For sure my malice, Lord,
Shrinks before your kindness.
I hope in you, with fairness,
Without fear of being turned away.

Prayer.

36. Like my forebears I hope in you,
And you will hear and answer me as well.
Should I have woes more bitter
Your glory is greater for it.

37. With the lightning in your hand,
Set to quench me with its might,
I could not bring myself
Not still to hope in you.

38. Against hope I hope in you,
When I should have lost the day,
If you do not come to my defense;
But no, your love I know.

39. My trust is utter and complete;
Forgive me if I seem rash,
But deal with me as I hope
In your sweet charity.

40. I hope for your grace on earth,
Blessings of soul and body.
I hope to see you face to face
And delight in all your treasures.

41. Through Jesus, through Mary
In you, O Lord, I hope in peace.
I shall hope throughout my life
And I shall never perish.

GOD ALONE.

# 8
# SPARKLE OF HUMILITY

1. In singing I discover
A rare beauty
Veiled and hidden:
Holy humility.
She is slight and small,
Barely can you see her,
Yet look at her grace
And her perfection.

The essence and definition of humility.

2. Man, by the light
Of this humility,
Discerns his woeful state
And wickedness.
Himself he then despises,
Views himself with horror,
And believes he merits
But hell and hardship.

1st Point. *The excellence and necessity of humility.*

3. Upon her are founded
A Christian's virtues.
Nothing in this world is great

Motives
1st motive.
She is the foundation.

If she does not uphold it;
Tiny though she may be,
Nothing is so glorious,
She is the true excellence
Of earth and heaven.

2nd motive.
The support.

3rd motive.
The excellence of the other virtues.

4. She is the virtue dearest
To the sovereign Lord,
In her dust he encounters
His honor most matchless;
He is the invincible one,
Yet his conqueror is the humble man;
With might transcendent
He wins his heart utterly.

4th motive.
God loves the humble.

5th motive.
He delights in them.

6th motive.
He is conquered by the humble.

5. The humble man mortifies his soul,
And God who loves him to it descends;
If he calls out to him and pleads,
He listens thus answering his prayer;
This humble reverence
Pleases him infinitely,
And even humble silence
Mightily delights him.

7th motive.
He descends to them.

8th motive.
He answers their prayer.

6. To him God opens up
The greatest of his secrets,
And fills him beyond measure
With his greatest benefits;
He shows him the tenderness
Of a virginal Bridegroom
And on him bestows
A generous master's bountiful gifts.

9th motive.
He reveals his secrets.

10th motive.
He showers them with gifts.

7. While with lightning in hand,
As a rigorous judge
He strikes and crushes
The haughty sinner,
Like a good father he goes out
To seek in lowliest regions
The humble man in his grime
To lift him up to heaven.

11th motive.
He lifts them up to heaven.

8. So great a majesty has
This most excellent virtue
That God himself had to come
And manifest its beauty;
For before the coming
Of the most humble Savior
She was unknown,
And men lived in dread of her.

12th motive.
God became man
out of love for
humanity.

9. God could not protect himself
From her charms so dazzling;
To enlighten us about her,
He became flesh on earth;
He was born in a stable,
He lived as a carpenter;
What a worthy model
For being the last of all!

13th motive.
The example of
Jesus Christ.

10. "I am most gentle
And humble of heart,"
Our loving Savior
Was wont to say.
How salutary a lesson
That brings us peace,
Complete victory,
And happiness everlasting.

14th motive.
The lesson of
Jesus
Christ.

11. He said to his apostles:
"I pray you, be humble;
Let the greatest among you
Be the servant of all.
I, Wisdom Eternal,
Have come to serve you;
Take me as a model,
Or you shall perish."

15th motive.
It is his
commandment.

12. In Mary God sees
But her humility,
As she made clear
In all its truth;
He takes her as his Mother,
Glorifies her name,
And makes her the foremost
Of earth and heaven.

16th motive.
The example of
Mary and
the saints.

13. O feckless creature,
Say grace and faith,
You are a disgrace,
And worthless. Bow low.
The Most High makes war
On every proud man,
While on earth his heart
And his eyes the humble possess.

17th motive.
Faith requires us to be humble.

God above.

14. A body conceived in filth,
A worm-filled sack,
Ghastly fodder,
Worms and infernos:
With all that, you ash heap,
Arrogant criminal.
Do you claim out of wrath
To scale heaven?

2nd Point.
*Subjects man has for humiliating himself.*

1st motive.
Above us is God in anger.

2nd motive.
Our body is corrupt.

15. In history seek out and read
What the saints did
To enter into glory,
And then think yourself perfect!
Or imagine rather at your side
A hundred righteous men,
The least of whom
Ought serve as an example.

3rd motive.
The example of the saints.

16. A source unfit
To produce anything good,
A wretched sinner
Who merits nothing,
A traitor, an infidel
Ready to be condemned;
Yours is a cruel folly
If you deem yourself saved.

4th motive.
Inside us there is incompetence, faithlessness, iniquity.

17. The falsity and ignorance
In your sinful spirit,
The coldness, the fickleness
And the malice of your heart;
With a memory
Filled with vanity,

Falsity, ignorance, coldness, fickleness, distractions.

Can you delude yourself
Amid all these infirmities?

18. Your poor soul is full
With a plenitude of sins,
That your benighted folly
Always well hides from you.
Among your colleagues
Have they confessed their sins?
Have you received forgiveness?
Are your sins all wiped away?

5th motive.
Within us are
unknown and
unatoned for sins.

19. You fear not, perhaps,
The judgments of a God
Before whom you will appear,
And in so short a time;
His boundless justice,
Without error, without appeal,
His sentence followed
By an everlasting hell.

6th motive.
Before us lie
God's
judgments.

20. Sinner, filled with crimes,
Man, enemy of God,
On the brink of the abyss,
Held back by a hair,
In hell you belong,
You have well deserved it!
Soul empty of grace,
Be proud of yourself.

7th motive.
Beneath
ourselves.

21. This fathomless virtue
Has cowed the flesh,
Has overwhelmed the world,
Has disarmed hell.
The man who looks down
On himself without pretense,
Ever eludes the clutches
Of the world and the devil.

3rd Point.
*Its victories and its fruits.*

1st
Over the world,
the flesh and the
devil.

22. Frenzied with rage, the demons
Frequently bemoan
That the humble have the profit
Of their former bliss;
That their surpassing anguish
Comes from the great pride,

2nd
It saves the soul.

Which hurls man himself
Into a similar torment.

23. Glory we cannot claim
Everywhere and every place;
Either we must descend
To climb up to heaven,
Or else delude ourselves
That we can climb in arrogance,
Only then to forfeit glory
And fall into the fiery pit.

3rd
Without it we are damned.

24. Only on the ladder
Of true humility
Does a humble, faithful heart
Attain holiness,
Reach victory
Over all iniquity,
And climb to glory
For all eternity.

4th
It is Jacob's ladder.

25. You will receive light,
O glorious unknown,
And total victory,
O worthy vanquished.
O refuse of the world,
God exalts you all;
The sky, the earth, the sea
And God himself are yours.

5th
The humble are glorified
and raised up.

26. God rejects and abhors
False humility;
Flee like the plague
This malignancy,
Avoid the surprise
Of a subtle pride,
Which shrewdly disguises
Its real allure.

4th Point.
*The practice of humility.*

27. Knowing our wretchedness,
Looking on ourselves with scorn,
Loving to be amid the ashes
And among the lowly;
Believing ourselves all-guilty

Interior practice.

And skillful in nothing
Believing ourselves ignoble
And unworthy of all good.

28. Hiding our fair grace
And showing our defects,
Loving that others pass us by
With their surpassing talents,
With good heart resigned
For the love of God:
These marks make known
The humility of the heart.

29. All gleaming virtue
Is bound to perish,
If the humble, prudent soul
Knows not how to mask it.
Hide far from praise
Your virtues peacefully,
And the Lord and the Angels
Will see them for eternity.

Exterior practice.

30. By deferring your opinion
To that of someone else
Who speaks with haughtiness,
You emerge the victor.
Suffer people to accuse you,
Without cries of complaint;
Suffer people to refuse you,
But without protestation.

31. What a praiseworthy practice:
Choosing the worst in beds,
At meals, at table,
At work, in dress,
The better to hide your grace;
Behaving in a saintly way,
Through menial deeds,
Even though in public.

32. Look upon yourself
As an ugly toad,
Horrid in the extreme,
Displeasing the Most High.
Say not for or against,

For you or against you,
For that is a vain display
Common to every fool.

33. Should misfortune come
And you fall down,
Have a timorous soul,
But do not be uneasy.
Say: "Forgive me, Father,
Here is all my skill."
And then, among the ashes,
Choose the least place.

34. Your best point,
O wretched sinner,
Is but mischief
In the eyes of the Lord;
Marks of self-importance
And willfulness,
Faults of negligence,
Sins of vanity.

Remedies to thoughts of vanity.

35. Whence come these expectations
And your bold desires?
Have you received some license
To be in Paradise?
The saints, full of innocence,
Were fearful until death,
And you, not being shriven,
Think you strong and upright.

36. It is in your presence,
O worshipful Lord,
That I feel the powerlessness
Of a woeful sinner.
Before your justice
And your holiness,
I am utterly spiteful
And full of wickedness.

Prayer.

37. The sin roots I have in me
Of all your foes,
Without your grace divine
I would have done them all.
Am I not guilty

Of all deadly sins?
Of them I am capable at least,
Like every criminal.

38. Wherever I go I am
Like an ugly snail,
Spoiling your grace
With a subtle poison.
And I delude myself
Like a haughty peacock
That we shall both now
Soon reach victory.

39. Your just judgments, Lord,
About me I venerate,
But humbly I implore
Your grace unceasingly;
Though I am worthy
Only of condemnation,
By a signal grace
I hope still to be saved.

40. I am a wretch
Unfaithful to your laws,
I sense and see
I'm unable of any good;
Yet, in my soul,
I feel a puffed up pride,
Like a filthy sewer
Unequaled in the world.

41. Lord, I beg you for
Humility of heart,
That I might give you
More perfect honor;
So that, from my place
Among the very least,
I may by grace one day
Become among the first.

GOD ALONE.

## 9
## CHARMS OF GENTLENESS

1. Here is the elder sister
Of all humility,
Her companion, arrayed
With utter charity.
Her name is Gentleness:
The sugar, the oil,
The balsam of the heart,
Without coldness, without bile.

The essence and definition of gentleness.

2. She is ever winning,
Without uneasy cares,
Never impatient,
Always full of peace.
Of all the virtues
She assumes the charms
By which hearts are won
As with so many weapons.

1st Point.
*Her excellence through the example of Christ and the saints.*

3. A God so kindly,
Filled with gentleness,
Came that she might
Triumph in our hearts.
He names himself Lamb,
Or rather gentleness itself.
How sweet and fair he is,
How much he deserves our love.

1st motive.
The example of Jesus Christ.

4. He is gentle of countenance,
Gentle in all his bearing,
Gentle in all his language,
Gentle in his conversation.
Gentle in every action,
Gentle in every woe,
Gentle in his passion,
Everywhere boundless gentleness.

Gentle to others.

5. From his infancy he charmed
Both shepherds and kings
With so much power

Gentle since his infancy.

That he made them subject to him.
His smile, his gentle manner
Had so much eloquence
That he won them all to himself
Without breaking his silence.

6. The children of his age
Wanted only him to see;
By his comely mien
Everyone was charmed.
His torturers, in fury,
And fearing his good nature,
Veiled his face,
The easier to strike him.

Gentle in His passion

7. How gentle his behavior
Toward all sinners!
No matter how far away he sends them,
He charms their hearts.
With what gentleness
Did he win over the Magdalene,
And conquer the soul
Of the woman of Samaria.

Gentle in his behavior toward sinners, the Magdalene and the Samaritan woman.

8. See him as a father
Gently forgiving
An adulterous woman.
Wishing to save Judas,
He weeps, he humbles himself,
He bows low to the ground.
O unheard of gentleness!

Judas

9. On the smoking wick
He gently blows,
And then relights it
Without any anger.
Break a stick,
He takes it, joins it,
And makes it fit again.
O infinite gentleness!

Comparison.

10. On the cross he summoned
The last of his strength
To gain forgiveness
For the poor sinner,

And for his own torturers
Full of rage and envy,
Who with untold suffering
Will make him lose his life.

11. With all this, my brother,
Will you still act harshly,
And behave with bitterness
Unlike the gentle Savior?
All bloated with pride,
And filled with arrogance,
Will you have no kindness,
Gentleness, or clemency?

12. In Mary did you ever see
A trace of sharpness?
The mother of life
Gentleness engenders.
Her mild and gladsome mien
Chased away all sorrow
And filled eyes and heart
Again with jubilation.

Example of the Blessed Virgin.

13. See the gentlest charms
Of the godly apostles,
They were the sole weapons
They used in their hands.
They were lambs
Even in the midst of wolves,
They showed in their distress
Surpassing gentleness.

Examples of the apostles.

14. If they won the world
It is with this virtue,
With their profound gentleness
They conquered everyone.
Are not all the saints
Quite free of gall and ire?
Moses was so gentle!
It was his quality.

The fruits of gentleness.

The example of the saints and Moses.

15. With neither ire nor war
She wins over the hearts
Of heaven and earth
By her gentle sweetness.

2nd Point.
*Gentleness sings victory over every heart.*

The heart of Jesus Christ
Wins all for himself through her,
She is his very spirit,
He is her true ideal.

1st
Over the heart of God.

16. With gentleness we charm
Our neighbor's heart,
Or else we disarm him
Without a weapon in hand.
The gentleness of children
Has such striking traits
That the most violent of men
Are rendered peaceful.

2nd
Over the heart of our neighbor.

17. A saint is very gracious,
Gentle, upright, winsome,
Amiable and obliging,
Without any agitation.
It is by this sweet means
That he wins over and beguiles,
That he does so much good,
At times without a word.

3rd
Over every heart.

18. Only fervor does he enkindle
With his mien so sweet and tender.
For souls' conversion
He becomes all things to all,
But without human respect,
Without mawkishness,
Or pride, or scorn,
And without any imprudence.

4th
She is all things to all men.

19. He is never bitter
In correction,
The zeal consuming him
Soothes with unction.
He corrects a friend,
Like a father he admonishes,
Not like a foe
Out of envy or in anger.

5th
She corrects usefully.

20. By anger man
Is driven from his home,
No more light, nor faith
Nor law does he possess.

6th
She wins the heart of one who is gentle.

The virtue of gentleness
Puts him in charge
Of both soul and heart,
So that all might yield to him.

21. Gentle patience,
Without bitterness or gall,
Is that very violence
Whereby heaven is ravished.
It is the true path
To life everlasting;
Any other is unsure,
Any other is untrue.

7th
She wins heaven.

22. The gentle have the benefit
Of living without ill-humor,
Without suspicion, without offense,
Without coldness toward their neighbor.
Never bad tempers,
Never impatience,
Even-tempered at all times
Even in suffering.

3rd Point.
*In practice she overcomes many sins.*

23. No indifference, no intimidation,
Without discord,
No semblance of stoniness
And without loathing,
They speak gently,
Without arrogance
or stubbornness
And are ready to comply.

24. When someone offends you gravely,
Bear everything gently.
You will win out
Over his behavior.
Gentleness has within
A secret strength
Which for all creates a charter
For a most perfect peace.

Practical advice.

25. In your wrath, my brother,
You correct another?
Alas, your anger
Will harm you all the more.

You provoke only
A crime with crime;
To charm him you want
A surpassing gentleness.

26. Be gentle of mien,
Without moodiness, or gloom,
Let your tongue be gentle,
Without haughtiness or spite.
Behave gently
And without misgiving
Suffer peaceably
And without concern.

27. Bitter is my soul,
And with harshness my heart abounds,
I am filled with rage:
My Lord forgive me;
Calm your wrath,
Grant me your graces
That I may be humble and meek,
Walking in your footsteps.

Prayer.

28. Rough as a bull I am
In my behavior;
Make me hereafter
As gentle as a lamb,
To preserve the peace,
With patience,
In all I do,
In all I think.

29. O heavenly Mary,
Give me gentleness,
It is my heart that begs you
Through your own heart.
Pour into it that sweet honey,
That holy tenderness,
That wins for heaven
A sinful soul.

GOD ALONE.

## 10
## MERIT OF OBEDIENCE

1. A cherub you would have to be
To tell the eminence
Of a most godly sacrifice:
Holy Obedience,
Which makes the Lord obeyed,
Either in doing or believing,
And tames the mind and heart
All the better to sing victory.

Its essence and definition.

2. Every man's and every Christian's
Greatest sacrifice it is;
Without it God welcomes nothing:
For he wants us to obey.
A great sacrifice, in truth,
Not of flesh or fatling,
But of our own will,
That grand mistress.

1st Point.
*Its necessity.*

Motives.
1st motive.
It is the greatest sacrifice of a man And of a Christian.

3. Making a vow of poverty
And of chastity as well,
Practicing austerity
In greatest hardship,
Enduring violent torments,
And even martyrdom;
Obeying is still worth more,
For that is God's desire.

2nd motive.
The greatest of the three religious vows, even greater than martyrdom.

4. To disobey in but one matter
Is the crime of crimes,
Without it God accepts not
Even the greatest victims.
Saul disobeyed in little,
But a prophet cried out to him:
"God has forsaken you."
And all he lost and life as well.

3rd motive.
Without this sacrifice all other sacrifices displease God.

5. By disobedience
Were we accursed,
But Jesus saved us every one
By his obedience.
Of the Savior's virtues
This is the model miracle,
Which holds the center of his heart,
It is of such necessity.

4th motive. Through disobedience Adam doomed us. By Obedience Jesus saved us.

6. He comes down and becomes an infant
In his mother's womb
In order to obey, by saying:
Father, I want to fulfill,
Your law, your will;
This law I love
And I set it, truly,
At the center of my being.

5th motive. The example of Christ.

1. At the beginning of his life.

7. Like the least of children,
He had his whole life long
Been subject to his parents,
To Joseph and Mary.
Greater nothing Jesus did,
This is his greatest miracle,
As the Gospel affirms,
And his greatest oracle.

2. During his life.

8. He obeyed until death
Without striking back,
His dying on the cross flowed
From his obedience.
God, for this compliance,
Made his name glorious,
A name above every name,
A name replete with victory.

3. Until death.

9. Obey truly,
And you save your soul,
For your own will
Shapes hell and its fire.
Obedience does away
With that cruel sweetheart,
Who debases all and makes us perish
Once she interferes.

6th motive. Obedience is the death of one's own will.

10. The mark of one predestined
Is his obedience;
The man who will be damned
Loves independence.
All saints have trod this road
To life everlasting,
The baleful mind takes another path,
As does the infidel.

7th motive.
It is the mark of the predestined and without it We do not imitate the saints.

11. Unless you become a child,
It is Jesus you must believe,
But a child most obedient,
You shall not have my glory.
Since it is Lucifer you follow,
That arrogant rebel,
You shall follow him to his hell
Into everlasting punishment.

8th motive.
Without it we cannot be saved.

12. How great a sin it is to disobey!
A sin of black magic!
God is stirred to the quick,
And it is God who makes it clear.
Whoever resists with passion
The lawful master
Does commerce with the devil,
What an appalling crime!

9th motive.
Disobedience is a great sin.

2nd Point.
*Its excellence.*

13. Without it virtue perishes
Or is but hypocrisy,
It is its source, its spirit,
Its merit and its life.
The more we obey, the more
We perform a worthy deed;
If in obeying we omit it
We still lose not its glory.

1st motive.
It is the summary, merit and the prize of virtues.

2nd motive.
It earns merit without effort.

14. Obedience leads to a safe haven
In the thick of a storm,
It is a bark where we slumber
As it sails along.
It brings peace to us entirely
In the midst of war
And uncovers by its secret ways
A Paradise on earth.

3rd motive.
It gives peace and reassurance in the thick of a storm.

15. In every woeful mishap,
When everything goes awry,
Where even earth and heaven
Would surely founder,
I obey, says the obedient soul,
I act with dependence
For the future and the present,
I sleep with self-confidence.

4th motive.
It brings joy to
the suffering.

16. He sings, says the Holy Spirit,
And histories tell us,
All victory in Jesus Christ,
And even victory songs.
Victory over the serpent of old,
Who cannot submit;
Wishing independence
He opposes God his Lord.

5th motive.
Victory over the
devil.

17. Victory over the world as well
And over self-importance,
Victory over the hard hearted soul
Who runs from independence;
All victory over the flesh
And its own bidding.
Victory at last over all of hell.
O most excellent triumph!

6th motive.
Over the world.

7th motive.
Victory over the
flesh and its
desires.

18. By this virtue we discern
What true merit is,
We can know or divine
The pious hypocrite.
To know holiness,
This is the touchstone,
Revealing its truth
Once touched.

8th motive.
It is the
touchstone of
virtue.

19. Were we to have the holiness
For working miracles,
Were men to ask our counsel
As from a great oracle,
Unless we are humble, obedient,
We are hoodwinked by the devil,
And cover with a winning lie
A lamentable calamity.

9th motive.
It dispels illusion.

20. In dying, the obedient sing,
All brimming with hope;
Effortlessly they die,
As I have witnessed.
Their peace, their joy and sweetness
Are a reward
The Savior won for them
By his obedience.

10th motive.
It gives peace at death.

21. On the great day of judgment
It is an instant excuse
Defending, and most mightily,
A man who is accused:
"Out of obedience, Lord,
Did I so act."
If he proves it, he is innocent,
And he has won his cause.

11th motive.
It is the right excuse on judgment day.

22. With his own hands Jesus gave
The crown to the obedient
And such alluring charms
That confound the heavens,
He gives them a name above all names,
The name of a true king;
In all of holy Zion,
His like, there will not be.

12th motive.
It gives incomparable glory.

23. Obedience is a secret,
A secure highway
For soon becoming perfect,
In little time, and painlessly.
Witness that saint who after five years
Of pure obedience,
Great gifts received from heaven,
And then immeasurable glory.

24. Oh, if only we knew what peace,
What grace there is in life,
What gifts, what happiness eternal
And glory unending
God gives to the obedient,
If we knew their great reward,
We should obey like children
Without ever holding back.

25. See only God himself
In the one commanding,
And like a saint you will do
What all God asks of you,
And you will do whatsoever He will say
Without complaint or murmur,
And nothing will seem
Beyond your strength.

3rd Point.
*The qualities of what God demands*

1st quality.
Obeying like a saint for God alone.

26. Obey completely,
That is essential;
God so orders without condition,
You must then comply.
Keep all his commandments
And without distinction,
Everywhere and every time.
If not, you offend him gravely.

2nd quality.
Completely obey everything good and possible.

1. God's commandments.

27. For your inner life follow
A friend learned and wise,
Open to him your full heart,
Simply, no holding back.
In all things obey the king,
God speaks in his person;
Submit to every law,
Though created by your peer.

2. The spiritual director.

3. The king.

4. Even your peers.

28. I mean here only
Every law that is good;
It makes us holy, and leads us to God,
It offends no one;
Better to be flayed alive
And lose the whole world
Than to commit but one sin,
No matter how someone may scold.

29. Obey most swiftly,
Without asking people to wait,
Obey doubly
The one who commands.
Obey gladly,
Without ill humor
Where you would surely lose
Your glory before God.

3rd quality.
Promptly and without delay.

4th quality
Joyfully and without ill humor.

30. Do all you are told
If it be good and possible,
Without grumbling, without question,
However harmful it may seem.
Obeying gladly and with joy
In a difficult matter
Is the most generous action
Of our whole Gospel.

5th quality.
Strongly despite hardships.

31. Obey blindly,
Without overbearing,
Without saying why or how,
"I could not," or "perhaps."
This kind of quibbling,
Sharpened by conceit,
Is a major indisposition
We mask and we disguise.

6th quality.
Blindly and without quibbling.

32. As long as men will hear you,
You can, through prudence,
Quite carefully express
Your reasons for exemption.
And then, stay calm
Without saying a thing,
Bear the yoke and the burden
A master lays upon you.

7th quality.
Prudently.

33. Agree with your Superior
In what he enjoins,
Compliant in mind and heart:
How great is obedience.
Take pains to obey,
It is God who commands,
Till the end, until death
And your heavenly crown.

8th quality.
Inwardly with heart and mind.

9th quality.
Perseveringly.

34. Do all you are required
With precision,
For that is surely from God,
Whose yoke is not harsh.
Do as Our Lord does,
Who lets not a whit go by
Without tending it ardently
And with very good grace.

10th quality.
Obey all your regulations.

35. Your rules are great laws,
Not one is too slight,
They are all of great import,
And all of great merit.
Faithful in much as in little,
With fealty unbroken,
You will hear your God
Say these words to you:

36. Dear son most obedient,
My servant most faithful,
Come now with me
Into my joy everlasting.
Upon earth as in heaven
Receive the dominion
Over even the blessed
In view of your obedience.

37. Trust not your mind,
Its light is misleading,
For this is how Satan
Beguiles a righteous soul.
Consult an enlightened man
And follow his lights,
You will be most secure
In all that you do.

11th quality.
Mistrust yourself.

38. We are clear-sighted for others
And know what should be done;
But for ourselves we are hopeless,
And see upside down.
While saints counseled others
In marvelous ways,
For themselves they consulted
With like-minded souls.

12th quality.
Consult a
spiritual director
in everything.

39. Forgive me, good Lord, I avow
My misdeed and wrongdoing,
Till now have I followed
The laws of my fancy.
Full of my own opinions,
And of my own worth,
My own willfulness I followed
In all that I did.

40. Henceforth, my God, I follow you,
    I walk in your footsteps,
    And obey like a child,
    But grant me your grace
    To see in my Superior
    Your very own plan
    And in my father director
    Your presence alone.

41. No, no longer will I listen
    To the laws of nature
    That have so made me defy you.
    Forgive this affront.
    Without quibble or waiting,
    With pleasure profound,
    Till death shall I obey
    Out of love for you alone.

42. Sure refuge of sinners,
    All powerful Queen,
    And most obedient
    Of the handmaids of the Lord,
    Drive out my own will,
    And make me obey,
    That I may be truly saved
    And render you service.

43. I want to obey so I may sing
    A full victory song,
    I want to be humbled so I may climb
    To the heights of glory.
    And make me rather die,
    My God, I beg you,
    Than ever to disobey
    Even one day of my life.

GOD ALONE.

## 11
## POWER OF PATIENCE

1. A noble princess I admire;
She smiles amidst her agony,
And without grief or sorrow
Turns her woe into winsome joys.
She is Patience unconquerable,
The message dying Jesus gave,
The foundation of hope,
The force of a true conqueror.

Its essence and definition.

2. Is this not the great sacrifice
Of man's to the Godhead
So to compensate his justice,
And glorify his bounty,
To expect his Providence,
And believe in his authority,
To surrender to his power,
And worship his majesty?

1st Point.
*Patience is glorious to God and salutary to man.*
1st motive
It glorifies the attributes of God.

3. What glory it is for God, our loving Father,
To see his dear child laugh,
And humbly kiss and reverence
The rods that beat him;
In the midst of blows he cries out:
"Blessed be God! My God, forgive!
Good Father, I thank you.
Oh, what a grace! How great a gift!"

2nd motive.
It glorifies God the Father.

4. The patient man glorifies
Good Jesus with his cross,
For thus he imitates his life,
Submitting to his laws,
And through suffering completing
What is lacking in his passion,
Since by patience does he vanquish
All the enemies of his name.

3rd motive.
It glorifies God the Son.

5. The cross protects and purifies
From self-will and from sin,
Makes the righteous humbled
And the sinner moved.

4th motive.
It is salutary for man.
5th motive.
It protects him from sin.

Through its radiance the cross
Makes us see both God in his splendor,
And the utter wretchedness
And deception of the sinner.

6th motive.
It humbles him.
7th motive.
It enlightens him.

6. Nothing is more meritorious
Than suffering for Jesus Christ.
Look about, read all of history
To satisfy your mind.
A day of the love of suffering
For the Christian is worth more
Than a hundred years of penance,
Or giving alms of all one has.

8th motive.
Its merit is greater than that of voluntary penance and almsgiving.

7. It is you, dear cross, that rule
Over all the enemies of God,
Yet in this lowly place no one knows
That your victory is divine.
The world deems you ugly,
Flesh is fearful of your strictness,
The devil looks at you with hate,
While your greatness I adore.

9th motive.
It gives victory over all God's enemies.

8. The cross has abounding power,
It is the spur of virtue,
It is the brace and hope
Of the poor despondent sinner.
This cross is heavy, it is true,
Yet when we love its holy weight,
The soul, abroad, is most at ease,
And both laughs and weeps.

10th motive.
It spurs on virtue.

11th motive.
The support and strength of his hope.

9. Believe, with deepest faith believe:
Without the cross we are not saved;
It is the battledore, the lye
With which God wants to cleanse us.
It is his loving purgatory,
It is his blazing fire, his crucible
Where even the most perfect man
God prepares for glory.

12th motive.
It is man's crucible and purgatory.

10. In vain a man sings victory,
If he is not patient in suffering
He acquires but vain glory,
Since his conquest is but a sham.

13th motive.
It is man's great and true victory.

Becoming master of an empire
Is not a feat so glorious
As suffering quite without a word,
Though wracked with pain.

11. O saving patience!
My verse cannot express
How imperative you are,
How much we are to love you.
Suffer we must, how great a maxim!
God's decree, a law most just
To which he subjects every man
In nature and in faith.

2nd Point.
*Patience is necessary.*

1st motive.
It is a universal decree.

12. On earth be as righteous
As that simple and holy Job,
Avoid every war as wisely
As the patriarch Jacob.
You are not able to fend off
Suffering always and everywhere,
For this is what man must expect
Until his advent in heaven.

2nd motive.
The most righteous must suffer.

13. "Will any come to live with me?"
Asked Jesus Christ quite clearly.
"Will any follow where I go?
Take up your cross and carry it.
With my cross I walk ahead,
I want your suffering like mine,
Without complaint
Or stopping to look back."

3rd motive.
Jesus' call to the cross.

14. "My head is crowned with thorns;
Away with you, squeamish soul!
Crosses are my divine weapons;
Away with you, feeble soldier!
The cross is my dearest friend.
Away with you, who cast it off!
On the cross I ended my life;
To you who tire of it, farewell!"

4th motive.
His example.

15. "True innocence am I,
For you, all have I done and suffered;
And you, sinner, so blameworthy,
You will suffer naught for me.

5th motive.
Man is Christian and sinful.

From the cup I was first to drink;
Now you take it, it is yours to quaff;
Help me in my sacrifice
And render me love for love."

16. "The least devoted suffering
Of the last one of my followers
Is richer and more precious
Than an emperor's treasure house.
Suffer now, this happiness exceeds
That of being loved by my heart,
It is the very high point of grace,
The highest grade of favor."

6th motive.
Nothing is as
great as
paticncc.

17. "I want you to receive a diadem
Or else a confining prison,
Or some dignity supreme,
Or the gallows for my name.
Take prison and the gallows
And trample vanity under foot,
That is the highest prudence,
Believe me, I am the truth."

7th motive.
Without patience
all is vanity.

18. "Never can you win my victory
If you have not fought like me,
No one comes into my glory
Save by the power of my cross.
If you grasp not my speech
To love the cross, and quell the flesh,
You will have to suffer the fury
Of hell's fire everlasting."

8th motive.
No victory or
salvation without
the cross.

19. Look at heaven and reflect
On that company of the blest.
Will you reign after their example?
Like them, then, you must suffer.
By fleeing the common road,
Through their crosses they reached
The zenith of good fortune
Which crowned them all kings.

9th motive.
The examples of
the saints.

20. One trampled riches under foot
And another ran from fame,
One from pleasures, and caresses
Another from honors and possessions.

With me as their only model,
They passed through fire,
And from the harshest death
They climbed to highest heaven.

21. Crosses of a highest merit have I,
The crosses of my favored ones;
All the noblest saints of my court
Had crosses of greatest price.
I made my mother suffer all with me,
I pierced her heart with grief,
Because she was so dear to me
And the tender object of my heart.

10th motive. Example of the Blessed Virgin.

22. See this hallowed throng
Of holy martyrs of first rank,
Whose robes are all flushed crimson
And dyed with their own blood;
With all the prophets, they have
Suffered all for Paradise,
And you, fool that you are, you think
To have it cheaply and without pain?

11th motive. Example of the martyrs.

23. They did all for the Gospel,
Suffered all to flee from sin:
One was roasted on a grill,
One run through, another flayed alive;
All died a brutal death
After myriad pains and labors,
All for everlasting life.
So now, feel sorry for yourself.

24. Behold those weighty fetters
With which the worldly chain themselves:
What griefs, what ills, what troubles!
And then only to be forever damned.
They suffer, yes, but they are forced
For the devil's sake, without reward.
But to suffer all for God without complaint,
Is to win all with nothing lost.

12th motive. The wicked all suffer.

25. A very slight suffering,
A short moment of distress,
Bring immeasurable glory,
An endless time of happiness.

13th motive. Paradise is the fruit of suffering.

The woes of most dreadful times
Are but the smallest woes,
In the light of the unfathomable blessings
God makes ready in Paradise.

26. Suffer in this world or the next
Either on earth or in hell,
Though holy as an apostle,
Though tough as iron,
Choose that petty trial
That wins God in a moment,
Or else his dreadful wrath
In hell without end.

14th motive.
Suffer or be damned.

27. Suffer all with patience,
In grace and without mortal sin,
Otherwise there is no reward
In heaven or on earth.
Natural patience
Is that of a pagan man,
Christian patience is supernatural:
It makes a Christian.

3rd Point.
*The qualities of patience.*

1. It is holy.

2. Supernatural.

28. The impatient man stops only
Before what his senses feel,
Thus imitating the beasts
Who see a stone and bite it.
From God's hands receive
Even your woes as his great gifts,
As signs that he loves you
Like a most cherished child.

3. Prudent.

29. There falls not a leaf
Without his express command,
His Providence watches over all,
But over us in a singular way.
All our crosses are measured
By his justice and his love,
In their weight and in their duration,
He himself transforms them in turn.

30. Should God punish his creature,
It is as a good Father, a good friend,
With reason and with measure,
And not as an enemy.

He knows each person's
Strength and his perfection.
His kindness metes out to him
His pain and his temptation.

31. But patience is universal:
To suffer all adversity,
A faithful friend's desertion,
The direst poverty,
The grimmest malady,
Loss of possessions, loss of honor,
Indeed, all the woes of life,
In a word, the cross of the Lord.

4. Universal.

32. Since it is God who sends,
And weighs and shapes our crosses,
We must bear them with gladness,
Without taking away their heaviness.
Let us suffer without groaning, without gloom,
Though we are showered with blows,
And let us quiver with jubilation:
All goes well, for God is on our side.

5. Joyful.

33. This amazing grace,
This joy in affliction,
We obtain through prayer
We make with humility.
To obtain it, let us pray to Mary;
Through her sorrow-pierced heart
She bestows life
And even the cross of the Lord.

6. Humble.

34. Let us be filled with gratitude
When God sends us off to suffer,
Let us ask for perseverance
To live on the cross, and there to die.
Let us beg him strike us as a father strikes,
And not as a wrathful judge;
If he is severe in time,
Let him be gentle in eternity.

7. Grateful.

35. Lord, I suffer at this hour,
But I bless your bounty for it;
I am on the cross, and there remain
But subject to your will.

Prayer.

Strike, O bountiful Father,
I worship and bless your blows,
I am your child, yet guilty,
With me you are still too mild.

36. You desire then, Jesus my master,
That I be with you on the cross.
I am content, deign to place me there,
It is for me too much honor by far.
In putting me there, give me your grace
And keep me there by your might,
That I may walk in your footsteps
In suffering most gladly.

37. I am a poorly polished stone,
Crude and without adornment,
Shape it, Lord, I beg you,
To set it in your building.
I want to suffer in patience,
Cut, shape, strike, slice,
But help my helplessness
And forgive me my sins.

38. Saint Andrew, let me cry out
With you: "How good the cross!"
Saint Paul, may I glory with you
In this hallowed wood!
Catherine, let me share with you
No crown of flowers,
But a crown of thorns
From the brow of the man of sorrows!

39. May I exclaim with you, Teresa,
"I want to suffer or else to die;"
Or like another in her furnace:
"Not to die, but to suffer well."
Pray for me, faithful Virgin,
Give me a share in your sorrows,
That in life everlasting
I may share in your majesty.

GOD ALONE.

# 12
# BEAUTY OF VIRGINITY

1. They think me a little girl,[37]
Without pleasure, without greatness,
Yet in the Gospel I am great,
And nothing equals my happiness.
Since my youth in my breast
I nurture a princess,
Royal beauty I possess
In my virginity.

2. I am a virgin, a virgin pure,
And Jesus is my Bridegroom,
He is all that is most sweet
In nature and in grace.
I have eternal Wisdom
Attached to my breast,
Royal beauty I possess
In my virginity.

Essence and definition of a virgin.

1st Point. *The excellence of virginity.*

3. I have the matchless name
Of bride of Jesus Christ,
I am a true virgin,
Virgin in body and spirit.
Without a sinful will
And without carnal blemish.
Royal beauty...etc.

1st motive. Her name.

4. Marvel at my marriage:
My Bridegroom is all bloody,
His cross is my legacy
And my peerless portion,
His Calvary my abode
Where we must die to live.
Royal beauty...etc.

2nd motive. It is a divine and eternal marriage.

5. The covenant is for ever,
Most heavenly is its bond,

---

[37] For the important context of this hymn, see the Introduction on page xv

Nor will the cruelest death
Ever see its end.
He embraces me, I embrace him.
He is all mine, in grace I am all his.
Royal beauty...etc.

6. Put your finger to your lips,
You know not who I am,
Since God himself has his bed
On my bosom among the lilies,
I am his lowly handmaid
And his winsome bride.
Royal beauty...etc.

3rd motive.
It is a great mystery.

7. What mind could fathom
A mystery so hidden?
God alone can make it felt
By a heart that he has touched;
It is heroic grace,
An evangelical counsel.
Royal beauty...etc.

4th motive.
It is a heroic virtue.

8. As a virgin, I have the glory
Of triumphing over my flesh
And of winning victory
Over the world and over hell.
I am queen and conqueror,
I am more than laurel-crowned.
Royal beauty...etc.

5th motive.
It is victorious over the devil and the flesh.

9. On men I make war,
Of me they are unworthy,
Never a mortal on earth
Will have my heart or troth.
The King of Heaven chose me
For his accomplished bride.
Royal beauty...etc.

6th motive.
Over the world.

10. Farewell, O world, I loathe
Your false and fleshly pleasures,
Full heavenly is my joy,
Eternal are my pleasures,
With them my soul is fragrant,
They set my soul ablaze.
Royal beauty...etc.

7th motive.
Over all the pleasures of the flesh.

11. A century of worldly pleasures
Are not even worth a day
Of the chaste and deeper peace
Of Jesus, my precious love.
Only the purest virgin
Can know what I affirm,
Royal beauty...etc.

8th motive.
It gives the
fullness of joy and
peace.

12. In my anguish, I cry out:
I am a virgin, what delight!
My misery fades away,
I no longer feel distress.
No grief, no pain,
I am a virgin and a queen.
Royal beauty...etc.

9th motive.
It dissipates all
pains

13. O marvel of grace!
August virginity,
You make us pass from mortality
Even to divinity.
A virgin God begets you,
Only God can understand you.
Royal beauty...etc.

10th motive.
It brings a soul to
divinity.

14. Mary was the first to make
A vow of chastity,
Alone she is its mother,
Its model and its beauty.
Only in and through her
Faithful virgins we become.
Royal beauty...etc.

11th motive.
The example of
the Blessed
Virgin.

15. Never would the angel have won her
To be the mother of God,
Had he not indeed assured her
That she would keep her vow.
The Blessed Virgin we call her,
And man she has never known.
Royal beauty...etc.

16. Jesus, a virgin like his mother,
His beloved John, a virgin too,
A virgin, Saint Joseph his father,
Every true virgin is his.

12th motive.
The examples of
Saint Joseph and
Saint John.

Oh, how joyful then am I
This pearl of great price to possess!
Royal beauty...etc.

17. For whom these powerful graces
That so sweetly and gently seduce?
For whom this winning tenderness
That God so rarely bestows?
These endless riches
Are for the faithful virgins.
Royal beauty...etc.

13th motive.
The virgins have
singular graces.

18. Fine company they possess,
For the angels are with them
To guard them in life
From every ill fortune,
As we love our fellows.
How glorious is their affection.
Royal beauty...etc.

14th motive.
The angels
accompany
them on earth.

19. Virgins were celebrated
By pagans in manifold places,
They were called the hallowed ones
And the companions of the gods
So much do grace and nature
Honor a virgin pure.
Royal beauty...etc.

(They were
honored even
by pagans.)

20. The virgin dies in the ardor
Of a holy and charming bridegroom,
While a husband or wife
Falls into the arms of a living God.
The wife is all a-tremble
Where the virgin laughs and sings.
Royal beauty...etc.

(The virgin dies in
the arms of her
bridegroom)

21. After their death, upon their shrine
No black cloth is draped,
White marks their grace
And their glory and their power.
For the wedded, black crape
For virgins, crown and glory.
Royal beauty...etc.

After their death
their shrine is
covered
in white.

22. The virgin sings alone
The Canticle of the Lamb.
How comely her voice!
How fair and tender her air!
What an angelic song!
How transcendent a hymn!
Royal beauty...etc.

15th motive.
Their heavenly
reward.

They sing the
Canticle
of the Lamb.

23. Whither Jesus fares
In all the universe
Virgins are his escort,
And his fairest ornament.
They stand nearby,
And form his crown.
Royal beauty...etc.

16th motive.
They follow Jesus
Christ.

24. On the virgins is bestowed
A ring of light in heaven,
A shining crown
Made for them alone.
Their joy is inexpressible,
Their glory without compare.
Royal beauty...etc.

17th motive.
The virgins have a
special halo in
heaven.

25. Alas! How many foolish virgins
And scatterbrained young men
Sell for trinkets and baubles
This treasure of Paradise!
In losing everything they revel
In their brutal pleasures.
Royal beauty...etc.

18th motive
The foolishness
and troubles of
those who marry.

26. What is lost in marriage?
Shall I tell the truth?
You put yourself in bondage,
You lose serenity,
You are tainted, you embrace.
Oftentimes you lose grace.
Royal beauty...etc.

27. My lady-friend gets married
How sorry I feel for her!
I prefer to lose my life,
Though people swear fast friendship.
The wife scoffs, and taunts me,

Yet I am free and she the slave.
Royal beauty...etc.

28. I am a maid and I am wise.
Dear God, how many fools I see!
No children, no housework,
Nor any jealous husband.
I am a virgin by grace,
Nothing at all encumbers me.
Royal beauty...etc.

29. It is not that I allege
Wedlock to be bad.
If God so bids you,
Be bound to your mate,
But follow the counsel of a sage,
Lacking any lewdness.
Royal beauty...etc.

Marriage is not an evil.

30. Oh! What dreadful ill fortune
To lose one's virginity!
The loss is beyond repair
For all eternity,
But it is a frail vessel,
And keeping it most arduous.
Royal beauty...etc.

2nd Point. *Means of preserving one's virginity.*

31. This flower wants to be enclosed
And more than you may think;
It is all but the same
To lose it or to flaunt it.
A virgin on display
Is a virgin half doomed.
Royal beauty...etc.

1st means. Flight from the world and retreat.

32. This fair maid is fragile:
A notion, a desire,
A carnal pleasure that flatters
Withers her and makes her perish,
But the pleasure people shun
Makes her stronger and more flawless.
Royal beauty...etc.

2nd means. Flee the least sensual pleasure.

33. The glamor and the world I flee
To preserve my purity,
And I am a virgin fruitful
In works of charity!
Poor outside, but joyful,
I work, I pray, I sing.
Royal beauty...etc.

3rd means. Attend to holy and charitable work.

34. Bah! to that vain finery,
To those crowns of vanity,
Those haughty hairstyles!
Oh! What shameless pomp!
I wear thorns on my head
And my crowns are divine.
Royal beauty...etc.

4th means. Never dress in the world's fashion.

35. Bah! to that freakish fashion
That changes at every moment!
The beauty which adorns me
Adorns me eternally.
My lilies never wither
Nor does my beauty age.
Royal beauty...etc.

36. Maidens, let us be wise virgins,
Fleeing the dance and games
And a hundred little pleasantries
That only fuel the flames.
Drinking, eating, sleeping, laughing,
Must be a great martyrdom for us.
Royal beauty...etc.

5th means. Fleeing dance and games of chance.

37. Let us avoid the diversions
And the presents of young men.
Their letters, their flatteries,
Their trysts, their songs,
How many virgins are lost
Just by their talk!
Royal beauty...etc.

6th means. Avoid the company of young men.

38. They promise the wonder
Of a future marriage,
To drop into the ears
A poison most impure.

7th means. Don't listen to their promises.

The demon who drives them
Wants only sin from you.
Royal beauty...etc.

39. From the flesh let us fear war,
Since, despite all we do, we are
More breakable than glass,
Less substantial than reeds;
Let us tend our lilies in fear,
In seclusion and with restraint.
Royal beauty...etc.

8th means.
Fear the flesh and mortify it.

40. My body has all it needs,
But with nothing in excess.
One must often displease it
In order to please Jesus.
In thorns, the rose,
In crosses, Jesus rests.
Royal beauty...etc.

41. I sacrifice to perfection
For this precious treasure,
My mouth, my ears,
My hands, my feet, my eyes;
My Bridegroom takes his delight
In these little sacrifices.
Royal beauty...etc.

42. I am always at prayer
To preserve this great gift,
To have total victory
Over the devil and the flesh.
I love to pray in secret,
In quiet, in my room.
Royal beauty...etc.

9th means
Pray always.

43. Meditating on each mystery
Of Jesus, my dear Bridegroom,
Each day I say the whole rosary;
Not everyone knows this,
But the effort is a sure help
To remain a virgin pure.
Royal beauty...etc.

10th means.
Say the holy rosary.

44. In the Eucharist I find
The lilies of my purity,
The sweet pleasures of my life,
The fires of my charity.
The more the virgin takes Communion
The more purified she is.
Royal beauty...etc.

11th means.
Receive
communion often.

45. The wise virgin is obedient
To the counsels of a director.
But the foolish one scorns him,
She finds in him her misfortune.
Let us flee the utter folly
Of being our own leader.
Royal beauty...etc.

12th means.
Obey a director.

46. Celebrity and limelight
For us are not the safest,
Let us hide in the dust
And a pure heart will be ours.
The virgin who humbles herself
Abounds with grace.
Royal beauty...etc.

13th means.
Hiding.

47. O virgin wise and celebrated
Do not be deceived,
Keep your lamp lighted
For the Bridegroom's knock.
Be watchful always
As you wait for him to come,
Burning with charity,
Deep in humility!

14th means.
Engage in good
works.

48. Farewell, then, wedlock
And you friends of Venus,
I have the gift and privilege
Of being Jesus' bride.
Bah! To man and his caresses,
Bah! To all his promises.
Royal beauty...etc.

Farewell to
marriage.

49. O holy sisters in religion,
Keep your threefold vow;
O victims of love,
Burn with love for God.

Your flowers' fragrance encircles him,
In you he has his kingdom.
Royal beauty...etc.

50. My God, I thank you
For my peerless state,
For having thus chosen me
To keep celibacy,
But keep my body spotless
And my heart without attachment.
Royal beauty...etc.

Prayer.

51. Choose another bride
Full of faithfulness,
And I shall not be jealous,
I shall praise your goodness:
Even take throngs to yourself
Of these beloved virgins.
Royal beauty...etc.

52. Hail, Mary,
Mirror of purity,
Replete you are
With grace and charity.
Glorious virgin, guard
This precious pearl of mine,
Preserve my chastity
For the Supreme Beauty.

53. O Virgins, I offer you
This small but priceless posy,
Composed of a dazzling rose,
Of a fair and snow-white lily,
And of a violet
No less flawless:
You breathe it in while singing
And beam with it at worship.

GOD ALONE

# 13
# NEED FOR PENANCE

1. Behold illustrious Penance
Whose name seems stern
Yet it is great and glorious
And gentler than you think.

Its essence and its definition.

2. All glory it gives to God,
And destroys every sin,
It makes a heart most touched,
Weep and sing victory.

3. It is called the Lieutenant
Of the Lord's Justice,
The plank that saves a sinner
From impending doom.

1st Point. *Its necessity.*

4. God twice orders it,
O sinners, convert,
Yes, all of you,
No one excepted.

1st motive. God commands it.

5. If you do not repent,
You will all be doomed together
Just as surely as you will die.
O dreadful judgment!

2nd motive. Jesus Christ orders it.

6. To teach us how,
He was the first himself.
Let us do likewise without delay:
He is our model.

3rd motive. Jesus Christ gave us the example.

7. The prophets proclaimed it,
Speaking out for God:
"Wherever you are, repent,
Or every soul is doomed."

4th motive. It is preached by the prophets.

8. Great Saint John, shining beacon,
Exclaimed along with Jesus:
"Without it you are doomed,
You vipers' tangle."

5th motive. By Saint John the Baptist.

9. Prompt penance and severe,
Or you will soon all perish,
Unable to escape
God's most righteous wrath.

10. The apostles, filled with ardor,
Preached this truth,
And proved its necessity
For the salvation of souls.

6th motive.
By the apostles.

11. Look at the saints, I pray you:
Though often most innocent,
They were all repentant
All their lives through.

7th motive.
The example of
the saints.

12. Penance is necessary
To repair, by its severity,
The Lord's glory and honor
And quell his wrath.

8th motive.
Necessary to
repair God's
glory.

13. It atones for the abuse
Of Jesus in his passion,
It is his consolation.
Oh! How great a boon!

9th motive.
To atone for the
scorn given to
Jesus on the
cross.

14. Once innocence is lost,
It cannot be won back,
Nor can it now be mended
Save by penance.

10th motive.
To repair lost
innocence.

15. It is a certain balm
For healing a sinner's soul,
And for changing its ugliness
Into a glorious glow.

11th motive.
To heal the soul's
wounds.

16. It retrieves lost grace;
Do all you want and moan;
You cannot receive it without repenting.
O power invincible!

12th motive.
To retrieve lost
grace.

17. It is the key, it is the door,
Whereby the sinner gets to heaven,
Though hell were his destiny.
How mighty its power!

13th motive.
To obtain glory.

18. Without it God does not forgive,
Nor has he ever done,
Without it is a sinner doomed
To everlasting flames.

14th motive.
Without it we are damned.

2nd Point.
*The necessity of not delaying it.*

19. It must not be put off,
That God specially forbids,
Or else, for every moment
A store of wrath.

1st motive.
God forbids it.

20. Sinner, God urges and is waiting;
Be then converted to him,
Prolong not his grief,
For he is full of tenderness.

2nd motive.
God wants us to be converted and is waiting.

21. Give God your youth,
To him dedicate your earliest zeal,
For an insulting gift
Are the leftovers of old age.

3rd motive.
The merit of conversion at a young age.

22. The young man growing older
Travels along the same road,
Always better or more shrewd:
So the wise man says.

4th motive.
We do not convert in old age.

23. Every leniency God pledges
But not for the morrow,
Without delay be certain
And do penance.

5th motive.
God does not promise for tomorrow.

24. "Tomorrow, tomorrow," say the ungodly.
Alas! Tomorrow is not theirs.
"From today on," says the wise man,
"I shall change my life."

6th motive.
The example of the ungodly who procrastinate.

25. Today God gives you grace,
Most ready to convert you:
Tomorrow, you cannot use it,
For it takes flight and is gone.

7th motive.
The grace of conversion is of the present.

26. Sinner, you defy God himself
Who speaks to your heart this very day,
You know not your ill fortune,
Alas! It is most intense.

8th motive.
When we will want to
We shall be unable.

27. O reckless defiance!
God may well avenge himself,
One day you will want to change
And be unable.

9th motive.
We defy God.

28. The weighty burden of your sins
Will grow heavier day after day,
And then finally overwhelm you
In the deepest pit.

10th motive.
The weight of sins
will increase.

29. Your sinful habit
In your heart will root itself
And bind you fast, unhappily,
With an everlasting chain.

11th motive.
Habit will become
stronger.

30. The devil will chain up your soul
With links so tough and strong,
That till death you will belong
To this loathsome tyrant.

12th motive.
The devil will be
the stronger.

31. In tarrying, your ills increase,
And the farther away God is each day;
Less help will he give you,
And weaker is his grace.

13th motive.
Grace weakens.

32. From sin to sin you will flounder,
From weakness to ungodliness,
From habit to compulsion
And from chasm to chasm.

14th motive.
We become
hardened.

33. Repentance put off
Is not often of much value,
It belongs to petty minds
And does not abide.

15th motive.
Repentance
postponed
is not worth
much.

34. But I see through your trickery:
You pretend to convert
Only when you are to die,
But death is like life.

16th motive.
As you live so
shall you
die.

35. The sinner dying, we are assured,
Is dying well, is remorseful.
But alas! He is only feigning,
It is only deception.

17th motive.
God mocks an
unrepentant
sinner at death.

36. At your death, unhappy sinner,
To all your cries of repentance,
God will only answer woe,
Only justice and retribution.

37. This very moment, then, without waiting,
No more make war on the Most High.
As you should, repent;
Sinner, you must give in.

Resolve.

3rd POINT.
*Usefulness of repentance.*

38. To righteousness, repentance
Makes an atonement of honor.
It is a settlement for its eminence,
It is its great sacrifice.

1st motive.
It remunerates justice.

39. The repentant sing victory
Over the heart of a God almighty,
And in repentant hearts
This God finds his glory.

2nd motive.
It glorifies his omni-potence.

40. God the Father, this father so kind,
Always accepts a penitent,
Embraces him as his child
And prepares him a great feast.

3rd motive.
It makes the eternal Father happy.

41. What joy for the faithful Shepherd,
After so much labor, to have
Led his sheep to the sheepfold
Of eternal life!

4th motive.
Jesus Christ.

42. Defying nature, the Holy Spirit
Enters into the heart of the true penitent
To make it his living temple.
How pure is his joy!

5th motive.
The Holy Spirit.

43. The holy angel had taken flight
Far from the sinner and from the sin,
But once he sees his heart is moved
He returns with him to stay.

6th motive.
The guardian angel.

44. Heaven provides a fine feast
When a sinner is converted,
It sings glory to Jesus Christ
For his fair conquest.

7th motive.
The entire heaven.

45. True repentance
Moves hearts of stone
And gravest sin forgives.
Oh admirable power!

8th motive.
It forgives all sins.

46. On the soul it bestows a grace
That sustains it, and leads it,
Adorns and informs it,
Enlightens and sets it on fire.

9th motive.
It bestows grace.

47. It grants life
To all merits lost
And restores brilliance to virtues.
Unbounded is its might.

10th motive.
It revives merits.

48. Nothing so gentle, so peaceful,
Even its turmoil is peace;
Its rigor is full of appeal
And no way to be dreaded.

11th motive.
It bestows peace and joy.

49. Yes, its sweetness has no peer,
And the tears of the penitents
Hold still greater delights
Than all the pleasures of this world.

12th motive.
It bestows a great sweetness on the soul.

50. With repentance all things are useful,
Everything merits heaven,
But without it a bountiful deed
Can bear no fruit.

13th motive.
It makes everything meritorious.

51. It shuts the door to the abyss,
Its weeping puts out its fire,
Its suffering satisfies God
And wipes away all sin.

14th motive.
It closes off hell.

52. It lays open heaven to us;
We must be truly repentant
Or else a most innocent saint
For life everlasting.

15th motive.
And opens heaven.

53. How rare a true penitent is!
All ill gotten goods he restores,
His enemies he forgives,
And he breaks with evil.

16th motive.
The rarity of genuine repentance.

54. He cuts off, uproots and knocks down
All things that make him sin
And everything that hinders him
From preserving grace!

55. Feigned repentance
Damns an infinity of people;
Be wise and wary of your company,
Predestined soul.

56. How many fruitless sacraments!
How many unenlightened confessors!
How many imprudent directors!
How many treacherous falls!

57. True repentance
Must have many qualities.
I shall tell them to you, give ear,
It is of consequence:

4th Point.
*Its qualities.*

58. It is prompt and supernatural.
Without hesitation or human respect,
Answering the divine spirit
As soon as it calls.

1st
Prompt.
2nd
Supernatural.

59. True repentance
Has its center in the heart,
Else its whole appearance
Is vain and blameworthy.

3rd
Internal and of the heart.

60. It is a conversion undivided,
For a divided heart will perish;
The Lord will refuse it,
For it dishonors him.

4th
Complete.

61. A humble heart without conceit
Is a truly repentant heart,
But the proud and pretentious
Have only its illusion.

5th
Humble.

62. When repentance flows
From the love of God alone,
And not from fear of punishment,
It is of great merit.

6th
Loving.

63. Love makes it strong and lasting
Without faltering or changing,
But timorous repentance is in danger,
It is unbearable.

7th
Lasting and strong.

64. It must be most severe
In order to uproot iniquity,
To transform an angry judge
Into a kindly father;

8th
Severe.

65. To exchange eternal pain
For the pain of a moment
And make a sinful soul
Live like a saint.

66. How many flattering penances
Without any severity
Or of one's own devising!
Deceitful penances.

9th
False penances.

67. Follow my helpful counsel:
Choose a good confessor,
A director firm and wise,
For you he is essential.

*Means for doing penance well.*
1st
Choose a good confessor.

68. Show him your soul's ills,
With candor and simplicity,
Totally and without concealment,
To the most loathsome detail.

2nd
Opening one's heart.

69. With utter obedience
Do all he bids you,
Accept what he gives
As your penance.

3rd
Total obedience.

70. Go often to confession,
But with a purpose of amendment
For to wish to do otherwise
Is ever to damn yourself.

4th
Frequent the sacraments with the purpose of amendment.

71. Bodily penances
Have most wondrous effects;
They make us a generous heart,
And give us wings.

5th
Corporal penances performed with discretion.

72. With counsel, with courage,
Practice one in secret,
In keeping with your strength, your taste,
Your state, your age.

73. Ask God, I beg you,
For heartfelt contrition,
A new heart in the Lord,
A new life.

6th
Ask for the spirit of compunction.

74. Mary has all in her power:
Ask of her this sorrow,
Without it a poor sinner
Dies impenitent.

7th
Through the intercession of the Blessed Virgin.

75. Would you delight this grace?
Give, and it will be given to you.
Almsgiving will fast obtain it.
Oh, efficacious secret!

8th
Give alms.

76. I am blinded by my sins,
I feel my heart quite callous.
Oh, Lord, shall I thus fall
Into the depth of the abyss?

Prayer and acts of contrition.

77. No more than prayer have I,
Come, Lord, to my assistance.
To you alone have I recourse,
In you I hope.

78. Let me see by your light
On one side your majesty,
And on the other my cruelty
And all my woes.

79. With a stroke of fear and ardor
Pierce my flesh, pierce my heart,
And penetrate with sorrow
My body and my soul.

80. Oh eyes, weep copious tears;
My wicked heart cries out and moans,
For forgiveness I am promised
But only with your aid.

## *NEED FOR PENANCE*

81. Against God himself have I sinned,
I have scorned my Creator;
My God, forgive this sinner,
Forgive, O supreme goodness.

82. Good Father, so cruel is my offense,
After so many blessings received;
I repent, and am confounded.
Forgive this rebel.

83. What! Dare I call you Father?
I am unworthy so to name you.
Forgive me, great God, forgive, forgive.
Stay your wrath.

84. Do not answer war with war,
See my heart humble and contrite,
Or rather see Jesus Christ
And not this wretched worm.

85. I borrow the voice of his passion,
The voice of his blood shed.
No, I cannot be lost
In his most sacred blood.

86. Lay down, Savior, lay down your arms,
Your blood is too precious.
Your name too glorious;
Forgive me, you see my tears.

87. Holy Spirit, nothing can I say.
How could I have betrayed you?
Lend ear to the repentance
Of my lamenting heart.

88. Pray for me, Virgin Mary,
Safe refuge of the sinner,
Speak a word in my favor,
And my soul is healed.

89. Put down your arms, Monarch Supreme.
Peace, peace, forgive me.
I am armed, against you no more,
But against my own self.

90. Mercy and penance,
I embrace you both,
To live and die with joy
And so full of hope.

GOD ALONE.

## 14
## TENDERNESS OF LOVE OF NEIGHBOR

1. I want to sing in vain no longer,
For in singing my heart expresses itself,
And love for my neighbor,
Opening my heart, creates this hymn:
Long live holy charity
With which I feel my heart expand.

2. Through this we love tenderly
Our neighbor just like ourselves,
For the love of God alone,
Because he commands us to love him
Without regard for his faults,
Without being horrified by his ills.

Its essence and definition.

1st POINT. *Excellence of charity.*

3. It is the absolute will of the Most High
That man should love his brother-man;
This is his greatest commandment
As Creator and as Father.
He punishes those who flout this
With the greatest rigor.

1st motive. It is the first commandment of God as Creator and as Father.

4. His authority alone suffices;
It is enough that he speaks and commands;
Woe to those who disobey,
For his vengeance will be great.
God declares himself their enemy,
Even though they may otherwise be great friends.

2nd motive. To transgress in this is to touch him to the quick.

5. Every human being, says this great Lord,
Is my beautiful portrait, my true image;
You touch me to the quick, to the very heart,
Whenever you offend him.
I will avenge this insult
On the great day of my anger.

3rd motive.
God punishes harshly those who transgress.

6. Charity contains within itself
The most perfect holiness;
It is the fulfilling of the law,
There is no law without it;
It is the only bond of virtues,
Without which they no longer exist.

4th motive.
It is the summary of holiness.
5th motive.
The fulfilling of the law.
6th motive.
The bond of virtues.

7. It is this charity which, by its beauty
And its shining purity,
Covers and destroys iniquity,
Even the greatest and the most numerous.
A heart is filled with purity
Once charity truly reigns there.

7th motive.
It covers a multitude of sins.

8. Have a mutual love
For one another, says Saint Peter.
There lies the essential point,
There is nothing greater on earth.
Love is the perfection
Of all religion.

8th motive.
It is the essence of the Christian.

9. The sign that one is predestined
Is charity for one's brother;
It is Jesus who has given us
This infallible characteristic,
To pick out his servants
From among those who are false adorers.

9th motive.
It is the sign of the predestined.

10. Here is my great commandment,
Says Jesus Christ himself to all of us,
That you love one another tenderly
In the same way as I love you.
It is new in its gentleness,
Though it is old in its greatness.

10th motive.
It is the new commandment of Jesus Christ.

## *TENDERNESS OF LOVE OF NEIGHBOR*

11. But how has he loved us?
Without self-interest and beyond measure,
To the point of dying, completely consumed
With the purest charity.
Jesus is filled with fire for us,
While we are quite icy towards everyone.

11th motive. Jesus Christ gives us the example.

12. Look at the love and the ardor
Of the first Christians in the Church:
They had but one heart and one soul;
Love alone was their motto.
Being quite ready to die for someone,
They placed their goods in common.

12th motive. Example of the first Christians.

13. Saint John preached only love
In his ordinary conversation.
He would say a hundred times a day:
Love one another, my dear brothers,
My little children, love one another,
My children, love everyone.

13th motive. Example of St. John the Evangelist.

14. This was his answer
To those who did not know this mystery:
Charity alone suffices,
You must speak of it and never be silent,
It is the commandment of the Lord
Which is enough for our happiness.

15. The saints were on fire with love
And with charity for their brothers;
Night and day they would give
Help to them in their trials;
The example of a God who died for us
Made them all things to all.

14th motive. The example of the saints.

16. Why would we not love our neighbor?
He is the vivid portrait of God himself,
The masterpiece of his hand,
A friend whom his heart loves,
The brother of Jesus Christ,
The temple of the Holy Spirit.

15th motive. Our neighbor is worthy of being loved.

17. He is the son of the eternal Father
By divine covenant,
The universal heir
Of his kingdom and his immense glory,
Who will reign some day in heaven
As a great and glorious king.

His qualities

18. Man is crimson with the blood
Of Jesus Christ my dear master;
If he does not have his rightful place in my heart
I am a Judas, or even more of a traitor.
Can a Christian do wrong
To those for whom God himself has died?

His price

19. Love your brother, good Christian;
Otherwise you condemn yourself, without any doubt.
It may be all right for a pagan
Who does not know the price paid for him;
But how can you know his worth
And have nothing but scorn for him?

20. What am I saying? The pagan without any faith
Shows more natural friendship;
In this he shows you the way,
On this point he is more faithful:
Look at the Turks in their charity,
And blush at your hardness of heart.

16th motive. Pagans and heretics have more natural charity than Christians.

21. My heart is beginning to burn
As my neighbor appears to me to be lovable!
Ah! Now I wish to love him;
It is too right and reasonable.
Nothing is so gentle or so pure,
Nothing so great, nor so sure.

22. But watch out! This sacred gold
Is counterfeited by hypocrites,
Whose gold glitters and seems refined.
At bottom it is without worth;
They call it charity,
But in God's eyes it is carnality.

2nd POINT. *The qualities of charity.*

23. If you only help your neighbor
By virtue of a natural principle,
Then, alas! you work in vain
And your alms are quite impure.
Charity goes straight to God,
A fire which ascends to his domain.

1. It must be supernatural.

24. To love people because they are relatives,
Or because they are civil, obliging, agreeable,
Because they are rich or wise,
Noble, powerful or respectable:
This is the charity of a pagan
And not that of a Christian.

25. Love your neighbor in a holy way,
Through virtue, not for sinful reasons;
For to love sinfully
Is to give yourself as a victim to the devil.
Put far away from you all carnal love,
For it is a pleasing fire, but a mortal one.

2. Just and innocent.

26. Love with your heart and hand
And not simply with your mouth.
Pour your alms into his lap.
Let whatever affects him, affect you!
Friendship which is only in speech
Is a ridiculous decoration.

3. Effective.

27. That your love may extend to everyone,
Entertain no coldness for anyone.
You say: He is my enemy;
Nevertheless, you must love, God
commands it.
Flee from singling out some,
For that destroys charity.

4. Universal and not particular.

28. Love is gentle and patient
And full of support for one's brother;
Docile and obliging,
Free from trouble and anger.
Put up with your neighbor's faults;
God makes you responsible for his burdens.

5. Patient.

29. You must love your friends,
And nothing is easier in practice;

6. Heroic.

But love also all your enemies:
This is the most heroic act,
Which you really must carry out
Or lose yourself for eternity.

30. You must love with all your heart
An enemy who wishes you harm;
This is the commandment of the Lord,
To which you must submit and subscribe,
Under pain of mortal sin
And eternal repentance.

3rd POINT.
*Necessity of forgiveness of enemies.*

1st motive.
God commands it.

31. God gives to all, even to sinners,
His gentle rain and his light;
Let us then love our persecutors
In order to imitate this good Father,
Who, in his immense goodness,
Overcomes all iniquity.

2nd motive.
He sets the example.

32. Without this love, this forgiveness,
God will not accept any sacrifice;
You will be the devil's martyr
Amidst the worst tortures;
The gift of all you have in alms,
Without this forgiveness, does you no good.

3rd motive.
Without forgiveness, all sacrifice is useless.

33. A person with animosity in his heart
Asks God in his prayer
To look on him without pity,
To rekindle his anger;
He never says the Our Father
Without condemning himself to hell.

4th motive.
All prayer becomes pernicious.

34. Animosity turns to poison
All the springs of life,
The Sacraments and mental prayer.
All become an impious sacrilege,
And the one who is vindictive in his heart
Will be lost in spite of all confessors.

5th motive.
All Sacraments become sacrileges.

35. The most wonderful action,
If charity is not involved in it,
Is pure illusion,
And God rejects and castigates it.
It has the external appearance of goodness,

6th motive.
All good acts are an illusion.

But within is nothing but iniquity.

36. It is only heroes
Who never exact vengeance,
Who suffer for God all ills
In peace and in silence.
When you take vengeance and become embittered,
You show your meanness of spirit.

7th motive.
Nothing is so heroic.

37. Did not the saints forgive?
Did they not pardon all injuries?
That is why God has given them
His blessings without number or measure.
God is liberality itself
To the charitable heart.

8th motive.
The example of the saints.

38. The one who forgives evil
Is more than human; he surpasses himself.
This victory is without equal
In nature and in grace;
Here is a victor so glorious,
To be found only in heaven.

9th motive.
The miracle of man in nature and grace.

39. Forgive, because the Lord,
Through pure goodness, forgives you.
For you he is all gentleness,
And will you show none to anyone?
Tell me: will you be saved
If God takes you on the hop?

10th motive.
God forgives us.

40. Jesus forgives his executioners,
And prays for them to his Father.
Be there ever so many ills done to you,
Ever so many causes for anger:
A dying God forgives everyone;
Sinner, calm your wrath.

11th motive.
Jesus Christ forgives his executioners.

41. What madness it is to scorn
A God who forgives and prays,
Who reaches out to embrace
Those who put him to death!
Vengeful one, go ahead and avenge yourself;
Go ahead and throw yourself into hell.

12th motive.
It is madness to avenge oneself.

42. Scorn the cross, scorn Jesus,
With the executioners strike out and shout
To avenge the injuries you have received.
Scold, speak ill, swear,
Demand a tooth for a tooth here below,
And you will burn in red-hot fires.

43. Take courage, you must forgive
Despite shudders and complaints;
You should not be surprised by these,
For this is contrary to nature,
But this generous forgiveness
Will delight all the blessed.

13th motive. This forgiveness will delight heaven.

44. Overcome "What will people say?".
Put a stop to your growling flesh,
And rise beyond reason
To the victory without parallel;
Forgive your enemies,
Love them as your friends.

14th motive. Will be praised by the just and the saints.

45. Good people here below will praise you,
The angels will sing songs of victory,
And the saints who are with God will cry out:
This man is worthy of glory
Because he imitates his Savior
In forgiving with all his heart.

46. Do not delay, go quickly,
See this adversary
And ask him humbly
For his pardon, but a sincere pardon;
And do not be afraid of being put off,
For God alone is your aim.

4th POINT. *Qualities of forgiveness.*

1. It must be prompt.

47. Should he reject your forgiveness,
You cannot avoid it,
For it will become like coals
To win him or reduce him to ashes.
You gain more by forgiveness
Than by force or by reason.

2. Strong and courageous.

48. But forgive sincerely
Without retaining any bitterness,
Completely from the bottom of your heart,

3. Sincere and cordial.

Without any freezing and consuming coldness,
With a serene countenance,
Opening your heart as well as your hand.

49. Forgive unconditionally,
Speak to him, visit him,
Serve him as occasion arises;
This forgiveness is in no way hypocritical,
Provided you avoid saying "But...",
Which condemns a soul for ever.

4. Absolute without conditions.

50. Try then to find a way
To render some service to this man;
For his injury, treat him well;
God speaks, we must obey.
A pardon which is merely polite
Is a bad pardon and a lying one.

5. Effective and of service.

51. Forget all the harm of the past
As soon as peace is made.
Often enough agreement is destroyed
By an indiscrete memory.
And think no more of the future
Except to love and support each other.

6. Prudent and permanent.

52. Be the first to ask forgiveness;
Do not wait for him to pre-empt you,
For the one who is last to forgive
Receives almost no reward;
And if you are not in the wrong,
Yours is the more heroic effort.

53. You are all love
Towards me, my Lord and Father,
And I am filled with hardness of heart
Towards my neighbor and my brother.
Forgive me, I know my sin,
And I am deeply touched by it.

Prayer.

54. I wish to keep for my neighbor
My goods, my body and my soul:
My goods so as to help him,
My heart to burn with his flame,
My eyes to let me be charmed by him,
All that I am so as to love him.

55. Lord, since I have no return to make
Which is worthy of your extreme love,
Grant me to go night and day
Calling everywhere for people to love you,
And to save by some effort of mine
The one for whom you died.

56. When an ass falls into a ditch,
We pull it out with haste.
My brother has fallen, shattered,
And I see him there without any sadness.
My God, I want to lift him up;
Send me to save him.

57. Grant to my heart every warmth,
To my spirit all light,
Even to my body, vigor
To help him in every way,
To lift him up from these depths
To the heights of heaven.

GOD ALONE.

## 15
## SPLENDORS OF PRAYER

Essence and definition of prayer.

1. Christian, here is the bread of the strong,
A delightful manna,
A store filled with treasures,
A copious spring,
A flight of the spirit towards its God,
A glimpse of his countenance: Prayer.
But after all this, I have not said enough:
It is indeed a treasure-house of grace.

1st POINT.
*Its necessity.*

1st motive.
It is necessary to adore God in spirit and in truth and to give him his due.

2. Prayer is a blessing for all,
Both men and angels,
The honor owed to the Immortal One,
The sweetest praise given to him.
It is that truly divine incense,
That pleasant perfume

Which renders sovereign worship
To this adorable Being.

3. We accept and demonstrate in prayer
That we are full of woes,
That we seek all the best things
From the Father of lights.
We sacrifice to his greatness,
In all reverence,
Our spirits, our bodies and our hearts,
Indeed our whole being.

4. It is here that, in body and spirit,
We offer ourselves in sacrifice;
We adore with Jesus Christ,
We tremble and humble ourselves,
Adore his majesty,
Calm his justice,
Beg his bounty.
Oh! the greatness of this sacrifice!

2nd motive.
To obtain mercy.

5. In prayer, a poor sinner
Ascends even to his throne,
And forces this powerful Lord
To give him relief.
Often he wrenches from his hand
The thunder and lightning
With which, as sovereign,
He might soon have reduced him to dust.

6. It is God's will that, outside of prayer,
No sinner should reach him;
But if he sees him praying and calling out,
He offers his mercy.
He turns him from being a child of the devil
Into a child of God himself.
Oh! the power of prayer!
What supreme power is this!

3rd motive.
To obtain grace.

7. Prayer is the great channel
Through which all good things come,
Through which a God who is so generous
Communicates his grace.
Without it, we are without virtue,
Without grace, without light;

We are weak, we are beaten.
Oh! how necessary it is.

8. Without prayer, the creature is no more
Than a corpse without a soul,
A sagging reed,
An extinguished torch,
A dropsical, famished wretch,
A weathercock blown by the wind,
In short, a soldier deprived of his arms,
Quite ready for defeat.

4th motive. Without it, nothing is possible.

9. Without prayer, you cannot
Retain your innocence,
You are weakened, you fall down low
Through your own powerlessness.
You fall into temptation,
You fall into sin,
And then into damnation,
Sinking lower and lower.

5th motive. Without it you cannot keep your innocence.

6th motive. To defeat sin and the devil.

10. Jesus prayed night and day.
Was this necessary?
Yes, his example teaches us,
He is our model.
The saints, night and day, like him,
Offered this sacrifice;
This was their strength and support,
Their sweetest exertion.

7th motive. To imitate Jesus Christ.

8th motive. To imitate the saints.

11. What! You ask me for nothing?
Said he to his disciples.
I want to do good to you,
Because my blessings are yours.
Seek then, and you shall find,
I am your assurance;
Ask and you shall receive
Every blessing in abundance.

9th motive. To obey Jesus Christ.

12. In prayer you must be persistent,
In spite of all obstacles,
Never tiring, never ceasing;
This is one of the great sayings.
Both Testaments,
Throughout almost all their pages,

10th motive. To obey the Holy Spirit.

Confirm this commandment
By the example of the wise.

13. Prayer heals all ills,
Even the most disgusting;
And when work is over
It relaxes body and soul.
It strips away the blindfold
Which sin alone creates,
To let you see this pernicious evil,
This monster so deformed.

2nd POINT.
*Utility of prayer.*
1st motive.
It heals.

2nd motive.
It relaxes.
3rd motive.
It enlightens the spirit.

14. It causes you to see the truth,
The beauty of grace,
And the lying and vanity
Of this passing world.
It carries the soul up to heaven,
Then down to the abyss,
And makes it see in all of these
The most sublime truths.

4th motive.
It gives knowledge of all mysteries and eternal truths.

15. Prayer brings gentleness
To the impatient soul,
Keenness and fervor
To the apathetic.
It is the fiery furnace
Of the brave soul,
Which makes of it a victim for God,
But a loving victim.

5th motive.
It strengthens, enlivens and sets the soul on fire.

16. Without it, you cannot uproot
Bad habits,
Habits of sin
Whose yoke is so harsh;
It is a mighty hammer
Which strikes and smashes,
A ravishing sun
Which melts the ice.

6th motive.
It destroys sin and sinful habits.

17. It gives to mortal man
Peace in the midst of war,
And makes him abide in heaven
Even when thrown down to the earth.
It enriches his poverty,

7th motive.
It brings peace and raises to heaven.

Not with perishable goods,
But with the benefits of eternity
And goods which are real.

8th motive.
It enriches with true goods.

18. It gives growth to, or sustains,
Virtue which is sickly;
It is the means to obtain
Grace in abundance,
To move on with giant steps
Towards God in this life,
And to rise from the depths of nothingness
Up to our homeland.

9th motive.
It sustains and increases virtue.

10th motive.
It gives grace in abundance.

19. On earth there is nothing so sweet;
It is the heavenly manna
Which truly contains all flavors,
But none which might be fatal,
Provided you can draw out the meaning,
Since this is also necessary,
And then put into practice with a good will
What it teaches you to do.

11th motive.
It is very sweet to the soul.

20. What marvellous wonders
Our fathers of old performed!
They opened heaven and earth
Just by their prayers.
By means of prayer and faith,
They were completely transformed;
In prayer they laid down the pattern
For every created thing.

12th motive.
It can obtain and accomplish everything.

21. What glory for a sinner,
This piece of dust and ashes,
To speak to God his Lord
When he enters into prayer,
To converse with the majesty
Of this all-powerful God,
Yet with a great freedom,
Without laying himself open to blame.

13th motive.
It is glorious for man.

22. How will you conquer Lucifer
Who hurls down fire and flames,
And casts down into hell
The majority of souls?
By fasting and prayer you will do it;

14th motive.
It is terrible for the devil.

You must believe what Jesus says,
And then you will be in the right
And will gain the victory.

23. Prayer it is which weakens him,
Disarms and puts him to flight,
Torments and punishes him,
Strikes home and knocks him down.
Oh! how he fears this heavy burden,
This burning sword!
What horror he feels for this executioner
Which torments him and puts him to death!

24. The devil has spoken often
Through those who consort with him,
Saying: I am furious, I am scorched,
My sufferings are made twice as bad;
When someone sets himself to pray to God,
And when he humbles himself,
He scorches me with rekindled flames,
And my suffering is unbelievable.

Recapitulation.

25. Let us pray then with fervor.
God wills it for his glory,
And it brings about our happiness
And our victory.
Following the example of Jesus
And his holy Mother,
We will gain all virtues
By a prayer that is good.

26. But what are the qualities of prayer,
I hear you ask.
Listen, and I will tell you,
For this is an important question.
To pray to God is not easy;
Often enough a prayer,
Far from appeasing God,
Redoubles his anger.

Kinds of prayer.

27. When we pray to the Lord in our hearts,
This is called mental prayer;
When we pray to him with voice and heart,
This is called vocal prayer.
Practice these with delight,

For both are very good,
And if sometimes you have to make a choice,
Do whichever God inspires.

28. Practice meditation:
This is very safe.
Rest in contemplation:
This is a higher form of prayer.
But take care not to put on a show
Of exalted styles of prayer,
For taking pride in this could cast you
Into the depths of hell.

Illusion.

29. You will know when prayer is good
By the fruit of a good life;
Either it is rooted in this,
Or it is mere deception.
Prayer which bring clear vision,
And an unblemished life,
Are like two sisters going hand in hand
So as to know and to act.

The sign of a good prayer.

30. But what must you avoid
In order to pray well?
Three words: listen carefully,
For this is for your benefit.
Never strive in contemplation
For an exalted form of prayer,
For often this false diamond
Is the cause of a soul's condemnation.

31. Let your meditation then be simple,
Without ostentation which might steal
from it;
But be faithful to it.
Let faith suffice,
Without any desire to see or to feel
Extraordinary things:
This snare has caused many to perish,
For it is too common a thing.

3rd POINT.
*Qualities of prayer.*
1st
Simple without affectation.

2nd
Pure without vision.

32. But make your prayer above all
A matter of patience,
Persevering to the end
Despite feelings of powerlessness,

3rd
Strong and patient without discouragement.

Despite the body or the spirit,
And despite the devil who calls to you.
Stand firm with Jesus Christ
Who prays in his agony.

4th Prudent.

1. in regard to the quality of prayer.

33. If you really want to be saved,
If salvation really matters to you,
Have the Our Father and the Hail Mary
Often on your lips,
Say the five decades of the Rosary,
Or even the full fifteen.
What a beautiful prayer for one who is perfect,
What a divine prayer!

2. in regard to the quality of the one praying.

34. To be heard by the Lord,
You must be in a state of grace,
For he does not listen to the sinner
Who prays in his disgrace;
But if you are in sin,
Pray that he grant you
A contrite heart, touched to the quick,
And mercy for your sins.

3. in regard to what one asks for.

35. Ask nothing but what is good,
Nothing but what is salutary,
For God alone and his holy name,
Which alone is necessary;
For to think only of temporal things
When you go to prayer,
Without submitting these things to the Eternal One,
Is a very brazen thing.

4. in regard to the manner of praying.

36. Pray fervently to Jesus
Through his divine Mother,
And through Jesus, very humbly,
Go up to God his Father.
For, using these steps of humility
And of holy prudence,
You cannot be rejected,
And you can pray with confidence.

5. in regard to the external comportment.

37. Pray with the virtue of religion,
And without any conceit;
Perfect adoration
Requires that you pray with your whole self,

Not turning around, nor leaning on your elbows,
Nor making faces,
Talking or looking about,
But with a straight back and a good grace.

38. If you do not pray from your heart,
You have no merit in praying.
God receives no honor from that,
And you are being hypocritical.
Go into your private room,
Close your door,
Pray to your Father in secret;
This kind of prayer is powerful.

5th
Interior, without hypocrisy.

39. To cease using vocal prayer
On the pretext of perfection,
Is quite false;
A subtle but fatal illusion.
Take the example of the Savior:
This was his practice.
Anyone who draws away from it is a deceiver,
No matter how ecstatic he may be.

6th
Exterior.

40. Do all you can
To pray in a hidden way,
Without let-up, when you come out
Of your seclusion.
Pray everywhere, to please God,
Without regard for persons;
Pray always, in every place,
And then your prayer is good.

7th
Edifying, but without vanity.

41. You should pray with charity
For the salvation of souls,
For those who, in their blindness,
Are destined for the flames,
For all those Muslims and pagans,
And all who are in schism,
For so many who are miserable Christians
Or bad Catholics.

8th
Charitable.

42. Pray with attention,
Without being distracted;
Pray with devotion:
This is very necessary.

9th
Attentive.
10th
Devout.

Realise that a distraction
Which you reject and chase away,
Does not take away at all from the attention
Required for a perfect prayer.

43. Pray with plenty of faith
And great confidence,
Saying frequently: "My God, I believe
In your presence here."
If you always humble yourself,
Believing yourself to be unworthy
Of obtaining the least comfort,
God will make you worthy of it.

11th
Faith-filled.

12th
Humble.

44. Pray always with a hope
That goes beyond hope;
God gives his excellent gifts
Only to perseverance.
Pray always in spite of the flesh
Which balks and becomes bored,
And in spite of the world and all hell,
And you will have life.

13th
Strong and
persevering.

45. It is from you that all good comes to us,
O Father of lights!
It is from you alone that I look for it,
O Father of my fathers!
Since I must ask of you
All that I need,
Deign to grant me, then, my God,
The grace to pray.

Prayer.

46. Cause to come down into my heart
Your Holy Spirit, Father,
There to create the true fire
Of holy prayer,
To bring forth groanings
Which are unutterable,
Sighs, and the stuttering
Of those who are really children.

47. My spirit is nought but blindness,
I deceive myself constantly;
My heart is nought but hardness,
Misdeeds and weakness;

But this evil arises from myself alone;
I have abandoned prayer.
Lord, increase my faith,
That I may pray well.

48. You who give lavishly
To the crow when he calls,
Hear me in this hour;
It is your child who is praying.
By your heart full of goodness,
By Jesus and Mary,
Let me not be rejected.
In you I rest my hope.

GOD ALONE.

# 16
# POWER OF FASTING

1. Join fasting to prayer,
Said an angel to Tobias,
Nothing is so sweet, nor so good.
I beg you, let us learn
Three secrets to gain ourselves a crown
And place ourselves upon the throne,
To wit: prayer, fasting,
And alms-giving.

Essence and definition of fasting.

2. Take care not to be caught off guard
By a very common error.
This is how I shall define
What fasting is:
One meal per day,
Abstaining from meat,
With a collation,
But not a large one.

1st POINT. *Its necessity.*

1st motive. God loves it.

3. Fasting is, in the Lord's eyes,
One of the beautiful sacrifices
Which human beings make to his greatness;

He takes delight in it.
This was the first commandment
He gave to the first man,
To abstain absolutely
From eating an apple.

2nd motive.
It glorifies him.

3rd motive.
It was his first commandment.

4. As soon as Adam, by misfortune,
Transgressed this holy fast,
He became a miserable sinner,
And lost all his fortune.
If fasting was necessary
In that garden of delights,
In truth it is even more so
In this place of torture.

4th motive.
It was necessary in the state of innocence.

5. Without fasting you are merely flesh,
Says our supreme God;
I cannot triumph over it,
I cannot even stay there;
But if, by your sacred fast,
You mortify yourself,
Then you are consecrated to me,
And I achieve my glory in you.

5th motive.
God lives only in one who fasts and mortifies his flesh.

6. Great and long were the fasts
Of the wise of yesteryear,
The prophets and the conquerors
And all those marked by greatness.
Fasting gave them their fire,
Filled them with grace,
Allowed them to speak with God,
Even face to face.

6th motive.
The example of the great saints.

7. But what should surprise us most,
And is worthy of our astonishment,
Is that God himself was pleased to fast
For forty days together,
Without anything to eat or drink,
In silence and in prayer,
Without sparing himself or seeking relief
In any way whatsoever.

7th motive.
The example of Jesus Christ.

8. He fasted so as to teach us
To fast in this same way;
He fasted to prepare himself

8th motive.
Christ's reasons for his fast.

For his divine baptism,
To vanquish the proud devil,
Puffed up with arrogance,
And lastly to be able to go anywhere
To preach penance.

9. Without fasting you cannot save
A soul which is so carnal.
Without fasting you cannot take captive
The flesh which is so rebellious.
A body deprived of fasting is as good as dead,
It brings forth only misdeeds,
It is a tyrant, cruel and strong,
Which casts down to hell.

9th motive. The soul cannot be saved without the body's fasting.

10. Had he fasted, Adam would have been able
To retain his innocence;
But without fasting, he was corrupted
By his own intemperance.
Without fasting you cannot bring forth
The worthy fruits of penance,
Worthy, that is, of Paradise
And its rewards.

10th motive. One cannot retain one's innocence without fasting.

11th motive. Nor do worthy penance.

11. It is by prayer and fasting,
Says the Savior of the world,
That the demon is conquered and chased away,
Along with every unclean spirit.
Without fasting, you will be so battered
That you will no longer be invincible;
You will in the end be destroyed
By a terrible misfortune.

12th motive. Without fasting, one is conquered by the devil.

12. Without fasting, you succumb to sleep,
Weighed down with sadness;
By fasting you are strengthened
And filled with joy.
Fasting, and every austerity,
Is like a lightweight wing
Which can carry up to holiness
The coarsest soul.

2nd POINT. *Excellence of fasting*

1st motive. It strengthens and brings joy.

13. Meat veils our reason
In a very dark cloud.
Fasting makes for a good mind,
Sharpens the memory,
Dissipates all obscurity,
Gets rid of every stain,
And causes us to see all truth,
Even the most obscure.

2nd motive.
It enlightens the spirit.

14. See what power fasting has,
And how incisive its strength!
It brings complete freedom
To the soul that is held captive;
It subjects the spirit to faith,
And the heart to its flame;
It subjects the whole person to the law,
And the body to the soul.

3rd motive.
It gives freedom to the soul.

4th motive.
It subjects the whole person to God.

15. Mark well that the body of the damned
Is really fattened up,
While that of the predestined
Has the fat trimmed away.
Fasting strips away from this animal,
This cruel beast,
The means of doing evil
To our immortal soul.

5th motive.
It saves body and soul.

16. A body which is thin and withered
Has sinful moods no more,
Which lead us all to sin,
Without anyone else to tempt us.
Fasting, in truth, draws us away
From every odious pleasure,
And clothes us in purity
Of body and of soul.

6th motive (a).
It kills concupiscence.

17. More miserable people
Have perished through gluttony
Than fearful enemies put to death
By the two-edged sword.
Our ancient fathers, fasting often,
Drove out sickness,
While we who fast little nowadays
Are shortening our lives.

6th motive (b).
It keeps at bay the evils of gluttony.

18. On the admission of any good doctor,
Or of a good apothecary,
There is no remedy so divine
As a salutary fast.
Have a good but sober dinner,
And take little in the evening,
And you will certainly live
Just as long as our fathers.

7th motive.
It brings health.

19. All who belong to Jesus Christ,
Mortify themselves in all things,
Fast in the body and in spirit,
Always crucifying themselves;
But the reprobate give in willingly
To their inordinate desires:
One will be drunk, another intoxicated;
They love only their bellies.

3rd POINT.
*Qualities of fasting.*

20. So fast, but in the right way;
Fasting imprudently,
Which is always displeasing to God,
Gains no reward.
The devil himself has his fasters,
Hypocritical ones,
Who, deceived themselves, are deceivers
And completely without merit.

1st
Prudent.
2nd
Humble and obedient.

21. Fast with severity,
Observing without equivocation
Both quantity and quality,
Following the advice of a wise person,
In accord with the commandments
Of God and the Church,
On Vigils and Ember-days,
And through the whole of Lent.

3rd
Complete.

22. Fast in humility,
Without appearing to do so;
Guard yourselves from vanity,
Do not fast to impress.
Conceal, as far as you can,
By washing your face,
All the fasts which you keep:
This fasting is filled with grace.

4th
Secret.

23. Fast without self-will,
For the Lord makes clear
That, when your fast is spoilt by this,
He hates and detests it;
And that, however good it may appear
In the eyes of creatures,
It belongs to the devil
And at bottom is nothing but filth.

5th
Obedient.

24. To fast well and with safety,
Observe obedience;
This is a great matter of holiness,
As well as of prudence.
A fast undertaken at the behest of another
Has much more merit
Than a thousand in which you follow
Simply your own choice.

6th
Prudent.

25. For a fast to be meritorious,
You must do it in God's grace,
Otherwise it has little merit,
Or even no glory at all.
Abstain from all sin:
This kind of fast is essential,
And no-one is incapable of this;
We can and must do it.

7th
Holy.

8th
Abstain from sin.

26. Fasting and austerity
Must be coupled with prayer,
Not forgetting charity
And alms-giving to our brother.
Through this threefold assistance, you will obtain
A renewal of grace,
And then, at the end of your life,
Eternal glory.

9th
Coupled with prayer and alms-giving.

27. If through sickness or infirmity,
Holy obedience,
Or some other necessity,
You are dispensed from fasting,
To make up for it, you should perform
Some other penance:
Pray more, or give alms

10th
Dispensations from fasting.

With greater generosity.

28. By fasting, here, I also mean
The hair shirt and girdle,
Keeping vigil and taking the discipline,
And sleeping on a hard bed.
This is what the saints did.
Follow in their steps,
And like them you will be perfect
And will receive the graces they did.

11th
What is included in fasting.

29. Either you break with God's spirit
Or with your miserable flesh:
Choose, beloved soul, there is no middle way,
If you wish to be happy
And have your God, eternal Wisdom,
To dwell with you;
Renounce yourself, lay down the law
For this rebellious flesh.

12th
Resolution.

30. Lord, I am thoroughly wicked
And full of weakness,
Sensual throughout,
And full of delicacy.
It is only right that a sinner
Should avenge you and punish himself:
I offer my body, I offer my heart
And all else in sacrifice.

13th
Prayer.

31. I want to keep watch, to fast, to pray,
For the rest of this my life,
To offer you in sacrifice
A divine host.
Grant, Lord, your blessing
On this living victim,
Deign to uphold me everywhere
With your all-powerful grace.

GOD ALONE.

# 17
# BENEFITS OF ALMSGIVING

1. I see a light descending,
Approaching, shining near.
Ah! Truly, it is charity,
It is heartfelt mercy.
She yearns to espouse us,
O! how kind she is,
We must not refuse her
For she is too charming.

2. Although awesome in her greatness,
Although God be her throne,
Because of her gentleness,
Almsgiving is her name.
She is compassion
For the wretched,
The tender abundance
Of a loving hand.

Essence and Definition of almsgiving

3. This queen seems forgetful
Of her divine birth.
She sacrifices herself
For the suffering poor;
She gladly clasps to her breast
The greatest miseries,
And how gently she dresses
The most repulsive wounds.

4. You miser with one foot in hell,
You would rather not believe;
But dear chosen soul, trust me,
For it concerns your glory.
Gently lend your ear
To everything I'll now explain,
So you may believe it perfectly
And put it into practice.

The Call

5. Almsgiving is necessary,
Our faith itself attests,
Everything confirms this truth
Even nature itself.

1st POINT
*Its necessity*

Our neighbor has the good fortune
Of having the same father as we,
So we must help him with all our heart,
As our own brother.

1st Motive
God, our Creator and our Father, obliges us by His power in creation to practice almsgiving.

6. Almsgiving is the commandment
Of Jesus, our Master,
Only the truly blind
Are ignorant of this.
Give and it will be given unto you,
That is my commandment.
Without it, you will be condemned,
No exceptions granted.

2nd Motive
Jesus by His wisdom and express command.

7. Transform iniquity
And transitory goods,
Into treasures for eternity
And friends, without a doubt;
Then no thief can pilfer
By force or by cunning,
Nor will the wealth ever spoil
From rust or from years.

8. Everything grants alms for God,
Each in its own way:
The air, the sea, the earth, the fire
And all nature itself.
Look at all the animals:
One gives us food, another carries us,
They all assist us in our needs
By lending strong support.

3rd Motive
The example of all creatures.

9. But what greater blessings
When it comes to grace:
The Father sends His Son
In spite of our disgrace,
The Son gives Himself all to all
Right up to the Eucharist,
The Holy Spirit comes upon us.
Oh! What alms so infinite!

4th Motive
Example of the Holy Trinity in the order of grace.

10. When I see heaven's Queen,
 (She is our only hope),
 Put in this world's poor
 All her confidence,
 Give all things to us in charity,
 And become our Mother,
 I say: Almsgiving, in truth,
 Is great and necessary.

5th Motive
The example of the Blessed Virgin.

11. Look at those star witnesses,
 Those irreproachable saints:
 They had no other needs
 Than those of the poor
 And happily shared the food
 They were eating
 In order to feed them.
 This example stirs me.

6th Motive
Example of the Saints.

12. To give alms to neighbors,
 They sold their possessions,
 No plans for the morrow.
 Their hearts were so tender
 They stripped almost naked
 To help the poor neighbor,
 And sometimes were sold
 As ransom for slaves.

13. Do you seek remission?
 The Lord only grants it
 To hearts with compassion
 And brimming with mercy.
 Your deeds make the Lord kind
 Or quite unrelenting.
 He lets you decide,
 So truly be generous!

7th Motive
Without almsgiving, God does not forgive.

14. What is a poor person? It is written
 That he is the living image,
 The representative of Jesus Christ,
 And His most beautiful legacy.
 But, to say it even more clearly,
 He is Christ Himself.
 In the poor, we assist or refuse
 Our supreme monarch.

8th Motive
In the poor, we are giving to Jesus or refusing Him.

15. Christ suffers poverty in one,
In another, vermin,
In another, prison,
And in another, famine.
Jesus, suffering in them
So many afflictions,
Appears the most needy,
The most wretched of them all.

9th Motive
Jesus Christ is
the poorest of all.

16. Keep not from the poor his due,
Says Holy Scripture;
This key statement is not grasped
Or is understood carelessly,
For in truth, we can not
Keep through greed
What we take from charity,
For this is unjust.

10th Motive
Almsgiving is
owed to the poor.

11th Motive
It is an injustice
to refuse it to
them.

17. What is besides our honest expenses,
Must be given away;
To do otherwise is an abuse
That cries to the Lord for vengeance.
It is the verdict of the great Saint Thomas
And even the holy Fathers themselves.
Rich people, if you do not believe me,
I pronounce you accursed.

12th Motive
The Fathers and
theologians
declare the same.

18. Know that anything you retain
Which you no longer need,
Belongs to the poor; it is theirs,
As the Gospel tells us.
You owe them this ornate furniture,
These precious pearls,
These beautiful, silky clothes,
This pretentious finery.

19. The poor have the right to claim
Anything you do not need,
A rich person can not keep it,
Although he believes otherwise.
He is only the steward,
Says Saint John Chrysostom,
Quoting another holy doctor,
Great Saint Jerome.

13th Motive
The rich are only
the distributors of
their superfluous
goods.

20. This lack of charity
Is very significant,
The saints say it is cruelty
And, with no doubt, stealing.
It is even malicious murder,
Says a holy Father,
Not to give food
To the starving poor.

14th Motive
Such lack of almsgiving is a mortal sin.

21. But let us now see
How useful almsgiving is,
And that it is assuredly
A most fertile field;
It's fruit is truly special,
It has no equal
Since it returns the hundred fold
To a charitable man.

2nd POINT
*Its usefulness*

1st Motive
Almsgiving conserves and augments temporal goods.

22. Almsgiving is a security box,
A trusty safe,
Which preserves everything in it
For eternal life.
It is where possessions, gold and silver,
Are kept on earth
From the thief and the bailiff
And the disasters of war.

2nd Motive
Comparisons which prove this truth.

23. It is the seed we sow
That multiplies,
At a high rate of interest,
Glorifying God;
A running stream
Never dried up,
A huge fire
Spreading wildly.

24. We can safely call it
The philosopher's stone
Which changes base metal
Into something precious.
Almsgiving changes earth into heaven,
The false into the true,
The temporal into the eternal.
O incomparable stone!

25. Giving alms, we lose nothing,
As we know from experience,
The more good we do by giving alms,
The more that good increases.
We become poor
When we are miserly and stingy;
But giving to charity,
We soon become rich.

26. Everyone greatly honors
Charitable men;
We call them, in the Lord,
Fathers of the poor.
We approach them
With confidence,
We ask them to preside
At our conferences.

3rd Motive
Almsgiving makes the donors praiseworthy.

27. To give life and health
Is a marvelous thing:
It is what makes charity
So miraculous.
To uphold the whole world
Is not so great a feat
As to uphold one's neighbor,
Giving him what he requests.

4th Motive
Almsgiving works miracles.

28. Almsgiving obtains contrition
And soul-felt sorrow,
It redeems all sin,
Extinguishes concupiscence.
Through almsgiving, all is forgiven,
It is a second baptism,
A sign of predestination,
It is God's own seal.

5th Motive
Almsgiving obtains the contrition and

6th Motive
The pardon of all our sins.

29. Without this oil of charity
Which the foolish virgins lacked,
The lilies of chastity
Are false and frivolous.
Without it, there is no holiness,
One is not authentic.
Without it, there is no resolve,
One is not persistent.

7th Motive
It makes a virgin pleasing and steadfast to her spouse.

30. Nothing speaks as powerfully
As the poor and almsgiving,
This prayer quickly
Rises to the throne of God,
Opens His hands, ravishes the heart
Of this loving God,
Changing Him from a just avenger
Into a sincere friend.

8th Motive
It is the most
powerful prayer.

31. It is a lance, a buckler,
A very powerful weapon,
Baffling and vanquishing
The devil who tempts us,
It impedes the devil from accusing
A soul in the next life,
And forces him to let it
Go to its homeland.

9th Motive
It attacks and
confounds the
demon.

32. The death of almsgivers
Is a very holy death;
They die gloriously,
Peacefully, fearlessly.
Their charities are their soldiers
Winning them the victory;
The poor are their advocates
Setting them in glory.

10th Motive
It renders death
peaceful and holy.

11th Motive
At death, the
almsgivers have
their soldiers and
advocates.

33. Almsgiving is a sacred trust
That God keeps safe and then returns;
He will surely return it,
For He cannot refrain from so doing.
Almsgiving is a promissory note
Which God Himself guarantees;
Its interest is hundred fold.
Oh! divine usury.

34. Here is the third pact,
Keep it well in mind:
To give alms is to buy
Heaven and its glory.
Almsgiving makes earthly goods
And a little manure
Eternal wealth in heaven
And happiness unending.

3rd POINT
*The evils of those who fail to give alms.*

35. A miser is without charity,
Without faith and hope,
He is filled with iniquity
And without repentance.
In his last moments he will cry out
And God will not hear him.
At His turn, God will mock him,
Doing to him what he did to the poor.

1st Motive
He has neither faith nor hope, etc.

2nd Motive
God does not listen when he prays.

36. He who leaves his neighbor
Without any assistance
Finds God heartless, unhelpful,
And without any pity.
He loses what he refused
To the poor in their misery
And is often crushed
By the weight of God's anger.

37. At death he will ask for pardon
But God will not grant it;
This hard heart will die abandoned
And without mercy.
God will judge him sternly,
Without fatherly kindness;
He will condemn him to misery
And eternal death.

3rd Motive
He dies in his sin.

38. Give alms, good Christian,
Believe me, be wise,
It is the way good things come to us
And all good things without limit.
Sins are redeemed by it,
The soul returned to grace,
All heaven's goods are purchased.
Woe to him who doesn't give!

39. On the great day of judgment
God will only remember
Our almsgiving,
So great is its glory.
He will reveal

The alms given sincerely
And will give them
Highest praise.

40. Come, the Lord will say to you,
Blessed of my Father,
Possess my own happiness
And all my glory.
For having helped me on earth
By giving me alms,
I will make you kings forever
And set you on thrones.

41. Give of your own goods;
This almsgiving is prudent,
Otherwise it is worth nothing
And is even revolting.
Pay Caesar, render to God,
Pay all your debts,
Give to the poorest of the town
And of the borough where you live.

4th POINT
*Qualities of almsgiving*
1st
It must be prudent.

42. See only God
In every poor person,
For Him alone give them
Your charitable help.
Whether they be good or malicious
You are giving to Jesus.
It suffices that He be within them,
In His own person.

2nd
Holy and pure.

43. Always be charitable
And give alms in secret,
Avoid the proud trumpet
Of vanity.
Otherwise, almsgiving is fruitless,
It is the almsgiving of a hypocrite
Who makes great fanfare and a lot of noise
But has no merit.

3rd
Humble.

44. Give alms very carefully
According to your means
And according to the needs of the beggar
Even though he annoys you.
Give to him joyfully

4th
Abundant.

5th
Joyful.

Without any bitterness,
Without telling him curtly:
Now get out of here, God bless!

45. Give to the poor promptly
Without selling your alms
By a harsh delay which hurts
The pleading, poor man.
Treat with great respect
The poor man begging you:
This almsgiving is more meritorious,
This almsgiving edifies.

6th Prompt.

7th Upright.

46. Exercise charity
For both the body and soul
Without excluding anyone
Either man or woman;
Give food to one,
Give drink to another.
Welcome the poor stranger
With honor and glory.

8th Universal.

*Corporal Works of Mercy.*

47. Have clothes made for one
To hide his misery,
Visit another, wasting away,
Sunk in despair.
Visit another, ranting
And raving in prison,
Pay the ransom of another
To free him from slavery.

48. Do not forget those who have died,
Almsgiving is salutary;
Try to bury their corpses
Or have them buried.
These works of mercy
Are called corporal,
Other good deeds
Are more spiritual.

49. Instruct the ignorant,
Enlighten him,
Correct the weak man,
But not by shouting or anger;
Give him friendly advice,

Forgive injuries,
Pray for your enemies.
This is the purest almsgiving.

50. Console the afflicted
Overwhelmed by sorrow;
Console hearts eaten away
By frightful scruples.
Pray to God for the wicked
To obtain their forgiveness,
Pray for the living and the dead
With no one excluded.

## 18
## CRIES OF THE POOR

1. You rich, wake up and hear
Our most pitiful sobs,
Alas! come to our aid,
For we are desolate.
All of us are Christians,
We are all your brothers,
Help us with your riches,
Answer then our prayers.

2. God made you important
But to be our fathers,
God made you powerful
To alleviate our woes.
Yet you enjoy yourselves,
Always midst abundance
While leaving us aside,
Always in dire need.

3. You are so richly-clothed
And sleep on feather beds,
We are almost naked,
Consumed by lack of food.
Everyone blesses you,
Honors and accepts you,
While we are cursed by all,

Mistreated and despised.

4. Nobody offers alms,
Rather, they rebuke us.
They think they're doing good
When they all bully us,
Chase us and arrest us,
Chaining us in prison.
We are even forbidden
To call attention to our woes.

5. The rich so often tell us:
I have no silver, no coins.
High class people curse us,
Treating us as riff-raff.
Get out of here, bold idlers!
Oh! You brazen, evil race!
That's the language many use,
And even the common folk.

6. Great God, please do help us
In this situation,
What! Will you forget us
As does all your creation?
Gaze on us from heaven,
For you are our Father,
Deign to cast your eyes
Even on our dust.

7. GOD
O dear poor of heart,
I hear your just complaints
And deeply feel your sorrow,
I suffer the same blows;
Have patience for a while,
Then you will see my anger,
Though I am almighty God
I also am your Father.

8. You are my elder sons,
My true and chosen friends,
My dear predestined souls,
My dwelling-places fair.
All the evil done to you
Is done also to me.

Anyone who helps you out
Is proof that person loves me.

9. THE POOR
O you rich, how good for you
When you give us alms;
For a corner in your house
You'll get a stunning throne.
For some of your old clothes,
A rich crown is your prize,
And all of Paradise
For a cup of water.

10. Now, do give us something,
Do not be niggardly,
This will be the sure way
Of becoming very rich.
The Lord Himself has promised
To grant the hundredfold
To all those who befriend
The miserable poor.

11. Almsgiving wins God over
And makes Him favorable;
Almsgiving also quenches
The fire of His justice;
It gives to all the sinners
A sincere anticipation
Of receiving from his Savior
The weight of heavenly glory.

GOD ALONE

## 19
## TRIUMPH OF THE CROSS

The cross is a great mystery.

1. The cross is a mystery
Most profound here below,
Without abundant light
It can never be known.
Only the noble hearted

Are able to comprehend it,
Yet understand it we must
If we are to be saved.

2. Nature abhors it,
Reason battles it,
Pundits ignore it
And the demon tears it down.
Often the most devout
Do not plant it in their hearts.
Professing to love the cross,
They are really lying.

1st POINT
*Its Necessity.*

1st Motive
God chastises all his children and gives them the cross.

3. The cross is necessary,
We must always suffer,
Either climb Calvary
Or perish forever.
St. Augustine proclaims
We are among the damned
If God does not chastise us,
If we are not tested.

2nd Motive
The cross is the way to heaven.

4. We go to our homeland
By the way of crosses.
It is the path of life,
The highway of the kings;

3rd Motive
The soul must be trimmed for heaven.

Each precious stone is cut
To precise proportion
So they may be the bricks
In building Holy Zion.

4th Motive
We must conquer ourselves in carrying the cross.

5. What value has the victory
Of the greatest conqueror
If he possesses not the glory
Of self-mastery through pain,
If his model is not
The crucified Jesus,
If, like the infidels,
He spurns this holy tree?

2nd POINT
*Its victories:*

Over the demon and the world.

6. Through the Cross, Jesus Christ
Has conquered hell itself,
Crushed the rebel forces
And won the universe;
He gives the cross as arms

To those who serve Him well,
It charms or it disarms
Both hands and hearts.

And the flesh.

7. You will conquer by this sign,
He said to Constantine,
Every signal victory
Is contained within it.
Read in history books
Its marvelous effects,
Its remarkable triumphs
On earth and in heaven.

Over its enemies visible and invisible, over the earth and in heaven.

8. In spite of feelings and nature,
In spite of politics and reason,
The truth certifies it:
The Cross is a great gift.
In this princess
We truly find
Grace, wisdom,
All holiness.

3rd POINT
*Its glory and its merit.*

1st Motive
The cross contains all sanctity and wisdom.

9. God could not resist
Her singular beauty,
The Cross made Him come down
To our humanity.
Entering the world He said:
Yes, I yearn for her, Lord!
Good cross, I thrust you
In the center of my heart.

2nd Motive
The love of Jesus Christ for the cross.

10. He considered her so beautiful
That He made her his honor,
His eternal companion,
The spouse of His heart.
From His earliest childhood
His heart longed ardently
For the cross' presence
Since He loved her fervently.

11. He has, from His youth,
Sought her eagerly;
He died of tenderness
And love in her arms.
I desire a baptism,

He proclaimed one day,
The dear cross I so love,
For which I so yearn.

12. He called Saint Peter
A scandalous Satan,
When he wanted here below
To turn his eyes away from it.
The Cross is to be adored,
His Mother is not,
O awesome grandeur,
Unknown here below!

13. This Cross, now scattered
Wide upon this earth,
Will one day rise,
Carried to heaven.
The Cross, on a cloud
Of blinding beauty
Will judge by its light
The living and the dead.

3rd Motive
The cross will be resurrected and will judge the world.

14. It will demand revenge
Against all its foes,
But joy and pardon
For all its faithful friends.
The cross will glorify
All the blessed in heaven
And proclaim victory
On earth and in the sky.

4th Motive
It will make the blessed rejoice and will confound the doomed.

15. During their life, the saints
Sought naught but the cross,
It was their great desire,
Their preferred choice.
Not content with those
That heaven had sent,
They sentenced themselves
To additional crosses.

5th Motive
The example of the saints.

16. Saint Peter's shackles
Gave him more honor
Than being on earth
The Savior's vicar.
O holy cross, cries out

Faithful Saint Andrew,
So I may attain life,
Let me die upon you!

17. Look! Saint Paul forgets
His great rapture,
Finding his glory
Only in the cross.
He is more praiseworthy
In his grim dungeon
Than in deep ecstasy
Ravishing him to heaven.

4th POINT
*The effects of the cross.*

18. Without the cross, the soul is sluggish,
Soft, cowardly and dull,
The cross makes it fervent
And full of strength.
How dull we are
If we do not suffer!
How bright we are
If we suffer well.

1st Motive.
It bestows fervor.

2nd Motive.
Light.

19. A soul untried
Is of little worth,
A puny soul
Of no learning.
O sovereign sweetness
Tasted by the afflicted soul
Taking comfort in suffering
Without knowing relief!

3rd Motive.
Knowledge.

4th Motive.
Tenderness.

20. It is by the cross that the priest
Gives us his blessing,
It is by the cross that God forgives
And grants us remission.
God wishes that everything be marked
By this sign;
Nothing appears beautiful to Him
Unless sealed by the cross.

5th Motive.
Blessing.

21. Bearing this sign
The profane is made sacred,
Stains are removed,
And God takes over.
He wants the cross signed

6th Motive.
Consecration.

On our forehead and heart
Before starting anything,
So it may share in the conquest.

7th Motive. Victory and success.

22. The cross is our confidence,
Our protection,
Our only hope,
Our perfection;
It is so precious
That a soul in heaven
Would joyfully return
To suffer here below.

8th Motive. The cross is loved by saints in glory.

23. This Cross has such charms
That a priest at the altar
Uses no other arms
To lure Jesus from heaven.
The priest signs the cross
Over the host many times.
By these signs of life
He gives orders to Jesus!

9th Motive. It charms and draws God to the altar.

24. By this adorable sign
The priest offers Jesus
A sweet-smelling aroma
Akin to none other;
It is the incense he offers
After the consecration.
This is the garland
He wishes to bear.

10th Motive. Its sign is a pleasing incense to God.

25. The Eternal Wisdom
Still seeks today
Faithful hearts
Worthy of this gift.
Wisdom seeks someone wise
Who loves only to suffer,
Who carries his cross
Courageously, till death.

11th Motive. God desires to bestow the cross.

26. O Cross, I must be silent,
I diminish you by words;
I am too bold,
I am insolent
Because I have received you

With a reluctant heart,
I have not appreciated you.
Forgive my transgression!

27. Dear Cross, at this time,
Now that I know you,
Come dwell in me,
Rule over me.
Fill me, my dear princess,
With your chaste love
And reveal to me
Your most secret wealth.

28. Seeing you so beautiful
I yearn to possess you
But my unfaithful heart
Keeps me in my place.
If you wish, dear mistress,
To enliven my lethargy
And endure my languor,
I give you my heart.

29. I choose you as my life,
My pleasure and my honor,
For my only friend,
My only delight.
Imprint yourself, please,
On my heart, my arms,
On my forehead, my face;
It will not make me blush.

30. I choose for my wealth
Your rich poverty,
And for my tenderness
Your gentle austerity.
May your wise folly
And your holy disgrace,
Be, for all my life,
Its glory and crown.

31. I consider it a victory
When by your mighty power,
And for your greatest glory,
You truly overcome me;
Dear Cross, I am not worthy

To die beneath your blows
Or of being a sign
Of contradiction to the world.

GOD ALONE

## 20
## TREASURES OF POVERTY

1. Here is the precious pearl,
Here is the treasure so hidden,
And the quality so generous
That I have sought for so long.
But it is not easy to take hold of;
Whoever wishes to possess it
Must, to do so, give away and sell
All he has, without any haggling.

The essence and the definition of poverty.

2. It is called voluntary poverty,
Or poverty of spirit,
Or the great saving counsel
Given to us by Jesus Christ;
It makes a wise man put aside
His goods and any desire for possessions,
So to follow in His footsteps,
Like a true Christian.

1st POINT. *Excellence of poverty.*

1st motive. It is the foundation of perfection.

3. Jesus Christ has founded on this
Both Church and Religion;
It is on this that the faithful Christian
Must build his perfection.
This is where one must begin
To attain holiness;
Otherwise there is only impotence,
Lukewarmness and instability.

2nd motive. The example of Jesus Christ.

4. This God who cannot resist
The charms of poverty,

And who loves it to the point of making
himself
Very poor in our humanity,
Enriches it in his own person
With the treasures of his truth,
And even adorns it and crowns it
With the fullness of his divinity.

5. Let us heed the stable and the crib
Where this lovable Savior was born:
Here everything demonstrates and preaches to us
Holy poverty of heart.
From the crib, go to Calvary:
He dies poor and naked on the cross,
He makes of the cross a pulpit
From which to preach at the top of his voice.

6. He is poor all his life,
His father a poor carpenter,
His mother Mary very poor.
He has not even a poor penny
To pay a modest tax.
The beasts have somewhere to hide,
But he, as he says, has not so much
As a poor bed to lie on.

7. For thirty years he prepares himself
To speak what is in his heart;
So this utterance must be very exceptional.
Here is this great word from our Savior,
His first beatitude,
The greatest word ever written
Which demands long and careful study:
"Blessed are the poor in spirit!

3rd motive.
His words.

8. For the kingdom of my glory
Belongs to their poverty;
The poor one is master, believe me,
Of all my bliss."
Notice that Jesus protests
That the poor person is, here and now,
Master of the heavenly kingdom,
So great, rich and powerful is he.

4th motive.
They are blessed
even in this
world.

5th motive.
Paradise is theirs.

9. He says that the spirit of his father
Has made him come for their salvation,
To announce his light to them,
And that this is his main aim.
If he utters great oracles,
If he opens the depths of his heart,
If he performs great miracles,
It is for them, for their benefit.

6th motive.
Jesus Christ
came for them.

7th motive.
It is to them that
he has revealed
his secrets.

10. While he rejects and scorns
The great and the rich lords,
He founds his holy Church
On none other than twelve poor sinners,
Who, to conquer the whole world,
Leave everything, possessing nothing,
And who, to defeat the foul spirit,
Strip themselves, keeping back nothing.

8th motive.
It is them he
chooses to found
his Church.

11. He says: Does anyone want a throne?
Does anyone want to be perfect?
Let them sell and give as alms
All they have: this is my secret.
You cannot be my follower,
If you are not willing to leave everything.
I have left everything; imitate me,
Otherwise you reject me.

9th motive.
He wants us to
leave everything
to be his
disciples.

12. At the birth of the Church,
The Christians were all fervor;
They left everything without reward,
Without arguing, with all their hearts;
But now we see a thousand weaknesses
In what poses as holiness.
Alas! we love riches,
Alas! we flee poverty.

10th motive.
Example of the
first Christians.

13. All having one heart and one soul,
One purse and everything in common,
They burnt with a pure flame,
And became holy Christians.
Having left behind those chilling words:
Mine, yours, someone's,
The fullness of all grace
Enriched them all together.

14. Their wholly divine poverty
Was the cause of their happiness;
Our greed is at the origin
Of almost all our unhappiness.
They gained victory over the devil
Because they went into battle completely naked;
If we fail to achieve victory and glory,
It is because we are well-clad.

11th motive. Poverty is the source of all good and of all victory.

15. Look at the saints, look at our fathers,
Those models of holiness
To whom the Father of lights
Revealed the truth.
They left all their wealth,
Or kept very little of it,
To embrace with tenderness
The holy poverty of a God.

12th motive. The example of the saints.

16. It was this charming poverty
Which Saint Francis preached everywhere,
That living image
Of a poor God dead upon the cross.
It was when he embraced this
That God showered him with treasures,
And that his soul was inflamed
With the most ineffable delights.

2nd POINT. *The happiness of the poor*

17. Despite the senses and nature,
We must believe the poor person to be happy;
This is certain, since God attests it;
This point is not open to doubt.
The poor are genuine portraits
Of Jesus Christ, become poor for us,
They are his brothers, like him in every way,
Worthy of being honored by all.

1st motive. God attests it.

2nd motive. They are portraits of the poor Christ.

18. By courageously leaving everything,
By scorning vanity,
They gain all things without exception
In time and in eternity:
In time, grace in abundance,
Whose kingdom is in their hearts;
And in eternity, immense glory,

3rd motive. They gain all things in time.

4th motive. In eternity, a special glory.

The glory of the Savior.

19. As imitators of the apostles,
They receive from their Savior
More glory in heaven than others,
More treasures, more greatness.
For being ready to follow him and to believe
In his most noble actions,
Seated on thrones of glory,
They will judge the nations.

5th motive. They judge the world with the apostles.

20. What bestows supreme happiness
On the friends of poverty,
Is that they receive from God himself
A hundred times what they have given up.
For a father, they find a hundred fathers,
And for one friend, a hundred friends:
A hundredfold in all things,
Just as God promised them.

6th motive. They receive the hundredfold promised by God in this world.

21. They have, even in this life,
A hundredfold in temporal goods,
And then, in heaven, in their fatherland,
A hundredfold in eternal possessions.
The truly poor person is master of the world;
Having all things without exception,
He has the sky, the earth and the sea,
And nothing can take these away.

And in the next.

22. This poverty creates wise people,
The great saints, people of worth;
It is the quality of the brave,
And not of mean-spirited people.
It is the source of wisdom;
Reason itself has understood this,
As witness those wise men of Greece
Who left all with scorn.

7th motive. It makes men wise.

23. While the rich sigh
In the midst of a thousand ills,
The good poor people rejoice
Amidst a thousand delights.
Peace, joy and abundance are the lot
Of the poor person who is always content,

8th motive. It delivers the poor from the troubles of the rich.

Worry, trouble and need
That of the rich person who is ever discontented.

24. Since God assures me it is so,
I hold the rich to be unfortunate;
I believe it to be a fatal thing
To become rich like them.
For wealth, so called,
Is the god of iniquity,
A subtle but cruel plague
Which destroys all holiness.

3rd POINT.
*The troubles of the rich.*

1st motive.
Wealth is the god of iniquity.

25. It is the formidable snare,
One of the most subtle and hidden,
But the greatest instrument of the devils
For bringing about the greatest sins.
This malignant cancer alone
Causes so many rich to perish,
And opens the gaping jaws
Of Hell to swallow them up.

2nd motive.
The snare of Satan.

3rd motive.
The jaws of Hell.

26. Riches are prickly thorns
Which cause the heart so many pains,
The fatal beginnings
Which give birth to the greatest ills.
Their pompous appearance
Is a smiling executioner,
A vanity full of flattery
Which soils everything and perishes.

4th motive.
Riches are thorns.

27. There is no lasting quality
In their malicious brilliance,
Yet their golden countenance
Leads hearts astray and charms the eye.
They are the great engine
Which causes the whole universe to rush onwards,
With more and more subtle malice,
To sin and to hell.

5th motive.
They seduce and damn souls.

28. But, O my God, what wisdom is needed
To unmask this treacherous boon,
When even the wise person is at pains
To acquire it, to his sorrow!
It is so true that you can find on earth
An infinite number of fools

6th motive.
The number of fools is infinite, and the poor in spirit very rare.

Who will suffer anything, and go to war,
To gain possessions which are the damnation of all.

29. What comings and goings!
Whence comes all this haste?
It is for money that everyone is running about,
Everyone is trying to get it for himself:
The greedy official at the Bar,
The artisan in his workshop,
The nimble-footed soldier in the army,
And the peasant in the market-place.

30. I have nothing to say about those leeches
Who suck blood day after day,
And by their elaborate shrewdness
Are robbers of the highest degree.
But, good God, what is this I see in the Church?
Oh, what monsters of iniquity!
I am astounded,
Not daring to speak the truth.

31. The doctor, the prosecutor, the notary,
Judge, advocate, bailiff, constable,
Every merchant and businessman,
All run and steal at the mention of money.
They brave any storm,
They undertake a thousand labors,
And all to find a beast
Which must bring them a thousand ills.

7th motive.
The poor in spirit
are content.

32. While a rich man will sacrifice
His time, his rest, his health,
And the happiness of the life to come,
To this iniquitous piece of metal,
The one who is voluntarily poor in spirit
Finds a holy rest in God,
There gaining without any bother
Both the earth and the heavens.

8th motive.
The would-be rich
person unhappy.
1st
He is gnawed by
grief and care.

33. See how this rich man is at his ease!
He has his money, he has his
possessions!
For him, all is laughter, he has no
burdens!
Wise person, don't you believe it.

His poor soul is eaten away
With worry and unnecessary cares,
Like a wave-tossed sea
Which can never again be calmed.

34. The more the rich person has, the more he wants;
His possessions only increase his desires,
And these are his constant martyrdom,
Never leaving him any pleasure.
His desire is like a miserable starving wretch
Who never cries: "That's enough,"
An insatiable hell-fire
Which cries: "Bring more, pile it up."

2nd
He cannot quench his anxious desires.

35. God tells us that there is nothing in this world
More wicked than one who is rich at heart;
He is a swine wailing and growling
In the midst of all his good fortune.
He has a mercenary soul
Which he would sell for a few pence;
His folly is more than bestial,
He is the greatest of all fools.

3rd
Nothing is worse.

4th
He is a swine.

5th
He has a mercenary soul.

36. He is full of idolatry
In regard to his God, his sovereign;
He is full of barbarity
Towards the poor and his neighbor.
Speak to him of money, and he will come running:
This is his idol and his god;
But speak a word about God
And he won't move an inch.

6th
He is an idolater.

7th
He is a barbarian all his life.

37. But when he loses all this wealth
By some annoying misfortune,
Oh, what regrets, what anguish!
What gnashing of teeth!
And when death comes, and he has to vomit up
These possessions which were in his heart,
He is disemboweled, and he groans over it,
But heaven laughs at his misfortune.

8th
He dies badly.

38. Wealth is very sticky
And the soul easily becomes glued to it;
It has a charming color
Which powerfully delights.
You can have it without being glued to it,
But that is where the difficulty lies,
The greatest difficulty I have ever known
With regard to holiness.

9th motive. It is difficult not to become attached to money.

39. Money is altogether soiled with the vices
Which it has brought about everywhere;
It is shot through with malice,
The friend of the Evil One.
One has to be a saint (but how rare that is!)
To avoid its poison;
It glitters, it sneaks in, and takes over
Both heart and mind.

10th motive Money is dirty and dirties everything.

40. This little bit of dirt, all made-up,
Seems to the eyes of the fool to be good,
But its worth is only in the mind,
For it is worthless to the wise,
It is a Proteus with a thousand faces;
At one moment up there, the next down here.
It is by these ever-changing posturings
That it betrays and wins the fight.

11th motive. It is changeable and is only good in the mind.

41. Mark well that it is more difficult
For a person rich in heart to enter heaven
Than for a camel to pass through the needle's eye.
So fundamentally unfortunate is he
Because of the ills with which God threatens him,
He ought to be howling at the top of his voice,
Begging for mercy and grace,
Because God looks upon him with scorn.

12th motive. The words of Jesus Christ and the Holy Spirit.

42. You poor people, quiver with joy,
Be content, go in peace;
You are piling up riches for yourselves
Which will never be stolen from you.
See, at your right hand,
Ten thousand rich people falling into the fire;
Follow the narrow path unshod:

13th motive. The poor are blessed, because they are on the narrow road which leads to heaven.

That is the way to get to heaven.

43. But make no mistake, my brothers:
There are many poor people who are damned,
For it is only those who are voluntarily so
Who are the chosen poor.
Many poor people, being forced to be so,
Complain in the midst of their loss;
Their virtue being only skin-deep,
They are the devil's poor.

4th POINT.
*Qualities of true poverty of spirit.*

1st
They are patient.

44. They do have money in this life,
Not in their hands, but in their hearts,
Because they are always wanting it,
And they love it with great ardor.
Often a poor wretch
Is more greedy in his destitution
Than a great potentate
With all his great wealth.

2nd
They have a heart detached from possessions and without desires.

45. Jesus does not want as his followers
The poor who are idle;
The idler is without any merit,
And is bound and cast into the fire.
God does not even want him to eat
If all he wants is to rest
And if, by a strange misfortune,
All he will do is play the beggar.

3rd
Hard-working.

46. Often enough the poor are lacking in piety,
Keeping away from the Sacraments,
Lying without any reason,
And sometimes cursing.
By these sins of theirs they are doubly
Unfortunate in their poverty,
And still more wretched in Hell
Throughout eternity.

4th
Devout.

47. Faithful poor people, give up from your heart
This money which fools look for,
And all these useless vanities
Which are unworthy of you.
Make a complete sacrifice,

5th
Detached even from the smallest things.

Let your heart not be attached to anything;
This would be an injustice
And an insult to your sovereign good.

48. Trample under foot, like brave people,
Gold and silver and all their friends;
Do not make yourselves their slaves,
But take them for your enemies.
Go, ascend the throne,
By the poverty of the Savior,
Where such abundance is prepared
For all true poor in heart.

6th
Enemies of money.

49. But try to put into practice
This holy spirit of poverty;
Otherwise your poverty is fanciful
And filled only with vanity;
When you lack something which is necessary,
Suffer it with joy,
Saying nothing which might be contrary
To the most perfect detachment.

7th
Joyful and content when they do not have all that is necessary.

50. How little I have known of the grace in you,
Dear poverty of my God!
But now I embrace you
With a heart all on fire,
For I prefer your livery,
Your rags, your pale colors,
To all the golden vanities
Which lead eyes and hearts astray.

Prayer

51. Away, little creatures!
You are unworthy of me.
Now I call down a thousand curses
On these creatures that enslaved me.
The Lord has come to teach me
How to be happy without you.
Away! I cannot take you back
Without numbering myself among fools.

52. I know that the world treats me
As scrupulous, a beggar, a fool;
And that is how I will treat the world
And how I will break its neck.

The more it tells me to feather my nest,
The more I will strip myself;
The more it tries to inspire me with its habits,
The further I will go from it.

53. Yes, I will do just the opposite
Of all it tries to inspire in me;
That will be my normal rule
Which will never deceive me.
It will have its vain outward show,
But I will have the truth;
It will have its foolish abundance,
But I will have poverty.

54. It may have its pompous garments,
But I will have nothing but an old rag;
It may have its numerous followers,
But I will live in neglect.
Money may be what inspires its victory hymn,
Mine will be sung in impoverishing myself;
Money may be where it finds its glory,
I will find mine in leaving it behind.

55. I find in my poor cottage
More charms than in the world's palaces:
I may have neither cellar nor kitchen,
Yet I feast on better dishes.
It is for goods that it torments itself,
Fearing that they might be stolen;
For myself, I neither sow nor plant,
Yet I harvest more than the world.

56. The world searches, steals, talks, shouts,
So as to acquire some goods;
While I, if I act or pray,
Do so to have nothing more.
It goes about in a carriage;
If it walks at all, it is with a pompous air.
While I laugh at this vain giant
And go my way barefoot like a beggar.

57. It is rich in the goods of the earth,
I am poor, but rich in God.
It has nothing but lawsuits and war;
While I have peace wherever I go.

It cries without ceasing: "More, more",
And I want nothing at all;
Its attachment to goods is very strong,
While my poor heart is out for nothing.

58. I have merited by my sins
To be a rich man here below;
Oh! what vengeance!
Lord, do not condemn me to that,
Calm your just anger
By the poverty of Jesus;
I take it for my dear mother,
I take it for my wealth.

59. Poor Jesus, I wish to follow you,
One poor man after another, even unto death.
Have mercy, poverty intoxicates me
And inspires in me this holy delight.
Either let me be like you in my life,
Or else deprive me of life right now;
By your heart and through Mary,
Grant me this great gift.

60. For fear that the common way
Might lead me astray from truth,
I come to make my fortune
With the wealth of your poverty.
Make my fortune very great,
That I may be poor like you
And all my belongings may hop along with me.
I shall be richer than all.

GOD ALONE.

## 21
## FLAMES OF ZEAL

1. May we all sing and be enflamed
With ardent zeal for souls.
Zeal springs from love of God;
Love cannot abide offenses

Definition and essence of zeal.

Hurled at God, our Mighty King,
Nor bear assaults on our neighbor.
Let us then scan (twice) zeal's excellence.

1st POINT
*Necessity and excellence of zeal.*

2. Saint Michael, armed with zeal,
Struck the rebel Lucifer,
And plunged him into hell.
Michael's great victory is shared
With those who live his great zeal,
We too shout, as Michael did:
To God all victory (twice) and glory!

1st Motive
Example of Saint Michael.

3. What bliss for God our Father
When our zeal joins in with His
To save a poor sinner!
It wins for Him a soul He loves
And honors Him perfectly,
And since He infinitely loves
All sinners (twice), Love spurs Him on.

2nd Motive
Zeal glorifies and gives joy to God the Father.

4. The angels celebrate as often
As zeal gains a victory;
Such joy for our sweet Savior,
For He sees His blood bear fruit,
He recovers His lost child,
The price of His shed blood.
How this return (twice) glorifies Him.

3rd Motive
Zeal gives joy to Jesus Christ.

5. Sometimes a single zealous word
Has opened wide the door
And touched some hardened heart.
Right then, the Holy Spirit enters
And through His secret touch,
The soul becomes most penitent
And peace (twice) forever reigns.

4th Motive
It opens the heart to the Holy Spirit.

6. Zeal is as reasonable
As our neighbor is admirable.
For who can know his value?
God alone knows his fathomless price;
He is the temple of the Holy Spirit,
The price of Jesus' blood,
A child of God (twice) beyond a doubt.

5th Motive
Our neighbor deserves our zeal for his salvation.

7. So then, shall this immortal soul
So noble, great, so beautiful
Perish through iniquity?
They trample on God's image
And do not even care;
And no one gives a hoot?
Blindness! (twice) What a catastrophe!

6th Motive
Beauty and immortality of our neighbor's soul.

8. Alas! so many of our brothers
Perish through their ignorance
Or through their own weaknesses.
We must then overflow with zeal
To help them see the truth,
To snatch them by our charity
From evil's clutch (twice), so deplorable.

7th Motive
Our neighbor needs our zeal.

8th Motive
To enlighten and strengthen him.

9. How many sinners by their deeds
Will fall in the abyss
Unless we truly help them!
We must break the brutal chains
That cruelly shackle them
Or they will be forever damned.
Help them (twice), faithful soul.

9th Motive
To rescue him from the gates of hell.

10. Ah! free them from their slavery
With wise and prudent zeal.
In charity, come to their aid.
Your help is almsgiving most divine
To rescue them from hell
And make them triumph finally
By giving them (twice) a heavenly throne.

10th Motive
And to help him reach paradise.

11. Zeal, so necessary,
Is also very salutary
For those who possess it.
Zealous hearts receive many graces,
The Savior's precious treasures,
The ardent flame of fervor,
The greatest gifts (twice) of innocence.

11th Motive
God grants great graces to the zealous.

12. The most abundant almsgiving,
The most fervent prayer
And intense austerity
Are far surpassed by proper zeal;
What could be so grand or so divine

12th Motive
Zeal is a very meritorious and divine virtue.

As converting one's neighbor.
Pure love alone, (twice) brings us there.

13. Zeal places in security
And covers with its innocence
Our sins, though they be many.
Charity is given to the charitable,
God is only love and tenderness
To a heart filled with burning zeal,
For God returns (twice) what He has been given.

13th Motive
It covers a
multitude of sins.

14. Of all deaths, the most beautiful,
Is the death of a zealous man.
Oh! How joyfully he dies!
His charity makes his case strong;
The sinner he converted,
At judgment takes his part,
Pays for him (twice) and is his crown.

14th Motive
The zealous have
a beautiful and
holy death.

15. No happiness can equal his,
His crown, beyond compare!
What glory for all preachers then!
They are in heaven the brilliant stars,
The suns shining brightly
And for all eternity,
In splendor (twice) ravishing.

15th Motive
They have special
glory in heaven.

16. Listen to Moses crying out
That his name be lifted from the book of
life
In favor of poor sinners.
Saint Paul yearned to be anathema
For his brothers according to the flesh,
To keep them out of hell.
O ardent zeal, (twice) love's extreme!

16th Motive
Examples of zeal.

17. False zeal is always reprehensible;
Pure and authentic zeal
Must be supernatural,
And must be modeled on
The sacred zeal of Jesus Christ,
Conceived by his Divine Spirit,
Or else (twice) the zeal is false.

2nd POINT
*Qualities of zeal*

1st quality.
Supernatural.

18. No bitterness can mar true zeal,
It springs from hearts consumed by love,
No harshness, all paternal,
Like that of God, our good Father
Or like that of Our Blessed Lord
Who converted sinners
With no bitterness (twice), no anger.

2nd quality.
Tender.

19. We must imitate this matchless model:
Our good Master compared himself
To a hen with chicks,
Day and night she shelters them
Beneath her wings; gently she calls them
And so tenderly feeds them
Without excluding (twice) the most rebellious.

Example of Jesus Christ.

20. A child may squander grace.
If he repents, our Lord embraces him
With delights most divine.
A ewe may leave the fold;
When Jesus finds it after its misfortune,
With no spite he brings it back
To the sheepfold (twice), back to life!

21. True zeal is creative in fostering,
Without being maudlin,
Salvation and divine love.
It is everything to all, with no borders;
Zeal considers sinners and also little ones
Of very great worth,
Which renders it (twice) very meritorious.

3rd quality
Industrious.

4th quality
Universal.

22. True zeal is full of wisdom,
Modesty and joy
To win over a neighbor.
Zeal does nothing for itself;,
God alone is the perfect motive
For what zeal says and does.
God alone (twice), nothing else.

5th quality
Modest.

6th quality
Disinterested.

23. True zeal is full of trust
In divine Providence,
In the care of our loving Father,
Counting for naught its own strength and
skill;

7th quality
Abandoned to
Providence.

Not counting on any human help,
Zeal places all its strength in God.
That is where (twice) wisdom is found.

24. Zeal is insurmountable,
Always agreeable and stable,
Its fire can never be extinguished;
It is a torrent which topples and shatters
Whatever blocks its course.
It speaks and always overcomes,
Allowing nothing (twice) to overwhelm it.

8th quality.
Insurmountable.

25. Neither hell nor the entire earth
Can ever conquer it in war;
Zeal is stronger than death,
It fears not the power of man.
Zeal fears God, it fears sin,
But for the rest, it is not moved.
Compared to God (twice) all else is a nothing.

26. In all it does, zeal has taken
Obedience for its motto,
It is, therefore, active and strong.
Whatever happens, it wins a glorious victory;
Even though no one is converted,
Although alone of its kind,
When it obeys (twice), it has won.

9th quality
Submissive.

# 22
# RESOLUTIONS OF A ZEALOUS MISSIONARY

1. My choice is made! I'll roam through the world,
Living just like a vagabond,
To rescue my poor neighbor.
Could I see my dear brother's soul
Perishing everywhere through sin,
My heart not being touched?
No, No, Lord, no, no, his soul is too dear.

2. Could I see his exquisite soul
Fall into hell, and forever,

Yet not one person distressed?
What! Could I see God's loving Blood
Poured out for us all, and wasted?
My brother's ransom for eternity lost?
I would rather, rather be damned.

3. Ah! Lord, everyone blasphemes you
By blaspheming your own image;
Should I bear this without a word?
Your foes now ravish your glory,
Should I cowardly take their side?
Truly, Lord, I would rather die.
Lord, Lord, I will be victorious!

4. O mighty God, give me your arms
To conquer the world with its charms
And all things against your law;
To convert souls, O Lord bestow
Your holiness into my soul,
The truth into my mind,
And pure fire, fire in my heart.

5. Grant me the gift of wisdom
And of fervent charity,
Creating a godlike man.
Great God, make my voice thunder
So evil may be destroyed,
And your holy Will be done
On earth, on earth and in heaven.

6. All I do, Lord is for you,
You alone are my concern,
You, with no human respect.
I stomp on the world and its show;
If, Lord, my zeal pleases you,
I will count myself as blest
To become, become the world's trash.

7. People travel land and sea
With limitless exertion
Only for a grain of sand.
Should I not have zeal for you?
Should I dare not take a step
So God's Blood be not wasted?
Oh! what contempt, contempt from the unfaithful!

8. When a heavy load fells a horse,
We pity and unburden it,
But what contempt for human souls!
When souls fall, and sleep in sin,
Who is there to lift them up?
Go off, poor souls, where you may
Die in sin, in sin, and fall into hell.

9. Ah! Everywhere the demon tempter,
Everywhere an abundant harvest,
Yet so few laborers for our God,
We must beg, beg our family's Father
To bring down, bring down the devil's pride
And send out into his harvest,
Laborers, laborers for the Gospel.

10. Wherever the soldier beats his drum,
People hurry up to gather arms,
Quickly, many regiments are formed.
Do we Christians form a regiment
To defend a God so offended?
Do we ready our holy arms?
Alas! Alas! no one even cares.

11. O you false Christian, carnal soul,
Why not side with the unfaithful?
Sleep in peace, you are not wounded.
You are neither harmed nor injured;
So who cares about his neighbor?
He goes to hell? That's his bad luck.
What callous, callous outrage!

12. I can not take an hour's rest,
Or stay that long within one house,
Seeing Jesus so offended.
Alas! so many battle Him.
Sin now is reigning everywhere,
Souls are falling into hell.
I want to roar, roar like thunder.

13. O my great God, for your Gospel,
From town to town, I would suffer
A thousand hardships and abuse,
If by my life and all my blood

I destroy even but one sin.
If through me you may touch one soul,
You reward kindly, too kindly, my toil.

14. If I were to save not a one,
I would still not lose the crown
You prepare for my labors.
You reward not success,
But the good seed we have sown,
And the many labors spent.
The wage matches, matches the pain.

15. O my God, although I love you,
I am apprehensive of myself,
Support me in my weakness.
If I were as holy as the apostles,
And were to gain the whole world,
I could still fall into hell,
In trying to save, to save poor souls.

16. In the exercise of my zeal,
Make me always very faithful
To the duties of holiness;
May my spring gush forth night and day,
Never leaving me depleted,
May I preach to transform hearts,
But by preaching, preaching, let me be renewed.

17. Far from me austere zealots,
Filled with harshness and anger
Used as pretexts of charity.
Little vinegar, much oil,
Converts the greatest sinners,
And wins both mind and heart
As we see, we see in the Gospel.

18. O my God only your grace
Can sustain me so that I may,
Above all else, do your holy Will,
Despite hell, the flesh and man.
I want to make you loved, dear Lord,
If my death will do you honor,
How happy, happy to be slain.

19. Everywhere may I have simple ways,

A most pleasant and heavenly zeal,
But with no varnish or vanity,
Never depending on flattery;
Let me be all things to all
With a gentle and accepting heart,
Open, open, to the worst degenerate.

20. I bind myself to obedience,
It is my one and only safeguard,
To preach in all security.
I know from my own experience
That ardent zeal is but an evil
When not truly humble and prudent,
According to the rules, the rules of sacred science.

21. Far from me, mercenary pastors,
Pastors, yes, but better business men,
They preach, but only for their profit;
For me, 'I am a God poor on earth,'
Possessing then not a penny,
Having no fear of any bailiff,
Not involved, not involved, in any wars.

22. Although I neither plant nor sow
I am richer than you wealthy.
Believe me, Sirs, if you please,
For truly my prudence is shrewd,
The wealthy are my landholders,
Mine whatever of their wealth I need.
With them I share, share, cellar and kitchen.

23. It is not that I despise you
If you do not have for maxim,
Perfect, total detachment;
But you must know that by your greed,
You gain so little by your work,
In fact, you cause yourselves great harm
And often, often, through injustice.

24. How many useless priests are there
Whose wonderful gifts are fruitless
Because they lack this detachment?
They preach well, no one does better,
Yet no sinner is ever touched
Even though they preached so well.

What fruit? fruit? Only flattery.

25. We no longer see among us
Those solid, true apostles
Who shone so brightly years gone by.
Why? There are no voluntary poor;
One seeks to be well settled,
Another seeks, though indirectly,
A little money, money for his business.

26. This money is but muddy slush
Which so sullies generous souls
It rules them and makes them grovel;
Money has something revolting
Which fully contaminates zeal.
Although it seems to be detached,
Its pure ardor, its ardor is cooled.

27. No money! this heavy heap
Both captures and dismays me;
The more I have, more I grovel,
The less, lighter is my soul.
Money is like a camel's load;
Penniless, like a bird soaring
Heavenward, heavenward, into Light.

28. My Jesus, I want to be wise,
I want You alone for my lot,
For my possession and my worth.
My God, you alone and souls' salvation!
No penny, then, of recompense.
What great wealth in my vocation,
For with your fire, fire, my heart is rich.

29. Grant me Lord, I entreat you,
A very ingenious zeal;
Please instruct me in all truth;
Enkindle me with new flame,
Teach me heavenly secrets
So I may be more perfect,
More vigilant, vigilant, more faithful.

30. Keep me from the great precipice:
From scruples concerning justice,
From a spirit of novelty

In my faith, my zeal, behavior;
Guard me then from all illusion
And from insincere devotion,
To follow you, follow you, alone.

31. I am ready, Jesus, my Lord,
To turn up preaching anywhere,
Supported by your power.
Make me, Lord, your missionary;
Even though it has no income
But only insults and rebuffs,
I am content, content, dear Model.

32. O Mary, O my good Mother,
Help me with a full army,
Hasten, I am now attacked.
May my word increase and bear fruit,
May I destroy iniquity,
May I grow in holiness,
And may God be always, always glorified.

GOD ALONE

## 23
## WISDOM OF SILENCE

1. Do you want to be perfect
And preserve your innocence?
Here is the secret:
Practice silence.
Do you want to give the Lord
Immeasurable glory?
Be silent. Close your heart
To every creature.

Essence and definition of silence.

2. How does one extinguish the fire
Of a cruel tongue
Which everywhere sullies and kills
The most faithful soul?
Only silence is the death
Of this murderer.
Without effort silence wins

1st POINT
*Silence is victorious over the tongue and all the evils it causes.*

1st Motive
The tongue soils and kills.

Full victory over the tongue.

3. O tiny bit of flesh,
O delicate tongue,
You burn with the fire of hell,
You lose the soul and flatter it,
Your darts are poisonous
With deadly venom.
Your witty remarks are flaming arrows
And snares of the devil.

2nd Motive
The tongue light
the fire of hell.

3rd Motive
It poisons.

4. Restless and cruel evil,
Furious murderer,
Tender but deadly dagger
By which the soul is devastated,
By your two-edged sword
You make more souls perish
With chains and flames
Than the wickedest tyrant.

4th Motive
It is a restless evil
and a two edged
sword.

5. You ravage your own house
And that of your brother.
Your toxin destroys everything
Even in the monastery,
O great university
Of all the greatest sins,
Summary of all the iniquities
That fill the abyss.

5th Motive
The university of
all sin.

Enumeration of
these sins.

6. You spit out oaths,
You spread scandal,
You enrage,
You insult,
You blaspheme, you curse,
You hate and you grumble,
Your sins are infinite,
The worst in the world.

7. Dear friends, will we perish
By this common evil?
To avoid its anger
Let us learn to be silent;
Silence is an infallible remedy
For this horrible evil,
It destroys this hellish poison,

6th Motive
Silence avoids all
the evils of the
tongue.

This terrible monster.

8. Often, a constant talker is no more
Than a strongbox without a lock,
A huge windbag,
A beautiful sack filled with filth;
Since he is often distracted
And without self discipline,
The devil soon traps him,
To his extreme misfortune.

7th Motive
And the miseries of constant talkers.

8th Motive
A great talker is compared to several things.

9. A gabby person is never
Controlled on earth,
His mouth casts arrows
Which he regrets;
He is often wounded by them
Even losing his life,
And his heart is pierced like a sieve
By his own folly.

9th Motive
He is conquered by the demon.

10th Motive
He is uncontrollable.

11th Motive
He hurts himself.

10. The wise man has his mouth in his heart,
He speaks there, he rests there.
However, a great talker
Has his heart in his mouth;
He argues, making plenty of noise
Like a swift waterfall,
But his noise brings forth no fruit.
He is a totally empty vessel.

12th Motive
He has his heart in his mouth

13th Motive
He brings forth no fruit.

11. The man who is wise according to God,
And filled with God's wisdom,
Speaks little or not at all.
The fool speaks incessantly;
The wise man is silent,
His silence edifies,
A chatterer is often scandalous,
And always so boring.

14th Motive
He constantly talks and he is a scandalous and annoying fool.

12. Oh! how a regulated silence
Is holy and salutary!
The Fathers called it
The divine school
Shaping divine thoughts
In the silent man's mind,

2nd POINT
*The excellence of silence.*

1st Motive
It is the seminary of good thoughts.

Secretly filling the heart
With ardent graciousness.

13. It can also be called
A divine school
Training its students to speak well,
And form their words;
A person only speaks rightly
When he has learned to be silent,
When a person wants to speak constantly
He often speaks brashly.

2nd Motive
The school of the word.

14. We rightfully uphold
Silence is necessary
To meditate well
Since it is the father of prayer.
Yes, it is silence that instructs us
To form our prayers,
That gives us quietly and in secret
The purest lights.

3rd Motive
The father of prayer.

15. Silence is the great director
And the support of a soul,
The sure guardian of its heart,
The keeper of its flame.
Wisdom is with silence,
Silence is never without wisdom,
Both are the glory and the support
Of a faithful soul.

4th Motive
The director of souls.

5th Motive
The companion of wisdom.

16. It is a marvelous book
That the ignorant can read,
An eloquent preacher
Who speaks without talking,
A sweet smelling balm
That perfumes the soul,
A secret gently charming
The sinner's soul.

6th Motive
The book of the wise and the ignorant.

7th Motive
The balm and the secret of pouring balm on the soul and converting sinners.

17. Without silence, religion
Is sterile and unsteady;
Without silence, devotion
Is sullied and straggling,

8th Motive
Without it, there is no religion, devotion or true joy.

But this divine balm
Never brings sadness;
It fills the saddest heart
With joy and cheer.

18. Exteriorly God speaks little,
But interiorly, always;
Oh! God's beautiful example!
O supreme model!
During thirty years Jesus Christ
Lived in silence;
Oh! how these startling examples
Prove the excellence of silence.

9th Motive
Examples of silence.

1. God.

2. Jesus Christ.

19. But the greatest miracle is that
The Mother of the Savior
Kept in her heart
The most divine oracles,
And rarely spoke;
We know it from the apostles,
Her heart pondered delicately
The words of others.

3. The Blessed Virgin.

20. Silence was the great lesson
Of the sages of Greece,
To obtain the gift
Of great wisdom;
To the saints, silence was
A beatitude,
To be silent they fled from the worldly
Even to solitude.

4. The philosophers.

5. The saints.

21. But how must one speak
When one can not be silent?
We must control ourselves;
Nothing is so necessary,
Since the tongue contains
Both death and life,
By reason and even by faith
Let us control it, I entreat you.

3rd POINT
*Rules for speaking well.*

1
Death and life are in the tongue.

22. The tongue speaks from the heart,
For the heart is its image;
The tongue's bliss or distress
Springs from the heart's plenty;

2
The tongue speaks from the heart.

If the heart is truly holy,
The tongue is innocent;
But if the heart is wicked
The tongue is very evil.

23. How we need prudence
To speak like a saint!
How we need vigilance
To speak prudently!
We speak so easily,
Our tongue is bold,
With one word spoken rashly
We can start a fire.

3
We must speak prudently.

24. What evil the tongue commits!
What vain lapses!
What useless plans!
What stupid blows!
Do you want to avoid
A thousand frivolous words?
Be very prompt to listen
But very slow to speak.

4
We must speak rarely.

25. Do you wish to excel
In this necessary skill?
Be sparing of your words
And generous in your silences.
Let your words be weighed
And passed through the strainer,
Then afterwards, speak the truth
Without lying or sinning.

5
After having weighed and meditated on our words.

6
Truly, without lying.

26. Speak to edify
Your neighbor, your brother,
Speak to glorify
The Lord your Father;
Seek God in your speech
And you will hurt no one,
Then speak and preach everyday,
Your speech will be virtuous.

7
For a good purpose.

8
Charitably.

27. To be annoying in speech,
To answer without understanding,
To interrupt someone
And speak out of turn,

9
Wisely, avoiding several faults.

Or to comment on everything
Are signs of foolishness,
Or at least they are great faults
Against the virtue of modesty.

28. Don't shout when you speak,
Speak in a low voice
Without bursts of laughter,
Without smirking or scowling,
Without affectation or vanity
Without showing off,
Graciously, with humility,
Without sounding bossy.

10
Modestly.

11
Humbly

29. Speak truthfully,
Without any hypocrisy,
Without wounding charity,
Without any flattery;
Speak without human respect,
But without being annoying,
Pay full attention to your neighbor
But without affectation.

12
In a holy manner,
without human
respect.

30. All that glitters is not gold.
Speak prudently,
Preserve your treasure
In profound silence.
Unless required to,
Or ordered by obedience,
Refrain from being an advisor,
[So easily] stuffed with conceit.

13
Modestly.

31. Try not to speak
When one should be silent.
Such as in bed or at table
Unless it is necessary;
But above all, say nothing
Unnecessary in church,
There, maintain Christian silence
And submissive faith.

14
Rarely speak in
bed or at meals.
Never in church
without necessity.

32. Whoever chatters in this holy place
Is quite irreverent
And commits a cruel offense
Against God.

He inflicts on Him a blow
For each vain thing he says,
And God always avenges with anger
Those who cause Him this sorrow.

TO FALSE DEVOTEES

33. Great devotees but poor saints
Who prattle constantly
I pity you before God,
Charity impels me;
What blind piety!
What stupid chatter!
Do you not piously damn yourselves
By your pious blather?

34. Not choosing the better part
Of a true, weeping devotee,
To speak of everybody,
To constantly chatter,
To look all around,
To be part of all the gossip
To inquire about the latest news,
O lost devotee!

35. Farewell to her devotion,
For her mouth is always open.
Farewell to her piety,
Oh! the terrible privation.
Farewell to her communion
And her inner ardor
Farewell heaven and perfection,
She is damning her soul.

36. The Lord will judge you,
O devout busybodies,
His justice will punish
Your idle words.
Prattlers of this age
If you are not damned,
Oh! you will suffer torments
For many, many years!

37. Oh! what a craving
To speak without end!

Is that not the venom
Impure women sip?
The wicked love to talk
And can not be silent.
To speak ill, to scold, to gossip,
This is her only business.

38. Devout people, even if you perform
All sorts of great miracles
And even utter
All sorts of great oracles,
If you gossip all the time
Without any restraint,
You lose grace every day
And you will be lost.

39. What badly digested words!
What useless talk!
What hysterical laughter,
And over such trivia!
After that, call yourselves
Saints, devout people;
Be known as saints among fools,
To me, you are fanatical.

40. This young woman speaks well,
She is holy and learned,
There is a charming graciousness
In her conversations.
As for me, I would not consider
A pagoda holy;
The up-to-date devout person
Is nothing but a baited hook.

41. She talks day and night
She is a flood of words.
Alas! her heart is seduced,
She is a foolish virgin.
She is a barrel, hollow and empty,
That echoes and re-echoes.
False devotee, will you open your eyes?
I'm talking to you.

42. She has read all the books,
This woman is smart,

She has her admirers.
Oh! the insolent woman!
She cites Augustine,
Jerome, Hilary,
Oh! what evil! Oh! what subtle toxin,
Alas, all too common!

43. I shall tell you the truth,
Annoying devotees,
The world and its vanities
Make you too common,
You would be of some value
Without a tongue and a head,
For they both heap you with scorn.
I have said enough, I must end.

44. Ah! leave vanity aside;
Leave this infamous world,
Seek the truth
Within your soul.
On the outside speak very little
But on the inside a great deal.
That is how one acquires
Great sanctity in God.

45. Ah! Lord, help me! — Prayer.
My tongue is against me,
Deign to stop its course
With a strong barrier,
Purify at this time
My sinful lips
With the fire and burning coal
Of the faithful prophets.

46. Lord, speak to my heart,
For it savors you alone;
Since all are liars
The heart listens only to you.
Speak, from now on I wish
To be silent to creatures
I hardly ever speak to them
Without suffering their insults.

47. I want to speak to you alone,
To be a wise man,

Although the world and its fools
Treat me as a bumpkin;
My tongue no longer speaks,
It is time to be silent
Unless it is to honor Jesus
And his holy Mother.

48. Eyes, no longer see
So much trivia;
Ears, be tightly closed
To all the latest news.
Blind, deaf and mute
To this passing world,
Let us become perfect
And men full of grace.

49. Silence then, to my eyes
Silence to my ears,
Be still, my tongue, everywhere
In order to speak marvels.
Speak, my heart, to the Lord,
From the depths of retreat,
No longer be heard by sinners
And your voice is now perfect.

GOD ALONE

# 24
# PRACTICE OF THE PRESENCE OF GOD

1. Do we want to be happy, preserve our innocence,
Even pass through fire without being burned?
By essence and power
God is present everywhere!
Let us then live in the presence
Of God.

Definition of the presence of God.

1st POINT
*Excellence of this practice.*

Motives

2. This is God's great secret, inviting us
To become holy, seeing Him everywhere,
Receiving more merit
Than one gains in heaven.
Let us then live in the presence
Of God.

1st Motive
It is more meritorious than the vision of God in heaven.

3. God sees me here; this thought alone
Prevents me from sinning, keeps me at duty,
My soul is restored,
Oh! how powerful this thought!
Let us then live in the presence
Of God.

2nd Motive
It makes us avoid sin.

4. A soldier fighting in the presence of his captain
Fights valiantly, doubles his strength,
Victory is assured,
Never is he conquered.
Let us then live in the presence
Of God.

3rd Motive
Gives us victory.

5. A loving child fulfilling his father's wishes
In all things and with joyful heart,
Can never displease him,
He has his eyes on his father.
Let us then live in the presence
Of God.

4th Motive
Characteristic of good children of God.

6. Are you distressed, do you feel weak?
Think of God's presence, in Him you will find
Buttress and brace,
Joy, exhilaration.
Let us then live in the presence
Of God.

5th Motive
It brings joy.

7. This holy presence is the soul's sunlight,
Destroying its sins, making thieves flee,
Enlightening, enkindling,
With gentle fervor.
Let us then live in the presence
Of God.

6th
It is the sun of the soul, enlightening it and curing it.

8. Forgetting our God, we fall into sin,
From sin to sin, even to godlessness,
Even to the bottom of hell
For all eternity.
Let us then live in the presence
Of God.

7th Motive
Forgetting the presence of God is the cause of all sins.

9. Forgetting the Lord has devastated the earth,
So full of fools. How relentless is evil!
Almost everyone wages war
Against their judge and in his presence.
Let us then live in the presence
Of God.

8th Motive
Forgetting God is the reason for an infinite number of fools.

10. Abraham heard God Himself tell him:
Walk in my presence and you will be perfect.
It was to instruct us
God told him this secret.
Let us then live in the presence
Of God.

9th Motive
It is a secret God gives to us to be perfect.

11. The presence of God is eternal life,
The glory and support of the angels;
They find in it everything
Needed for happiness.
Let us then live in the presence
Of God.

10th Motive
It is the nourishment of angels.

12. Saints made it their constant concern,
Seeing God alone everywhere, always:
All their fulfillment was found
In pleasing Him.
Let us then live in the presence
Of God.

11th Motive
The example of saints and prophets.

13. Prophet and saint proclaimed at all times:
Long live God who sees and sustains me!
In life or in death,
With Him nothing I fear.
Let us then live in the presence
Of God.

14. The presence of God strengthened their souls,
Filled them with joy in their labors,

Even when engulfed in flames,
And during their greatest trials.
Let us then live in the presence
Of God.

12th Motive
The example of martyrs.

15. We live in God's presence in so many ways,
Nearby, in heaven, outside, in one's heart,
And according to the light
Given us by the Lord.
Let us then live in the presence
Of God.

2nd POINT
*Different ways God is present.*

16. We can consider the person of Jesus Christ
And picture Him visibly.
This is a good practice
When done with simplicity.
Let us then live in the presence
Of God.

1st Practice
Or the manner of the presence of God: picturing Jesus Christ present.

17. We can see Him on heaven's throne,
With his eternal gaze fixed upon us,
Seeing our victory,
Counting our sins.
Let us then live in the presence
Of God.

2nd Practice
See Him in heaven.

18. We can consider Him as a powerful refuge
Where sinners risk no danger,
Or as a just judge,
Ready to judge us.
Let us then live in the presence
Of God.

3rd Practice
To picture Him as judge.

19. Outside of this presence, we are outside our center;
Take a fish out of water, its only home,
And the fish will certainly die
Unless returned to the water.
Let us then live in the presence
Of God.

4th Practice
As one's center.

20. A sublime practice: We picture ourselves in God,
And plunged into the ocean of holiness,
Into the bottomless abyss

5th Practice
To picture oneself in His immensity.

Of His immensity.
Let us then live in the presence
Of God.

21. You can see this supreme monarch everywhere,
Higher is he than heaven, deeper than hell,
For He goes even beyond
This whole vast universe.
Let us then live in the presence
Of God.

22. We can consider God in each earthly creature:
By one He feeds us, through another instructs us,
In one He affirms us,
In another He leads us.
Let us then live in the presence
Of God.

23. God resides in us more than anywhere else,
So in our hearts we must seek Him,
It is there He reveals Himself,
In all glorious splendor.
Let us then live in the presence
Of God.

6th Practice
In our heart.

24. God has chosen our hearts for His throne and domain,
Luring us there night and day, bidding us taste
His sovereign beauty
And His divine love.
Let us then live in the presence
Of God.

TO SINNERS

25. O sinner, God hears you; sinner, God sees you;
He observes your actions, He counts every step,
And you really don't care,
You don't even think of Him.
Let us then live in the presence
Of God.

26. You can avoid neither his eyes nor his anger,
Judge and witness is He of all your sins,
Even the words you say,
Yet you are tranquil!

Let us then live in the presence
Of God.

27. You fool, when you speak, you astound me;
You say: No one saw me, there's nothing here.
You consider God nobody!
He sees you, He saw you.
Let us then live in the presence
Of God.

28. In this hidden nook, in that dark room,
Or hiding in a dismal desert,
The King of glory, the Judge,
Has seen all your sins.
Let us then live in the presence
Of God.

29. Sinner, when about to fall, recall
The presence of God; you will be very strong,
Chanting full victory
Over hell and death.
Let us then live in the presence
Of God.

30. Christian, if you desire true holiness,
Have God always present in mind,
O awesome secret,
Gift of the Spirit!
Let us then live in the presence
Of God.

PRAYER

31. Lord, do you seek among men
Someone wise in your sight, who walks in your presence?
Imbeciles that we are,
We all forget you.
Let us then live in the presence
Of God.

32. To your eyes, Mighty God, nothing's invisible,
Since you fill both heaven and earth,
It is then impossible
To hide from your sight.
Let us then live in the presence

Of God.

33. I adore you here, O Father of my fathers,
O almighty Lord, before whom all things are nothing,
O Father of lights,
From whom all good proceeds.
Let us then live in the presence
Of God.

34. Your divine Providence feeds me,
You probe my mind and test my heart,
Nothing ever escapes
Your knowledge, Lord.
Let us then live in the presence
Of God.

35. To all, you give being, movement and life,
Your immensity holds everything, everywhere,
And the earth is full
Of your majesty.
Let us then live in the presence
Of God.

36. Can someone offend you, even in your presence,
Sin and disobey you before your eyes?
O cruel arrogance!
I would prefer death.
Let us then live in the presence
Of God.

37. Lord, engrave in me your divine face,
So I may calmly possess your presence everywhere,
With nothing ever effacing you,
No, not even death.
Let us then live in the presence
Of God.

38. Enter into your heart, my soul, leave the trifles;
All exterior goods, in your eyes, belong to others.
God calls to you in your heart,
All your good is in Him.
Let us then live in the presence
Of God.

39. Let us all calmly enter our hearts

To meet God present there more than anywhere else.
To preserve our innocence,
Or soon to regain it.
Let us all live in the presence
Of God.

GOD ALONE

## 25
## PLEASING FRAGRANCE OF MODESTY

Essence of the virtue of modesty.

1st POINT
*Its excellence*

1. Gaze at this face and these eyes
So gentle, docile and joyful,
Behold the virtue of Modesty;
Behold the traits of the overflow
Of virtues that fill the soul
And its inner glory.

Motives
1st Motive
It is the ornament of virtues.

2. Modesty is the adornment
And the most noble attire
Of truly sublime virtues;
It is the virtue of the perfect,
Those untroubled and sinless,
Those filled with mildness and peace.

2nd Motive
The virtue of the perfect.

3rd Motive
The fruit of the Holy Spirit.

3. It is the Holy Spirit's fruit,
As the great apostle writes:
"The Holy Spirit in a soul,
Makes His gentle flame's glow
Gush forth onto the body,
From the inner, they light up the outer."

4th Motive
The presence of God calls us to modesty.

4. Be modest with everyone,
For the Lord is nearby;
He knows all things by His light,
Nothing is hidden from Him.
He is watching you right now,
So be modest and sinless.

5. Admire the modesty
And gentleness of Our Lord;
It is His shining weapon
Which ravishes on sight;
It is his eloquent mouth
Which convinces by its silence.

5th Motive
The example of
Jesus Christ.

6. He had this sacred brilliance
To such a sublime degree,
His modesty was so striking
That Saint Paul regularly
Preached and implored with modesty
And so persuaded mightily.

6th Motive
St. Paul prayed
through the
modesty of Jesus
Christ.

7. Even the Lord's fuming slayers
Veiled His face and eyes,
Fearing the appeal of His charms,
Fearing His wise and meek air
Would make them stop the torture
In spite of their rage and anger.

7th Motive
His executioners
covered His
modesty.

8. They say that Heaven's Queen,
While she was here on earth,
Was so wise and modest,
Anyone who gazed on her
Felt the celestial flame
Burning within her heart.

8th Motive
The example of
the Blessed
Virgin.

9. Great Saint Denis affirms
His soul was so ravished
When contemplating her,
Had he not known the truth,
He would have thought
She was some great divinity.

9th Motive
Proof from Denis
the Areopagite.

10. By this virtue, saints have
Disarmed all, conquered all
Without any violence,
Trouble, yelling or shouting;
Their modesty and silence
Gently ravished hearts.

10th Motive
The example of
the saints.

11. Since modesty everywhere
Is so lofty and rich in God,
It puts in the heart, the sage says,

11th Motive
It is a rich virtue
before God.

Fear and love of the Lord,
Glory, life, plus the promise
And pledge of happiness.

12. The modest man is a winner,
His modesty, a fragrance
Speaking more loudly than his mouth.
Oh! how eloquent the preacher
Speaking in silence yet touching
The eye and heart of his hearers!

12th Motive
It wins every victory.

13. Look at great Saint Francis
Preaching at full volume
Yet only making an appearance.
Just seeing him, people are ravished,
He becomes the saintly master
Of all hearts, without making a sound.

13th Motive
Example of Saint Francis.

14. Without modesty how vain our work
To sanctify our neighbor,
Which as most people know,
Happens more through eyes than ears.
Modesty is so necessary
To raise hearts to heaven.

14th Motive
Without it, we do not help our neighbor.

15. Often, far from curing evil,
We cause horrible scandal
Through lack of modesty,
Though we preach holiness;
If the appearance does not edify
How much time is wasted.

15th Motive
Without it we scandalize our neighbor.

16. It is a brightness teaching us,
The rind protecting the fruit,
The beautiful glow confirming
The soul is truly healthy.
It is the hand of the clock
Telling us it's working.

16th Motive
It is as necessary as peel is to fruit, as bark is to a tree.

17th Motive
It is the mark of virtue

17. Without modesty we are unhinged,
Our poor heart is assaulted
By innumerable trifles.
Modesty is sanctity's bastion
Where all faithful souls
Preserve their purity.

18th Motive
It is a rampart and a guardian of the heart.

18. It is the sign of the chosen,
The elect's brilliance arrayed
By the inspiring Spirit;
Often, the carefree reprobate
Has immodest, sinful ways
Etched on his brow and in his eyes.

19th Motive
It is the sign of the chosen.

19. But what are Modesty's traits?
I will tell you, listen well:
This supernatural virtue
Seeks only to please the Lord,
For natural wisdom
Has no value before God.

2nd POINT
*Qualities of modesty.*

1st
Supernatural

20. Either in manner or posture,
In look or in speech,
It is always edifying
And without affectation,
It is gentle, it is pleasing
Without any dilution.

2nd
Edifying without affectation or hypocrisy.

21. Everywhere, a godly man
Is modest, even when alone,
For God sees him there;
He flees useless pastimes,
He is unruffled and restrained
Everywhere, at all times.

3rd
Continual, even in secret.

22. The sage seems so serene,
Always unflappable
In his gait, gestures, speech,
In his body, behavior;
Nothing appears childish,
Not even his smile.

4th
Universal in everything.

23. Chosen soul, we must heed
The advice given to us
By great and holy people,
If we are not learned
Let us try to be wise
By observing the following:

3rd POINT
*Practices of modesty.*

24. Acquire a gentle and joyful air,
Never haughty or disdainful;

1st
Modesty of the head and face.

Do not hold your head high
With pride or arrogance,
Hold it straight, a bit lowered
But not turned aside.

25. Be modest when you blow your nose,
Even when you cough or spit;
Whistling is undignified,
Laugh little, never bursting out,
Your brow you must not wrinkle
And try not to scratch.

2nd
Of the mouth and other senses.

26. Do not be too serious,
Be somber, also full of joy
And have a certain polished air,
No harshness nor vanity,
No affectation nor smirking,
Full of gentleness and kindness.

3rd
Of one's general appearance.

27. Don't fidget like fools
Constantly in motion,
Let your hands be well arranged,
But never at your sides,
Rarely stretch out your hands
Unless the necessity is urgent.

4th
Modesty in one's posture, hands and feet

28. Stand up straight ordinarily,
Without slouching indecently,
Never should you cross your legs
As the proud people do,
But keep them gently posed,
Not stretched out lazily.

29. Do not speak too much nor too little
For both displease God.
Never interrupt anyone;
Listen before responding,
Speak in a kindly manner,
But before speaking, reflect.

5th
Modesty in words.

30. Do not speak in too low a voice
But at the same time, do not shout;
Do not take a pedantic tone,
Imperious and contemptuous,
Do not use a rustic tone,

6th
In the tone of voice.

Nor saccharine or languishing.

31. Leave aside amusement,
Laughter and buffoonery,
Silliness and bagatelles
Which sully the ear and the heart
And all sorts of novelties
Spoken by the deceiving world.

7th
Leaving aside trifles and worldly news.

32. In order to be a perfect person,
Be deaf, blind and mute
To a thousand little witticisms
Made for children and for fools;
Treat these games with contempt
And disgust, as wise people do.

8th
One has to be blind, deaf and mute.

33. Speak simply
Without affectation or vanity;
Be modest in giving advice,
Do not give it sternly;
Give in to those who argue,
To overcome more nobly.

9th
Modesty in words, advice and arguments

34. Be modest in your clothes,
Let them not be too costly;
Do without lace and cloths
Shiny and luxurious,
The fancy airs and new styles
Seen in the outfits of the worldly.

10th
Modesty in clothing.

35. Walk without rushing,
Unless avoiding
A menacing danger;
Walk without affectation,
Sloth and daintiness
And without emotion.

11th
Modesty in walking.

36. Everywhere preach humility,
Wisdom and holiness;
When you walk through the towns,
Avoid laughter and childish games,
The many useless amusements
And the thousand cheeky things.

12th
Modesty in town.

37. Wisdom and cleanliness
Are two sisters of holiness
Which always go together;
Flee then disorder,
For it tarnishes modesty,
But avoid pompous cleanliness.

13th
Modesty and cleanliness.

38. Be modest at meals,
Eat what is set before you,
Without complaining or grumbling
And without rushing.
Observe good posture
And speak rarely at table.

14th
Modesty at meals.

39. Be filled with piety,
Respect, devotion
And modesty in church;
With a serene and gentle expression,
Head bent submissively,
Try to pray on your knees.

15th
Modesty in church.

40. Before the Blessed Sacrament
Bow profoundly,
Without saying a word,
Unless it is necessary,
Without doing anything childish
Before the God of majesty.

GOD ALONE

# 26
# OBLIGATIONS OF GRATITUDE

1. I sing and sing again
Always and everywhere,
Regardless of anyone,
The charities of my God.
He is here, listening to me; sing louder, my tongue.
Chosen soul, sing with me,
Let us sing, and renew our faith,
It is love that moves us.

2. Leave aside, I beg you,
All ungrateful sinners,
Flee their company,
They are but fattened swine,
Gulping down our master's riches
And do so with a hardened heart,
Without giving Him any thanks.

Exhortation to gratitude.

3. What gratitude
To offer the Lord?
Everything is in His power,
Everything is for His grandeur;
Though man has nothing, the Lord seeks an offering:
Man must recognize His gifts
And always bless Him for them.
That is all He asks.

1st POINT

1st Motive
Gratitude is the great sacrifice that God asks for His Glory.

4. He knows our weakness,
Our inability,
Our pettiness
Our poverty;
He wants as gifts nothing extraordinary,
He wants us to bless Him for them.
And to acknowledge them:
That is what we can do.

5. In justice, man owes
His generous God
The perfect sacrifice
Of a grateful heart:
Offer to Him in sacrifice the purest praise,
Fulfill one's vows to the Most High,
Adore God as we should
And as the angels do.

2nd Motive
It is owed to God by justice.

6. Jesus was faithful
In fulfilling this duty,
He is the best model
We could ever have;
Night and day He gave thanks to God His Father
By the oracles He spoke,
By the miracles He worked;

2nd POINT
*The examples of Jesus Christ and the saints.*

1st Motive
The example of Jesus Christ.

They were His prayer.

7. The more a soul is favored,
The more it must make return.
We see that in Mary
Brimming over with love;
Night and day she was filled with gratitude.
She blessed her Lord,
Proclaimed His kindness
And His immense power.

2nd Motive
The example of the Blessed Virgin.

8. The faithful Virgin
Encouraged everyone
To praise with her
Their common benefactor:
Deo gratias was her ordinary greeting;
Many saints, following her example,
Often said: Deo gratias.
O most salutary word!

3rd Motive
The example of the saints.

9. The Church militant
With the Church triumphant,
The Blessed in heaven,
Sings in joyful tones:
Thanks to our God whom we adore and bless,
Praise to our Creator,
Praise to our Redeemer.
Oh! holy practice!

4th Motive
The example of the Church militant and triumphant.

10. Both grace and nature
Inspire this return,
Everything mutters
If it does not happen.
The river runs to the sea as if it were its parent,
The flowers turn to the sun,
As the author of their being,
As their own father.

5th Motive
The example of creatures without reason.

11. Everything returns to the earth
That produced it,
Even the thunder
Returns with a loud bang
Teaching mortals to receive and give back,

To give back to God, as their end,
The gifts received from His hand,
Not keeping or taking anything.

12. Everything here below leads us
To this heartfelt return.
All land provides
Fruit for the laborer;
To the one manuring it, it says silently:
"For your manure and for your toil
I give you new fruit;
It is my thanks."

13. Animals are wise,
They are grateful,
Even the wildest
And the most voracious;
How well they remember favors.
We see this loyalty in dogs
And even in lions and bears,
As we read in history.

6th Motive
Example of the animals.

14. To love and give thanks
Are proper to all mortals;
Perhaps nothing in the world
Is as natural.
Our hearts are touched by another's kindness,
But for the kindness of the Lord
We have neither tongue nor heart.
O horrendous ingratitude!

7th Motive
Gratitude is natural for man.

3rd POINT
*It helps to avoid the sins of ingratitude and the faults of ungrateful people.*

15. We recognize gratitude
In the humble of heart,
But ingratitude
In the pride of the sinner;
A grateful heart avoids all the wrongs
And misfortunes of thankless people,
It wins victory in its combats,
And obtains sublime gifts.

1st Motive
The ungrateful are proud.

16. The ungrateful person wastes his efforts
And the Lord's favors.
He dries up the fountain
Of the Savior's graces;

2nd Motive
They waste their efforts and the goods they received.

God withdraws from him His grace and justice
And he falls into blindness
And then into obstinacy
And then into the abyss.

3rd Motive
They dry up the fountain of grace.
4th Motive
They fall into blindness and obstinacy.

17. A good heart, on the contrary,
Always grateful,
Obliges God to give him
Some new gift. Since he returns
What he gets, God always gifts him;
He loses nothing of what he has received
He advances from virtue to virtue
Even to the crown.

5th Motive
Gratitude is the opposite.

18. Sinners resembling
The ill-fated Judas,
Despite their innumerable gifts,
Are always ungrateful.
But chosen souls are full of gratitude,
They do what they will do in heaven,
They imitate the blessed
In their beatitude.

6th Motive
The chosen are grateful but the doomed are not.

19. There is no small grace,
God's gifts are great,
The wise man profits
From the least talent.
We must not use our gifts of grace and nature
To offend His Majesty,
That would be blasphemous,
A cruel insult.

7th Motive
The wise profit from the least goods.

20. Give praise and glory
To God for His favors,
Remember them,
Reflecting on them peacefully.
Let us glorify everywhere His paternal goodness
Not with pride and vanity
But with the simplicity
Of His faithful children.

4th POINT
*Acts of gratitude.*

1. Offer to God the glory of His gifts.

2. Keep them in mind.

3. Humbly proclaim them for the glory of God.

21. What shall I render, holy angels,
What shall I render to the Lord?
I have no praise
Worthy of His greatness.
Oh! Would that I had your purest flames
To render Him a worthy return,
To praise Him night and day
In the name of all creatures!

4. Use them to practice virtue.

5. Call the angels, man and other creatures to thank God for us and for all.

22. Praise God, all my faculties,
Bless God, my heart,
A thousand thanks
To our Creator.
Oh Christians, bless with me His tenderness,
It is He who made us Christians,
It is He who fills us with good things.
So let us praise Him constantly.

23. How many unfaithful men,
How many wretched ungrateful people
How many rebellious sinners
Are found everywhere!
Oh! we receive from God all the goods of
this world
But without praising our benefactor,
Without regard for the giver,
Like a vile beast.

6. Lament over those ungrateful to God.

24. Let us praise God, I beg you,
Both for ourselves and for all people,
Though Jesus and Mary
Let us calm His anger
And sincerely say: Deo gratias,
As many times as drops of water in the sea
As atoms in the air
As grains of sand.

## 27
## THANKSGIVING FOR GOD'S GIFTS

1. God of goodness, having nothing
To offer your majesty,
Humbly, I would like to intone:
Deo gratias,
Deo gratias, Deo gratias, Deo gratias.

Avowal of the incapacity to thank God.

2. For the excess of your great love
I possess no worthy return
So I want to chant forever:
Deo gratias,
Deo gratias, Deo gratias, Deo gratias.

3. Great God, you made me from nothing,
I received everything from you.
You alone are my sole support.
Deo gratias,

1
Blessings, creation.

4. I am your image, O great King,
And with lively faith I believe
You have imprinted it in me.
Deo gratias,

2
Man is the image of God.

5. Your love, O eternal Father
Surrendered Your Immortal Son
To give His life for criminals.
Deo gratias,

3
The Eternal Father has given His Son for us.

6. O Jesus, you have ransomed me
And freed me from captivity
By bearing my iniquity.
Deo gratias,

4
Jesus Christ has redeemed us.

7. If you had not willed to save me
If you had not washed me clean
I would be forever condemned.
Deo gratias,

5
Jesus Christ has saved us and washed us in His blood.

8. You lived in such cruel poverty,
   And died a contemptible death,
   You did it all for me alone.
   Deo gratias,

6
Jesus lived in poverty and died a horrible death, for us.

9. It was for me, divine Spirit,
   That you have fashioned Jesus Christ
   At the words of Mary's consent.
   Deo gratias,

7
The love of the Holy Spirit has formed Jesus Christ for us.

10. You anointed me with mildness,
    And adorned me with all splendor,
    You have filled me with your favors.
    Deo gratias,

8
The Holy Spirit has been given for us.

11. You alone had me baptized,
    And then and there had me espouse you,
    And later had me catechized.
    Deo gratias,

9
Baptism
10
The covenant with God.

12. Why, Lord, am I not a pagan?
    Why did you make me Christian?
    I have not deserved this favor.
    Deo gratias,

11
Catechism.
12
Chosen to be a Christian.

13. The flood of my iniquity
    Has not limited your goodness
    Or put limits on your bounty.
    Deo gratias,

13
Forgiveness after sinning.

14. You have often prevented me
    From plunging deeply into sin
    In spite of my inclination.
    Deo gratias,

14
Preservation from sin.

15. Fallen down, you lifted me up,
    When falling, you kept me up,
    And about to fall, held me back.
    Deo gratias,

15
The graces received from God so that we may avoid sin.

16. My talents of mind and body,
    Both inner and exterior
    Are all your gifts, all your treasures.
    Deo gratias,

16
Interior and exterior graces.

17. I received strong inspirations,
Many holy, urgent graces,
All your gifts and all your presents.
Deo gratias,

17
Inspirations for virtue.

18. From you, O My Lord, comes my health,
All my wealth and prosperity,
All my wonderful happiness.
Deo gratias,

18
Health and prosperity.

19. If I have been educated,
If I follow my vocation,
It is all through your protection.
Deo gratias,

19
Education and vocation.

20. Whatever other gift I have,
If I have vanquished the devil,
It is by virtue of your name.
Deo gratias,

20
The grace of the Cross.
21
Victory over the world and the demon.

21. What is this great joy and sweetness
Savored at times within my heart?
It is the effect of your grace.
Deo gratias,

22
Sweetness and interior joys.

22. What can I offer for these gifts,
For many other hidden ones,
Except to chant forever:
Deo gratias,
Deo gratias, Deo gratias, Deo gratias.

GOD ALONE

## 28
## ABANDONMENT TO PROVIDENCE

1. Let us admire Providence
Guiding all things to their goal.
This supreme prudence
And sovereign order,
Knows, rules and arranges

Essence and Definition of Providence

Everything, even the least,
Strongly and gently,
Without any confusion.

1st POINT
*Truth of Providence*

2. The entire universe proclaims her,
At all times and everywhere
The entire earth is filled
With her marvelous order
The seasons, one after the other,
The skies, rolling on forever
All beings, influencing one another
And lending each other aid.

1st Proof.
Order of the universe.
2nd Proof
Succession of the seasons.
3rd Proof
Movements in the heavens.

3. The worm of conscience affirms it,
As does punishment for sin
We believed well hidden
And unknown to anyone;
Finally, every creature
Tells us, although silently.
God leads me, God sustains me,
God always within me.

4th Proof
Testimony of conscience.
5th Proof.
Punishment even of hidden sins.
6th Proof
All creatures for God is present in them.

4. This wisdom, extended
From one end to the other,
In the blink of an eye, in a flash,
Knows and orders all.
She disposes and arranges
In such beautiful array,
From the greatest archangel
To the tiniest worm.

2nd POINT
Its *universal extension from the angels in heaven to the* least *things on earth.*

5. She watches over everything
Yet fools are unaware;
Without it, the smallest leaf
Can not fall to earth.
She controls the thunder,
The wind and the clouds,
The dust of the earth
And the gales on the seas.

3rd POINT
*The confidence we must have in Providence.*

6. God knows our wretchedness
And all of our needs,
And since He is our Father,
He takes great care of us all.
He joins His immense power
To His wonderful kindness,
We must place our hope then
In His supreme goodness.

1st Motive.
God knows all our miseries.

2nd Motive.
He is our good Father.

7. Put complete hope
In His paternal love;
He wants us to expect from Him
Even temporal goods:
All the goods of nature
Which we use every day,
Clothing, nourishment
And all other help.

3rd Motive.
His infinite power.

4th Motive.
He wills that we expect everything from Him even temporal goods.

8. Above all, try to understand
This great secret of the Savior
That He came to teach us
(What a remarkable favor!):
Hope in God so faithful,
Rest at peace in the bosom
Of His paternal love,
With no worry for the morrow.

5th Motive.
Abandonment to Providence is the secret Jesus came to teach us by

6th Motive.
His words. Do not worry about tomorrow.

9. Avoid being anxious:
Worrying like pagans
Primarily concerned
With loving and seeking earthly good.
Not having faith to trust,
They worry about the future;
Tomorrow, what will we have to drink,
To eat, what will we wear ?

7th Motive.
Pagans think about the tomorrow; do not imitate them.

10. Please, do not be concerned
For your body,
Since your soul is worth far more
Than your body and your wealth.
I have filled your soul
With my infinite treasures,
How can I forget
Its food or clothing?

8th Motive.
God, caring for the soul, more noble, He also takes care of the body.

11. Consider, if you will,
The millions of birds
Lacking for their sustenance
Both reserves and granary.
Your charitable Father
Makes sure they lack nothing;
And you, worth so much more,
Would lack what you need?

9th Motive.
Example of the little birds.

12. What! You think you can on your own,
Grow in good and in virtue
You, who can not add
A hairsbreadth to your height?
I do everything with no one noticing,
Your efforts are too human,
All depends on my power,
I hold all things in my hands.

10th Motive.
Our incapacity to do the least thing.

13. Consider the splendor
Of the flowers, the lilies of the field,
Solomon in all his glory
Was not arrayed as one of these.
If the fields are so clothed
Without working or spinning,
You who are worth so much more,
Must I not also clothe?

11th Motive.
Example of the lilies of the field.

14. Do you desire abundance,
The increase of temporal good?
First, and before all else,
Seek eternal good,
The Lord and His justice,
His kingdom and His love;
Earn by this sacrifice
Your daily bread.

12th Motive.
Means to be nourished by divine providence and to have all temporal goods.

15. Begin first by believing,
Putting your trust in God,
Seeking only His glory,
Loving Him alone.
Then He will see to your affairs
And He Himself will give you
All that is necessary
And all that will please.

16. How many are miserable
Because they think otherwise!
How many wretched guilty
Who are justly chastised!
They think only of the earth
But God curses all their work;
Their sins attack Him,
God engulfs them with woes.

13th Motive.
Misery of those
not trusting in
providence
as they should.

17. Follow the adorable example
Of heartfelt abandonment,
That the Savior gave us
With His admirable Mother.
Imitate the holy apostles,
Those models of virtue,
And the example of so many others
Without goods or revenue.

14th Motive.
Example of Jesus,
Mary, the apostles
and saints.

18. It is on holy Providence
That the saints cast their cares
And God by His almighty power
Supplied all their needs.
Living from day to day,
Like courageous soldiers,
They received their crowns
At the end of their struggles.

19. They nursed at the breast
Of this loving mother,
The milk for faithful souls,
And their daily bread;
They easily obtained
Their food and clothing
And the sovereign sweetness
Of perfect detachment.

20. Man is a fragile reed
Which of itself bends over,
Man is a clay vessel
Which does not endure;
Cursed are those who trust in man,
The Holy Spirit tells us,
But blessed those who depend
On God alone through Jesus Christ!

15th Motive.
Human support is
useless and
hurtful.

4th POINT
*Qualities of trust in Providence*

21. The trust you have placed
In God, must be united
With prudence,
According to time and place.
Although God fulfills a task
And we do hardly anything,
It is still necessary for us to work,
And even most diligently.

1. Prudent and hard-working.

22. In God our Father,
Infinitely generous,
We place our total trust
For every good in general,
For grace and light,
Interiorly and exteriorly
And for all that we need
Both for soul and body.

2. Universal.

23. Be calm and at peace
When your plans are upset
For anxiety is most harmful,
God alone suffices.
Love only God who loves you
And never abandons you;
Cast yourself entirely on Him
Without anxiety or fuss.

3. Peaceful.

24. Humble yourself constantly
Under the hand of the Almighty,
Be thankful for His tenderness
And His compassionate heart.
Filled then with gratitude,
Peace and humility,
You will praise His Providence
In spirit and truth.

4. Humble.

5. Grateful.

25. So, my soul, let's be wise,
Flee this deceiving world;
It has only its own advantage
And its own interest at heart.
No one is concerned
For the interests of God.
Alas! we forget Him everywhere
Or so seldom keep Him in mind.

Prayer and resolution.

26. Concern for land
And cupidity
Kindle wars everywhere
And cause all iniquity.
How fatal this vengeance!
For it hardens the heart,
It makes the soul dishonest,
Plunging it into evil.

27. This diabolical concern,
Widespread everywhere,
Infects even clerics
And often leaves them crushed.
It hides within a thousand thorns
By which hearts are flayed,
And also the accursed roots
Of the greatest sins.

28. Why is the liturgy and other tasks
So shoddily fulfilled?
Why so many benefices
So poorly served?
Alas! a mercenary
Forced the lock by golden key,
So he can live high
And make a fortune for himself.

29. This church needs a roof,
The altars are stripped,
The walls are crumbling,
The vestments are tattered,
Everything so poor and filthy
It makes the heart wince;
Then look at the chambers
Of the rector or the lord!

30. What ignorance and malice
Among the poor peasants,
What sins of injustice
Among the small and the great.
Good God! What diligence
To seek temporal goods,
While people show only lethargy
For their eternal salvation!

31. How do these disorders begin?
(Pastors, allow me to comment,
Even though you didn't ask)
Money leads you, pushes you
Only for your own interest.
Without such selfishness, you would be strong,
But it now drags you everywhere
And may well land you in hell's bottom.

32. Friends of God, without delay
Let's plunge deeply into self-abandon,
So you will not be entrapped
By these snares of the devil;
We must empty ourselves of malice
To receive the Holy Spirit,
The kingdom and the justice,
Jesus Christ proclaimed.

33. We must rid ourselves of selfish interest,
Then grace will surely follow;
We must put aside all creatures,
Then the Lord will come near;
We must never seek our glory
Or our own ambitious grandeur.
We must seek but the glory
And the victory of our God.

34. Flee the ordinary custom
Of temporal revenue;
The joy of full surrender
Must be our only wealth,
Let's despise the stupid nonsense
Motivating all the fools,
Let's renounce the illusions
Which dupe so many hearts.

35. Never put your human hope
In friends or in relatives,
Never place your worldly hope
In the powerful or famous.
God alone, God alone and His grace
And the work of salvation!
No matter what they say or do,
This must be our only aim.

36. Providence, I cast myself
    On your most loving breast.
    Let the world reject me,
    All the happier will I be;
    The more the world abandons me,
    The more I hope for blessings,
    And when I will have no one,
    You will be my sole support.

37. Deceiving creatures,
    Withdraw far from me;
    Your flattering promises
    Have ruled me for too long.
    The Lord is my good Father,
    Jesus is my dear Savior,
    Mary is my good Mother,
    Could I have greater joy?

38. The Lord is my only resource,
    My wealth, and my income;
    Spending His treasure,
    I am sustained,
    Like a bird on a branch
    Without thought of the morrow;
    Whether the economy is good or bad
    I have daily bread.

39. I have everything in abundance
    And more than a king.
    The world is in my power
    Since its Master is within me.
    Rich people will protest,
    They must be my landholders
    So I can take what I need
    From their heap of coins.

40. Clerics and lay people,
    You despise my way of life,
    And I detest your practices
    Leading you to death.
    Oh! if you could understand
    All my joy and all your woe,
    On the spot you would free your hearts
    From all of your possessions.

41. O secret of Providence,
O holy abandonment to God!
You are considered imprudent,
And are so little known.
Ah! for many years
I wander the earth seeking
Souls fully abandoned
And I find almost none.

42. Priests, we must follow
A poor crucified God,
Since He invites us;
We must listen to his voice
And think only of His interest.
Let us march under his banner
As the voluntary poor;
Behold the better part.

43. My soul, lose yourself in God,
Totally and for ever.
Expect all your help from God alone
Even though you will be censured;
Do not be fond of the world;
Fly then, free as a bird,
In supreme peace,
Poor even to the grave.

44. How we would perform marvels
If we were detached from the world!
We would then destroy sin
Almost without work or vigils.
We would then be apostles
And remarkable men,
Worthy to teach others
And lead them to heaven.

GOD ALONE

## CONTEMPT OF THE WORLD

## 29
## CALAMITIES OF THE WORLD

1ST POINT

*The evils of the world.*

Prayer to God.

1. Great God, come to our assistance,
Arm yourself with your thunder;
Everyday, far and wide, cruel war
Is waged against us by the world.
The world is our most hateful foe
Because it is the most human.

Exhortation on the evils of the world.

2. Friends of God, courageous soldiers,
Let us unite and take up arms,
Never let us accept defeat;
Let us combat the bewitching world.
Since God Himself is with us,
We will conquer. Let us all do battle.

Arm oneself with the truth.

3. We must arm ourselves with truth
Against the friends of lies,
Through love we must convince them
Their goods are only dreams;
We must arm ourselves with lively faith
So that faith will be their law.

Empty oneself of errors and false ideas.

4. But to be truly victorious
And gain the advantage
Let's drive out from our minds and hearts
The world's childish, false ideas.
Let's vomit this cruel potion
Or else we fight in vain.

1st EVIL

*It is evil in itself.*

What is the world.

5. What is this deceiving world?
It is the global gathering
Of sinners waging war,
Atrocious and cruel, against the Lord;
Sometimes very openly
But more often secretly.

6. The Holy Spirit called the world
The chair of pestilence itself,
The broad road where souls perish

Without giving it a thought,
The synagogue of Satan,
And the kingdom of this tyrant.

7. The great church of the wicked,
The infamous, great Babylon,
Where the devils, as the lords,
Are so cleverly enthroned,
Where all good is opposed
And all the sins are taught.

8. The world is Satan in disguise
To make himself acceptable;
It is his army and his minions
Hailing him a mighty prince,
Enlisting the whole universe
To follow him to hell.

9. O God! How he enlists people
In this crew so diabolical!
Many simple people, far more the notable,
The peasants, politicians,
The half-devout, the learned,
The libertines, the bons vivants.

10. Their novice master is the devil,
Who inspires them and leads them;
They offend God but in the devil's name,
Although they think they hate him!
He their prince and their king,
Who, they don't know it, rules them.

2nd EVIL
*It is the enemy of God and of His Son, Jesus Christ.*

11. The world fought against Jesus Christ
While He lived on earth;
The world is always the Antichrist
And constantly wars against Him;
The world always contradicts Him
In what He does and says.

1. The world hates God.

2. It contradicts Him.

12. The world destroys or disguises
His sentiments and maxims;
Whatever God does, the world undoes
In order to justify its crimes.
It distorts His sacraments
And His divine commands.

3. It destroys what He had done.

4. It poisons or distorts.

13. All the servants of the Lord
Are attacked by Satan's malice;
He does them wrong and frightens them,
He flatters them, he helps them,
He gives them a thousand reasons
So they may drink his venom.

5. It combats God's servants in several ways.

14. He makes their devotion
The object of his ridicule,
He calls it an illusion
Or farfetched devotion;
He condemns their good actions,
He misinterprets their intentions.

15. To destroy their holiness
He uses a thousand ruses;
To win them over to his side
He invents a thousand wrongs;
Good God, how many he has uprooted
Through all his evil snares!

3rd EVIL
*It is totally penetrated with malice and is the enemy of the truth.*

1. It slyly destroys truth.
2. By inventing all sorts of injustice.

16. He so cleverly covers up
Sin with virtue itself;
So sin can enter easily,
He flatters them, asserts his love.
By his smiles, this great deceiver
Thrusts a dagger to the heart.

3. By covering sin with virtue.

4. By pretending to be a good friend by flattery.

17. The world is the great incendiary
And the important tool of devils
Who sanction far and wide
The most detestable of crimes;
Worldly people call others scrupulous
If their actions are not like theirs.

5. It is the great means by which the devil sows sin everywhere.

6. Those who are not on his side, the devil calls scrupulous.

18. Among the famous the world sows pride,
As well as effeminacy and arrogance;
Among the peasants, it sows ignorance,

7. It sows sin everywhere and in everyone.

Drunkenness and scandal;
It sows envy and division
Even in religious orders.

19. It sows injustice in the palace,
And scandals in public places,
The filthiest impurities
In beds and secret places;
The insolence of libertines
In the church and holy places.

20. It sows indolence and idleness
As well as excess among ladies,
Chitchat and vanity
Among almost all women,
Greed among the merchants
And pride among the clever.

21. It sows swearing among soldiers,
Blasphemy, and violence,
Thousand disorders far and wide,
Gambling, balls and impudence,
All things are flooded with these sins,
Even the wise are sullied.

22. What am I saying, alas! I say too little,
Men and boys, girls and women,
Almost all burned with the fire
Of the world's infamous concupiscence.
It spreads vanity high and low,
And impurity almost everywhere.

23. Since the world is in decline,
Being only sin and bias,
It has never been so cunning
Nor so imbued with malice.
Whoever sins most secretly
Is considered the most proper.

4th EVIL
*The world is blind.*
1. Blind, but it thinks itself wise.
2. It rejects reprimands.

24. The wicked world is blind
Yet believes itself wise,
It has become hardened;
Whoever corrects it, outrage...
Alas! it neither sees nor hears,
And this multiplies its evil.

25. The world labels evil as good,
The salvific as harmful,
What is a nothing as happiness,
And what is true as false.
All these errors have blinded it,
Its sins have put it in disorder.

3. It badly judges all things.

26. It does not comprehend the vanity
Of the things this earth offers,
It ignores the cruelty
Of the tempter evil spirit.
Since it sees only with its senses,
The world misjudges present goods.

4. It does not see the great truths taught by the faith.

27. It fears its deceptive ghosts;
If God threatens, it knows no fear.
It is lawless, faithless, fearless
Before this Holy Majesty;
It does not fear His judgments
Or His terrible chastisements.

5. It fears what it should not fear and does not fear what should be feared.

28. Its judgments are distorted:
It believes fools are wise,
And the wise are foolish,
Bigoted and stupid people,
Since it believes this so firmly
The world makes rash decisions.

6. It is wrong in all its judgments.

29. This blind world is proud and tough,
It wants no one to correct it,
Although it is completely stupid,
We waste our time correcting it!
It is, as is written,
Incapable of the Holy Spirit.

7. It is hardened.

8. It cannot receive the Holy Spirit.

30. Surprisingly, the world cannot
Receive any light;
It will remain until death
Like the devil, its father,
Ungodly, proud, scandalous,
Blind, hardened, wretched.

31. Woe to the world, God has said,
Because it causes scandal;

5th EVIL
*It is scandalous.*
1. God has so said.

It forever vomits infernal rage
On everyone, both far and near;
The scandals shock all people,
The wise as well as fools.

2. God has cursed it because of its scandals.

32. The trades and occupations,
Are filled with revolting snares
The world has decreed mandatory,
So to damn miserable souls!
Its scandals are so clever
Even saints have been deceived.

3. Its scandals are universal, found everywhere, in all jobs, in all sorts of persons.

33. Beneath the snare there is a hook
Which traps a soul unawares.
With its wine, it mixes poison,
Concocting concupiscence;
The world can hide a mighty toxin
Under a single flippant word.

4. Its scandals are sly and well camouflaged

34. It covers up impurity
With quite clever pleasantries,
Luxuria with frivolity,
Candor or simplicity;
Greed and pride of heart
With a nice home and point of honor...

35. It draws the sinner's bow
Against innocent souls,
Stabbing their eyes and their hearts
In a thousand different ways;
The world creates evil snares
For their eyes, their mouth and hands.

5. They are natural.

36. The world, so skillful at deceiving,
Its bait so luscious and tender,
We can barely escape it,
We can barely be safe.
Happy those who have fled
To some far desert place.

6. They are cruel and almost insurmountable.

6th EVIL
*Its riches are vain and deceiving.*

37. It promises its followers
Honors, pleasures, rotting goods
Which are basically deceiving,
And make people awfully wretched.

1st Their vanity.

O vanity of vanities,
The greatest of truths!

1. They are really nothing but vanity.

38. What is all the gold and silver
That we call wealth?
A bit of dirt changing hands;
The surface looks beautiful,
But only a bit of gilded dirt,
A bit of metal, more highly polished.

2. They bring no peace to hearts.

3. They make people miserable.

4. The truth of gold and silver:

39. Coins are nothing but a passing good,
They always want to change masters;
When no longer valid to exchange,
Coins become the cruelest traitors,
Kept over a long time,
It is a poison in reserve.

40. Some cast-off skins of animals,
A few mounds of mud and clay,
Some wood cut into planks,
Some white and yellowish dirt,
These are the fools' great possessions
Damning most of them to hell.

Precious clothing, magnificent homes, gilded furniture.

41. We lose our goods in many ways:
A thief robs them or ruins them,
Rust eats them away.
How strangely they change!
They last but a moment
Then are forever lost.

5. They are all transient and perishable.

42. Do you see this rich Cresus?
His money makes him honored;
He will soon lose all his coins
And die just like a wretch.
Will he take along his riches?
Alas! a shroud; alas! Nothing else.

6. They are necessarily lost.

43. All these possessions have something
Inexplicably pernicious;
They hide within them deadly toxin
Which sullies and stinks horribly.
This is what our faith teaches us;
The wise person understands.

2nd Their malice

1. The goods are really malicious.

44. These goods, passed from hand to hand,
Have damned the ungodly and the greedy,
They have contracted so much poison,
Even the wise can hardly leave them.
Possessions are called, truthfully,
The gods of all iniquity.

2. Because of the malice they have contracted.

3. They are the god of iniquity.

45. From the time we seek to acquire them,
From that time on, we sin and are guilty,
Since when someone seeks more riches
He is entrapped in the devil's snare.
Evil it is to desire riches,
What greater evil to possess them!

4. One sins in wanting to possess riches since they are a snare of the devil.

46. These goods are the pitch, the glue,
Binding and then destroying souls,
Their power to cast souls to hell
Must be considered almost absolute.
One can hardly touch them
Without sticking to them and sinning.

5. One sins by being attached to them, which is very easy.

47. The utmost difficulty,
And the greatest one I know,
Is to acquire sanctity
While owning wealth without addiction;
It takes a miraculous effort,
What a marvelous prodigy.

6. They are an obstacle to holiness.

48. Do you have many possessions?
Do you live comfortably, even lavishly?
Then farewell to faith and charity,
Farewell to penance and to hope;
That is commonly the case,
Although how it happens, I do not know.

7. They almost always bring about the loss of faith, hope and charity.

49. Today we see so many people
Making wicked use of their possessions,
Keeping property of another,
Never making up for his loss.
So many slick and clever thieves
Yet all canonized by this world!

8. They damn people by the wicked use they make of these goods, even if they were honestly acquired.

50. I say nothing to the usurers,
So rampant in the world,
To pirates, to fat land holders,
Who steal both on land and sea;
They have so many stolen goods,
They'll never profit from my words.

9. By the thievery they cause in several ways.

51. Even if justly possessed,
Riches are but stinging thorns,
Secretively pricking
Even most innocent souls.
What efforts to acquire them!
What trouble to preserve them!

3rd The evil of riches.

1. These goods sting.
2. They are with difficulty acquired.
3. They are preserved only with trouble.

52. Money is the divinity
To which the world sacrifices
Its time, its rest, its health,
Even the goods of the life to come,
With no concern for one's neighbor,
Or even for its Sovereign Lord.

4. Everything is sacrificed to them.

53. Speak to the rich about increasing wealth,
They'll run, risk all and swear;
But never speak to them of God,
They cannot even grasp the language!
Their hearts belong to their gold,
For gold is their treasure and their god.

5. Riches make people insensitive to God.

54. The more revenue a man has,
The more the devils bewitch him;
The more superfluous concerns,
The more they annoy and abuse him.
His wealth is his cruel tyrant,
Even more cruel than Satan.

6. They are a kind of tyrant and witch during life.

55. When the rich lose their wealth, what sorrow!
Their souls incredibly tormented;
But when they're dying, O what fury!
Their poor souls are torn to shreds;
What despair! What struggles
Stalk the pitiful rich at death!

7. They bring unhappiness at death.

56. Oh! what terrible words God will speak

To those sinfully using this world's goods
And in hell what punishment they'll know;
What despair and what rage!
After all this, damn yourselves
Like fools with their false treasures!

8. They lead to eternal pains.

57. How great the vanity of wealth
Offered by this world,
Always avidly seeking more,
Without ever being happy.
But the world's pleasures are as false
And cause as much woe.

7th EVIL

*He is unhappy even in his pleasures.*

58. The greatest pleasures are deceiving,
They only seem to be pleasures,
For they never satisfy the heart
But make the heart crave pleasure even more.
They make us feel, in the end,
Remorse, boredom, and dejection.

1. Pleasures are really vanity.

2. They do not make the heart happy.

3. They result in bitterness in the end.

59. The world has only carnal pleasures:
Nothing but stinking garbage
Making many people criminals,
Rendering their souls ignoble;
Such pleasures flatter the external senses
And soil both the soul and body.

4. They are carnal.

5. They are criminal.

They are injurious to God.

60. Worldly sinners boldly dance,
Laughing, at the abyss' edge,
With the God of Judgment looking on;
He is armed with justice all divine.
Yet the worldly stomp on the crucifix,
Despising all God's holy laws.

6. They draw the curse of God and His vengeance.

They are injurious to Jesus Christ.

61. To its own misfortune, the world invents
A thousand pleasures and a thousand fads,
Like tobacco and scented powder,
A thousand pleasing sophistications.
Its sole concern it to protect itself
From anything inconvenient.

7. They are sought after and invented by sensuality.

62. The worldly spend their time thinking
Only how to please the body;
Drink and eat! laugh and dance!
Seem to be their only business;
While they fattens their bodies
They plunge the soul deep into hell.

8. Their desires are continual.

9. Riches are deadly for the soul.

8th EVIL
*With all its pride and honors, the world is unhappy.*

63. The world is always proud,
Even when acting humbly,
Flaunting before people's eyes
Its candor and its skill.
It is thrilled that people see
Its talents, goods and power.

1st Its pride.
1. In itself, the world is always proud.

64. It covers and hides its flaws
To show off all its glory;
It puts down all its peers
To increase its own importance.
Its haunts are only for the great,
It despises all the poor.

2. The world hides its defects.

3. It shows off and vaunts whatever it has that may be beautiful.

65. The worldly proud can be recognized,
By their vain, bogus glory,
By their bearing, clothes, allure,
The manner they walk and talk,
Exuding only grandeur,
Pride, show, and hauteur.

4. It lowers its equals, its ambitions are higher than the great and it rebukes the lowly

5. Its pride shows up in everything that pertains to it.

66. Only most reluctantly
Obedient and humble,
They love to give orders,
Believing they have wisdom,
Assuming they are always first
And even in humility.

6. He hates obedience and humility.

67. But what is all this honor
But reverie and whimsy,
A puff of smoke, a mist,
A wind, flimsy foam,
A dazzling and pompous glow,
Deceiving hearts and eyes.

2nd Its honors.

1. They are only vanity. Comparisons.

68. It is the most shrewd of hooks
The devils use as bait,
The most subtle poison
Offered everyone to take.
Satan, fallen by his pride,
Dashes the world against the same reef.

2. They are a sly hook and the subtle venom of the demon.

69. God hides his secrets from the world,
In His wisdom, He combats it
And prepares the most vengeful flame
For the world, for eternity;
As much it glorified itself,
As much will the world be punished.

3. They stop man from knowing the secrets of divine wisdom.

4. They damn people forever.

70. How deceived is this cursed world!
All the days of its life
Are wasted or preoccupied
With nothing but stupidities.
If not lost in idleness
It is busy with wrongdoing.

9th EVIL

*The world is lazy*

1. The world does nothing but evil.

71. It lives only on the outside,
Never turning thoughts to God,
Concerned with the body only,
Neglecting its poor soul.
Despising true happiness,
Only occupied with lies.

2. It concerns itself with the body, never with the soul.

72. O blind world! O hypocrite!,
Preferring earth to heaven,
Creature to Creator,
War, to God's peace,
Lies, to the truth,
And time to eternity.

3. It thinks evil of everything and is vain in its thoughts and judgments.

73. We can hear it chatting night and day
About The Gazette and the news,
The army and the court,
About a thousand bagatelles,
Money, meals, and baubles,
About games, clothes and hobbies.

4. It is vain and idle in its words.

74. How filled with wild enthusiasm
For temporal affairs,
How dim-witted and bored
For eternal concerns.
When playing, it enjoys staying up late;
When praying, it just can't stay awake.

5. It is vain and deceiving in its actions.

6. Insensitive to God and to necessary salvation, it thinks and speaks only of trifles.

75. The world is never occupied
With the one thing necessary,
But with conceited amusements,
Doing wrong or doing nothing,
With gawking and gossiping,
Visiting and primming.

10th EVIL

*It is hardened.*

76. The world, its heart so hardened,
Doesn't admit to any sin,
Doesn't smell its great stench
Nor the burdens that oppresses it.
It cannot believe that within
The devil reigns as king and father.

1. It doesn't even know its crimes and does not smell its stench or its burden.

77. Never fearing hell or judgment
Not even God, the devil, retribution,
The accursed world sins boldly,
Insolently snickering;
It sings its verses as it sins,
Making sin its song.

2. It has no fear of God.

3. It sins joyfully and boldly.

78. The worldly say they are too strong
To ever whine or weep;
They fear neither hell nor death,
Not even its forewarnings;
The good God, they say, is so good;
At death, we will be forgiven.

4. The worldly excuse their hardness.

79. Fully insensitive to truths
Which make all good souls tremble,
From stupidity to stupidity,
From sin to infamous crimes,
They die without any dread
Then fall into damnation.

5. They add sin to sin and die hardened.

80. He harshly treats his neighbor
Although he sees him suffer,
Speaks disdainfully to the poor,
If he gives alms, it's out of anger;
Come what may, he feeds his dog,
Yet nothing for his brother.

6. They are hard toward their neighbor.

81. He is totally hard-hearted
Toward the souls in purgatory,
At their expense, he can be seen
Gladly eating, laughing, drinking;
He will repay with a De Profundis
His poor, blockhead relatives.

7. Hard towards the souls in purgatory.

8. Cruel even toward their deceased relatives.

82. He finds their wills excessive
So weakens or negates them
On his own, or through a court
Appealing against his parents;
Oh poor deceased mother, father,
Your children have abandoned you.

83. He makes sin his pleasure,
His heart never bothered
By offending and outraging God,
Unless he gets hurt himself.
Never the Lord's but his own interest
He holds close to his heart.

9. Insensitive to offenses against God.

84. Although the world be cursed,
Condemned by the Savior,
He is engrossed in its amusements,
Dancing through this curse.
So blind is his spirit!
So disordered his heart!

10. Insensitive to the anathemas of God.

11th EVIL

*The world is unhappy in this world and at death.*

85. Secretly it is the devil
Misleading and steering him,
Binding him invisibly,
Holding him tightly by a chain
To work hell's iniquity
According to the devil's whims.

1. The worldly have the devil for father, master and leader.

86. Peace, peace, he cries to everyone,
Without having a tuppence's worth
himself,

2. The worldly do not possess true peace.

How many thousand hidden regrets!
His greatest joy is upheaval;
The worldly man is a stormy sea,
Never to be calmed.

87. No matter what he does to stifle
The remorse of his conscience
Never can he win,
Never can he relax.
Although he appears so cheery
Within, nothing but misery.

3. The worldly are tormented by the remorse of conscience.

88. This fraud, no matter how he tries
To achieve perfect peace,
His past sins make him afraid,
The future makes him anxious,
Unable, even for an instant,
To know true happiness, fulfillment.

4. In spite of all, the past upsets, present sins weigh heavily, and the future causes anxiety.

89. During life he can only know
Some illusory, passing pleasure,
But at his death, what despair,
What rage, what excoriating pain,
O! what troubles, and what torments,
And after death, what chastisement!

5. The worldly are unhappy at death.

90. To replace his pleasures,
His honors and riches,
Hell bestows a thousand evils, thousand woes,
Thousand spiteful afflictions;
For a moment of vanity,
Wretchedness for all eternity.

12th EVIL

*The worldly are unhappy for all eternity.*

91. Thus is the world and its afflictions.
Can we really love this wretch?
Can we follow its many lackeys
In their so appalling misery?
We must all then cry out: woe, woe,
Woe to this deceiving world.

92. Here are several malicious snares
The world slyly uses to entrap us,
Drawing us into its service,
Then finally casting us to hell;

To protect us from these dangers
We now uncover its wicked secrets.

## 30
## FIRST SNARE: GAMES OF CHANCE

1. Games in themselves are not wicked,
They contain nothing lethal,
In fact, it is just the opposite:
They are a recreation
Without effort, without strain,
A fitting relaxation,
Enabling us to work the harder
When such labor's necessary.

Definition of games.

1st POINT
The purpose and the qualities of games for them to be good.

2. Games God has not forbidden,
If played at time and place
That do not offend His Wisdom,
So we can gently relax,
Innocently have fun,
Enliven our neighbor,
Chasing away sorrow,
Troubles and sadness.

1. God has not forbidden games.
2. Games help to relax.
3. To have innocent fun.
4. They are also recreation for the neighbor.
5. They also chase away our problems.

3. Some saints, even though quite serious,
Have at times played games,
As their biographies relate;
Inspired by the Spirit,
Their charity invented them;
But they were games most innocent,
Charitable and compassionate,
Full of grace and glory.

6. They imitate the saints.

*Qualities of games*

4. Games must have certain qualities
For them to give God glory
And be salutary:
Games of chance you must avoid,
For sooner or later the soul is lost,

1. Avoid games of chance and play games of the mind.

Games of mind are the best;
God rejoices in His servants
Who play, hoping to please Him.

2. Games must be pleasing to God.

5. Games should not be passionate,
But, gentle, prudent, moderate,
Played at fitting times,
Without argument, full of grace,
Without trickery, full of honor,
Simply, without addiction,
Without malicious purpose,
Charitable and honest.

3. Games must be played with moderation.
4. With prudence.
5. With justice.
6. With kindness.
7. With freedom.
8. With honesty.
9. With charity.

6. In place of cards and dice
Choose checkers, chess,
Or the like;
Do not play without stop,
But only at certain times and places,
And play with those who are God's friends,
For then, not only may you play,
But perhaps you even should.

10. We should not play games continually.

7. Yet how many games are forbidden!
How many people have been lost
Not even noticing their vice!
Games of chance are subtly used
By the devil and the doomed,
To make us lose the precious time
God grants us to gain heaven
By doing deeds of righteousness.

2nd POINT
*The troubles with forbidden games.*

1. Few know the malice of forbidden games.

2. The devil is their author.

8. O time, O gift of Spirit Blest,
O price of Jesus' Blood divine,
O immensely precious time!
Players at cards or dice
When you die, a thousand regrets
Having wasted so much time
In your games and useless hobbies,
And never doing penance.

3. It is a loss of time.

4. Time is the most precious thing in this world.

5. The regrets for having lost time.

9. If the damned in hell
Had an hour you squander,
Would they copy your stupidity?
You would see them weeping, moaning,

Fasting, filled with mortification.
Ah! what would they do if they had time?
As they would, so use it well
For the time you're still alive.

10. A player is always troubled,
Anxious, moody, so upset,
All depending on his luck;
He loses, by his crave to win,
Charity for his brother;
He seeks only to trap him,
Surprise him, trick him,
Barring nothing.

A player loses peace.

6. Charity.

11. How many sins commits a player,
Through his hands, his mouth and heart,
Almost without thinking!
Blasphemy, oaths,
Shouts and fits of anger,
A thousand disguised lies,
A thousand clever, cunning thefts,
Filled with hatred and revenge.

7. Holiness

12. A player, in fact becomes his game,
He is no longer for himself or God
But for the game that consumes him.
All his delights, his whole soul
And body are in the game;
It is only for the game he lives,
The game alone captivates him.
It is his cruel chain.

8. Freedom.

13. A player thinks he'll win some good,
But as often as not, his own is lost,
As experience always proves.
Money won at games of chance,
Cannot be seen as blessed by God,
Sooner or later it's used for evil.
The saints call it a theft,
And of all, the sneakiest.

9. Even goods.

10. Justice.

14. A player who loves gambling
Is a clever thief of Satan,
And such a thief in point of fact,
That from his own children he would steal,

And even from poor wife and family,
Holding all possessions as his own.
He dies clutching others' goods,
O deplorable disaster!

15. Toward God, he is full of coldness,
Too full of laziness and boredom
For the good of his own soul;
Mass lasts far too long,
Sacraments neglected;
Wicked, hardened, lazy,
He drifts along from game to game
And then from games to hell.

11. The love of God and his salvation.

16. Players are the tinderboxes,
The do-nothings, and the scandal-mongers,
In every republic;
They reveal every kind of sin
By teaching idleness.
These public games and poker
Make many people perish,
It is a public loss.

12. It scandalizes the neighbor.

17. Kings have condemned games
With punishment severe,
Fitting for a subtle plague.
Councils by their laws,
The holy fathers in their writings,
Hurled anathemas at games of chance.
Yet everywhere throughout the world
The deadly venom spreads.

13. It disobeys:

1st The King.
2nd The holy fathers.
3rd The Church.

18. Deceiving world, be gone,
You will not rule me
By your games so diabolical.
Never any part of you!
Woe to your games of chance!
Woe even to all the players!
In order to avoid their fall,
I never follow their example.

GOD ALONE

## 31
## SECOND SNARE: THE DANCE AND THE BALL

1. Lord, the world wants to damn me
By the snare of dance.
Free me from this devious trap
Set to snatch my innocence.
Worldly people dance, snubbing You,
O Lord, help us.

Prayer

2. Behold the incense to Venus
And her pleasant school,
Behold the plaything of Bacchus,
And the devil's circle,
Behold his clever invention
For our damnation.

Definition of dancing.

3. Yes, Satan is the inventor
Of malicious dancing.
He is the principal creator
Of this happy plague,
Damning people joyfully
And so subtly.

1st POINT
*The source of dancing is wicked.*

1. The devil is the author

4. At dances, he is king,
Where he is rendered homage,
Where he promulgates the rules
Of joyous wantonness,
Here he holds court,
His throne right at the center.

2. He is the king of dancing.

3. He is the conductor.

5. The devil sets everything in motion
In this accursed practice,
Slipping in his poison,
His malice and his flames.
From him flows the desire
For this deadly pleasure.

6. He incites the dancers
To dance, to sing and cackle;
There he wins their hearts,
Their bodies and his empire,
Performing all the movements,

4. Different works of the devils in the dancers.

All the steps and whirls.

7. He slips into the voices
So all sing gracefully,
He enlivens the oboist
To perform without fatigue;
He executes the harmony
And the instruments' tunes.

8. He slips into the body
Of men and women dancers,
Kindling the rapture
Of his flaming passion;
He directs the feet and eyes
Of these poor wretches.

9. Their body is bewildered,
Their mind is bedimmed,
Their heart is bewitched:
That is what the devil does,
Making them call scrupulous
Whoever does not follow them.

10. Among the pagans, the devil
Ordinarily receives this tribute,
He doesn't seek their goods
But that they dance to please him;
Satan may even promise them
Some reward for dancing.

5. Dancing is the tribute that the devil demands from pagans.

11. At Saturday's late hour, witches,
It is said, have the practice
Of dancing after meals
A diabolical bop;
Dancing is the incense, the deadly cult
Of this infernal spirit.

6. And from witches.

12. Almost all the doomed
Believe that dancing is permitted;
But those who will be saved,
The Church's true children,
All loathe it, holding it
In abomination.

7. And from those on the way to hell.

2nd POINT
*Sins which are committed at the dance: dancing in itself is not bad but it is almost impossible to dance without sinning.*

13. Now speaking in general,
Dancing is neutral;
In itself, it is not evil,
And can then be innocent,
For David danced with fervor
Before the Ark of God.

14. But dancing without sinning
Demands so many conditions
That one can hardly refrain
From sinning by dancing.
Ordinarily, it is bad,
An immense disorder.

15. The manner, time, and reason,
Plus the person dancing,
All spit out so much venom
That innocence is lost;
Misfortune follows dancers
And even those who watch them.

1. Wicked in the disposition with which one comes to the dance.

16. How does one get involved
In this clever, shameful decadence?
By dousing with perfumed powder,
Smearing make-up on the face,
By cunning nudity,
Extravagance and vanity.

2. In the manner of dancing.

17. How do worldly people dance?
The style is so notorious:
Everything kindles the toxin
Of a most impure passion:
These sweet, piercing glances,
These hold-me-close dances.

18. The steps are so measured,
The beat is so pleasing,
The dancers so well dressed
And the song so up-to-date!
Who could refrain from loving,
Burning, being set on fire?

19. What about those kisses

At the dance's end,
These cruel, accepted signals
Of a foul passion?
Are they not the devil's seals
Imprinted only in his name?

20. We well know the motives
Why many people dance;
They are hidden but so lewd:
Yearning to love, to please,
To arouse or be aroused,
To see, or better, to be seen.

3. In the purpose and motive one has in dancing.

21. Bouncing to ballads
Filled with love affairs,
Dancers easily get hooked
By this notorious nonsense;
After dancing they dare say:
"God was not offended."

4. In the words that one says or hears.

22. Dances are held on days it's forbidden
Even more than on others;
During this time lost
Satan does business;
So we make the Day of the Lord,
The Feast of the Tempter.

5. In the days when people dance.

23. Alas! all think nothing of time
Wasted in dancing,
Although time is a great gift
And of immense price;
Time so short, time so precious,
Given to win heaven.

6. In the time lost.

24. If dancing among pagans
Is always to be condemned
What among Christians?
Oh abominable sin!
Traitors, renouncing the vow
They made to their God.

7. In the person who dances: a Christian.

25. Have they not renounced
All the devil's pomps?
Dancing has always been considered
The most notable of them all.

Dancing is a cruel dishonor
To the Most Holy Lord.

26. Dancer, caricature of a Christian,
Jesus Christ is not your master.
But Satan has claimed you as his own
Like an apostate, a traitor.
Be gone, disciple of the evil spirit,
You're a disgrace to Jesus Christ.

3rd POINT

1. *(missing)*

27. A criminal dies
Swaying on the gallows;
In deadly peril,
A soldier dances and laughs.
O folly, O cruel misfortune
Of dancers so criminal!

2. A condemned criminal dances.

3. An attacked soldier dances.

28. Oh giant fool, twirling on the edge
Of the eternal precipice,
Without fearing death,
Nor even God in His justice!
Ah! Satan has blinded him,
He will kill the fatted calf.

4. The unhappy man at the precipice of hell dances.

29. The dancers, in their frenzy
Of arms, feet and head
Plus the rest of their body,
Are crazier than animals;
A lot less spirited are horses;
They're calmer than the dancers.

5. Dancers are more stupid than animals.

30. Both New and Old Testaments
Condemn all dancing
And strongly threaten
With terrible vengeance
Dancers, buffoons,
Their patrons and spectators.

6. The Old and New Testaments condemn dancing.

31. God curses their finery,
Their perfume, their rhythms,
Their romantic affairs,
Their imprudent gestures.
He forbids us to copy them,
To frequent their shows.

7. God curses all the gestures of the dancers.

32. Dancing is even a tyrant,
Perhaps the most cunning of all;
It caused the death of Saint John,
Our Master's Precursor.
O great God, how it has caused ruin
Both of soul and body!

8. Dancing is a tyrant.

33. The holy fathers, the doctors,
The canons, the Church,
Have all condemned dancers,
Declared them anathema
Together with buffoons,
Actors and jesters.

9. Dancing is condemned by the holy fathers of the Church and by the canons of the Church.

34. Men are blinded
By dancing, says one of fathers,
Children are confused,
They despise father and mother.
Women lose their honor
And the grace of the Lord.

35. Dancing makes one transgress
All the laws of the Church,
It also makes one break
The entire law of Moses;
A dancer has lost the faith
And no longer obeys the law.

10. Dancing makes one transgress all the commandments of God.

36. Whenever there's dancing, wherever,
Heaven weeps with grief;
At this affront to God
All hell rejoices,
While the saints lament
And the ungodly screech.

11. When one dances, heaven and the angels are weeping and the devil rejoices.

37. God often severely punishes
Dancers with sudden death,
In a moment vomiting
Their accursed souls.
From balls and games,
Suddenly they fall into hell.

12. God punishes dancers in this world and in the next.

38. Be gone, world and your friends,
In spite of what I have said,
Tell everyone that it is permitted

Both to dance and to cackle;
Be gone, scandalous world,
Be gone, unfortunate world!

## 32
## THIRD SNARE: THEATRE AND PLAYS

1. But what shall we say of the ball
And of evils and the theatre,
This infernal treasury
Of all shame?
It is there that the strongest heart
Weakens and becomes impure.

2. It is the treasury of sin,
For it knows the way
To present sin so subtly
That it has become up to date,
So cleverly clothed
With the garments of virtue.

Evils of the theatre.

Definition of theatre

3. Diabolical invention,
Wretched theatre,
Oh! cruel illusion!
Oh! infernal blaze
Where every iniquity is committed
Cheerfully, with joy!

The devil is its author.

1st To beguile one's spirit.
2nd To bewitch hearts.

4. Opera House, accursed place
Where the lilt, the voice and the gesture
Freely inject
The most deadly poison:
"What gorgeous arias," "What lovely verses!"
Oh! Sirens of hell!

5. O source of the greatest evils,
Babylon's furnace,
Where new honors
Have enthroned Satan!
O sharpest hook!
O sweetest poison!

3rd To enthrone himself.

4th To joyfully damn souls.

6. To put on a deceptive mask
   Disfiguring one's face
   So to rebuke the creator,
   Altering his work,
   Bears the seal of the devil
   And puts on his livery.

5th The evil of masks.

7. This mask of the doomed,
   Which resembles the devil their father,
   Appears for applause;
   No, it is Satan who entertains;
   The accursed, so disguised,
   Invites us to take part.

8. Listen to Satan declaiming
   Through this actor reciting.
   It is through him that Satan burns
   The body as well as the soul;
   Subtle snake slithering beneath the flowers
   And the most vivid colors.

6th Diabolical evil in the stage settings and in the speeches.

9. The most perfect of actors
   Performing his role flawlessly
   Is the most slippery of liars,
   Hiding his passion well,
   Cleverly slipping into the heart
   The most deceptive bane.

10. Everyone admires the dance
    Of this wretched woman,
    She will enkindle everything
    With her romantic passion.
    Her poison seems sweetest;
    It is the cruelest of all.

7th The theatre is a sly school of sordid sin.

11. The laughing and sparkling eyes
    Of this fair ballerina,
    Her tender and saccharin air
    And her melodious voice
    Strike blows and shoot arrows,
    Always well accepted.

12. The gestures and the movements

Performed by this Lady Buffoon
Are true charms
Of an evil so cunning;
Her eyes, her song, her twirls,
Sermonize her romantic follies.

13. A person sees her and looks again,
The devil comes and lights a fire;
The heart burns and then bends,
Then comes crashing down into sin.
And it's said that at the ball
No one does whatever wrong!

14. In hell, how many thousands
Of those male and female dancers
Burning in those fires
And harsh flames!
In spite of it all, dance, you idiots,
Without believing what I say.

8th They send people to hell.

TO FATHERS AND MOTHERS

15. Despite all these great dangers
And the sinfulness of dancing
Go ahead, father, teach your son
This deadly beat.
And tell him, if he is scrupulous,
That he must, that you demand it.

16. Mother, don't listen to me,
Go ahead, make your daughter dance.
Train her body and her steps.
What will they say in town?
What beautiful skill! This civility
Befits her rank.

17. Without this skill, no boyfriends,
She'll just be a wallflower;
Without it, the young men
Will laugh her to scorn.
To marry her off, she must have this skill;
Otherwise, you'll be taken to task.

18. Take her yourself to the ball
To learn about the world.

Why, dancing isn't evil,
Although scrupulous people rant.
Whatever can be wrong
In dancing and ditties?

19. Flee from the scrupulous,
Don't adopt their ways,
And never be glum;
Dance, keep up with the world!
It's what I want of you, you must obey;
What's wrong with having some fun?

20. The daughter of a laborer
Has such rough country manners.
Shame! Don't act like a peasant,
Get her to a dance teacher
To learn to be polite,
Courteous and gracious.

21. The confessor whom I go to,
Knowing very well I dance,
Finds nothing wrong at all with it
And doesn't in the least forbid it.
This is how, wretched parents,
You damn your own children.

TO BUFFOONS AND ACTORS

22. Buffoons, actors,
Worse even than witches
And magicians
Who hide their tricks,
Doomed, scandalous men,
Skillful thieves.

23. Yes, wretches, you cleverly steal
From your countrymen,
Bewitching them
With your infamous practices.
Clever thieves who fool the fools,
All of you should hang!

24. Eminent teachers of all sin,
Worse than any heathen,
Rotten members, cut off

From the Church and her faithful,
Accursed, excommunicated people,
Woe to you who smirk!

25. Oh! God's great enemies,
Oh! brood of vipers,
Who spread abroad fire,
Lies and misery,
You pillage by your skill so fine,
Both the widow and the orphan.

26. Satan's dupes,
Foes of the Gospel,
Go forth to gain money,
Appear from one town to the next,
No fear of anyone scrupulous!
You are supported everywhere.

27. You will be welcomed
By the city of Babylon,
You will be well looked after.
In spite of the pastor's sermons,
You, Babylon's great preachers,
Will have a large audience.

28. At the pastor's sermons, the poor,
The devout, the peasant women;
But at yours, renowned people,
Influential gentlemen and important ladies.
Though you are the greatest fools,
Everyone will follow you.

29. And although excommunicated
By the Church and by wise people,
Drink, dance and chortle
As you perform your roles,
Saying, The Lord is good,
All will be forgiven.

30. On condition, however,
That, in full measure,
You will go in an instant
From dancing to hell,
To burn forever
And bitterly weep.

TO PRIESTS

31. Barking dogs of the Lord,
Holy priests filled with zeal,
Let us, with heartfelt voice,
Wage war on this rebel world,
On dancers, on actors,
Worse than all pagans.

32. Those blind folk take us
For visionary fools,
And perhaps they will say to us:
Mind your own business!
Let's hold fast, let's bark constantly,
God will come to our aid.

33. We do not have the power
To stamp out these worldly sins;
Nonetheless, it is our duty
To bark, though the world complains.
Then, if the world does not believe us,
To lament it till we die.

34. If we don't hamper these games,
These stage productions, plays,
God will punish us like them
And more than them in the next life;
We will have to answer for everyone
And bear all His anger.

GOD ALONE

## 33
## FOURTH SNARE: LUXURY

1. Behold the cleverest snare
The devil has set,
The greatest witchery
Spread far and wide.

2. Behold all the proud pomp,
The stupid vanity

Definition of luxury

Of sick, empty minds,
Thinking themselves fit.

1st POINT
*The evil of luxury*

3. Lavishness in decorations,
In attire and in food,
In a hundred passing things
We make use of here below.

1st motive
It is contrary to religion

4. Extravagance goes beyond
All moderate attention;
It's what the wise man does without
And what decorates the fool.

1. God condemns it in Holy Writ

5. All the books of Holy Writ
Deplore this disorder,
The Holy Spirit Himself assures
That luxury will be punished:

6. He will transform these delights,
This fine stuff, these adornments,
Into hair shirts highly coarse,
And torments truly piercing.

2. Babylon falls because of luxury

7. Babylon is among the fallen
For its purple and fine linen,
All the wicked are so clothed,
Their end will be the same.

3. The wicked rich man is condemned because of luxury.

8. By such fastidiousness
The rich evil man perished;
For this self-indulgence
He was doomed by the Spirit.

4. It is condemned by the saintly Fathers.

9. With differing tactics
All saints have fought
This brood of vipers,
This poison of virtue.

5. It is contrary to the baptismal promises.

10. Luxury is the delirium
Of the proudest people,
And worse still, the betrayal
Of baptismal promise.

6. Contrary to the spirit of Jesus Christ.

11. Luxury forbids living
As true disciples of the Savior,

It betrays our good Master,
Poor and humble of Heart.

12. Christians forsaking His thorns
Become spineless followers,
Stripped of divine armor,
They are cowardly soldiers.

7. With luxury we are not members of Jesus Christ.

8. Nor one of His good soldiers

13. In luxury and abundance,
Festooned in stylish clothes,
What specter of penitence!
What specter of penitents!

9. Nor a true penitent

14. The body becomes an idol
When it is so flattered
By frivolous adornments,
The incense of vanity.

15. To make this rotting flesh
Our idol and our incense,
What horrible idolatry,
What insult to our God!

10. It is idolatry insulting to God.

16. This monstrous idol
Often enters churches,
Setting up the devil's throne,
To fulfill his designs.

11. Which disputes the glory of God even in His temple.

17. Madame enters: room! room!
For her train, her cushion.
All make way, she strolls by
And all stand there gawking.

18. She is the adorned idol,
Near a decorated altar,
Adored by everyone,
God not even considered.

12. Diabolical ways of worldly women

19. Everyone gapes,
Their backs to the Tabernacle;
She fidgets coquettishly,
Adjusting her looks.

20. This insolent worldly woman
Has rejected all laws;

Even on her smelly flesh
She profanes the cross.

21. Abominable, ungodly,
She vies for God's glory;
Her rank immodesty
Blasphemes His sacred place.

2nd motive
It is contrary to wisdom.

22. Luxury is child's play
Where children make-believe,
A ludicrous hodge-podge
Of many scissored pieces.

1. It is child's play.

23. Double is the wickedness
In these miserable times;
Double then the affectation
Even in one's clothes.

2. It is a fraud.

24. Cloth is measured, cut and mixed,
Feigning this, masking that;
Styles change every day,
Confusing us so cunningly.

25. Natural beauty
Is far more attractive
Than all phony pretense
Decked out with ornaments.

3. It is a destruction of modesty and of nature itself.

26. Modest cleanliness
Holds a charm divine,
And not the deadly air
Of worldly cosmetics.

27. Prefer the body to the soul,
Time to eternity;
That is what ungodly display
Does by its malignity.

4. It is an unjust preference.

28. Luxury's emblem
Is the shrewdest of evils,
Since it camouflages
All evils and flaws.

5. It is the mask of all evils.

29. It is the natural sign
Of a poor, empty head,

6. It is the sign of folly and pride.

Of a superficial soul,
Of a proud, haughty spirit!

3rd motive
It is contrary to strength.

30. Luxury tells of spineless souls
Who have no gumption,
Souls full of fetishes,
So wide-spread here below.

1. It is the characteristic of the lax.

31. Luxury turns the soul wretched,
Idle and haughty,
Unworthy, even incapable
Of great things for God.

2. It makes the soul lazy and incapable of great deeds.

32. Luxury makes the faithful
Captive of human respect,
Captive of trifles,
Captive of the evil spirit!

3. It is godless.

33. It destroys temperance
Which moderates pleasures,
It inspires the overflow
Of pleasures, desires.

4th motive
It is contrary to:
1. Temperance and sobriety.

34. Luxury with its delights
Dispels sobriety
And destroys the sacrifices
Of holy austerity.

2. To austerity.

35. In these times so full of misery,
Of luxury and vanity,
We no longer see our ancestors'
Holy frugality.

3. To the frugality of our ancestors.

36. Their souls were filled
With honor, humility,
Holy thrift
And humble simplicity.

4. Customs of our ancestors.

37. By an admirable secret
They joined the useful with beauty,
Brick and mortar with delight
And glory to their tombs.

38. Their conduct was steady,

Simple, no pretense,
Charitable, no envy,
Firm, no stubbornness.

39. Under serge and rough clothing,
They concealed more greatness
Than us under the adornments
Of this deceitful world.

5. Difference of our customs.

40. Good God, what a difference
Between our ancestors and us!
They were so wise,
We are almost all fools.

41. Their sole need
Was to be virtuous,
We seek only to please
This miserable world.

42. They considered as trivia
And vain amusement
So much frivolous baggage
So much stupid affectation.

43. Their finery, their riches,
Were the virtues of their hearts;
Their pleasure and their tenderness
Was the love of the Savior.

44. They wisely considered
Affected adornments
As silly child's play
And occasions of sin.

45. Each one lived tranquilly
Happy with his lot,
Following the holy Gospel
Without frills or quarrel.

46. Do we have their character?
Ah! we abandon them!
We no longer bear their ways
But only their names.

47. Now, a thousand whims,

Thousand deceiving goods,
Thousand useless cares,
Are lodged within our hearts.

48. Luxury has become the master
Of an endless crowd of fools;
A vain desire to show off
Enlivens and controls them.

49. Luxury has confounded man:
The craftsman now's the merchant;
The bourgeois, the gentleman;
The nobleman, the steward.

5th motive
Luxury has confounded situations and is contrary to order and humility.

50. In magnificence, another
Equals a royal prince;
Few, by humble prudence,
Now keep to their rank.

51. One must address the wife,
Of co-worker, or clerk,
By the fancy title of "Madame,"
In order to be friends.

52. The simplest women pretend
Airs of distinction,
Decked out and coiffured,
All yearning for praise.

53. They pile on themselves
Gold, silver, fabric so fine,
Silk, pricey lace,
Velvets and satins.

54. Their weird style demands,
As do their proud friends,
Everything more exotic,
More expensive and rare.

55. These sad worldly ladies
With their silk and fine linen
Are almost all thieves,
But their theft is so clever.

6th motive
It is contrary to justice.
1. Worldly ladies are almost all thieves.

|  |  |
|---|---|
| 56. Hundreds of purchases<br>To look better than others,<br>Yet not paying their debts<br>Or returning what's borrowed. | 2. They do not pay their debts. |
| 57. For their ridiculous outfits<br>So stylish and pricey,<br>They steal deceitfully<br>From children and husbands. | 3. They steal from their children and husbands. |
| 58. Their desire, their craving<br>To own new finery,<br>Puts their decency on sale<br>With their foolish affairs. | 4. They often sell their purity. |
| 59. Their luxury, their arrogance<br>Never say: "It's enough."<br>God will wreak vengeance<br>For these needless expenses. | 5. They make bad use of their goods. |
| 60. What insult, what nerve,<br>Toward their Creator!<br>They dare alter His work<br>By deceptive attire. | 7th motive<br>1. It is contrary to the Providence of God. |
| 61. They spoil nature<br>By masking it;<br>It's only a fraud,<br>A trap to cause scandal. | 2. They spoil nature.<br>3. They cause scandal. |
| 62. O luxury, so infamous,<br>You sully purity<br>Enflaming body and soul<br>With the fire of impurity. | 8th motive<br>It is contrary to purity.<br>1. It soils body and soul. |
| 63. O most evident mark<br>Of immodest women!<br>O dazzling livery<br>Of haughty ugliness. | 2. It is the sign of a prostitute.<br>3. Of a proud woman. |
| 64. O devils' great snare,<br>And amorous venom,<br>Making hearts guilty,<br>Seizing them by their eyes! | 4. It is the snare of the devil to enflame them. |

65. It's the devil's secret plot
To overturn the strong,
Their lethal contraption
Putting everyone to death.

5. It is his secret plot and contraption.

66. They ready their canons
Upon the powdered face,
Striking others with envy
When it is admired.

6. It is their battery of canons.

67. Devils have cunningly set
Their throne in these vanities,
Their home office is located
Amidst all the nudity.

7. Slyness of the devil.

68. From scantily clothed bosoms
Devils cast burning arrows,
Piercing the heart through the eyes,
Making thousand men perish.

69. To inject even more
Their amorous venom,
They make faces shine,
Adding dazzle to finery.

70. Through ladies' lips, devils chat,
They twinkle in eyes,
Whose luster stirs men,
Creating lovers galore.

2nd POINT.
*Extent of luxury.*

71. Luxury has made its way
Through the styles of this era;
It thrives in meals, hansoms,
In furniture, and knick-knacks.

1. Luxury in women's clothes.

72. Young ladies dressed
In their harlequin costumes
Parade through the streets
In their pointed laced-boots.

73. Madame appears bloated
In her large, heavy mantle;
She groans, overcome,
Under her stylish burden.

74. See their trains dragging,
Their stunning, sheer linen;
All these various materials
In three or four layers.

75. Their scarves are arranged
From all different pieces,
Through ingenious pleating,
In hundreds of ways.

76. Their three-story hair-do's
And beautiful rich necklace;
Their ostentatious display,
Their black hair all bleached.

77. Their tight-fitting sleeves, lace nets,
Their fringes of gold, their braids,
And many other trimmings
Whose names we don't know.

78. Oh! what a heap of nonsense,
Of feminine gear, and trinkets!
Every day these daydreams
Increase more and more.

2. Luxury in men's clothing.

79. Babylon's daughters
Are fancied by men;
Each has his Amazon
To make him unhappy.

80. Men imitate sugared ladies,
In luxurious dress,
In powdered wigs,
And costly materials.

81. Their style must change
At least once a month;
Bothersome perhaps,
But demanded by fashion.

3. Luxury in parish priests and ecclesiastics.

82. Parish priest, I'll let you alone
With your make-up and powder;
Seeing your laxity,
Makes the Church weep!

83. Your pompous soutane,
Your well-pressed rabat
Stitched by the best seamstress,
Your so shiny hat.

84. Your streaming sash,
Pretty shoes so well-shined,
Your elegant ways;
No use elaborating.

85. Luxury is now the butler
Of almost all banquets,
No longer can you find a feast
Which serves simple food.

4. Luxury in banquets.

86. Pride and gluttony,
Pleasure and lust,
Dispel innocence
And also frugality.

87. What superb table settings,
What silver-gilt plates,
These stews, these displays
Of pleasure and pride.

88. This useless abundance
Of fine dishes and wines,
This excessive extravagance
And for only one meal!

89. Excesses at table
That luxury seeks,
Make dining miserable
And cause many sins.

90. Oh! what arrogant retinues,
So many horses, so many dogs,
So many lackeys with pages as many!
Oh! what disastrous expense!

5. Luxury in retinues.

91. Luxury is on the pinnacle
Among those of high rank;
What miracle it would take
To change luxury to thrift.

92. How filled the houses of the great
With furnishings most precious:
With jasper and porcelain,
And with furniture exotic;

6. Luxury in furnishings.

93. What rare architecture!
Suites so enormous,
With jewels, and miniatures,
Plus countless curiosities;

94. With new-fangled weaving gear,
With novel suspended beds,
And many new pretenses,
Or rather the latest abuses.

95. Luxury, completely diabolical,
Is accepted everywhere,
Its practice is lauded,
So not to look scrupulous.

7. It is universal.

96. Almost no one follows the path
A good Christian should follow;
We are Christian in looks
But pagans at heart.

97. Luxury proclaims victory
Over humble simplicity;
The world has set its glory
In skill and vanity.

3rd POINT
*Causes of luxury*

98. Whence this common evil?
We want to be admired,
We want to be pleasant,
We want the world's love.

1. The desire to please.

99. When in public appearance,
Beautiful clothes, long train;
When alone, simplicity
Replaces worldly airs.

2. Human respect and parties.

100. We want to live in style,
Following the latest trends,
Fearing to look awkward,
And displeasing to anyone.

3. The custom.

## FOURTH SNARE: LUXURY

101. Often, ostentatious envy,
Seeing another better dressed
Is the unfortunate source
Of luxury in clothes.

4. Pride.

5. Envy.

102. Under the guise of cleanliness
The devil pushes us
To this elegance
And excessive affectation.

6. The demon.

103. He makes us drink carelessly
This prepared venom,
He makes us impale ourselves
On this gilded hook.

104. But if to please yourself,
As is commonly done,
You accept this adornment
So that you are looked at and loved;

105. From then on, you are guilty,
Unworthy of the sacraments,
Slave and handmaid of the devil
Deserving his torments.

106. Luxury has bewitched you,
You see no wrong in it;
But at your cruel death
You'll know it is deadly.

107. In spite of your follies
And bodily pleasures,
Your souls are filled
With woe and remorse.

108. Stand with your hair-do's high,
Never think of being humble;
Soon, heads swollen with pride,
Soon, you will fall into hell.

109. There, you will reap your reward,
For your make-up, your finery,
For the hours you've wasted
At games with your lovers.

## *FOURTH SNARE: LUXURY*

110. Shrewd women, pretty young ladies,
How cruel are your charms!
How your faithless beauty
Draws sinners to hell!

111. You will pay for those souls
You have dragged into sin,
Whom your wicked habits
Have finally made stumble.

112. As long as I'm alive,
Idols of vanity,
Armed with the truth,
I'll wage war against you.

113. If you will not believe me,
Reading these simple verses,
I await victory over you
When you land in hell.

114. Tear away, noble soul,
Everything that's useless,
Force yourself to be adorned
With sovereign good alone.

115. Flee the world in its splendor,
Enter deep in your own heart;
May it be your oratory,
Your distinction, your joy.

116. Flee disastrous luxury,
But maintain cleanliness.
Be humble and be modest
With no affectation.

117. Make certain your family
Is your principal duty,
Form it with Gospel laws
And tolerate no evil.

118. Always give it the example
Of all sorts of good works
So the family deems you
Its mirror of Christian.

GOD ALONE

## 34
## FIFTH SNARE: HUMAN RESPECT: FIRST HYMN

1. Great God, ever since I've served you
And decided to be faithful,
Man, and almost all creation,
Wage a cruel war against me.
Hasten, hasten, lend me a hand
To conquer human respect.

2. O Children of the chosen saints
We are so attacked by people,
Let us not become their slaves,
Let us not forget who we are.
Friends of God, brave soldiers true,
Let us not be conquered.

3. Poor sinner, held captive bound
By frivolous "what will they say"
Try to be very attentive
And very docile to my words,
Since only the truth itself
Can set you free.

4. Your name I cannot explain,
Human respect, accursed brood.
O devil's greatest favorite,
Who disparages penance;
O great enemy of virtue,
You overcome the strongest.

5. O most subtle poison
Causing us to swallow sin,
O most clever hook
Plunging us in the abyss,
O most traitorous friend
O enemy, the greatest.

6. I can not describe the evil

That human respect spreads,
The wisest, the most devout,
Almost all of us, life-long,
Suffer the maliciousness
Of this iniquity's monster.

7. What insult to the Creator
To fear his creature more than He,
To respect his greatness less
Than we would a wiggly worm's.
To prefer a really nothing
To this unique and sovereign good!

8. What outrage to his majesty
To prefer reveries to Him!.
What outrage to his truth
To thus believe a horrid lie,
Letting truth depend on human strength
And on mere idle words!

9. What insult to his charity!
Is that the heartfelt gratitude
We owe for His goodness,
For the blessings of Providence?
This good Father is abandoned,
Banished, this faithful Friend.

10. That is what happens, sinner,
When, through human fear
You disobey the Lord,
Serving Him reluctantly,
Lazily, by halves, lacking
Fervor and steadfastness.

11. I would serve the Lord well, you say,
But I fear this man or woman.
I would embrace all virtue
But I am afraid of their scorn;
Lord, I would be your friend,
Were it not for your foe, the world.

12. In spite of your almighty arm
I fear the man who threatens me;
In spite of your ravishing love,
I offer you an icy heart;

But I agree to serve you,
Whenever man approves.

13. I shall serve you, my Jesus,
Following you everywhere,
Provided I'm no longer treated
As a devotee or hypocrite;
If everyone approves of me,
Then I am yours forever.

14. Worldly man! Behold the greatest scorn
Of sovereign majesty!
Behold the sin you commit
When human respect drives you
To transgress His holy law,
Even to renounce your faith.

15. If neither God, nor religion
Can move you, enlighten you,
At least pay some attention
To your own wretched misery.
O wretched man, you lose all good
Through human respect.

16. Farewell to all the sermons,
Farewell to all the basic truths,
Farewell to all the inspirations,
Farewell to all the graces,
Farewell to all the absolutions,
And to so many Holy Communions.

17. So many good impulses followed,
So many victories won,
So much merit acquired,
So many heavy crosses well carried,
For a mere word, all is lost,
And for a nothing!

18. You were climbing with giant steps
To the most sublime of virtues.
Alas! you fell into sin,
Fearing to displease a nothing,
You fell so surreptitiously
Into the greatest laxity.

19. Often, after having lived
    Virtuously in one's youth,
    In old age, merit-filled,
    We are conquered by this snare;
    And so we lose in a moment
    What had value infinite.

20. Alas! if we were mocked
    And by this world ridiculed
    Alas! if we had practiced
    Virtue, even though disparaged,
    God in his generosity
    Would have filled us with grace.

21. God seeks true fidelity,
    He prefers it to all else,
    He grants to its steadfastness
    What is ordinarily refused.
    It is only to those tested
    That He gives His precious gifts.

22. To him who conquers, says the Lord,
    To him who remains faithful,
    I will share my tenderness,
    My grace and eternal glory.
    Far from me, worldly spirit,
    I look upon you with disdain.

23. What glory, at final judgment,
    Robes the victors of the devil and the world.
    When God will make clearly seen
    That their victory is unequalled,
    That, like good soldiers, in spite of all,
    They have walked in His footsteps!

24. What rightful joy then will be theirs
    To have the victory won,
    Despite the world and its perils,
    Despite all that was believed,
    And to see condemned to hell
    All worldly people of the earth!

25. To hear them sigh with moans so bleak:
    Alas! how totally wretched are we
    For having failed to persevere

Because of man's scorn,
For having followed vanity
Under pretext of the truth!

26. Today we see too late, too late,
Our worldly, criminal discretion;
It has only propelled us
To our eternal loss.
Oh! wretched human respect,
You put us in these flames.

27. Everyone will lament misfortunes:
Sons who followed fathers,
Brothers who believed sisters,
Daughters who believed mothers,
Everyone for having followed error
Instead of Jesus their Savior.

28. One day, they will see with surprise
Those wise devoted people
They considered with contempt;
Then they will cry out in rage:
What! are they the ones we ridiculed
Those whom we despised?

29. What! They dwelt upon this earth
Like so many fools (we thought!)
But now shine like God's children,
Like kings, adorned with greatest glory?
Wretches, how was it possible
To mistake the wise for fools?

30. In hell, how many wretched souls
Now seeing the entire truth,
Would wish, if it were doable,
To enlighten those still on earth
And cry to them: Do not believe
What we believed on earth!

31. Alas! we have been seduced
By these horrible, damned teachings
And we have mistaken darkness
For the brightness of true light,
We have falsely thought logical
What was only poison.

32. If you can't see, foolish man,
How clever and treacherous this snare,
At death you will be obliged
To realize it, but all too late!
These men whom you respect so much,
Will all perish at that moment.

## 35
## HUMAN RESPECT: SECOND HYMN

33. Are you inclined to gaze upon
A nothing, an iota?
Do you fear an illusion,
A transparent, empty ghost?
For such defines human respect,
And all worldly judgments.

34. Unjust and liars are we all
But with His exquisite fairness
Our only judge is the Lord,
Despite all human insolence.
Let us then despise the nothings,
They do neither harm nor good.

35. What! Are we better off
If the world decides to praise us?
What! Are we the worst of sinners
Because mudslingers filthy us?
Let them speak of us as good or bad,
Both have the same effect.

36. Suppose someone speaks ill of you:
They are but passing words,
Which can harm only fools
But not prudent souls
Who, pitying the speaker,
Consider them an honor.

37. One speaks, another carries out

An Injustice or some insult;
It is God who permits it,
Against Him then we grumble;
Man is only the instrument
God uses at that moment.

38. The Lord who comes to save us
Permits this sinister injustice,
Wishing so to test us,
Thus preparing us for glory.
But the devil is tempting you
Only to provoke you.

39. By patience, you gain the upper hand,
And edify your neighbor,
The devil is routed,
God is glorified,
Anger is calmed
And the mockers disdained.

40. By always doing your duty
By never giving just cause,
Try not to notice
Their ridicule and scorn;
This is the secret of great souls:
To contemn the world's contempt.

41. The wise man appeals in everything
To the tribunal of God, his judge;
Letting the carnal man judge,
He finds refuge in God alone;
All his glory is within
In spite of the greatest slanderers.

42. On the contrary, a carnal soul,
All worldly and all base,
Is offended by a random word,
By a glance or smirk;
Leave well enough alone
So as not to be despised.

43. The fool yearns not for his own glory,
But for the world's and his mouth's;
If someone robs him of this honor
What a fatal, cruel blow!

He has no other preoccupation
Than what people think and say.

44. Wise people, never fear
This world's persecution;
Wisdom lies in this truth,
On which Christianity is founded:
Truly, a good Christian
Lives with persecution.

45. Today, there are no assassins
Who as of old pour out our blood;
But there are plenty of new foes:
Those whose values are worldly;
Their mouth, worse than their hands
Inhumanely attack us.

46. The world, persecuting us,
Thinks it weakens and destroys us,
But its blows are not fatal,
Provided we can keep our smile;
He who suffers them gladly
May be called a martyr of charity.

47. Using all sorts of calumny,
Some disparage our honor;
Others become our critics,
Laughing outrageously.
They believe they have ruined our honor;
By suffering, it glows more splendidly than ever.

48. No one can steal from a Christian
The honor he holds within.
The world's honor being a nothing,
Who cares if we're cursed by it?
Christian, what an honor for you
To be mocked by fools.

49. A thief stole our possessions
By an unjust legal ruling,
Another robbed us of our funds,
Our clothes and all our food.
So what? These are temporal goods
Traded for eternal wealth.

50. Gold and silver have no worth,
For the world esteems them,
They produce a thousand evils
Leading multitudes to sin.
Would you call poverty evil
Even though it buys heaven?

51. That envious person got our job
By subterfuge and betrayal,
That proud person told us off
And acts as if he were boss;
So what? The greatest among you
Will be everyone's servant.

52. God says: If the world hates you,
Rejoice, rejoice because of it.
No subject are you of this world
For your soul is not worldly;
You will receive in heaven above
A reward of marvelous glory.

53. Thus the world has mistreated
All the saints in glory.
Reduced to begging,
Often forgotten,
Exiled from all lands,
They fled into the deserts.

54. People criticized their virtues,
Treated them like hypocrites
And attacked them everywhere
By jealousies kept secret,
Twisted what they thought, said and did
So it would appear as evil.

55. Gaze only upon Jesus Christ,
He is our perfect model:
What does the Spirit teach us
About Christ Eternal Wisdom?
The world calls him a sinner,
Drunkard, magician and a phony.

56. I'd like the world to slap you,
Smack you, torture you,
Though wrongly, undeservedly.

True, the insult is so glaring,
But you will gain infinitely,
If you suffer all patiently.

57. If someone wants to strangle you,
Fear not so much his fury
As God, who alone settles scores
Both in this world and the next,
Who can put aside a soul and doom it,
Kill the body and condemn it.

58. The Christian like his Savior,
Disciple like his master,
Both the slave and his lord
Must suffer from the traitors;
The world has always, everywhere,
Attacked those who serve their God.

## 36
## HUMAN RESPECT: THIRD HYMN

59. Human respect generates
An unreal, whimsy fear,
But also brings along with it
The most diabolical shame.
Once human respect subdues us,
We become ashamed of virtue.

60. Ashamed of serving God?
To serve this adorable Lord
Is it not to reign over all?
Nothing is more honorable!
O wretched human respect,
You are the one so shameful.

61. What! Be ashamed of God Himself
To please some mindless person!
What! Be daring for the world,
Letting all know you love it,
While trembling even at the word:
'Religious' or 'devotion!'

62. If you are ashamed of Jesus
And of serving Him today,
You may still declare for Him
At the final judgment hour,
But on that great Day, at His turn,
He will be ashamed of you.

63. Though filled with shame or craven fear,
Secretly, you still do some good,
You live just like all the spineless,
Fleeing the perfect path,
Shunning the title 'religious'
As much as 'fool' or 'stupid'.

64. One day you'll see but all too late
That this ugly shame is sinful,
For you'll have nothing in common
With Jesus and his faithful.
On that Day He will renounce you
And curse you, forever.

65. How can you be so ashamed
Of loving virtue, so beautiful
That none can esteem it fully?
Whose birth is from eternity
And ravishes the universe
From heaven even to hell?

66. In all ages, in all climes,
Virtue alone should be esteemed,
Land and water, air and sky
Proclaim that it is lovely
And you, so wretched, worldly,
Would look on virtue with disdain!

67. It is an infinite treasure
And a most precious pearl
Whose brilliance never tarnishes
If truly loved by a soul;
The Lord casts His loving eyes
On those who possess it.

68. By this sovereign good
The angel pleased his Creator,
Mary's heart overflowed with it

And God chose her for His mother.
It is through virtue that the saints
Have accomplished all their plans.

69. Virtue has protected them
Against their greatest foes,
Virtue always consoled them
In their most bitter woes;
Virtue chose them as elect
And virtue crowned them all.

70. Virtue, so often criticized
By the greatest sinners,
Is esteemed deep in their hearts,
As are even those who live it,
Although because of virtue's rigors
Sinners are quite repelled by it.

71. Evil men sometimes consult
Good people whom they trust
In order to conquer sin,
Even emptying their conscience;
In dialogue with the virtuous
They find new strength, new joy and good.

72. Pagans, the most barbarous,
Believed that virtue was the start
And source of all good things,
Even, that it was so divine,
They placed among their gods
Those they considered virtuous.

73. Virtue alone has credit
And insurmountable strength;
Everyone submits to it, without opposition,
The great and little, just and guilty.
And still, wretched Christian,
You are ashamed of virtue?

74. Grace and faith and also reason,
Show how excellent it is;
Virtue should rule all people
Bringing all things under its power.
How happy are its friends.
How wretched virtue's enemies.

75. Virtue is impossible in hell,
So devils and the doomed rage;
How they crave for its adornment
To lighten their eternal gloom;
But their torments and despair
Consist in virtue's total absence.

76. Evil spirits, always jealous,
Seeing a soul clothed with virtue,
Strike that soul, doubling their efforts
To bring that person into hell.
The envy of the ancient serpent
Falls on those most virtuous.

77. Friends of the great God Whom I serve,
Heads held high, let us practice
The most exalted virtues,
As all true Christians should,
Despite the world and fiery hell,
With no embarrassment or fear.

78. What do you expect from a mortal
For your cowardly indulgence,
For your sinful respect,
For your disastrous deference?
That he will esteem you more?
You are wrong; you'll only be abused.

79. Seeing you so weak and fickle
So ready to commit sin,
Because of one offensive word,
He will lose all esteem for you;
If he praises you with his lips,
It is surely not from his heart.

80. If you do what pleases him
Through fear of his ridicule
He will praise you through self-interest
Through politics or flattery;
In secret he will laugh at you
Judging you the weakest.

81. He will say to himself:
I thought this man an apostle,

A servant of Jesus Christ,
But he is like any other.
Human respect has changed him,
Befuddled him and made him fall.

82. He is our friend, our relative,
A noble and divine soul,
A person of high rank,
But when the world dominates him,
No matter! the wise pity him,
In spite of blood and friendship.

83. If no one reprimands you
For this accursed habit
It is self-interest that intrudes,
Or prudence, or politics.
Will an evil become a good
Because no one says anything?

84. It is foolish to depend
On a man, a fragile reed,
To take for your shield
A clump of mud and clay,
Who very often deceives us
And who changes like the breeze.

85. It's foolish to seek friendship
From a slimy earthworm
Who can not prevent God
From waging war on you,
Despoiling you of everything
And plunging you in hell.

86. When you have fallen into sin
Just to please a mortal creature,
When you have been so stained,
Will he make you pure again?
Will this worldly man absolve you?
Or save you from all peril?

87. When death attacks you,
Will he help you in any way?
When the Lord will judge you
Will he come to plead your case?
Then you will feel, worldly soul,

Human respect's wretchedness!

88. Do you still expect to find
Some way to please everyone
And Jesus too? And then be saved
Without one or the other grumbling?
It's an unknown secret that
Those who tried to do so, couldn't.

89. You can not, Jesus said so,
Please the world and please God too;
God and the world are contradictions,
Accursed you are by one or other.
Is the world your enemy?
Then God is your great Friend.

90. Unworthy Christian, choose your side,
You are making a horrible pact,
You are a monster in disguise
With the lovely title of penitent;
If Jesus Christ is your Savior
Renounce this deceiving world.

## 37
## HUMAN RESPECT: FOURTH HYMN

91. All the saints have been attacked
By contempt and grumbling.
Even their virtues so rare,
Suffered much criticism;
I say more: even the greatest sinners
Are not exempt from critics.

92. Do you think that by human respect
No one will despise you,
That the world will leave you in peace
And no one will bother you?
You are terribly mistaken,
In fact, you are blind.

93. Proud people will belittle you,
The envious will rage,

The learned will criticize,
You will be corrected by the wise.
Trying to please all the fools
Makes you the greatest fool of all.

94. Since the time of your conversion,
I have admired your refinement;
In concealing your devotion,
You use a thousand subtleties,
You always manage to disguise
The signs of a true penitent.

95. What! You committed the sin,
Despite all advice given,
Even though it shook some people,
And made yourself look like a fool;
You were, and very openly,
In the greatest immorality.

96. And now you dare be ashamed
Of God Himself and of His service?
This change is truly astounding,
Full of error and injustice!
Bold for all iniquity,
Ashamed of whatever holy.

97. Concerning temporal matters,
You have no fear of criticism;
But for eternal matters,
You fear the slightest murmur.
You flee like a total coward
At any hint of 'what-will-they-say'.

98. "But I want the whole world
To approve of your conduct."
Are you won over by this?
Would it really make you happy?
"What does it matter to gain the world
And suffer the loss of one's soul."

99. How I fear for a penitent
Who is universally esteemed,
Whom the world flatters as much
As it does a sinful person!
I believe that his conversion

Is nothing but illusion.

100. Know that the world and the flesh
Attack a converted soul,
That the devil and all hell
Often join in with those
Convincing him to leave His God
Whom he has just embraced.

101. You do whatsoever you please
And no one ever questions you;
Oh! how that sign displeases me!
I fear that God is reproving you;
His true friends are mistreated,
Slandered and persecuted.

102. Since worldly people are for you,
You are of their ilk,
They are all in your favor,
Because you follow their lead;
But if you were truly converted
They would all be against you.

103. Far from us, deceiving penitents,
Complacent and political,
Also those whose hearts you invite
For fear of suffering their criticism,
And who, despite the Holy Spirit,
Dare equate 'world' with Jesus Christ.

104. As for you, generous penitents,
Who serve God completely,
Flee the wretched worldly people,
Trample under foot their proud speech;
Confront hell, and here and now
And from now on, serve our God.

105. Listen to Jesus with faith,
Do not fear if you are cursed:
Whoever turns and look back
Has become His unworthy servant.
He wants all those who serve him
To confront the world and its fright.

106. When they turn their backs on you

And attack you here on earth,
You should not fear these evils
If God is not against you;
For if the Lord is for you
We will have victory over all.

107. Do not fear, do good boldly,
For God alone and to please Him,
Without cowardly fearing
What others think, say or do,
In order to be the sweet perfume
Of Jesus Christ your Savior

108. Since 'what-will-they-say' is much in vogue,
Choose well, faithful soul,
Not those things of world and devil:
Leave those for the unfaithful;
Choose the pattern of pious people
And of the Kings of Eternity.

109. What will the just say here below?
What will the saint in glory say?
What will these courageous soldiers say,
Who have already won the victory?
What will God, my Creator say?
What will Jesus, my Savior say?

110. If I do not make such an effort
For fear of feeling guilty,
What will I say at the moment of death?
What will my just Judge say?
What will be said at judgment?
Ah! the delightful 'what-will-they-say'!

111. Do not let yourself become captive,
Fight again, I beg you,
For, finally, you must be saved,
Although others rant and rave.
For God, be all things to all people
But keep yourself from sin.

112. It is the way to expiate
The scandals of your brothers,
To live well and persevere,
In the footsteps of your elders,

To reign forever as they do,
With the Lord in heaven.

## 38
## HUMAN RESPECT: FIFTH HYMN

113. What is human respect's taproot?
Perhaps worldly pride or envy,
The limelight or worldly profit?
Attachment to life's pleasures?
Deep-seated love of the world
Is its principal cause.

114. This toxin is injected
By a promise, a threat,
Or a specter of truth,
Or by criticism, a smirk,
An insult, an action mimicked,
Or by nicknames so silly.

115. If a person is not beaten
By this whole battery,
His virtue is then attacked
By ugly stinging jokes,
By most bloody outrages
And most exhausting blows.

116. This poison, spread everywhere,
Sets the entire earth afire,
Almost everywhere it is now
The master of souls most holy;
The most saintly nuns and priests,
Even they are contaminated.

117. Ah! what subtle venom,
And how effortless to drink!
For some reason or other
It is gulped quite unawares.
Traveling from the ear to the heart
The sinner is defeated.

118. Will I also succumb, Lord?

Take up arms in my favor
To conquer this world full of lies,
Its human respect and its charms.
So that I may better serve you,
This is what I now promise:

119. I shall act very simply
Following you, Divine Wisdom,
No craftiness nor subterfuge,
No politics nor cunning,
No contempt for my neighbor,
And most of all, no human respect.

120. I want to give evidence
Of being devout, most truly,
Of acquiring perfection
As much as I can,
And of advancing in holiness
Never looking aside.

121. To do that, in the footsteps of saints
I'll follow a director's advice
So he can lend me a hand
To serve God with all my heart.
Without any recklessness
Or any illusions.

122. I hope to be all things to all
Without cowardly smugness,
To try to win them all
To Jesus Christ by penance.
All things to all, without sinning
Or blocking any good deeds.

123. A useful deed, neither right nor wrong,
Yet scandalous to my neighbor,
Is, prudent man I pray to be,
An action I will not repeat,
For fear that I am doing harm
To those for whom my Jesus died.

124. I will support and very strongly,
A weak man about to fall,
Gently correcting him,
Not caring if I'm mocked;

In routing all iniquity
I will be most unbending.

125. Away with those vain compliments
That human wisdom uses,
And all that sophistication
That causes so much trouble;
Although studied with great fanfare
It is utterly so useless.

126. Away with those people so polite
With all their graceful bows,
Their pretty, gallant manners
Their contortions and their rhythms.
Honesty I love very much
But never worldliness.

127. Away with those wicked soldiers
Who fear some passing word,
Surrendering their arms
Because of some slight comment,
Trembling with abject fear
Of all the lying ghosts.

128. I despise everything they say
And all their worldly maxims,
As I would a cursed language,
Or at least like illusions
Seeming reasonable at first
Although basically they're poisons.

129. The world speaks very powerfully
To get across its maxims.
It so subtly uses virtues
Even to advertise great sins;
It has thousands secret detours
To ensnare us in its clutches.

## 39
## AXIOMS OF THE WORLD

130. You, converted? Very nice! Very nice!
A good fellow never changes;
And this change is just too much!
Everyone finds it weird.
Be wary of this hidden lie,
It smiles at us, but damns us.

131. Nothing but scruples of the pious,
All that is nothing but straw fire;
Do you want to look like a zealot,
And be the laughing stock of all?
Be wary ...

132. Your confessor is so scrupulous,
In the pulpit he damns us all;
They'll treat you like an airhead
And someone most abnormal.
Be wary ...

133. Now God doesn't ask of you
This good act or penance,
It's your own pride, disguising
Self-love and self-sufficiency.
Be wary ....

134. Good God, what devotion!
Good God, what piety!
Good fellow, you are deluded.
If you only knew how much they're howling!
Be wary ....

135. Abandon meditation,
It's really quite dangerous,
And prone to temptation,
For it makes the soul sluggish.
Be wary ...

136. What good in many rosaries?
Brother, better you be at work;
Surely, you should be satisfied

With your ordinary prayers.
Be wary ...

137. Flee such eccentricity:
True virtue is always hidden,
Watch out for yourself and vanity
For what a show you're making.
Be wary ...

138. You are so very gifted.
You should frequent society.
Be polite and gallant
Otherwise they'll grumble.
Be wary ...

139. By your clothes, your manners,
You're making everyone laugh,
They'll even write ditties about you;
It's far worse than you imagine.
Be wary ...

140. If you want to lower your eyes
And live just like a savage,
You should become a Carthusian
Or go into a hermitage.
Be wary ...

141. Believe me, I am your friend,
Now imitate so and so,
Don't let yourself be governed
By such mere trifles.
Be wary ...

142. I'm not the only one who says this:
So and so does, also your father.
What! You think they're all stupid,
Not knowing how to get things done?
Be wary of this hidden lie,
It smiles at us, but damns us.

143. The world, impostor, so verbose
In sanctioning its conduct,
Too bad it would be impossible
To write it all in many volumes.
We could then refute so easily

All its random lies.

144. O damned respect for the flesh,
Accursed brood of vipers,
Accursed offspring of hell itself,
Accursed source of misery,
O destroyer of good intentions,
O great persecutor of the saints!

145. I realize you are my enemy,
And I declare you damned;
I choose God alone as friend
And publicly, despite your rage
Without any fear of what you'll say
Or even what you'll do.

146. To follow the example
That Jesus gives to me,
I always do good everywhere,
Without fearing anyone,
In order to bear the sacred title:
A man without human respect.

PRAYER:

147. Help me, Queen of Heaven,
Help me, most Holy Virgin,
Against the wretched world,
Its human respect and fear,
To conquer them, with your Son,
In spite of all the risks.

148. O mighty God, lend me a hand,
Your all-powerful hand,
To conquer human respect,
That charming beast.
Trusting in you, my dear Jesus,
I will never be confounded.

149. Truly I will be blessed
If, living this life,
I am contradicted everywhere
By calumny and envy;
If, despite what they say
And in spite of hell, I carry on.

150. Ah! let me not be fooled
By this intricate spell;
Let me not be trapped
By this human being, by this cunning snare,
But let me die faithful to your laws
In the shadow of your cross,

151. Hated by the world and despised,
Contrary to the world's maxims,
Poor, suffering and abandoned,
Burdened with crosses and trials,
But, upheld by your arm
I shall never fall into hell.

152. If someone is truly converted,
Let him believe me and take up arms,
Let him join rank with me
Against the world and its alarms,
To follow a God victorious
Both on Calvary and in the heavens.

GOD ALONE

# THE LOVING DEVOTION TO THE HEART OF JESUS

## 40
## TREASURES OF THE SACRED HEART

1st POINT
*The infinite treasures of the Heart of Jesus Christ.*

1. Here is the greatest marvel
Expressed in my verses.
Chosen souls, listen
And mingle your voices with mine.

Motives.
To honor the Heart of Jesus.

2. Rising far above myself,
I ascend even to the saints,

Higher still, to the Great High King,
Higher than all the heavens.

3. What do I see? All heaven admires it,
All heaven's astonished!
I see what cannot be described.
Come, come and gaze, chosen souls.

1st Motive
It is the object of adoration and admiration by the angels.

4. Angels, tell me, I entreat you,
What is this lovely blazing fire?
It is the Heart of Mary's Son,
And of the only Son of God.

5. Mortals, adore with angels
This Heart, which we too must adore,
Cry out and sing praises
To a Heart that love has rent.

6. O great mystery of glory
Not grasped here below!
Faith is needed to believe it
If a heart has yet to taste it!

2nd Motive
It is an unknown mystery.

7. This Heart, as man approaches,
Exalts God its Creator,
Glorifying His mercy,
Offering perfect homage.

3rd Motive
It glorifies the mercy of God.

8. How startling! The Heart is humble
At all times before its Father;
It praises, adores, entreats,
Speaking for us mightily.

4th Motive
It adores the Majesty and prays for us.

9. O overwhelming marvel!
O Heart Most Divine,
Infinitely adorable,
Within the Trinity all holy!

10. O! What flames rise to the Father
From this Heart night and day!
O! how it loves man, his brother,
With pure and burning love!

5th Motive
It loves God Its Father and man Its brother.

11. O great Heart! O burning furnace!
O miraculous inferno

6th Motive
It enflames heaven and earth.

Shooting forth abundant flames
To set earth and heaven afire!

12. Since it is Heart, it loves us
Without ceasing for an instant;
It loves us as much as itself,
Exceedingly, infinitely.

7th Motive
The Heart loves us as Itself.

13. It is the Heart of hearts sublime,
The Heart of the truly chosen,
The greatest of their victim souls,
Through Him, our sins are pardoned.

8th Motive
It is the Heart of great hearts and great souls.

14. In this Heart, the holiest souls,
The best friends of the Savior
Have found their purest flames,
Their most inexpressible fervor.

15. Here is the real treasury
Of the grace of Jesus Christ,
Here is the admirable fount
Of all the Holy Spirit's gifts.

9th Motive
The treasury of Jesus Christ and the Holy Spirit.

16. Here is the fount of life
From which all the saints have drunk,
Here is the marvelous fire
Where their hearts became enflamed.

10th Motive
The source of life.

11th Motive
The fire of pure love.

17. We find in this Heart all weapons,
It is the great arsenal;
We find in it the holiest delights
To charm, and conquer evil.

12th Motive
The arsenal of all arms.

18. Here is the holiest hideaway
Where we avoid all sin,
Where even the imperfect soul
Becomes holy, at bargain prices.

13th Motive
The retreat of the perfect.

19. Here is the town of refuge
Where no one is ever hurt,
And the true ark of deluge
Where no one ever drowns.

14th Motive
The refuge of sinners.

20. This pierced Heart enchants
And disarms the God of vengeance,
Its wound forms its divine mouth
Which victoriously pleads.

21. In this Heart, God the Father
Never strikes the sinner,
This Heart calms his anger,
Obtains his grace and favor.

22. Here is the sacred entrance
To the Spouse's inner chamber,
Where the pure soul is inebriated
With love's most pleasing wine.

15th Motive.
The Chamber of the spouses of Jesus Christ.

23. In this Heart the soul is laced
With perfume's sweetest scent.
In this Heart the soul is lit
With extraordinary fire.

24. This Heart is our living ark
Containing the entire law,
The innocent soul's secrets
And the mysteries of the faith.

16th Motive.
The Ark of the Covenant.

25. In this Heart our Master planned
All the secrets of his love,
Before disclosing them to us,
Before bringing them to light.

17th Motive.
The Hall of the secrets of Jesus Christ.

26. His Heart formed His oracles
Before He ever uttered them,
His Heart formed His miracles
Before He ever performed them.

27. In this fount of all light,
The favorites of Jesus Christ
Have drawn the deepest mysteries,
The Holy Spirit's greatest gifts.

18th Motive.
The source of all lights.

28. In this pure treasure of innocence
All the saints have been formed,
It is there that they were born

19th Motive
The treasury of innocence.

And accomplished all their plans.

29. This Heart is the rock's cleft
Where gentle peace is found,
It is earth's paradise
Where dwell all the elect.

20th Motive
The paradise of good souls and their bed of repose.

30. This Heart is the bed of rest
For Jesus' intimate friends;
In this Heart they acquire
Their most sublime virtues.

31. O great Heart, O deep abyss
Of profound humility!
O great Heart, O sublime throne
Of perfect charity!

21st Motive.
The treasury of all virtues.

32. Oh miracle of the world, great Heart
Which truly contains everything,
Heaven, earth and sea,
All the Holy Trinity!

22nd Motive.
The miracle of the world.

33. Praising this adorable Heart,
I praise in proportion
The Heart of His admirable Mother,
So intense is their union.

23rd Motive
Union of the Heart of Jesus with the Heart of Mary.

34. It is you alone whom I adore,
Heart of my God, glorious Heart,
But, adoring you, I also honor
The Heart of heaven's Queen.

35. Christians, by Mary's Heart
We love the Heart of Jesus,
Since Jesus took life
In her most virtuous heart.

36. From the blood of her flaming heart,
The Heart of Jesus was formed;
They have but one heart, but one soul,
One and the other should be loved.

37. Soul, lose yourself entirely
In these two miraculous hearts,
One and the other convince you

Resolution.

To see but one in the two.

38. Dear soul, mount secretly,
By this tender heart to the Heart Most High.
You will soon become perfect,
Loving this Heart as one should.

GOD ALONE

## 41
## LOVING EXCESSES OF THE SACRED HEART

2nd POINT
*Motives to love the Heart of Jesus.*

1. Let us go deep within the Temple,
Let us enter this marvelous Heart,
So that we may love as it does,
Let us gaze at its excess of love.

1st Motive
In the womb of Mary.

2. See in Mary's womb
This tiny Heart aflame.
Filled with the Spirit, it cries:
Love, love, love of God.

3. My God, my Father, my Heart is set
To carry out your will.
Here in my mother's womb
I submit to it with all my Heart.

4. I adore you and I love you,
Here I am, do with me as you please.
In the center of my being
I set your cross and your rule.

5. You let me see even now,
That the cross must be embraced,
And on it I must even die.
I yearn for it, my God, it is my choice.

6. What, man would lose life itself?
My love can not abide it!
I want to die, I am dying of desire
To keep them all from perishing.

7. My mother, most dear to me,
I am filling you with gifts
So that you may be the mother
And the refuge of sinners.

8. This Heart impelled by love
Journeys to John, its herald,
It fills John's heart with joy,
With grace and with meekness.

2nd Motive
At the sanctification of St. John.

9. From His infancy Jesus reveals
The excesses of his love
By his excessive suffering
And his great poverty.

10. In the stable, everything proclaims:
His Heart is so loving
He is so poor in this crib
He seems sad on account of it.

3rd Motive
In the stable.

11. Love makes this Heart sigh
For it delays his death,
He hastens to be circumcised
To shed his blood and suffer.

4th Motive
At the Circumcision

12. In the Temple, he is the victim
Calming God's wrath,
Rendering God sublime honor,
Offering himself entirely for us.

5th Motive
In the temple.

13. When he flees from Herod, love impels him,
He seeks us, he yearns to find us;
Under an infant's weakness, he hides
His eagerness to save us.

6th Motive.
The flight into Egypt.

14. How gentle and docile is this Heart!
Jesus chats with other children,
How affable and loving,
How winning his charms!

7th Motive
In His conversations.

15. To win victory for us,
He obeys his parents;
To make us shine in glory,
He stays hidden for thirty years.

8th Motive
In His hidden life.

16. Running wherever love draws him,
He longs to find us eventually,
He is weak, he is out of breath
So weary is he from the journey.

9th Motive
In His missions.

17. He sits down by a well,
Not so much to rest
But for the Samaritan woman
Whom he wills to save and win.

10th Motive
In His conversation with the Samaritan woman.

18. With what skill and wisdom
This kindest of all hearts
Wins over this sinful woman!
A miracle of love!

19. By the sovereign meekness
Of his most tender and gentle Heart,
He converted the Magdalene
And shielded her from others.

11th Motive.
In the conversion of the Magdalene.

20. Admire the gentle way -
No harshness is shown -
He rescues the adulterous woman
From the hands of her accusers.

12th Motive.
In the salvation of the adulterous woman.

21. Do you see him humbly bowing
At the feet of wretched Judas?
His Heart tells him, his Heart calls out:
"My friend, do not damn yourself."

13th Motive.
In His conduct toward Judas.

22. He sighs, his tears flow down
But Judas is not moved.
O tender Heart, O charming Heart,
Truly you are not known!

23. Love robs Jesus of life
Yet bestows life after death:
He lives on in the Eucharist.
O Heart, how strong your love!

14th Motive.
In the institution of the Holy Eucharist.

24. In a garden, he weeps and cries,
Struggling brutally for us
Even to the depths of agony;
He is overwhelmed by our blows.

15th Motive.
In the Garden of Olives.

25. He weeps not for himself,
Although his blood flows in streams;
Since this Sacred Heart so loves us,
He can not abide our woes.

26. In terrible combat, his Heart
Overcomes all, draining his strength;
He is mindful only of us!
He rises, hastening to his death.

27. He is dragged to the slaughter
Like a silent lamb,
They treat him viciously;
He neither speaks nor complains.

16th Motive.
In His arrest and sufferings.

28. Alas! he is taken and bound,
Overwhelmed with thousand blows,
They nail him, they crucify him;
His Heart is always so gentle.

29. As nothing, he counts his suffering
And all the woes he has borne,
His Heart full of immense love
Cries: "Strike, strike even more.

17th Motive
His Heart desires even more suffering.

30. I am happy to be battered,
That all my blood be shed,
Provided man be forgiven
Provided man not be lost."

31. See how this Heart gathers
His meager strength and vigor
Only to obtain grace
For his executioners and sinners.

18th Motive.
In His prayer on the Cross.

32. More than his lips, his Heart cries out:
"O my Father, forgive them,
So that as their evil affects me,
You will diminish my sorrow."

33. Finally, his Heart stops beating
But life is not lost
Since his Heart is still eager
To suffer after death.

19th Motive
At His death.

34. His Father grants his prayer;
Behold! His side is pierced,
And from the gash, a river flows
Of water, blood and love.

20th Motive.
When His side
was opened.

35. Finally, the furnace opens up!
Finally, this great Heart unlocks;
Finally, the reason is clear
Why Jesus has so suffered.

36. By piercing His Heart, he is consoled:
The passageway carved by the lance
For his Heart's devouring fire,
Leads straight to the heart of the sinner.

37. Through this bleeding mouth,
His Heart has been speaking for two thousand years,
With a voice both dying and living,
Words that I hardly understand.

GOD ALONE

# 42
# WORDS OF JESUS CHRIST THAT REVEAL THE GREAT BENEFITS OF DEVOTION TO THE SACRED HEART

3rd POINT

*Motives for devotion to the Heart of Jesus.*

1. Let us journey, sinners, journey
To the Heart of Jesus Christ,
Through His Heart Jesus speaks,
Creating in us a contrite heart.

1st Motive
The Heart of
Jesus desires this
devotion.

2. My Heart burns with ardent thirst,
"I thirst" is my constant cry;
To you, dear penitent soul,
My Heart looks for relief.

He calls penitent
souls.

3. Mix my blood with your tears
Since you weep over your sins;

Fear not, I lay down my arms
Since your heart is so moved.

4. To double your penitence,
Enter my Heart so penitent.
To love me with immense love,
Enter my Heart which so loves you.

5. You are my sweetest conquest
By doing penance, as you do,
Heaven and my Heart rejoice,
I take pleasure in your tears

6. Although I love you and forgive you,
Groan constantly even so,
For it is the finish that I crown,
And not the starting point.

7. My Sacred Heart is my breast
I offer you for nourishment
To make you strong and true,
To practice penance, faithfully.

2nd Motive
His Heart is His
Breast.

8. Where do you flee, criminal sinner?
Why do you run away from me?
You will fall into the abyss,
My heart calls you: Draw near.

3rd Motive
Appeal to sinners
Whom He loves.

9. What! Must you offend me
Because I am so merciful?
My Heart defers vengeance
To grant you forgiveness.

10. Cry to your God: "Mercy!"
Do you hear me? I am your Savior,
Through me alone God grants mercy
Through me alone sinners find favor.

11. In my Heart forgiveness lies;
Outside of it, nothing is pardoned.
In my Heart hope has its home;
Outside of it, damnation looms.

12. If my Heart, by its gentle flame
Can not finally win over yours,

How cruel! You rip out my spirit,
And your heart transfixes mine.

13. My Heart, against its nature,
Will forever cry for vengeance
Against you, vile creature:
You did not accept my peace.

4th Motive
His threats if one is not devoted to Him.

14. For your excess of impenitence,
And my excess of charity,
I will return an excess of punishment
For all eternity.

15. At the end of the world, I will open
My ardent Heart to sinners
But for those who do not respond,
My Heart will be ice cold.

5th Motive
His lamentation

16. They scorn all my sufferings,
My blood, my Heart, my love,
In spite of my own blood,
They overwhelm me with sin.

17. Come to my Heart, faithful soul,
Would you also abandon me?
Come, drink at the eternal fount,
Not meant for hardened hearts.

6th Motive
Appeal to pious souls.

18. Soul, do you need light?
My Heart is a divine sun
Where the crudest soul
Will see clearly as a cherub.

7th Motive
This Heart gives light.

19. My Heart alone strengthens,
It powerfully charms;
My Heart alone restores peace
It is the center of peace itself.

8th Motive
It strengthens.

9th Motive
It pacifies.

20. Quick! To my Heart, far from bedlam,
Enter this home of saintly souls
Where sin and insult are unknown:
Secrets by the world ignored.

21. Rest, my dear soul, rest
In my Heart, a bed of flowers;

10th Motive
It is a bed of flowers.

All good dwells in my Heart:
Don't squander your life elsewhere.

22. Is your heart lukewarm, weary?
Or perhaps completely lazy?
My Heart sets souls on fire
Turning dwarfs into giants.

11th Motive
It sets souls on fire.

23. Is your heart melancholy
Through the devil's tricks?
My Heart brims with joy,
Banishing all worry.

12th Motive
It gives joy.

24. Are you really thirsty? Come,
Drink from the Savior's fountain
A liquor made of glory
With fire and holy fervor.

13th Motive
It quenches thirst.

25. Do you yearn for divine wisdom
Making you wise in God's eyes?
Do you relish divine delight?
My Heart is its burning throne.

14th Motive
It bestows wisdom.

26. To blaze joyfully with love,
Would that be your desire?
Quickly, lose yourself in my Heart,
The furnace aflame with winning Love.

15th Motive
It conquers everything by love.

27. If you want to love Mary
With almost infinite love,
Love with my Heart, I beg you,
For my Heart is one with hers.

16th Motive
Mary must be loved.

28. Our hearts were but one victim
When they lived on earth,
So intimately united, they form
But one love in the heavens.

29. Let everyone love and adore
My Heart, through divine delights;
I promised, I still promise
All my treasures to the pious.

30. If you wanted, Princes of France,
To love my victorious Heart,

17th Motive
It assures victory.

Victory in abundance
Would follow your troops far and wide.

31. In my Heart is all victory
Over your enemies and mine;
In my Heart is all my glory
All my riches and my grace.

32. Open your heart, pure soul,
Rather, enter into mine;
Abandon all created things,
Possess all good in my Heart.

33. I have borne countless insults
So I may be all yours today;
Make amends by your worship,
My Heart ardently entreats you.

GOD ALONE

# 43
# OUTRAGES AGAINST THE SACRED HEART

4th POINT.

1. Listen to my holy lament,
Friends of my Savior's Heart,
I open up my soul to you:
May my own heart be consoled.

2. Speak, O my heart, speak, O my tears,
Sigh, weep, a thousand times, weep;
How utterly distraught I am!
Both words and voice now fail.

3. You have asked me, friends,
Why my heart is so afflicted,
Why I sigh and weep.
Ah! My Jesus is insulted!

4. The idolatrous ignore Him,
They know not the King of Heaven,
Turks and Jews deny Him,

Jesus is blasphemed among them.

5. How many infamous heretics
Have profaned His sacrament!
Oh! how their diabolical rage
Should ever astound us!

6. All heaven and earth together
Weep over these indignities;
My heart weeps, my hand trembles
As I write about these cruelties.

7. How cruelly they insult
His paternal testament,
Deeming Him only as a sign
In the Blessed Sacrament.

8. What grave insult to His words
To deny the reality!
They treat as things so frivolous
His oracles of truth.

9. No longer having faith to rule them,
They outrage Him a thousand times;
By their fury and anger against Him,
They nail Him back upon the cross.

10. Some throw consecrated hosts
To animals so furious,
Others throw them piece by piece,
In the mud and in the streets.

11. One, with a penknife, O shocking act,
Pierces this most loving Heart,
Another throws it into boiling water,
Another throws it into fire.

12. Alas! how many by black magic
Have handed over the Host
To the devil, or by sorcery
Have made of it cruel poison!

13. Ponder now unfaithful Catholics
Who, by their piety, should
Defend it from the heretics.

They are alas, more cruel.

14. Our churches are neglected,
Our God is without adorers,
For days, what do I say, for years,
No one adoring His majesty.

15. If many come into our churches,
It is not so much for Jesus Christ
But through custom or example,
Jesus is not in mind.

16. Often this Master, King of glory,
Is abandoned on our altars,
No one recalling He is there,
Deserted by all mortals.

17. While the Sacred Heart plans
To shower us with favors,
We really do not care,
And even treat Him harshly.

18. How many impious opposed to this Heart!
How many infamous actions!
How much indecency everywhere!
How many profanations!

19. Look at this wretched man swearing
And blaspheming God's Holy Name!
Yet the insult upsets no one,
They laugh at it with the devil.

20. No one has ever seen the earth
So full of God's enemies,
Everywhere but crime and war,
Jesus bemoaned this recently.

21. But no one is shocked by this,
The greatest crimes are nothings.
Who pities Jesus? Alas! no one,
We're only thinking of ourselves.

22. If only He'd be spared in church!...
Alas! no, it's in His palace
That He is pierced by many darts,

And no one is even shocked.

23. Look at that worldly woman
That idol of such vanity,
Who by her haughty ways
Challenges the Divinity.

24. Do you see her all decked out
Near an altar unadorned?
See how she is adored.
Jesus is not considered.

25. How many infamous trysts
In the church of our God!
How many men and women
Lose their souls in this holy place!

26. What giggling, what chatter!
Talking there as if at market.
What unbounded insolence!
And God suffers all these sins.

27. Even Turks in their mosques
Practice modesty,
Respect and attention,
As for us, what disorder!

28. See the church, so poor, so filthy,
Next to the pretentious castle,
For the Lord and Lady must possess
Abundance in their homes.

29. Alas! how many wretched priests,
Wolves in lamb's clothing,
Judases, wretched traitors,
More cruel than executioners!

30. Is this then how man offends
The loving Heart of the Savior?
Is this what man calls gratitude?
What outrage and what heartbreak!

31. What cruelty! The ungodly
Vent all their fury in the church,
Where banished from many hearts,

Jesus seeks sure refuge.

32. Will we then have hearts of stone,
And not share in His sorrow?
Ah! Let's suffer with Him on earth
Mingling our tears with His blood.

33. He speaks as to the apostles:
I am abandoned, my friends,
Do you want to leave me also
And join my enemies?

34. Ah! I will suffer these insults
From my declared enemies,
But those I love without measure
Grossly insult me! Weep, my friends.

35. Ah! my Heart is in agony,
For they attack me in my home.
There I am betrayed, denied;
They change my blood to poison.

36. In bitterness my Heart cries out,
It is overwhelmed by sin,
Will you all have hearts of lead
Will no one of you be touched?

37. If you, the faithful, desert me,
I am left completely alone,
Shall I go to the infidels?
They know me less than you do.

38. My heart loves you, desires you;
It is for you that it was pierced.
It sighs so strongly for your heart,
And what! Shall I be forsaken?

GOD ALONE

## 44
## DEVOTION TO THE SACRED HEART

5th POINT
*Practices of devotion to the Sacred Heart*

1st Practice.

1. Come to this Heart, earth's sinners,
Or else misfortunes shall be great;
I can see the rod and thunder
About to fall on sinners.

2. Love this Heart, for it loves us,
Love is repaid with love.
Love with overflowing love,
Purely, night and day.

1
Love the Sacred Heart.

3. All heaven kneels before this Heart,
Calling earth to adore it,
Let us in justice then adore,
For It is the Heart of God.

2
Adore It.

4. Both through love and in justice
To this Heart, we consecrate ourselves.
Let's offer, offer this oblation
Totally and from now on.

3
Consecrate oneself to the Heart of Christ.

5. Let us chant with angel choirs
The grandeur of this divine Heart,
Let us take part in their praises
So that their fervor may be ours.

4
Sing Its praises.

6. Speak of this Heart, preaching boldly
Its greatness and delights.
Let us sigh constantly, lamenting
How few people know this Heart.

5
Promote this devotion.

7. How often we should visit Him
For so many wretched Christians.
This good Heart begs us to do so,
He wants to fill us with His blessings.

6
Visit this Heart in the Blessed Sacrament.

8. With a pure and faithful heart,
A heart filled with devotion,
Let us taste His eternal sweetness,
In our Holy Communions.

7
Receive Holy Communion.

9. Let us go to melt our coldness
In this Heart, the burning bush,
Let us there all graces draw
From His Heart's abundant store.

10. Let us be most grateful
For His innumerable gifts,
Always aware of His presence
In our hearts and in our homes.

8
Give thanks to this Heart and honor Its images.

11. Let us be united, I beg you,
Together vanquishing the devil,
By joining the confraternity
The Church erected in its name.

9
Unite oneself to this Heart in one's actions.

12. In our troubles, and afflictions,
In our most painful trials,
In this Heart, let's place our hope;
It is our Heart, it is ours.

10
Hope in the Sacred Heart.

13. For hope to be sincere,
We must avoid all sin,
And no matter what the cost,
Lie hidden in this wound.

11
Avoid sin and hide oneself in Its wound.

14. This Heart is our life's model,
Let us all assume its mind;
Heart to heart, we follow it
In all its ways and actions.

12
Imitate the Sacred Heart.

15. In famine and abundance
In joy as well as sorrow,
In what we do and what we think,
We stay one with it always,

16. So that our heart may be called
'According to the Heart of God,'
So that we may become people
Filled with grace and all aflame.

13
The purpose of this devotion.

17. The most useful practice,
Most glorious for the Lord,
Most conformed to the Gospel:
Make amends to His honor.

14
Make amends to His honor.

18. Try to make up for the insults
    Hurled against this divine Heart,
    Despite the flesh and nature,
    Despite the world and the devil.

19. While a thousand carnal souls
    Seek only their own pleasure,
    Faithful soul, let us seek Jesus,
    Sparing nothing to adore Him.

## 45
## CONVERSION OF A SCRUPULOUS WOMAN

1. At last I see that with all my scruples
   I get nowhere and hinder all good.
   I'm stuck in the mud, my faults increase.
   *Or:*
   *I live without peace, and my troubles accumulate,*
   *I lose heart and my faith withers.*
   REFRAIN: Wretched scruple, be gone,
   Wretched scruple.
   I obey and love God,
   I obey and I love.

2. When I want to move forward, backwards I go,
   In no way can I advance;
   I swing back and forth like a pendulum.
   Wretched scruple, be gone,
   Wretched scruple.

3. But I am no longer the scrupulous woman,
   A nuisance, a heartache to all;
   I have become affectionate Magdalene.
   Wretched scruple, be gone,
   Wretched scruple.
   I obey and I love God,
   I obey and I love.

4. My troubled ways, my sullen face

Would scare wolves away;
A trifle would upset me.
Wretched scruple, be gone, etc.

5. But now my face is smiling,
Without trouble or care;
I am at peace, I am happy.
Wretched scruple, be gone, etc.

6. When I'd commit a fault or blunder,
Through the effort of the evil one
I used to be troubled, convinced I was lost.
Wretched scruple, be gone, etc

7. But now, when I have fallen,
I ask forgiveness;
I humble myself and God lifts me up.
Wretched scruple, be gone, etc.

8. I only wanted to do as I pleased,
I was always right.
Oh! what a wicked beast I was!
Wretched scruple, be gone, etc.

9. But now I would not want
To take an imprudent step.
I want nothing; Father, tell me what's right.
Wretched scruple, etc.

10. When I had evil thoughts
Which really upset me
I would be troubled, I believed myself doomed.
Wretched scruple, be gone, etc.

11. My thoughts no longer worry me
Taking no pleasure in them,
Renouncing them without scruple or shame.
Wretched scruple, be gone, etc.

12. The evil spirit would twist me in circles
And at his pleasure.
He made me annoying to everyone.
Wretched scruple, etc.

13. As a child at the breast

I obey simply,
Never sly or rebellious.
Wretched scruple, etc.

14. A trifle seemed dreadful to me,
A mole hill, a mountain.
Even good deeds upset me!
Wretched scruple, etc.

15. But now I walk with confidence
I act quite simply,
And that is why I am confident.
Wretched scruple, etc.

16. I regarded God as a severe judge
Always ready to strike,
Lightning in hand and always angry.
Wretched scruple, etc.

17. But now I love God as a Father
Whom I fear to offend
He is my good Father and Mary my mother.
Wretched scruple, etc.

18. Before, I only acted through fear
Almost never through love;
Shame and fear were in my heart.
Wretched scruple, etc.

19. But now the love which rules me
Guides me night and day,
Making me holy and free.
Wretched scruple, etc.

20. Love makes me love obedience,
And seek poverty,
Flee pleasures, embrace suffering.
Wretched scruple, etc.

21. With love, I run through the countryside
With incredible joy,
I cut through the wind, I cleave the mountains.
Wretched scruples, etc.

22. Expect little from a scrupulous soul

For the glory of God;
She is neither strong nor courageous.
Wretched scruples, etc.

23. A trifle exhausts her, a bagatelle offends her,
Because she loves little.
Let us love greatly, then we'll have courage.
Wretched scruples, etc

24. Whoever wishes to leave scruples' abyss
Must reject her own will;
That is the source of scruples and sin.
Wretched scruples, etc.

25. The obedient will chant victory,
They are safe,
They will receive crowns of glory.
Wretched scruples, etc.

26. I would prefer to follow the plow,
Directing the oxen,
Than to direct a headstrong woman.
Wretched scruples, etc.

27. If I tell her, "I want you to obey me,"
She moans, "Father, I can't.
I know myself, and I am so wicked."
Wretched scruple, etc.

28. Both scruples and gloomy nastiness
Come from the evil one,
By one and the other he wins the victory.
Wretched scruple, etc.

29. Let us not fear the Lord with servile fear,
But with a reverence very childlike.
Let us love much; Everything then will be easy.
Wretched scruple, etc.

30. O Jesus, my love, I love you
From the very depths of my heart,
I love you above all, out of love of you.
Wretched scruple, etc.

31. Expand my heart, Virgin Mary,

So I may love Our Savior more,
Guard me from all scruples, the rest of my life.
Wretched scruple, be gone,
Wretched scruple.
I obey and love God,
I obey and I love.

GOD ALONE

## 46
## CONSOLATION OF THE AFFLICTED (1)

1. THE AFFLICTED PERSON:
Oh! How sick I am!
How miserable!
I'm so weary of this bed.
What have I done to the Lord?

2. THE DEVIL:
Weep now, grumble and rage,
Your illness is dangerous.
No one here to console you,
You are wretched indeed.

3. THE FRIEND OF GOD:
How you suffer, brother!
Suffer without languor.
God will be your Father
If you will suffer for Him.
Holy Cross of Calvary,
As long as it, as long as it,
Holy Cross of Calvary,
As long as it will last.

4. To suffer and grumble
Resembles the devil,
Our God is insulted
His name is attacked.
Holy Cross, etc.

5. Oh! the beautiful legacy
   You are winning for heaven!
   Suffer well, have courage
   And try to be cheerful.
   Holy Cross, etc.

6. THE AFFLICTED SOUL:
   My head is killing me,
   I burn like a fire,
   Like a poor animal
   How I suffer! O my God!

7. THE DEVIL:
   No more can you do,
   You are wasting your time;
   What about your mother,
   Your wife and your children?

8. (a) THE FRIEND OF GOD:
   God is punishing you
   But only to test you,
   He strikes, humiliates,
   But only to save you.
   Holy Cross, etc.

8. (b) A year's work
   Although excellent
   Is not worth one day
   Of a cheerful invalid.

9. If you know how to suffer,
   God takes care of your own,
   By himself or by others,
   He knows how to sustain them.
   Holy Cross, etc.

10. THE AFFLICTED PERSON:
    Ah! my pain overwhelms me.
    How horrible my lot.
    How miserable I am!
    How I wish I were dead.

11. THE DEVIL:
    Look, how you are abandoned
    Just like a poor dog,
    No one even offers you
    Help or support.

12. THE FRIEND OF GOD:
    Your hell is beginning,

God is armed against you
And your impatience
Increases His wrath.
Holy Cross, etc.

13. See our Good Jesus
Dying on Calvary.
There is your model,
Do you suffer as much?
Holy Cross, etc.

14. Your place is in hell,
Deign to look at it;
You have the audacity
To complain and to grumble?
Holy Cross, etc.

15. THE AFFLICTED PERSON:
Other misfortunes pass on,
But still to be sick, alas!
No, a saint in my place
Would not tolerate it.

16. THE DEVIL:
To suffer without complaint
Demands flesh made of iron.
So blaspheme, twist and thrash
Like a demon from hell.

17. THE FRIEND OF GOD:
Your cries, your black mood,
Add sins to your soul,
Hell proclaims victory,
You double your ills.
Holy Cross, etc.

18. The wise man embraces
His Cross at all times,
God endows him with grace
Proportioned to its weight.
Holy Cross, etc.

19. A little patience,
Your ills will pass on,
But your great reward

Will last forever.
Holy Cross, etc.

20. Suffering is called
God's divine will,
As long as it's loved,
Received in good spirit.
Holy Cross, etc.

21. THE AFFLICTED PERSON:
My sick bed is worth nothing,
Who cares for me anyway?
Outright scum, you scoundrels,
For this you'll really pay!

22. THE DEVIL:
Your distress how I pity!
Nothing but cold broth, stale bread,
And such rancid meat; you're right,
There is no one who cares.

23. THE FRIEND OF GOD:
What curses! What sins!
Angels weep and flee.
You open the abyss,
And devils laugh loudly!
Holy Cross, etc.

24. The devil inspires you
To distort everything,
And so make you furious
Toward the whole universe.
Holy Cross, etc.

25. If your sickness so bothers you
Say: May God always be blessed!
You will gain not only merit,
But infinite happiness!
Holy Cross, etc.

26. THE AFFLICTED PERSON:
Gout, aches in the belly,
Fever and toothaches,
Asthma, sciatica,
How great are my pains!

27. THE DEVIL:
Yes, your illness is strange,
Succumb under its weight.
You'd have to be an angel
To suffer in peace.

28. THE FRIEND OF GOD:
It is only fair
That a sinner like you,
So filled with malice,
Suffer quietly some blows.
Holy Cross, etc.

29. God disciplines like a father,
Not like an annoyed judge,
Never chastises through anger
But through absolute goodness.
Holy Cross, etc.

30. Heaven takes delight
Seeing you on this bed,
Offering sacrifices
Worthy of Jesus Christ.
Holy Cross, etc.

31. THE AFFLICTED PERSON:
I no longer know what to do,
I will die of sorrow.
Quick, call a pharmacist!
Quick, a good doctor!

32. THE DEVIL:
Keep far from his door
A father confessor,
His presence brings only
Fear and great sorrow.

33. THE FRIEND OF GOD:
What care, what concern, what zeal
For the health of the body!
And for the immortal soul
Not the least effort!
Holy Cross, etc.

34. A patient truly wise
Goes first to confession,
Then filled with consolation,
Prepares for his death.
Holy Cross, etc.

35. The victory you will win
By suffering well,
Thus becoming the glory
And the honor of God.
Holy Cross, etc.

36. Oh! how wise are His blows!
How joyful they make us!
They render Him homage
When suffering is loved.
Holy Cross, etc.

37. THE AFFLICTED PERSON:
My God, I adore you
In your judgments so just;
If you strike me again,
Grant your powerful help.
Holy Cross, etc.

38. In your Most Precious Blood,
I drown my sins and my woes,
And I embrace joyfully
Any new pain.
Holy Cross, etc.

## 47
## ACT OF REPARATION TO THE SACRED HEART

1. O Heart of God, adorable Heart,
Heart, the goal of all my love,
O infinitely lovable Heart,
Who loves me, loves me always.

2. Although so poor and wretched,

Although the greatest sinner,
I now make an act of reparation
To your Heart so full of grandeur.

3. Pardon for all the unfaithful,
Who, though created for you,
Attack you, and damn themselves,
Despite your paternal goodness.

4. Pardon for the schismatics
Estranged from your unity,
Pardon for the heretics
Who contradict your truth.

5. Ah! pardon for their malice,
Pardon for their scandal,
Pardon for all their fury,
Pardon for their cruelty.

6. Pardon, pardon, divine Heart,
We forget you in the Tabernacle;
Pardon for the ungodly Christian
Who constantly profanes you.

7. Ah! pardon for these insults,
For these criminal rendezvous;
Pardon for our irreverence
Which stains your holy altars!

8. They pierce your very Heart,
Which even the devil dare not do.
For this perjury and blasphemy,
Your pardon, Lord, I pray.

9. Pardon for the wayward priests
And all your hidden foes;
Pardon for a thousand traitors
Who receive you, though in sin.

10. Alas! Your life is shattered
In many hearts, despite your love;
Alas! They crucify you there.
O weep my eyes; O flow my tears.

11. Pardon for the cowardly souls

Who sleep next to your altars;
Who, by their hearts so sullied,
Incite your Heart to vomit.

12. Mercy, mercy, for myself,
Frequently approaching you
With so much indifference,
And with a heart so filled with sin.

13. Forgive me my negligence
My lack of preparation
And my cruel indifference,
At the time of Holy Communion.

14. Pardon my ingratitude
For receiving many graces,
Yet hardly even caring
To follow in your virtues.

15. O MY JESUS, MERCY, MERCY!
For all the sins I have committed;
If your Heart does not grant it,
I will be forever lost.

16. My heart, are you insensitive
To Jesus' Heart so despised?
No, no, it is not possible!
His self-surrender was for you.

17. If an infidel Turk's heart
Had loved you as much, you would
Return the love, O rebellious heart;
But this Heart, you do not love!

18. Loving Heart, I now embrace You,
I give myself entirely to you;
How right that I should do so,
For you have first loved me.

19. Alas! Would that I had as many tears
As drops of water in the ocean!
I see so many who attack
This Heart so worthy of our love.

20. Would that I could run throughout the earth

To cry out far and wide:
Sinners, stop all your attacks
On Jesus' loving Heart!

21. Would that I by a thousand praises,
As I crawl along in a hangman's noose,
Make amends for these awful scandals,
Even though I'd be treated like a fool!

22. O Heart, why can I not enthrone You
In every mind and heart on earth!
Why can I not bring to your feet
The hearts of kings and emperors!

23. May at least all these verses
Be as so many preachers,
Making amends for all the scandals
And giving grace to all their readers!

24. Go everywhere to melt the cold,
Go everywhere to destroy all sin,
Go, render homage to your God,
Go, no longer be afraid.

25. Must I refrain from saying
What I taste and what I feel?
Speak, relieve my martyrdom,
Speak, you are the Almighty.

26. Produce by your great power
Some new preachers for the Church,
To proclaim your immense love
And to proclaim your grandeurs.

27. Through the Sacred Heart of Mary,
Honor to your Heart, my Jesus,
Listen to Mary's heart who begs you,
And surely honors you the most.

28. O Sacred Heart, by her breasts,
By her womb which bore you,
Forgive your unfaithful people
The excesses of their cruelty.

29. Enthralled by the divine flame

With which I see your Heart so filled,
It is decided, I now open my breast,
O Divine Heart, enter in.

30. Finally, my request is bold:
Remove from me my sinful heart,
May I have in this life
No other heart than yours.

## 48
## TO THE RELIGIOUS OF THE VISITATION

1. O most holy Religious,
My verses cannot name you,
For I consider you so blest:
This great Heart is yours to love.

2. He has taken you for his own,
Has made his palace among you,
He is also your inheritance
Which not all can claim.

3. From the height of Calvary's Cross
He descended, through MARY,
To your holy father's heart,
And gave Himself completely.

4. This holy, kindly father *[St. Francis de Sales]*,
Like a good, loving master,
Gave you this loving Heart
So you would burn with Its fire.

5. Your Rule is so attractive,
Francis is not so much the author
As is meekness, humble and innocent,
With neither pride nor harshness.

6. What immense glory!
The Heart of the Lamb
Has been born in your home:

Your house is His crib.

7. Since your home He chose for birth,
There He must grow and increase,
You must make His Heart be known,
You must reveal Him to the world.

8. Among you His Heart takes refuge,
Banished as it is from many hearts;
He has found a home among you,
Burn, burn then with its flames.

9. God chose you as depository
Of this most exalted treasure;
It is your task, Reverend Mothers,
To make this gift increase.

10. As, thank God, you do this,
I shall not admonish you;
But do try to be more perfect,
More faithful on this point.

11. Among three Hearts, take your place;
Jesus, Augustine and Francis;
May the first, so full of grace,
Make you as one and not as three.

12. Here are my verses, which I present
To your hearts, all united as one;
If this offering is excellent
It is because as one you share it.

13. If any heart by its own spite
Is not one with the community,
I do not offer my sacrifice
For this evil monster.

14. That soul has left its Center,
This Heart so full of love;
May it now return immediately
Through the opening in its side.

15. Without concern for any rhyme,
Meditate well my humble verses;
Understand their sublime meaning

Making them your own sweet song.

16. If these verses have no impact,
    Let all the fault be mine;
    But may I not be the cause
    Of your refusal to believe.

17. But if my verses enlighten you
    Render glory to the Lord;
    Spread their truths everywhere,
    And make up for what I lack.

18. A priest has such need for wisdom,
    Please include him in your prayers,
    The Heart of Jesus urges you,
    Obtain for him this gift of gifts.
    Amen.

GOD ALONE

## 49
## OUR OFFERING TO MARY AND JESUS' OFFERING TO HIS FATHER BY MARY'S HANDS

1. Today we offer you,
   Blessed Virgin Mary,
   All that we have
   And our very lives.
   Consider this poor place
   Your own realm,
   Where you will be, under God,
   The only Queen.

2. Look upon your dear Son,
   O Father of Lights,
   Answer his soft sobs,
   Grant His prayers.
   We offer Him to you now
   By Mary's hands.
   Be appeased: this dear Child offers you
   Infinite glory.

3. My God, I offer myself to you
By Mary's hands,
To immolate myself
As victim for all people.
Behold my body, behold my blood,
Behold my dear Mother:
Immolate everything from now on
As you wish, my Father!

## 50
## ON THE PERFECTIONS OF GOD

1. Let us adore forever
The Lord in all His gifts. (twice)
Let us bless His mercy,
Proclaim His meekness
Adore His majesty
Honor His might.
Let us adore forever
The Lord in His very being

2. He is good by nature,
Meek without harshness,
Beautiful without blemish,
Great without limit.
Let us adore forever
The Lord in his very being.

3. He has no equal.
When forgiving or punishing,
Creating or destroying,
He is lovable in everything.
Let us adore, etc.

4. He is holy in Himself,
Just in His punishments,
Generous in His gifts,
Gentle to all who love Him.
Let us adore, etc.

5. By His power, He is

Present everywhere,
Both heaven and earth
Are filled with His presence.
Let us adore, etc.

6. His anger is extreme
When He is offended,
But in Himself, He is
Only goodness and love.
Let us adore, etc.

7. His being is more sublime
Than the heavens,
More vast and deeper
Than the sea and the abyss.
Let us adore, etc.

8. How immense is His glory!
The highest seraphim,
All the heavens and the saints
Quiver in His presence.
Let us adore, etc.

9. Oh! how adorable He is!
How sovereign!
How holy, how splendid,
But also how awesome!
Let us adore, etc.

10. Oh! How great a Master!
He has always been
From all eternity,
He will not cease to be.
Let us adore, etc.

GOD ALONE

## 51
## PRAISES OF GOD FOR HIS DEEDS

1. Let us exalt the Lord forever
For His marvelous, wondrous deeds.
With but one word He has drawn
All things from nothing,
The heavens, the sky,
And also both poles.
Let us exalt the Lord forever
For his marvelous, wondrous deeds.

2. By Him alone all things subsist,
There is naught He does not rule
And that includes his enemies;
Nothing resists Him.
Let us exalt, etc.

3. His gentle Providence
Orders all things firmly,
Leads everything wisely,
Without any one being aware.
Let us exalt, etc.

4. He produces and orders
All things even the tiny fly
And without mixup
Knows every item.
Let us exalt, etc.

5. This great God makes the towns,
He stocks the air with birds,
The earth with animals;
He even made the snakes.
Let us exalt, etc.

6. His arm shapes the lightning,
The thunder in the sky,
The tempest on the sea
And the dust of the earth.
Let us exalt, etc.

7. He takes as much trouble
   In making a tiny worm
   As he does a big whale
   In the depths of the sea.
   Let us exalt, etc.

8. He supports all people
   And the whole sky
   As easily as he does
   The smallest of the atoms.
   Let us exalt, etc.

9. Showing no prejudice,
   He seeks only to forgive,
   His great joy is to give;
   He is happy when he does so.
   Let us exalt, etc.

10. He bestows gifts in abundance
    Without ever becoming poor,
    He defers punishment
    But never through weakness.
    Let us exalt, etc.

11. As a clap of thunder,
    This God who settles scores,
    Crushes the emperor
    As well as the worm.
    Let us exalt, etc.

12. This holy Majesty
    Before whom I stand
    One day will judge me;
    I shudder with awe.
    Let us exalt, etc.

13. He searches the dust
    For the innocent poor
    To exalt them on high
    Resplendent with light.
    Let us exalt, etc.

14. In heaven He displays glory
    On earth He shows mercy,
    In hell, His severity,

And everywhere, victory.
Let us exalt, etc.

GOD ALONE

## 52
## PRAISES OF GOD FOR HIS BLESSINGS

1. Let us forever bless
The Lord for his great gifts.
Bless him, holy Angels,
Praise his majesty;
To his kindness render
Unending, lasting praise.
Let us forever bless
The Lord for his great gifts.

2. Oh! How good a Father!
He takes great care of us!
He supports us one and all
Even in our misery.
Let us forever...

3. Like a faithful Shepherd
He has, with greatest toil,
Led back into the sheepfold
The most rebellious sheep.
Let us forever...

4. He has broken all my chains,
Like a mighty conqueror,
And as a kindly Savior
Has saved me from distress.
Let us forever...

5. My poor soul He has healed
Like a kind physician.
Like a benign master,
My calm He has restored.
Let us forever...

6. He has taken for his temple
   Both my body and my heart,
   It is there that his great splendor
   Shines brightly night and day.
   Let us forever...

7. May all things praise in my stead
   A God so filled with love;
   He grants me every day I live,
   New graces for my soul!
   Let us forever...

8. He is my dearest Father,
   He takes good care of me,
   He holds me close to Himself,
   Helping me in my distress.
   Let us forever...

9. His kindness upholds me,
   His light instructs me,
   His beauty ravishes me,
   His love enraptures me.
   Let us forever...

10. His gentleness caresses me,
    His grace heals me,
    His power strengthens me,
    His charity urges me.
    Let us forever...

11. God alone is my tenderness,
    God alone my support,
    God alone is all I have,
    My life and my wealth.
    Let us forever bless
    The Lord for his great gifts.

## 53
## EVENSONG

Let us forever bless
The Lord for His goodness.
Oh! what a good Father!
What great care He takes of us!
He guards us all,
Sustains us all,
Instructs us all,
Forgives us all,
Despite our wretchedness.

## 54
## LOVER OF JESUS

1. Jesus is my only love,
Jesus is my treasure,
Night and day
I repeat, over and over:
Love.
Jesus is my love
Both night and day.

2. Let us go, O my soul,
Let us go to true joy,
Let us love gentle Jesus
Let us love the true and only
Love.
Jesus is my love
Both night and day.

3. Let us speak of Jesus
Despite all the critics
Both in places unknown
And in the public squares.
Love, etc.

4. Let us tell of His virtues,
Proclaiming all His triumphs,
Let us praise all His grandeurs,
Let us celebrate His feasts.
Love, etc.

5. In good times and in bad
To man and to angels
To fools and to sages
Let us sing his praises.
Love, etc.

6. O members of my Body
Holy Love impels you
Enter into rapture,
Love Jesus, and forever.
Love, etc.

7. Love Jesus, O my heart,
Seek His glory in all things
Let this tender conqueror
Sing victory over us.
Love, etc.

8. O my eyes, now be blind
To all things visible;
Leave them for the fools,
Look at God invisible.
Love, etc.

9. O my ears, now be deaf
To all malicious gossip,
Let the many fools chase
After stupid trifles.
Love, etc.

10. O my tongue, speak loudly
To praise our good Savior;
Compose in His honor
A saintly exhortation.
Love, etc.

11. O my hands, keep busy
With some virtuous work
Which makes our Spouse more loved

And renders Him all homage.
Love, etc.

12. Seek, O my feet, seek
This supreme beauty;
Run quickly, go up close
To make my ache cease.
Love, etc.

13. Lastly, sing, O my heart,
Sing this song night and day
Jesus is my conqueror
And He is my only love.
Love, etc.

14. Jesus is my love
Both night and day.
Mary is my love
Both night and day.
Love, etc.

GOD ALONE

## 55
## LOVER OF JESUS

15. Who is my good Jesus?
No one can really say.
For every mind falls short,
Angels do not suffice.

16. From all eternity
This is His holy name:
The Unlimited Truth,
The Eternal Wisdom.

17. He is Supreme Beauty,
Also the Supreme Light,
And the Supreme Goodness,
True God of God the Father.

18. He was born of Mary,
In time He is called
Jesus, Incarnate Word
And the Son of Man.

19. Who is my good Jesus?
His name is the God of armies,
He is the God of strength
Of all the crowned heads.

20. The Lord of lords,
Who gives kings alms,
Master of emperors;
He puts them on their throne.

21. My Jesus is so beautiful,
He is beauty in itself,
He is the meekest lamb,
His tenderness extreme.

22. He is the Almighty,
Doing as He wishes,
Absolutely everything
Stands subject to His rule.

23. I condemn forever,
The prudence of this earth,
For my good Jesus is
The Eternal Wisdom.

24. He is my kind physician,
My adorable leader,
He is my divine spouse,
He is my faithful friend.

25. This infinite treasure
Encloses all things good,
It is in Him alone
That I keep rest and vigil.

26. Since Jesus is in me
I cannot be quiet
For in Him I am king
Of heaven and of earth.

27. O mortals, all now say:
My Jesus, I love you.
If you don't, I will shout:
You are cursed! You are cursed!

28. I love only Jesus
I love only Mary
Do not bother to tell me
Of any other love in life.
Love.
Jesus is my love
Both night and day
Love.
Mary is my love
Both night and day.

GOD ALONE

## 56
## LOVER OF JESUS

29. Be quiet, traitorous world,
I trample on your glory,
Jesus, the great conqueror
Sings over me victory
Of love.
Jesus is my love
Both night and day.

30. Bah! to exterior wealth
My own heart is my kingdom,
In my body, what do I love?
Only Jesus who perfumes it.
Of love, etc.

31. Speak to me no longer
Of the grandeur of this world
For I find in Jesus
All the heavens, earth and sea.
Of love, etc.

32. Speak to me no longer
Of the sages of this earth,
For I know only Jesus,
Jesus on Calvary.
Of love, etc.

33. He has his sanctuary
Deep within my heart,
It is in this secret place
That I love Him in return.
Of love, etc.

34. It matters very little,
Whether I live or die,
Provided the holy fire
Of love remains in me.
Of love, etc.

35. I find in his Holy Name
A powerful weapon
To conquer the devil
And whoever tempts me.
Of love, etc.

36. His conversation I find
Filled with immense sweetness;
None can imagine this joy,
Except by experience.
Of love, etc.

37. Soul, I am yours, He tells me
In His own loving words,
You are my Spouse, love me,
Love me more and forever.
Of love, etc.

38. I tell Him in turn:
My Jesus, I'm Yours,
You are my sole love,
I want no other.
Of love, etc.

39. Money, pleasure, fame,
I reject all of that,

To have in my heart,
Jesus and His Mother.
Of love, etc.

40. Live Jesus in my heart!
Live Mary in my heart!
Speak to me no longer
Of any other love.
Love.
Jesus is my love
Both night and day.
Mary is my love
Both night and day.

## 57
## NOEL OF ANGELS

1. The Most-High, the Incomprehensible,
The Eternal and Almighty
Has just been born.
Is it possible?
The Eternal is one day old, the Word is silent,
The Almighty has become an infant.
Let us acknowledge,
Adore, praise,
Praise, love,
Let us acknowledge
Our God reduced to infancy.

2. Since this good God is born for men
To make them happy,
We owe Him, just as they do,
All that we are.
Let us place at His feet our glorious crowns
Telling Him joyfully:
Gentle child,
All that we have is yours,
Reign over us;
All that we have is yours,
From you alone comes our victory.

3. O Seraphim, in the midst of your fire,
Let us sing glory to God in high heaven,
Grace and peace on earth
To souls of good will.
O Son of the Almighty, O eternal Wisdom,
How glorious your name!
We praise
And bless your name;
We praise
And adore your name,
Even though in mortal flesh.

4. O shepherds, O faithful band,
Join your singing to ours,
God is born for all:
Good news!
Leave there your lambs, seek the true lamb,
Seek Him well, He is yours,
He awaits you
Although He is so great,
He awaits you,
This little child
On hay in a stable.

5. How praiseworthy this day is for us!
The God of all majesty
Becomes in human nature,
One of us.
Let us all then adore Him, acknowledge Him,
Bless His love,
And pay court
To this God of love.
Let all of us, each in turn,
Pay court to Him
Since He is master of us all.

6. O pure and divine Mary,
We admire your happiness
For having given birth
To your Savior.
Singular purity, deep humility,
You have delighted the Lord.
Beloved heart,
He gave himself,
He became incarnate,

Let us proclaim this miracle to the world.

5. GOD ALONE

## 58
## NOEL OF SHEPHERDS

1. THE SHEPHERDS:
   Shepherds, whence come these melodies
   Echoing in these lonely fields?
   Friend, they are angel choirs,
   God has just been born for us,
   It is He they are praising.
   Shepherds, shepherds, why delay?
   Hasten, hasten, let us seek Him.

2. The angels notified us
   That He was born nearby
   And He lies in a stable.
   A King born in a stable?
   Friends, that's hard to believe!
   Let's go, shepherds! Believe me,
   He is there. Let's have faith.

3. Let us bring to this new Infant
   Some fruit, or a lamb,
   As sign of our gratitude,
   Since it is for us
   He becomes a little child.
   Let's go offer this Savior
   The best that we have.

4. Good day, dear awaited Child,
   We all want to welcome you.
   We're here to pay you homage;
   We are only country folk
   All we have are simple things.
   Don't mind our strange accent
   Or our meager presents.

5. JESUS:

Welcome, welcome, shepherds,
You are the first I've called
By my shining angels,
For in your simplicity
You please me no end.
Please, please come close to me,
All of you, don't be afraid.

6. THE SHEPHERDS:
Lord, what are you up to?
Are you not the Sovereign King?
Why be born in a stable?
Why have you taken on
This condition, so poor and wretched.
None of us understands it.

7. JESUS:
Shepherds, I could have chosen
To be born a powerful King
In a rich comfortable palace,
But I have chosen humility
To make it fashionable,
I have chosen poverty
To enrich it with holiness.

8. THE SHEPHERDS:
Although we used to think otherwise,
We believe you completely,
Accepting, according to your wisdom,
Our low state as an honor,
Our poverty as wealth.
Shepherds, shepherds, what great happiness
To resemble our meek Savior.

9. Shepherds, isn't this Child beautiful,
How good to be near His crib!
If only we could stay here!
We would enjoy the holy pleasure
That its little master offers,
We would all see Him freely,
Ah! Let's satisfy our desire.

10. Let's sing, sing with one voice:
We bless you a thousand times,
O Holy Virgin Mary;

You grant life to us all
By giving us the fruit of life.
Please, would you permit us
To remain here near you.

11. JESUS:
Stay here, shepherds, stay
Near me as long as you want,
It makes me very happy too.
Only give me your hearts,
That is the gift I love.
It honors me immensely
That you love me so tenderly.

12. THE SHEPHERDS:
Here are our hearts, Child Jesus,
But hearts of no great worth;
Enrich them, then, we beg you
So we may sing each in turn,
Since you make room for us here:
Child Jesus, by your love,
Reign over us night and day.

GOD ALONE

## 59
## NOEL OF CHILDREN

1. Children, I have been told
That God has just been born,
Whoever loves me, follow me
To this little Master.
Let's go quickly,
Let's go right away.

2. Let's go, dear children,
And kiss His swaddling clothes.
Let our stammering
Form His praises,
Let's say to Him, Good Day!
Let's be His royal court.

3. Little King of heaven,
Everything worships you,
Accept the good wishes
Of our infant hearts.
We greet you,
We bless you.

4. Who put you
In this stable?
Who made you
Poor and wretched?
We all beg you
To come to our homes.

5. We'll shelter you
And your mother,
We'll serve you
In every way.
You'll be happy there,
And have everything you want.

6. JESUS:
God that I am,
I love poverty,
I love contempt,
I love suffering.
I am fine here,
For I've chosen it.

7. My little friends,
Your kindness
Will receive its reward
And recompense.
Although I am a child,
I am almighty.

8. Here, you see in me,
Your own childhood.
Let me also see
In you, innocence,
Simplicity
And love.

9. Prepare your heart,

It is my dwelling place,
Where my grandeur
Always takes pleasure,
It is my gift,
It is my glory.

10. THE CHILDREN:
Accept, O King of heaven,
Our infant hearts,
Reign over them
By your power.
All that we have
We give you.

11. Children, how wonderful
Here in this stable!
O little doll
How lovable you are!
O little lamb,
How beautiful you are!

12. No, I no longer wish
To be caressed;
I have found Jesus
Filled with tenderness.
Oh! how kind He is!
Oh! how divine!

13. Before leaving,
Our kind brother,
Deign to bless us
With your Mother.
O Jesus, Bye bye!
O Mary, Bye bye!

GOD ALONE.

## 60
## NOEL OF KINGS

1. O great kings, do you see a brilliant star in the sky?
How new it is! How mysterious!
It announces that a Savior has been born,
Let us go, let us go adore this great Master.

2. Let's hurry, leave everything without delay,
No disputing over this event.
Do you not feel a new tenderness?
It is the voice of God who calls us.

3. We confidently follow this heavenly light
And in its brilliance, seek the newborn Child.
He comes from afar to show us his love,
Let us travel far to show Him our love.

4. The star stops. What! At this poor place?
Is it here our God is born?
This can not be, it's beyond belief!
Whatever, let's enter the stable.

5. Truly, here is the one we seek.
He is our God; we shall dismount, halt,
Lie prostrate at the feet of this infant,
With respect, love and silence.

6. JESUS:
O kings, you have endured much for me,
I greatly admire your faith.
Stand up, please come near,
Come to me so I can embrace you.

7. THE KINGS:
Hail, O dear Child, O mighty King of kings,
We come to surrender to your kingdom.
We adore your almighty power
Under this lowly appearance.

8. All powerful King, deign to accept this gold,
As true God receive this incense,
As mortal receive this myrrh,

Our scepters are under your command.

9. JESUS:
I take these gifts, I accept these honors;
I want to shower you with favors too,
I will be very generous to you,
You will enjoy my most tender caresses.

10. THE KINGS:
Friends, do you feel the ineffable charm
One tastes near this meek Savior?
Our palaces offer no pleasure
Equal to our bliss in this stable.

11. Let us adore, adore this loving Lamb,
Let us kneel, kneel at the foot of His crib.
He is an infant, but adorable,
He is wretched, but all lovable.

12. Mother of fair love, may everything praise you
For having given us this Infant-God,
For having given birth to the light,
Humanity to the true God, life to our Father.

13. Your example, O Jesus, clearly shows
That greatness exists in lowliness,
Happiness lies in suffering,
True wealth is found in poverty.

14. You raise up our hearts by your humility,
You conquer them by your poverty;
Let your victory reign over us,
Bless us through your Holy Mother.

15. Since we can not linger here
Gazing at your charming features,
Before we leave, bless us, please,
And dwell in our hearts forever.

16. JESUS:
Friends, go in peace with my blessings,
Preach my name's glory everywhere,
Believe in me, bring one and all to believe,
And you will be great kings in heaven.

GOD ALONE

## 61
## NOEL OF PIOUS SOULS

1. Do you see this dear infant
   Lying in the manger?
   He is the almighty Lord
   And the true God.
   Of all crowned heads
   He rules as sovereign Master,
   His hands cup the universe,
   He is the God of armies.

2. Today this dear infant
   Speaks to us in silence,
   All things tell the virtues
   Of His divine infancy:
   We read in His poverty,
   His extreme love,
   All things say: look at His love,
   See how He loves us!

3. The two poor animals,
   These swaddling clothes and stable
   Are the new cantors
   Which now form His praises.
   "Love this little king,"
   They tell with tender tune.
   But one must have great faith
   Or else you will not hear it.

4. How good to see the Savior
   On His mother's breast!
   He presses against her heart
   With loving gentleness,
   He kisses her tenderly,
   Hugs and embraces her.
   His smiles, His tender, charming ways
   Fill His mother with grace.

5. How great is this King of heaven!

Oh! how adorable!
How little He is now,
But how lovable a child!
How attractive
His divine face!
His gentle eyes are mysterious charms
Speaking without words.

6. He preaches humility,
He preaches innocence,
He preaches charity,
He preaches suffering.
Oh! how eloquently He speaks,
Since He speaks by example!
He ravishes, touching to the quick
Those who gaze upon Him.

7. Who can understand His cries
For us to God His Father,
Since He became so small
To calm His Father's ire.
To offer God today
Glory infinite,
He lets Himself be seen
Only as a victim.

8. Behold your beloved Son,
O Father of light,
Listen to His whimpering,
Listen to His prayers.
He entreats you silently,
Speaking by His tears;
Be calmed by His present state
And cast away Your arms.

9. O Jesus, the reason for your plan
To be born in a stable
Is to find in my heart
A pleasing place to stay.
Then come to me now,
Rest in me with glory.
May I be conquered by a child,
O sweetest victory!

GOD ALONE

## 62
## NOEL OF ZEALOUS SOULS

1. You came from heaven
To this place, great Master,
So that you may teach us
The way to be happy;
But I notice no one
Studies your lessons.
What! They abandon you?
Pardon, Jesus, pardon.

2. O adorable Lord,
I make amends
To your grandeur
For all poor sinners.
Loving infant,
Allow me to go
Tell the whole world
To come and talk with you.

3. Miser, you only think
Of money and possessions,
You live in abundance
Nothing do you lack;
And this loving infant
Comes in severe poverty,
In the middle of a stable,
To melt your hardened heart.

4. Proud creature,
Come meet your pitfall
In the loving eclipse
Of the divine Sun.
Can you delude yourself
And lord it over others
Yet see the King of glory
Humbled to our level?

5. Worldly soul, come gaze upon
This infant, it is your turn.

Your life and your example
Boldly attack his love.
Jesus in all his sufferings
Is satisfying his desires,
But you find your pleasure
In wealth and in abundance.

6. O princes of this world
You live in splendid palaces,
All good things in abundance,
You boast of uniformed valets.
The stable is the refuge
Of the Lord of lords,
His food in short supply,
Not one servant to assist Him.

7. O unfaithful Christians,
Why do you pay attention
To a thousand trinkets
You will have to leave behind?
Come into the stable
To discover in an infant
Authentic pleasure
And never ending happiness.

8. He tells you through my lips
That He loves you ardently
And that what touches you
Touches Him infinitely.
Are you miserable?
He will console you.
Are you wounded?
He will heal you.

9. He is so kind:
He is all things for all,
He is an adorable Master,
He is a most chaste Spouse,
He is a very tender friend,
He is a kind physician.
So let's go without more delay
To surrender everything to Him.

## 63
## NOEL OF CHILDREN OF MARY

1. Dear children of Mary,
   Praise the Lord
   For He has filled her
   With grace and gentleness.
   She just gave birth to this adorable Lord,
   Let's all go to congratulate her,
   Let's humbly go to visit
   This admirable Mother.

2. O marvelous Virgin,
   O wondrous prodigy,
   O blessed Mother,
   Your happiness is great;
   Ours is also, you give us life
   Since you break our bonds,
   You shower us with a thousand blessings,
   May you be praised!

3. Finally the prophecies
   Of the Old Testament
   Have been accomplished
   In your giving birth.
   Heaven receives through you a new glory,
   You crush the head of the devil,
   And you obtain forgiveness
   For the faithless sinner.

4. Offering no resistance,
   You have achieved by your consent
   What the whole world
   So ardently desired.
   May we glorify, honor and praise your faith!
   The Savior came to us
   Only because you believed
   The word of an angel.

5. How charming you are
   In your purity!
   How powerful you are

In your humility!
You ravished God, you drew Him from heaven.
Attracted by your beauty,
He took on our humanity,
He could not resist you.

6. Through you, powerful Queen,
God comes to our world
And human nature
Is raised to heaven.
O astounding miracle! God becomes our brother,
You form your Creator,
You give birth to your Savior
And your own Father.

7. This supreme monarch
Shows that He is truly great
By making you
His excellent masterpiece.
Everything in you is mystery, an enormous mystery:
You give birth painlessly,
You beget with the honor
Of remaining virgin and mother.

8. Jesus loves the stable
But above all, your heart,
It is His pleasant bed,
It is His palace of honor.
Your womb is His most glorious throne;
It is there that He makes his greatness known,
It is there that He forgives sinners,
It is there that He distributes alms!

9. O the sweet tenderness,
O the tender smiles,
O the holy caresses
Your dear Son gives you!
Blessed is your womb, pure and faithful Virgin,
For having contained immensity,
For having nourished, for having borne
Eternal Wisdom!

GOD ALONE

## 64
## NOEL OF SPIRITUAL SOULS

1. In order to save man, God
Decided on a marvelous mystery:
He becomes what we are,
Making us become what He is.

2. The most high Lord lowered Himself
To raise us to heaven.
He came into our lowliness
To grant us His glorious life.

3. He became powerless
To make us all-powerful,
He became an infant
To make us immortal.

4. To shower us with riches
His majesty became poor;
In order to caress us
The great Lord became poor and small.

5. To break our chains,
He was bound himself
He took on our sufferings
To give us His pleasures and riches.

6. God became like us
Through infinite love.
It is right and fitting
To imitate and resemble Him.

7. Let us bring Jesus
A diadem to crown Him,
Since He takes off His own
To crown us with it.

8. Rather, let us give Him our souls,
They are His loveliest adornment.
Let us surrender our hearts to His fire,
He yearns to make them His dwelling.

9. Let us go in spirit to the stable
   To kiss His little feet,
   And say to Him: Gentle Child,
   Reign over us as Sovereign King.

10. Gentle Jesus, now is the time
    To ravish our hearts;
    Dwell in them
    For you are the kindest of conquerors.

11. Be blessed, O Mary,
    You are our bliss.
    And you give us life
    By giving us this gentle Savior.

GOD ALONE

## 65
## NINTH NOEL

1. A great Master
   Has just been born for us,
   A new King
   Calls us to the crib.
   Quick, quick, we must get ready,
   Let's go see Him, let's go on our knees.

2. All the angels
   By their praises,
   And their joyful songs,
   Make this place resound.
   Quick, quick, we must get ready,
   Let's go see Him, let's go on our knees.

3. He is called
   God made man,
   The Son of God
   Incarnate in this place.
   Quick, quick, we must get ready
   Let's go to see Him, let's go on our knees.

4. We must hurry,

He is Wisdom
Whose gentleness
Ravishes our hearts.
Quick, quick, we must get ready,
Let's go to see Him, let's go on our knees.

5. Let everything ring,
Let everything resound,
God is made flesh
To save us from hell.
Quick, quick, we'll all bow low,
For He is God, for He is born for all.

6. On the straw,
No nickel or penny,
Poor and small,
In the middle of the night.
Quick, quick, we'll all bow low
For He is God, for He is born for all.

7. I admire Him
As He sighs,
He yearns to have
Some power over us,
Quick, quick, we must get ready
He wants to speak, speak to us all.

8. But we must listen,
He requests
Not some money
But a very fervent heart.
Quick, quick, let's give a heart
A fervent heart to this gentle Savior.

9. Light
In darkness,
Immensity
In captivity,
Quick, quick, let's give a heart
A loving heart to the loving Savior.

10. All power
In powerlessness
Brilliance
In obscurity,

Quick, quick, lets give a heart
A humble heart to this most humble Savior.

11. Poor stable,
Lovable palace,
Your poverty
Is truly rich!
World, world, withdraw,
Don't come to the stable with me!

12. O Mary,
Completely filled
With holiness,
With grace and beauty!
Quick, quick, take my heart,
And give it to Jesus, my Savior.

13. Virgin Mother
I revere you
I bless you
With your dear Son.
Quick, quick, take my heart,
And give it to Jesus, my Savior.

14. May every age
Give Him all praise,
Small and great,
Simple and learned!
Quick, quick, let's give a heart
A loving heart to this loving Savior!

15. Let someone give Him
A crown,
A scepter in His hand,
He is Sovereign King!
Quick, quick, offer your heart;
It's the gift this gentle Savior loves.

16. At my pleasure
Let me kiss Him!
I am delighted
To see this Beloved.
Quick, quick, my gentle Savior
Yes, for ever, take, take my heart.

17. All glory,
    All victory,
    To the gentleness
    Of this conquering child!
    Mother, Mother, take my heart,
    And give it to Jesus, my Savior.

## 66
## NOEL OF SCHOOL CHILDREN

1. Friends, I hear the song of Angels,
   How sweet and melodious!
   They announce in their praises
   A new born babe, King of the heavens.
   They say that he is in swaddling clothes,
   Let us go adore Him with them.

2. Let us then all quiver with delight
   For we have a new King.
   Let us go, His love urges us,
   To adore Him with faith.
   Let us tell Him tenderly:
   Dear Master, rule over us.

3. What do we have to pay Him homage,
   To honor His majesty?
   Our heart is all He wants,
   Let us offer it as pledge
   For He wishes no other guarantee
   Of love and fidelity.

4. Do you see Him in the stable?
   His Mother holds Him in her arms.
   Oh! how beautiful He is, how lovable!
   His face, how full of charms!
   Oh! how sweet He is, how gracious!
   Let us go to Him now, and not tarry!

5. Behold infinite might
   In extreme weakness,
   Behold greatness in miniature,

A sun in darkness,
Whose eclipse invites us
To approach Him confidently.

6. Is it you there, our dear Master,
Our God, our Creator?
Why were you not born
In an emperor's palace?
Your love reveals you,
You seek but our hearts.

7. We are filled with hope
And completely astounded
To see you reduced to infancy.
Love alone accomplished this change,
In order to be, in this powerless state,
Our powerful consolation.

8. Filled then with gratitude,
We kneel at the foot of the crib,
To contemplate in silence
How beautiful its little guest!
Let us offer Him willingly
A contrite heart, a new heart.

9. Having nothing, meek lamb,
That could be a worthy return
Here are our hearts, deign to make them
Your cradle and your dwelling place;
But to make them more pleasing to you
Enkindle them with your love.

10. We have left our school
And our teachers' lessons,
To hear your word,
To become holy and wise.
Speak, nothing will be unimportant,
We believe as children.

11. 1. I am wicked, I want to learn
Your lesson of purity.
2. I am poor, I want to understand
Your lesson of poverty.
3. I am rich, I want to hear
Your lesson of charity.

4. I am proud, I want to accept
   Your lesson of humility.

12. Lord, here is a sacrifice
That each one offers you in his heart:
1. Without naming it, I will avoid a vice.
2. I reject my haughty air.
3. And I, my stubbornness and my whims
4. I want to be kinder.

13. 1. I, for love of you, will give up
This companion and these toys.
2. I, to please you, offer you
My outfit, too expensive and splendid.
3. For you, I gladly forgive
A child from whom I want revenge.

14. Child Jesus, what hinders you?
Take our hearts right now
Please make them a manger
Where you can rest peacefully,
And pierce them with an arrow
To make them love you ardently.

15. JESUS:
Today I am victorious
Although I am but a babe.
I enter your hearts gloriously
And I accept your gifts with delight
Always be ready to believe me
And you will become powerful kings.

GOD ALONE

## 67
## SUNDAY: JESUS IN AGONY

*Refrain:*
It is I who am guilty!
Jesus is innocent.
O how miserable I am!
And with groans I declare it.

## *SUNDAY: JESUS IN AGONY*

God Alone

1. Jesus sees horrendous death
   Closing in with threatening look
   To conquer Him,
   The Almighty though He be.
   Sinners, it is for us
   That He suffers these sorrows.

2. He sees all the crimes
   Of ungrateful man,
   The disdain for His pains,
   His death and his blood.
   It is I who am guilty!
   Jesus is innocent.
   O how miserable I am!
   And with groans I declare it.

3. He foresees that He will be cursed
   Even in the Most Blessed Sacrament
   He has yet to bequeath us as pledge
   Of his so ardent Love.
   It is I who am guilty, etc.

4. At this sight, he shouts
   With choking cry:
   "O My Father! How I beg you
   To spare me all these crosses."
   It is I who am guilty, etc.

5. But this Savior, loving to excess,
   Brimming with charity,
   Now says: My Father, I yearn to do
   Your Holy Will.
   It is I who am guilty, etc.

6. Within this mystifying Agony,
   Ready then to die,
   This great God permits an angel
   Come and comfort him.
   It is I who am guilty, etc.

7. O Christians, Who could ever plumb
   The depths of all His pains?
   Do you see his tender Body

Sweating drops of Blood?
It is I who am guilty, etc.

8. Have we then no feeling,
Are we not moved
As we gaze on the horrible evils
Which our sins inflict on him?
It is I who am guilty, etc.

9. O Jesus, so pitiful,
Why must you suffer so
For you are not the guilty one
But upright and so innocent?
Yes, we are the ones, O sinners,
Who merit all these pains.

10. Jesus, beg your Father
To have mercy on us all,
Or that He flash his anger
On us, rather than on You.
It is I who am guilty, etc.

11. Forgive us for all these sufferings,
O Jesus, caught up in Agony,
For it is our own crimes
That plunge you in such torment.
Ah! We are the ones, O sinners,
Who merit all these pains.

## 68
## MONDAY: JESUS SCOURGED

1. We shall all go to the pretorium,
Hearts overcome with sorrow,
To contemplate the King of glory
Mistreated like a thief.
It is for us, O sinners,
He will suffer these pains.

2. Four executioners full of rage
Like ravishing wolves

Insultingly tear off
All his poor clothing.
It is for us, O sinners,
He endures these pains.

3. This insolent rabble,
Having stripped Jesus,
Rejoices by mocking Him
To confuse Him even more!
It is, etc....

4. They tie Him up, they affix Him
To an infamous post!
They mock Him saying:
Do you see Him? How comely He is!
It is, etc...

5. One has knotted cords,
Another, iron chains,
And all are armed
Like devils from hell.
It is, etc...

6. O how dreadful, how dreadful!
This group of soldiers
Strike with all their strength
His innocent flesh.
It is, etc...

7. They cover Him with wounds,
They tear Him with lashes,
One sees only bruises,
Welts, gaping wounds.
It is, etc...

8. He can do no more, this good Master,
His blood flows in streams,
His bones are visible,
His flesh torn to shreds.
It is, etc...

9. Alas! From weakness
He falls in His blood,
Yet they do not cease
To batter innocent Jesus.

It is, etc...

10. Oh pitiless executioners,
    Stem your wrath;
    We are the guilty ones,
    Strike us instead.
    Yes, we are the ones, O sinners,
    Who merit these pains.

11. Consider that He endures
    This appalling torment
    Without complaint or murmur,
    So ardent His love.
    It is for us, O sinners,
    He endures these pains.

12. O Sovereign Clemency
    See Jesus, your Son!
    Cease your vengeance,
    Or let us be punished.
    It is, etc...

13. The executioners, exhausted
    Can strike Him no longer
    But through his immense love
    He would suffer still more.
    It is, etc...

14. Sinners, these are our offenses
    And our sensuality
    Which cause such sufferings
    To this man of sorrows.
    It is, etc...

15. Come, loathsome sinner,
    Consider the pain
    You cause the only Son
    Of the Sovereign Creator.
    It is you, ungrateful man,
    Who bring Him to this state.

16. Come! In the blood of His veins
    Find your cure,
    Do not increase the suffering
    By following your passions.

It is you, etc...

17. Let us, let us do penance,
    We must weep over this evil night and day;
    How grateful we must be,
    Returning love for love.
    It is you, etc...

18. O meek Savior,
    By this body bruised by blows
    Calm your anger
    And pardon us all!
    For we are the ones, O sinners,
    Who merit these pains.

## 69
## TUESDAY: JESUS CROWNED WITH THORNS

1. Jesus, is painfully clothed again
   With His torn garments;
   O look how they drag Him
   So harshly, kicking Him.
   It is for us, O sinners
   That he endures these pains.

2. Christians, we must follow in the footsteps
   Of this most innocent lamb,
   For every place He walks
   Remains stained with his blood.
   It is, etc.

3. As with an animal,
   They drag Him, whipping Him.
   They stop him, numb with cold,
   At the palace gate.
   It is, etc.

4. He is hardly in the hall,
   In the midst of these criminals,
   When he is dressed up like a king

So they may scream their contempt.
It is, etc.

5. With gross insults, they throw
A ragged cloak over him,
First ripping off his garment
Glued to his blood-soaked skin.
It is, etc.

6. A jagged rock serves
As a royal throne;
Being more easily seen,
More blows he receives.
It is, etc.

7. In his sacred hands, they put
A frail reed as a scepter;
Mocking him, they screech:
Ha! Isn't he pretty!
It is, etc.

8. They crown him with thorns
Pounding it in with a stick,
Mocking him constantly,
Howling like demons.
It is, etc.

9. This cruel crown
Pierces his skull,
His brains are seen oozing
With blood and water.
It is, etc.

10. With a filthy rag
They blindfold him,
Shrieking: You wretch,
Guess who struck you!
It is, etc.

11. Are you not a false prophet
Who wants to rule over us?
Comrades, be rough!
Let no one stop striking!
It is, etc.

12. They all spit in his face
    Horrible, filthy spittle,
    Showing their homage
    With incredible shrieks.
    It is, etc.

13. They mockingly adore
    By slapping his face;
    Hail, O King of Judah!
    Ah! How handsome you look!
    It is, etc.

14. They shout at him
    Their insolent tirades.
    A guard sticks out his tongue,
    Another grinds his teeth.
    It is, etc.

15. No, these aren't men
    But furious devils!
    Do you see those who smack him?
    One hits harder than the next.
    It is, etc.

16. At this pitiful sight
    Will we not be moved?
    Even reason demands it.
    And alas! it is for our sins.
    Yes, O sinners, we are the ones
    Who cause Him these pains.

17. He suffers extremely yet endures it
    Without even raising his eyes,
    Without complaint or murmur
    At all these harsh torments.
    It is for, etc.

18. From head to foot
    He is wounded by blows.
    Oh! if this were a beast
    We would all pity it!
    It is for, etc.

19. Our intolerable pride
    Always seeks prominence;

That is the real executioner
Who causes him sorrows.
Yes, it is we, O sinners,
Who cause Him these pains.

20. Proud people, come, be overwhelmed
As you gaze at your God so despised;
How then will you answer,
You, who crave to be praised?
It is for, etc.

21. Our bitter heart with stinging remorse
Now sees the difference
And is torn to shreds
Watching Jesus suffer.
For it is you, etc.

22. We must always remember
This loving Savior,
May contempt be our glory
And suffering our joy!
For it is you, O sinners
Who cause him these afflictions.

23. O most pitiful Jesus
Suffering unjust contempt,
Look with favorable eye
On our bowed, contrite hearts.
For it is we, O sinners,
Who cause Him these afflictions.

## 70
## WEDNESDAY: JESUS SENTENCED TO DIE

1. Let us follow our dear Master
Led with a noose around his neck
So that he will appear to all
As nothing but a fool on trial.
It is for us, O sinners,
That he endures these sorrows.

2. In this wretched state,
Wreaked by the executioners,
None can recognize Him
So beaten is He!
It is, etc.

3. Pilate, even though ungodly,
Moved to pity on seeing him,
Strives to save his life, realizing
Jesus is innocent
It is, etc.

4. Trying to calm the rage
Of this rebellious people,
He displays Jesus garbed
As the torturers left him.
It is, etc.

5. As soon as they look on him,
Only howls fill the air;
Mocking and scorning him,
Grinding their teeth.
It is, etc.

6. His Face so disfigured,
Covered with spittle,
His flesh itself torn:
The thankless mob is not moved!.
It is, etc.

7. His sorrows and misery
Not touching their hearts,
Increases their anger
Making them furious.
It is, etc.

8. Pilate cries: Behold the man!
Have pity on him!
Pilate has to so name him,
Otherwise they could hardly tell.
It is, etc.

9. At these words, the people
Shout, stomping their feet,:

Do away with him! Take him away!
Crucify him!, crucify him!
It is, etc.

## 71
## THURSDAY: JESUS CARRYING HIS CROSS

1. All abandon Jesus!
Will he die under this weight?
No one is not horrified
By the heavy cross he bears.
It is for us, O sinners,
That He endures these sorrows.

2. A foreigner who passes by,
Called Simon the Cyrenean,
Coerced by promises and threats,
Helps in shouldering the cross.
It is, etc.

3. Jesus utters to some women
Weeping over His sufferings:
Shed tears rather for your own souls
And for those of your children too.
It is, etc.

4. Look upon the pitiful state
Which befalls the guiltless Jesus!
What will happen to the guilty
And to the arrogant sinners?
It is, etc.

5. Veronica, so enflamed
With strong and fervent love
Boldly pushes through the crowd
To see Jesus, whom she loves.
It is, etc.

6. She wipes His holy face
Bloody and disfigured;
Jesus as a tribute

Leaves his face imprinted.
It is, etc.

7. What then! Is it possible
Oh miserable sinner,
That your heart be unfeeling
Toward the sorrows of your Savior?
It is, etc.

8. Since these are our offenses
Weighing heavily on his back
How could we fuel His torment
By offending Him again!
It is, etc.

9. Jesus, your immense love
Bore our sins and offenses.
Show us your mercy!
May they all be forgiven.
For it is we, O sinners,
Who deserve these afflictions.

## 72
## FRIDAY: JESUS CRUCIFIED

1. That arrogant rabble
Tears from Him again
His poor bloody robe
All stuck to His skin.
It is, etc.

2. While the most barbarous
Ready everything for his death
A few of the most greedy
Draw lots for his clothes.
It is, etc.

3. His murderers cry out
While pulling his hair:
Finish off your miserable life!
Accursed! Lie down there on the cross!

It is, etc.

4. They throw him on the ground
To nail him to the wood
But see how ardently
He embraces this cross.
It is, etc.

5. They stretch his sacred hands
With great cruelty
To attach them directly
On the readied holes.
It is, etc.

6. O cruel barbarism!
His limbs pulled out of sockets,
His flesh all torn;
Look! His tendons are bare.
It is, etc.

7. Now lying on the cross
At the feet of these monsters,
They bore with nails
Both His hands and feet.
It is, etc.

8. Oh what cruel suffering
These sharp nails cause!
His body pierced like a sieve
Loses blood. It can endure no more.
It is, etc.

9. Come, sinner, and contemplate
Gentle Jesus as He dies,
Begging you in His misery
To consider His torments.
It is, etc.

10. To make Him suffer more
Instead of wine and honey
They give Him as drink
Vinegar with gall.
It is, etc.

11. Do you see how He endures

Such contempt and mistreatment?
Instead of cursing
He prays for his murderers.
It is, etc.

12. The presence of his Mother
Increases his torments
Seeing that in some way,
Every second, she dies.
It is, etc.

13. I see Him surrendering his soul
Heaving a deep sigh.
I feel my heart swooning
As I watch my God die.
It is, etc.

14. Heaven and earth together
Manifest their sorrow:
The earth quakes
The sea is furious.
It is, etc.

15. Even the sun and the moon
Lose their brilliance
In this universal grief;
Only man is not moved.
It is, etc.

16. Sinners, let us do penance,
Since He has suffered for us.
Let us share His sufferings,
Kissing His feet and the nails.
It is, etc.

17. To kiss us tenderly,
He lets His head fall low.
Do you see how He implores us
Stretching out His arms to us?
It is, etc.

18. We no longer disturb the silence
Except to say, sighing:
Almost no one thinks
Of gentle Jesus as he dies.

It is, etc.

19. Let us all make our hideaway
Within his sacred side,
A lance prepared it for us,
We shall be safe within.
It is, etc.

20. Let us all cry mournfully:
Forgive us our sins!
O pitiful Jesus,
Forgive us our sins!
For it is we, O sinners,
Who deserve these afflictions.

## 73
## SATURDAY: JESUS DIES AND IS BURIED

1. O abominable sinners,
It is finished. Jesus is dead.
We are all guilty.
What will become of us?
It is for us, O sinners
That He died in torment.

2. Let us not leave Calvary,
Let us all die here,
Hoping to satisfy
The justice of God.
It is, etc.

3. Do you see His holy Mother
Who, sighing, kisses Him?
Bitter, bitter is her sorrow,
For her love is so great.
It is for us, O sinners
That she endures these sorrows.

4. She groans and swoons,
Fainting, she says:

Oh! beloved of my soul,
Is that You? I am about to die.
It is, etc.

5. Do I see the adorable body
Of my beloved Son?
Alas! it is so pitiful!
Yes, it is He, now I recognize Him.
It is, etc.

6. I see on your Face only
Spittle and blood
No beauty, no grace.
Oh my Son, how changed you are!
It is, etc.

7. Whence come these gashes,
These dislocated arms
The caked blood, these wounds
And the pierced hands and feet?
It is, etc.

8. Let us mingle our tears with hers,
Let us embrace His sacred feet
And in the blood from His veins
Wipe away our sins.
It is, etc.

9. To avoid the vengeance
Of God the angry Father,
Let us put all our trust
In His sacred side.
It is, etc.

10. Let us seek profound peace
With Jesus in the tomb,
And live there, far from the world,
To acquire a new heart.
It is, etc.

11. Obtain for us, O Mary,
Forgiveness from your Son!
We want to change our lives,
Answer our contrite hearts.
It is, etc.

12. O gentle Jesus, may an arrow
    Of love from your heart
    Breach ours, so we may
    Die of sorrow.
    It is, etc.

13. Engrave in our memory
    Your passion and death
    So in heaven we may
    Share in your grandeur.
    From now on we are determined
    To acknowledge your blessings.

## 74
## SUFFERINGS OF THE BLESSED VIRGIN AT THE FOOT OF THE CROSS

1. Contemplate Mary suffering
   Near the Savior's holy cross,
   See her saintly soul pierced
   By the sword of sharp sorrow.

2. She groans, she sighs,
   With throbs of love,
   She suffers a great martyrdom,
   Not apparent to our eyes.

3. Jesus dying is her torture;
   Love, her greatest torment,
   Her heart, her great sacrifice.
   O my God, how great her torment!

4. Seeing on a wicked gibbet
   The object of her desires,
   In her soul, she suffers more
   Than all martyrs together.

5. She feels the same wounds
   As her beloved dying Son,

She is the unique echo of His groans,
The true portrait of his pain.

6. Her tears flow in abundance,
She trembles, turning pale.
Her body is about to faint;
Her great love sustains her.

7. Sinners, by our offenses,
We make Mary and Jesus
Two very innocent victims.
Ah! never again shall we sin.

8. Oh our divine Mistress,
We all sympathize with you.
May your heart filled with tenderness,
Entreat your dear Son for us.

9. Pierce our heart with an arrow
Of love from your heart,
So that our breached heart
May share in your sorrow.

10. Let us share in your sufferings,
O Mother of Fair Love,
To expiate our offenses,
Offering you some return.

AMEN.

## HYMNS IN HONOR OF THE BLESSED VIRGIN

## 75
## RECOLLECTED DEVOTEE

1. Although the world
And all hell rant,
Glory o'er the earth
To Heaven's Queen!
Hasten, hasten, let us beg her
To calm God in His just anger,

*Or:*
Hasten, hasten, let's all greet her
With a thousand *Ave Maria.*

2. May we proclaim
Her everywhere
For her beauty
And her great love.
Hasten, etc.

3. Would you believe it?
She is my oratory
Consumed with fire
Where I burn for God.
Hasten, etc.

4. She is my mother,
She is my light
She nourishes me,
Enlightens and guides.
Hasten, etc.

5. How beautiful she is!
And how faithful!
She is my dwelling,
She is my loving rest.
Hasten, etc.

6. She is my glory,
She is my victory,
By her holy name
I crush the devil.
Hasten, etc.

7. Under her wing
And her care
Nothing do I fear
And I find all good.
Hasten, etc.

8. It is through her
That I have recourse
To the goodness
Of the angered Lord.
Hasten, etc.

9. Everything through her
And nothing without her,
This is my secret
To become perfect.
Hasten, etc.

10. She is my ardor,
She is my soul,
She is my honor,
She is my all, my heart.
Hasten, etc.

11. Even more,
I have her image
Engraved in me
To show me the King.
Hasten, etc.

12. Good women,
Faithful souls,
Chosen ones,
You will believe me.
Hasten, etc.

13. O Mary,
Completely filled
With holiness,
Grace and beauty.
Hasten, etc.

14. Amiable virgin,
Admirable mother,
Your charms
Are beyond words.
Hasten, etc.

15. O Servant
All-powerful,
You have only to wish
And all is done.
Hasten, etc.

16. Let all ring out,
Let all resound:

Mary has the first place
After God.
Hasten, etc.

17. God appoints her
Sole mistress
Of all His goods,
Nothing excepted.
Hasten, etc.

18. Her prudence
Grants and bestows
All His treasures,
Despite the free thinkers.
Hasten, etc.

19. She was born
Immaculate
Sin has never
Tarnished her beauty.
Hasten, etc.

20. I am astounded
That this is disputed:
God could easily do it,
I maintain that he should.
Hasten, etc.

21. She is the Queen,
The Sovereign
Of the universe,
Of heaven and of hell.
Hasten, etc.

22. Her speech
Is not frivolous,
What she says
Is without question.
Hasten, etc.

23. The impossible
Becomes possible,
Everything is easy
When Mary has spoken.
Hasten, etc.

24. She is rich
    But not stingy,
    Oh! what joy
    To be her servant!
    Hasten, etc.

25. By grace
    She surpasses
    The blessed
    Of earth and heaven.
    Hasten, etc.

26. To her charms
    All surrender,
    Sinners are converted
    Devils are crushed.
    Hasten, etc.

27. Whoever imitates her
    Is her disciple
    All her friends
    Are also her Son's.
    Hasten, etc.

28. Mercy
    Is only accorded
    To those who follow her,
    Pray and praise her.
    Hasten, etc.

29. No affronts,
    No shipwrecks,
    No tribulations
    For her good servants.
    Hasten, etc.

30. Anathema
    To him who loves her not.
    Accursed will be those
    Who neglect her.
    Hasten, etc.

31. Virgin Mother
    I revere you

I bless you
With your dear Son.
Hasten, hasten, accept my heart
And give it to Jesus my Savior.

32. I love you
More than myself
More than my own heart,
After Jesus, my Savior.
Hasten, hasten, pray for us
And calm God in his just anger.

GOD ALONE

## 76
## MARY'S TRUE DEVOTEE

1. I love Mary ardently,
After God, my Savior;
I would surrender my life
To win for her a single heart.
Oh! what a kind Mistress!
If she were known
Everyone would rush
To serve her. (*twice*)

2. To be dependent on her,
God became man here below,
How could I refuse
To follow in his path.
She is the faithful Virgin
Whom I must imitate.
Every grace comes through her
To her I must then pray. (*twice*)

3. Jesus finds his glory
In the honor shown to her,
It is an error to believe
Or to say otherwise.
But to place her first,

Or to love her without imitation,
Is such an error gross,
It cannot be pardoned (*twice*)

4. Far from me the heretics,
The fickle, scrupulous persons,
The proud spirits, the critics
And all haughty people.
I invoke her constantly,
I imitate her everywhere,
I love her, O so tenderly
And I delight God. (*twice*)

5. She is tender and merciful.
Everything in her so gentle.
She never sends someone away,
She is the helper of us all.
Jesus, her Son urges me
To love her tenderly,
My own good demands it,
How can I do otherwise? (*twice*)

6. She is the Sovereign
Of the whole universe,
In her domain
Lie both heaven and hell.
She has in her power
The graces of Jesus.
She gives and lavishes
The Holy Spirit's gifts. (*twice*)

7. She is the tabernacle
Where God became a child.
She is the greatest miracle
Of His almighty arm.
She is Daughter of the Father
The Mother of Jesus Christ
And by a profound mystery,
The Holy Spirit's Temple. (*twice*)

8. Mary has no equal
Among all the blessed.
She is the great marvel
Of all earth and heaven.
She is the great enemy

Of the wretched devil.
Just the name of Mary
Plunges him to hell. (*twice*)

9. Saint Austin proclaims
And rightfully so:
She is the brilliant image
Of the Divinity,
She is the very splendor
Of the Lord of Lords.
She is the immense ocean
Of all His magnificence. (*twice*)

10. Although garbed in light
Near God her Son,
She is the mother
Of earth's little ones.
She enters Purgatory
To break its chains;
She proclaims victory
Even in hell. (*twice*)

11. She is more brilliant
Than all cherubim,
She is more afire
Than all Seraphim.
Lastly, she outshines
All that is not God;
After Him, by grace,
She holds the first place. (*twice*)

12. Under her patronage
Never will I fear;
My hope is to crush
The Tempter everywhere.
Staying faithful to her,
Then will I be blessed
And by her I will rise
To the highest heaven. (*twice*)

13. Accept, my loving Princess,
My feeble stammering,
Excuse my total weakness
For I am but a child.
May everyone, in my stead,

Tender you honor
And offer to you
The gift of his heart. (*twice*)

GOD ALONE

## 77
## DEVOUT SLAVE OF JESUS IN MARY

1. Sing out my soul! Make known
To the glory of my Savior,
Mary's great mercy
Toward her poor servant.

2. Would that I had a voice of thunder
To proclaim far and near:
The happiest people on this earth
Are those who serve her best.

3. Christians, open your ears!
Listen to me, chosen souls!
The marvels I shall now relate
Of her who gave you birth.

4. MARY is my greatest fortune
And my all at Jesus' throne.
She is my tenderness and my honor,
The treasure house of all my worth.

5. She is my Covenant Ark
Where all holiness I find,
She is my robe of innocence
Concealing all I lack.

6. She is my divine oratory
Where Jesus is always found,
I pray there all times blissfully,
Never fearing a rebuff.

7. She is my city of refuge
Where I cannot be harmed.

She is my ark in deluge;
There, I shall never drown.

8. On her I am totally dependent,
On my Savior more so to depend,
Leaving everything to His care,
My body, soul and all my joy.

9. When I rise to God my Father
From the depths of my iniquity,
On my Mother's wings I'm carried,
Thanks to the goodness of her support.

10. To soothe Jesus in His anger,
Comes so easy with Mary.
I tell Him: "Behold your Mother"
And He is calmed at once.

11. This kind Mother and Mistress
Greatly helps me everywhere
And when I fall through weakness
She raises me up right away.

12. When my soul is troubled
By my daily sins,
It becomes unruffled,
Saying: Mary, help!

13. She tells me in her own way
When I am in a struggle:
Courage, my child, courage,
I shall not abandon you.

14. As a baby at the breast
I am held so close to her.
This pure and faithful Virgin
Feeds me milk all divine.

15. Here is something hard to grasp:
In my heart's center I carry her
Etched with strokes of glory,
Yet in faith's darkness still.

16. She makes me pure and fruitful
By her pure fecundity,

She makes me strong and docile
By her deep humility.

17. Mary is my clear fountain
Where I discover all my flaws,
Where I delight so freely
And temper all my passions.

18. I go through Jesus to his Father,
Never am I rebuffed;
I go to Jesus through his Mother.
Never am I spurned.

19. I do everything in and by her,
What a secret of holiness,
Keeping me ever faithful
To always do God's holy will.

20. Christians, provide, I implore,
For my huge infidelity;
Love Jesus, love Mary,
In time and in eternity.

GOD ALONE

## 78
## PRAYER REQUESTING WISDOM

O all-powerful Father, O most gracious God,
From heaven bestow Divine Wisdom on us,
Grant her to us, grant, (*twice*) love urges you.
Answer, (*twice*) answer the sighs of the poor.

Gentle Virgin Mary, answer your children's plea,
Obtain from God, Divine wisdom for us.
Pray for us, pray, (*twice*) love urges you,
Be merciful (*twice*) to our pressing needs.

## 79
## SINNER CONVERTED THROUGH MARY'S PLEA

1. Listen, poor sinners, to the goodness of Mary:
   She has filled me with blessings,
   And it is from her that I have
   Life, life, life.

2. My sins deserved only eternal damnation,
   Hell was justly my due.
   I would be already lost
   Without her, without her, without her.

3. God was about to damn me; our most tender Mother
   Prayed to Him so much, insisted so much
   That He felt constrained
   To delay, to delay, to delay.

4. Who now understands how good she is to me,
   Will he now proclaim her mercy
   And her generosity?
   No one, no one, no one!

5. Mary is my only support in my great misery,
   In all my pressing needs
   Like a child I call to her:
   My mother, my mother, my mother!

6. Does the devil with his minions tempt me?
   I invoke her without end.
   At the name of Mary,
   He flees, he flees, he flees.

7. She guides and leads me to eternal life,
   For in dangerous places
   I glance quickly
   Toward her, toward her, toward her.

8. Seeing that I owe much yet am always untrue,
   She becomes my ransom,
   My supplement, and my faithful

Pledge, pledge, pledge.

9. If I suffer some ill, she helps and consoles me;
If I am about to drown
She comes herself to calm
The storm, the storm, the storm.

10. If the devil tempts me, if I fall or have fallen
She comes benignly
To raise me and offer me her powerful
Hand, hand, hand.

11. Above all, she fills me with deep peace,
With love for Her dear Son,
With horror and contempt
For the world, the world, the world.

12. What causes this dear Princess
To take care of a sinner?
It is the love of her heart
Bent low, bent low, bent low.

13. Does any sinner want to smash his shackles
And keep from perishing?
Let him come then to serve her.
Let him come, let him come, let him come.

14. If my serious sins and my extreme woe
Have not limited her kindness,
Let him hope with confidence
For the same, the same, the same.

15. Does anyone want to taste her maternal kindness?
Let him imitate her fervently
And be to her always
Faithful, faithful, faithful.

GOD ALONE

## 80
## MARY'S ZEALOUS DEVOTEE

1. CHRISTIANS, do you want happiness?
Then obey Mary faithfully.
For she is the gate of heaven
And the path to eternal life.
She is a merciful mother
No one is ever turned away.

2. Ah! if we could comprehend
All her maternal kindness
We would endure anything
To be her faithful servants.
She is, etc.

3. Christians, are you troubled?
Then cry out for her help
And you will be consoled
Almost beyond all hope.
She is, etc.

4. Are you tempted by the devil
And on the brink of the abyss?
You will conquer the temptation,
If you choose her as your patron.
She is, etc.

5. Hasten, hardened sinners,
Beg her with confidence,
To obtain from her Son
A heart contrite and healed.
She is, etc.

6. Her mercy stretches forth
Even to the earth's end,
She heals and she protects
All over land and sea.
She is, etc.

7. She is the devils' terror
The ruin of all heretics,

The honor of Holy Sion
The firm support of Catholics.
She is, etc.

8. Do you yearn for fervor,
A penitential spirit?
Then serve her faithfully;
Be not fickle or lukewarm.
She is, etc.

9. She lavishes her favors
On her most faithful servants;
She captivates their hearts
By ever new delights.
She is, etc.

10. Let us imitate little children
Who rely only on their mother:
Mother! Mother!, they always cry,
It is their ordinary prayer.
She is, etc.

11. Let us humbly tell her:
Dear Mother and Mistress,
Be our consolation,
All our strength and our wealth,
Although sinners, accept us
- - - *[verse cut during the binding of the manuscript]*

12. Pray to your dear Son for us
And keep us in His grace
So one day we may be with you
To love and see Him face to face
For all eternity,
For all eternity.

GOD ALONE

# 81
# BLESSED VIRGIN HYMN TO BLESSED GODRIC
# (AN ENGLISH HERMIT, TO HEAL HIM OF THE SORROW HE WAS EXPERIENCING)

1. O holy and divine Mary,
   When I behold all your beauty,
   When I hear speak of your kindness,
   My poor soul is wholly ravished.
   Let me be your lowly servant,
   May I offer you, after God, all honor!

2. The Word, in God his Father,
   Rests eternally
   And has chosen you, in time,
   For his resting place and mother.
   Happy the womb that bore him
   And clothed him in humanity!

3. Among the purest virgins,
   Your purity shines forth
   As the holy humanity
   Shines among all creatures.
   Your womb, so pure and virginal,
   Ravished God from his royal throne.

4. You alone are all-beautiful,
   Without sin, without any fault,
   Never displeasing the Most High.
   Wholly faithful in everything,
   During your sojourn here on earth
   You always loved God, night and day.

5. You alone are the virgin mother,
   Your splendor is a mystery
   That no one will ever understand.
   You are, by a great mystery,
   The flower of virginity,
   The marvel of maternity.

6. You alone are sovereign Queen
In heaven and on earth,
You have power over hell.
Everything depends on you,
God has placed all in your hands,
You distribute all his gifts.

7. O Mary, tree of life,
Heal poor sinners, guard them
From all calamities.
May your Child give them life.
Be their support on earth
And their refuge at death.

8. You alone are my Queen,
Your Son alone my King,
May you both govern me,
He the King, you the Queen.
I fear no enemies
With such powerful friends.

9. Allow me, my good Mistress
To find grace with the Savior.
Fill my heart with great fervor
And banish from it all gloom,
So that I may contemplate
Your kind beauty for ever.

GOD ALONE

## 82
## FROM A CHILD OF MARY

1. Divine Mary,
Most fruitful Virgin,
Divine Mary,
I love your beauty
For it enflames,
O Holy Lady,
All my soul
With charity.

My heart is wholly ravished.

2. O my good Mother
I love and revere you.
O my good Mother
I render you all honor.
O my Mistress,
Your tenderness
Constantly nourishes
My poor heart
With its grace and gentleness.

3. Would that I could say,
Everywhere I wish,
Would that I could say:
O mortals, beg
With confidence
Her help
And her mercy,
For you will obtain
All that you ask for!

4. She is a gentle refuge,
So safe and accessible,
She is a gentle refuge
Open to all, no need to fear.
The troubled soul
That finds her
Is consoled,
The sinner
Receives favors through her.

5. Come, everyone, hear
How loving she is to me!
Come, everyone, hear:
She is my help and support,
She is my faithful one,
My most beautiful one.
Under her care
Nothing do I fear.
In her, I find all treasures.

6. It is through her
That I adore and love,
It is through her

That I speak to the Lord.
What riches,
What caresses
What tenderness
In her holy Heart!
Oh! How happy when I dwell there.

7. A humble silence
Full of confidence
A humble silence
On her loving breast
Calms God our Father
Of His anger.
This prayer
Pierces the heavens
And obtains all I desire.

8. She is my oratory
Where I pray joyfully
She is my oratory
Where I am never refused.
She is my petition,
She is my offering,
But, hear me
For I say even more:
She is my dear all toward Jesus.

9. O my protector
My mother and nourisher,
O my protector
Nothing do I have to give you!
In my place,
May each one give something.
Would you please permit
That your love
Reign in all hearts night and day.

10. Be blessed then
May everything glorify you,
Be blessed then
On earth as in heaven.
May you be blessed,
May you be loved
And honored
Here on earth

So we may all be blessed in turn.

GOD ALONE.

## 83
## MEMORARE
## OR THE POWERFUL PRAYER OF SAINT BERNARD

1. Remember, Virgin Mary,
   Your heart is so benign,
   Never has it been known
   To pray to you in vain.

2. No one has implored you,
   Confiding in your help,
   Not blest with your assistance,
   Not delighting in your love.

3. With contrite heart, O Mother,
   I dare invoke your name,
   And despite my sins, I still hope
   Your protection to attain.

4. Show then to me your mercy
   By obtaining from your Son
   Contrition and forgiveness
   For the grave sins I have done.

5. Please look on me with favor.
   O let me not be rebuffed,
   For all my sins and malice
   Are far less than your great love.

GOD ALONE

## 84
## REGINA COELI

1. O glorious Queen of heaven
   May your loving heart
   No longer be sad,
   Let it leap for joy,
   Jesus is risen!
   O most blessed truth!
   Let us all sing ALLELUIA!
   And then, Ave Maria!

2. Our sins are forgiven,
   The devils are crushed,
   Jesus, clothed in glory,
   Has won victory over them all.
   The proud are humbled,
   They will not rise again.
   Let us all sing ALLELUIA!
   And then, Ave Maria!

3. He has closed hell,
   Freed our fathers from fetters,
   Opened eternal glory and
   Won universal peace.
   At last, Jesus is Conqueror
   For the salvation of sinners.
   Let us all sing ALLELUIA!
   And then, Ave Maria!

4. O Mother of Fair Love
   Thrill with joy on this day.
   May the angels, may man,
   May all of us, whosoever we may be,
   Each respond in turn
   And solemnly celebrate this day
   By singing ALLELUIA!
   And then, Ave Maria!

5. O worthy Mother of God,
   May all things praise you everywhere,
   O most glorious Virgin,

O thousand times blest,
For having borne
This magnificent King of majesty.
Let us all sing ALLELUIA!
And then, Ave Maria!

6. Obtain for us from Jesus
A share in all his virtues,
A share in his new life,
So that everyone may proclaim
For all eternity:
JESUS IS RISEN!
Let us sing ALLELUIA!
And then, Ave Maria!

GOD ALONE

## 85
## MAGNIFICAT

1. My soul magnifies
My Sovereign Lord,
And God has filled it
With grace and meekness;
For, after groaning so long in wait,
His sovereign majesty
Has looked upon the humility
Of His servant's heart.

2. Generation after generation,
By marvelous accord,
Will call me blessed
On earth and in heaven,
For the mighty Lord has wrought deep within me
Stunning wonders.
How holy and powerful His name!
May He be adored and loved!

3. He has shown mercy
To those who fear Him,
He is their protector,
He Himself upholds them.

But who would not fear His wrath?
His just, mighty arm
Scatters the haughty
In heart and mind.

4. Like a clap of thunder,
This just God who settles scores,
Has overturned on earth
The prince and the emperor.
He has placed the lowly at the summit of glory,
Enriched the innocent poor,
And impoverished the arrogant rich.
Oh God, what a victory!

5. As he did to our ancestors,
God made a promise
To pluck from misery
All His suffering people.
At last He granted us what he had promised,
He takes fatherly care
Of His servant, Israel.
What mercy!

6. May everyone adore and bless
Our one true God!
May everything resound
And all sing throughout the world:
Glory to the eternal Father, glory to the adorable Word!
And the same glory to the Holy Spirit
Whose love unites them
With an ineffable bond.

## 86
## IN HONOR OF THE NAME OF MARY

1. To the beautiful name
Of amiable Mary
I shall, throughout my life,
Be completely devoted.
O charming name

You fill my heart
With amazing joy,
I have savored
Your great sweetness,
Your fragrance engulfs me.

2. I can neither explain
Nor understand
How tender this name,
Nor what its charms.
O sacred name,
Sure remedy
For the greatest afflictions.
This name provides
In the midst of our labor,
Buttress and brace.

3. This divine name
Gives angelic joy
To anyone gloomy,
By scattering sorrow.
Are you tempted?
Invoke this name:
Safety is yours.
In it is found
Consolation
When we are troubled.

4. The devil takes
Shameful flight,
With his underlings,
As soon as he hears it.
If we are afraid,
This holy name braces us,
Making us brave.
We fear nothing
Even at midnight
When the name is well prayed.

5. In sum, the name offers
All gifts for all, without reserve:
It protects, it guards,
It teaches and strengthens;
We should then bow
And doff our hats

Whenever we say it,
Giving example to others.
O what joy is ours,
Carrying it always
Engraved in our heart!

## 87
## IN HONOR OF JESUS ALIVE IN MARY AT THE INCARNATION

1. Let us adore Jesus
Alive in Mary's womb.
Consider with amazement
The Almighty made tiny.
Adore God become infant
Giving us life.

2. A sacred temple is this womb
Where God takes all delight,
A sky always radiant
With the Sun of justice;
Our refuge certain,
Where God, most merciful, dwells.

3. In this womb, night and day
He takes delight.
Mary, in turn, loves Him
With all her might:
What loving return
Of mutual affection!

4. Oh! how generous Jesus is
To His Mother most pure!
He bestows on her virginal womb
His grace without limit.
Her heart becomes his royal throne,
His dwelling-place unfailing.

5. While totally attached
To her undivided heart,
Which the slightest sin

Had never sullied,
He painted there with no restraint
His own authentic image.

6. Their hearts stoutly united
By intimate bonds,
Jointly offer themselves
As two victims,
Abolishing the punishment
Our sins deserve.

7. In this mystery
The elect were born.
Mary, united with Jesus,
Chose them beforehand
To share their virtues,
Their glory and their power.

8. How stunning this mystery!
What marvelous bliss!
What blessed raptures
Of these two loving hearts!
Only in heaven shall we know
These awesome secrets.

9. They both seem to merge.
How beautiful their union!
Mary is totally in Jesus,
Her most faithful lover,
Or better, she no longer is,
But Jesus alone in her.

10. Between these two hearts
We warm our coldness,
Share their ardor,
Their virtues, their graces.
Let us go, they love sinners,
We shall find a place there.

11. O Mother of Divine Love,
O rich sanctuary,
Bearer of our Sovereign,
And of our salvation,
Send this meek Lamb
Into our hearts.

12. O Jesus, our dear spouse,
    Our God, our brother,
    Come, come, be born in us
    By your Holy Mother,
    So that by you we can
    Go to your Father.

13. Come by your humility,
    Making us childlike;
    Come by your holiness
    Restoring our innocence.
    Come by your charity
    To reign over us totally.

GOD ALONE

## 88
## LITTLE CROWN OF THE VIRGIN MARY

1. Joyfully we all sing
   A melodious hymn
   To divine Mary,
   The giver of Life.
   Let's sing as best we can,
   Imitating the blessed.

2. Since we are all her servants,
   We show her endless honors
   May each of us offer her
   A sparkling crown.
   Or at least add a flower
   To her crown of honor.

3. She is the great masterpiece
   Of the Almighty God.
   May each one of us offer her
   A sparkling crown.
   Or at least add a flower
   To her crown of honor.

PATER NOSTER

4. She has conceived her Savior,
   Her Father and Creator.
   May we proclaim her blessed,
   A thousand times blessed.
   She has conceived her Savior,
   Her Father and Creator.

AVE MARIA

5. Virgin during birth
   Virgin after birth.
   May we proclaim her etc.

AVE MARIA

6. Never has the slightest sin
   Sullied her purity.
   May we proclaim her, etc.

AVE MARIA

7. She is the mirror of the virtues
   And the splendor of Jesus.
   May we proclaim her, etc.

AVE MARIA

8. Glory be to the Father, to the Holy Spirit
   And also to Jesus Christ.
   To God alone let us offer homage,
   Mary is His masterpiece.
   Glory be to the Father, to the Holy Spirit
   And also to Jesus Christ.

GLORIA PATRI ET FILIO

9. When we render her homage
   It returns to her creator,
   May each one of us offer her
   A sparkling crown.
   Or at least add a flower
   To her crown of honor.

OUR FATHER

10. She is the Queen of Heaven
And the honor of this earth.
May we proclaim her, etc.

HAIL MARY

11. Grace and divine gifts
Are all bestowed through her hands.
May we proclaim her, etc.

HAIL MARY

12. She calms in an instant
The wrath of the Almighty
May we proclaim her, etc.

HAIL MARY

13. She crushes the devil,
All hell trembles at her name.
May we proclaim her, etc.

HAIL MARY

14. Glory to the Father, to the Holy Spirit,
And also to Jesus Christ.
To God alone let us render homage,
Mary is His masterpiece.
Glory be to the Father...

GLORIA PATRI ET FILIO

15. After God, among the Saints,
Mary has the first place.
O charming Mistress!
O powerful Princess!
After God, among the Saints,
Mary has the first place.

PATER NOSTER

16. She is the sure refuge
Of the despairing sinner.

May we proclaim her, etc.

AVE MARIA

17. She is the Mother of All Christians
Who showers them with all good.
May we proclaim her, etc.

AVE MARIA

18. She is filled with tenderness
To win hearts for God.
May we proclaim her, etc.

AVE MARIA

19. She is the haven of the living
She is the support of the dying.
May we proclaim her, etc.

AVE MARIA

20. She is the Mother of Jesus,
One can not say more.
That is the glory of glories
The victory of victories
The crown of crowns.
Let all mortals chant:

21. In heaven, on earth and everywhere:
Mary is the Mother of God.
She is the Mother of Jesus,
One can not say more.

AVE MARIA

Glory be to the Father, etc.

GLORIA PATRI ET FILIO

PRAYER

O merciful Mother,
Can you look on us
And not be touched

By our prayers?
We all call out to you, we sigh constantly.
Come, come to our aid
To defend and protect us
Charity impels you,
Grant us Wisdom.

GOD ALONE.

## 89
## TRIUMPH OF THE AVE MARIA

1. Let all sing out and proclaim
With lofty, noble voices,
The greatness of the Ave
In praise of Holy Mary.
By the Ave Maria
Sin will be destroyed.
By the Ave Maria
Great Jesus will reign.

2. O divine prayer,
If you were truly known,
Everyone on this earth
Would pray you night and day:
By the Ave Maria
Sin will be destroyed.
By the Ave Maria
Great Jesus will reign.

3. Never have the heretics,
Never have the doomed
Truly experienced
Its angelic sweetness.
By the Ave, etc.

4. O soul by God chosen,
It is yours to praise,
Yours it is to relish
The Ave, God's hidden manna.
By the Ave, etc.

5. Angels in glory,
Man in the world,
Devils in hell,
Souls in purgatory.
By the Ave, etc.

6. God redeemed the world
By the Hail Mary.
By it, He will renew
The earth and the seas.
By the Ave, etc.

7. The Ave ravished Mary
And her faithful consent,
And now she is still ravished
When she hears the Ave prayed.
By the Ave, etc.

8. By its grace, it makes fertile
Everything here below.
Yet it is not valued
Though its grace has no equal.
By the Ave, etc.

9. The earth was once sterile,
But when the angel said Ave
It brought forth its Fruit,
The earth became fertile.
By the Ave, etc.

10. By the Ave, now listen well,
Sinners are converted,
Devils are defeated,
And hell is running scared.
By the Ave, etc.

11. The Ave profoundly enthralls,
Making everyone surrender;
The greatest enemies of God
It strips and disarms.
By the Ave, etc.

12. God himself in his wrath,
Cannot resist its power;

When He hears the Ave,
From judge, he becomes father.
By the Ave, etc.

13. What a powerful weapon
In fighting temptation,
And in all afflictions,
A delightful balm.
By the Ave, etc.

14. Whoever prays the Ave
With solid devotion
Crushes the devil,
Putting all hell to flight.
By the Ave, etc.

15. It makes angels rejoice,
Also Mother and Son;
And all Paradise
Cries out its praises.
By the Ave, etc.

16. It obtains forgiveness
And grace for the sinner
And for the just, fervor
And true perseverance.
By the Ave, etc.

17. The Ave enlightens, enflames,
It protects and it nourishes,
It comforts, it heals,
It grants the soul grace.
By the Ave, etc.

18. The Ave does everything.
If one prays it often
And very devoutly,
It turns ice into fire.
By the Ave, etc.

19. The Ave quickly wins over
A heart most rebellious,
The obstinate heretics
Soon become believers.
By the Ave, etc.

20. When you pray it well
You're rich and so wise,
Although, as you say,
You can't even read!
By the Ave, etc.

21. As for me, no matter what's said,
In order to please God,
I pray it everywhere,
At home and in church.
By the Ave, etc.

22. When I arise or retire,
Go out or come home,
Outdoors, in the house,
It is always in my mouth.
By the Ave, etc.

23. I am invincible,
Having prayed my Ave,
I am full of spirit,
No fear of the devil.
By the Ave, etc.

24. The devil and the world
Have often attacked me
To take my Ave away;
When they rant, more Aves I pray.
By the Ave, etc.

25. O salutary advice!
O marvelous secret!
To become perfect,
Say a rosary a day.
By the Ave, etc.

26. Whoever does this faithfully
Will advance quickly,
Will live perfectly,
Will die peacefully
And will surely obtain
Eternal life.
By the Ave Maria
Sin will be destroyed.

By the Ave Maria
Great Jesus will reign.

## 90
## ROSARY OR CROWN OF MARY

1. O most faithful Virgin, (*twice*)
All of us have come to greet you
And to praise you
In a novel way.
May our praises,
Through our holy Angels,
Serve only to crown you.

2. 1st PATER:
We praise your masterpiece,
Eternal Father, all-powerful God;
We offer you more fitting homage
By praising her.
Everything in Mary
Glorifies you
Forever, perfectly.

3. 1st AVE
Hail Mary,
O daughter of the eternal Father,
Look upon, I beg you,
A criminal
Offering you
A crown
With the Archangel Gabriel.

4. 2nd AVE
Hail Mary,
Worthy Mother of God the Son,
May everything glorify you
Here on earth.
O beautiful Dawn,
Break anew,
So Jesus may shortly reign over us.

5. 3rd AVE
Hail Mary,
Dear Spouse of the Holy Spirit,
May you be blessed by all
Without exception.
Without delay,
Through you, may the spirit of Jesus
Come down upon me.

6. 2nd PATER
We praise your masterpiece,
Eternal Word, all-powerful God;
We offer you more fitting homage
By praising her.
Everything in Mary
Glorifies you
Forever, perfectly!

7. 1st DECADE – 1st AVE
Hail Mary,
In your glorious mysteries!
Let everyone pray them
As best he can.
My faith increases
Because I'm singing
With a faithful and joyful heart.

8. 2nd AVE
Hail Mary,
Pure in your Conception!
May my lips proclaim it
Even to Sion.
I believe it
For your glory
Despite the world and the demon.

9. 3rd AVE
Hail Mary,
At your birth!
Virgin brimming over
With holiness.
Break, O Dawn,
So that the Sun of Truth
May shine.

10. 4th AVE
    Hail Mary,
    At your Presentation!
    As a pure victim
    Of holy abandonment.
    O virgin and mother,
    By this mystery
    Grant me piety.

11. 5th AVE
    Hail Mary,
    In the temple where the Holy Spirit
    Completely filled you
    Without a sound!
    Mother of Grace,
    Make yourself at home
    In my heart with Jesus Christ.

12. 6th AVE
    Hail Mary,
    At your Annunciation!
    Virgin completely full
    With the unction
    Of Wisdom
    Who caresses you
    And who comes to you from Sion.

13. 7th AVE
    Hail Mary,
    At your Visitation!
    Your soul proclaims the greatness
    Of God's Name.
    Virgin faithful
    And most beautiful,
    Grant me the gift of prayer.

14. 8th AVE
    Hail Mary,
    At the birth of the Savior!
    May everything sing and proclaim
    Your happiness.
    O Virgin and Mother
    I am in awe of you,
    Give birth to Jesus in my heart.

15. 9th AVE
Hail Mary,
At the Purification!
I adore the Victim you bear,
He is a baby.
I declare him the master
Of my entire being,
For he makes himself my bail.

16. 10th AVE
Hail Mary,
At the finding of Jesus in the temple!
Perhaps, Mary, my friend,
I have lost him.
May I find him,
May I relish him
In the tenderness of His virtues.

17. 3rd PATER
We praise your masterpiece,
O Holy Spirit, all-powerful God;
We offer you more fitting homage
By praising her.
Everything in Mary
Glorifies you
Forever, perfectly.

18. 2nd DECADE – 1st AVE
Hail Mary,
At the foot of the Savior's cross
Where you are
The fragrant victim.
O Mother of bitter grief!
On Calvary!
Let me share your sorrow.

19. 2nd AVE
Hail Mary,
When Jesus was laid low
By grief at the agony
In the garden.
Alas! my sin
Made him victim
By the working of divine love.

20. 3rd AVE
Hail Mary,
When your Son was scourged.
Oh! what atrocity
My sin caused!
May God grant me
Mercy
Through His holy body, all flayed.

21. 4th AVE
Hail Mary,
At His cruel crowning,
You were moved to pity
On seeing Him.
May Jesus grant me,
By His crown,
A more humble and fervent heart!

22. 5th AVE
Hail Mary,
When my Savior was condemned
To die on the cross
Like a thief!
Accursed world,
Though you growl,
I say to you: woe upon woe!

23. 6th AVE
Hail Mary,
When Jesus fell beneath his cross
You were stricken
To the depths of misery.
What sorrows,
What agonies,
You both suffered together!

24. 7th AVE
Hail Mary,
Near your dying Son,
Tearful and transfixed
On contemplating
The ignominy,
The barbarism
Of his cruel crucifixion.

25. 8th AVE
Hail Mary,
When your Son rose
And by infinite grace
Visited you.
What elation
Dear mistress,
Then ravished you!

26. 9th AVE
Hail Mary,
When Jesus ascended into heaven,
In His new life
Most glorious.
By you I hope,
My dear Mother,
To ascend to the joys of heaven.

27. 10th AVE
Hail Mary,
The Descent of your Spouse
Has completely filled you
Even for us;
By your requests
His gifts descend.
Pray: nothing is granted without you.

28. 3rd DECADE - 4th PATER
We praise your masterpiece,
Eternal Father, all-powerful God;
We offer you more fitting homage
By praising her.
Everything in Mary
Glorifies you
Forever, perfectly.

29. 1st AVE
Hail Mary,
In your divine communions,
Throughout your life.
Your actions
Are a model
Pure and faithful.
We fashion ourselves on you.

30. 2nd AVE
Hail Mary,
Deceased through a transport of love!
O Divine Fire
Of pure love,
Burn my soul
With your flame,
Everywhere, night and day.

31. 3rd AVE
Hail Mary,
At your Holy Assumption,
Raised up and ravished
To Sion.
O great Queen
And Sovereign!
On us all, a blessing!

32. 4th AVE
Hail Mary,
Enthroned and crowned in heaven!
Be also blessed
On earth.
Grant us grace,
Grant us place
In your glorious reign.

33. 5th AVE
Hail Mary,
Both Virgin and Mother.
O infinite marvel
Of the King of kings!
Fruitful Virgin,
With no peer,
Make me obedient to your rule.

34. 6th AVE
Hail Mary,
Admirable Mother of the Savior,
May everything sing and proclaim
Your splendor!
You gave being
To your Master,
You form your Creator.

35. 7th AVE
Hail Mary,
Full of grace and beauty,
Virgin brimming
With holiness.
Faithful Virgin,
Your patronage
Grants a sinner safety.

36. 8th AVE
Hail Mary,
Sovereign of the Universe.
May everything glorify you
Even hell!
Purgatory
Gives you glory,
You can break its fetters.

37. 9th AVE
Hail Mary,
Treasurer of divine gifts.
Open for us, I beg you,
Your holy hands.
And may grace
Pass through them
To us, making us holy!

38. 10th AVE
Hail Mary,
You alone crush the devil.
The evil one then screams
In his prison.
Behead
This beast,
And arm us with your name.

39. 4th DECADE - 5th PATER
We praise your masterpiece,
Eternal Word, all-powerful God;
We offer you more fitting homage
By praising her.
Everything in Mary
Glorifies you
Forever, perfectly.

40. 1st AVE
Hail Mary,
Mirror of the Divinity.
Virgin brimming over
With charity.
O Holy Lady,
May my poor soul
Love you for all eternity.

41. 2nd AVE
Hail Mary,
Amiable Mother of Christians!
Share with us, I beg you,
Your riches.
Our troubles are increasing,
Everyone looks to you,
Come, break all our bonds.

42. 3rd AVE
Hail Mary,
Dear advocate of sinners!
Take, I entreat you,
Take our hearts.
In everything
Plead the case
Of your faithful servants.

43. 4th AVE
Hail Mary,
Our refuge and firm support
During our entire life,
Right up to death.
Dear Mistress,
Great Princess,
Bring us safely to shore.

44. 5th AVE
Hail Mary,
Refuge of us all.
Virgin all blessed,
Pray for us.
Be the Mother
And the light
Of those who have recourse to you.

45. 6th AVE
Hail Mary,
Full of humility.
Share it with me, I beg you,
Through charity.
Dear Mistress,
Great Princess,
I will bless your goodness.

46. 7th AVE
Hail Mary,
Full of strength and fervor.
Bestow some of it, I beg you,
On my heart.
Dear Mistress,
Great Princess,
Free me from being lukewarm.

47. 8th AVE
Hail Mary,
Full of grace and beauty.
Share these with me, I beg you,
Through charity.
Dear Mistress,
Great Princess,
Be generous.

48. 9th AVE
Hail Mary,
Full of the gift of prayer.
Share with me, I beg you,
A ray of it.
Dear Mistress,
Great Princess,
Do not deny me this gift.

49. 10th AVE
Hail Mary,
Mirror of Virginity
Most gifted Virgin,
Have pity.
Hands, generous
And virginal,
Adorn me with purity.

50. 5th DECADE - 6th PATER
We praise your masterpiece,
O Holy Spirit, all-powerful God;
We offer you more fitting homage
By praising her.
Everything in Mary
Glorifies you
Forever, perfectly.

51. 1st AVE
Hail Mary,
Filled with the gifts of the Holy Spirit,
Share them with me, I beg you,
Without exception.
Dear Mistress,
Great Princess,
For the glory of Jesus Christ.

52. 2nd AVE
Hail Mary,
All wisdom is in you,
You are filled with it
Even for us.
All for the victory
And for the glory
Of Jesus, dead on the cross for us all.

53. 3rd AVE
Hail Mary,
Filled with all virtues.
May you be blessed
With Jesus.
Dear Mistress,
Great Princess,
May my enemies be overcome.

54. 4th AVE
Hail Mary,
Full of all gentleness.
I beg you, fill
Your servants with tenderness.
Gentle Mistress,
Great Princess,
Win our hearts for Jesus Christ.

55. 5th AVE
Hail Mary,
Contemplating your rich poverty,
May each one of us cry out:
What goodness,
What wealth,
What bounty,
What generosity!

56. 6th AVE
Hail Mary,
Sure Refuge of sinners
Whom God Himself has filled
With His tenderness.
God our Father
Is angry,
Calm His just wrath.

57. 7th AVE
Hail Mary,
Great Miracle of the living God,
O awesome mystery
Of the All-powerful!
May men and angels
Offer praise
To your tremendous Maker.

58. 8th AVE
Hail Mary,
Paradise of the Trinity
In all Its infinite glory.
O truth
Most astounding
Most consoling!
Glory to God forever.

59. 9th AVE
Hail Mary,
All transformed into Jesus!
Jesus is your life,
You are no longer.
O marvelous,
O blessed Mary!
Your mysteries are beyond understanding.

60. 10th AVE
Hail Mary,
I offer you my poor heart,
I offer you my life
And my honor.
Allow, please,
That all good things pass
Through you to God, my Creator.

61. GLORIA PATRI
Honor, glory, praise
To the Most Holy Trinity
By every man and angel
With total truthfulness,
Since Mary
Glorifies the Trinity
Much more than all creation.

62. JOYFUL TRANSPORT
Our crowns are made
Of roses, violets, lilies
And of a thousand little flowers
Of Paradise;
The good angel
Arranges them,
Adding no showy flowers with them.

63. Mary is crowned,
She holds our bouquets in her hand
And her head is adorned
With our chaplets.
May everyone give her
This crown
That never, never wilts.

GOD ALONE.

# HYMNS FOR SEVERAL PERSONS OF DIFFERENT STATES OF LIFE WHERE THEY CAN SEE, IN SUMMARY, THE RULES THEY MUST KEEP IN ORDER TO LIVE THEIR STATE OF LIFE ACCORDING TO GOD

## 91
## GOOD MISSIONARY

1. I roam through the world
   Like a lost little child,
   Seeking, though scolded,
   Neither income nor wealth.
   Having nothing
   I possess everything.
   All that I own
   Is my obedience.

2. I am a hunter of souls
   For Jesus my Lord;
   Contempt and censure
   I get in return.
   Having nothing
   I possess everything.
   All that I own
   Is my obedience.

3. O wealthy people,
   You are my landlords
   But neither lawsuit nor fighting
   Will get you your rent.
   Having nothing, etc..

4. To one, then to another,
   Carefree I go,
   Like an apostle, yet
   Have my daily needs met.
   Having nothing, etc.

5. I envy no one
His wealth or good fortune
And I strive only to be
Like the poorest of heart.
Having nothing, etc.

6. Since God my father
Cares for me infinitely,
I let Him do everything
To take care of me.
Having nothing, etc.

7. God's interests alone
Are my own interests,
And I say be cursed
To whatever annoys Him.
Having nothing, etc.

8. My prudence is surely quite clever:
Giving up all things, I have everything,
Without cellar or kitchen,
Without income or dwelling.
Having nothing, etc.

9. I live quite comfortably
Like a small bird;
Without money's burdens,
The higher I fly.
Having nothing, etc.

10. Without baggage I travel,
My walking stick in hand,
With nothing of comfort,
But also without grief.
Having nothing, etc.

11. I preach and explain
Simply, without fuss;
I just don't bother with
"What will they say."
Having nothing, etc.

12. Neither man nor woman
I notice at all,

I see God alone and their souls
And speak as well as I can.
Having nothing, etc.

13. If the world condemns
What I say or I do,
I cry: Move on, brother ass,
Don't fall under the load.
Having nothing, etc.

14. If a town or village
Cares not to hear me,
Not creating an uproar
I go elsewhere to preach.
Having nothing, etc.

15. Since the whole earth
Is chock-filled with sin,
There's no lack of work,
Every town excites pity.

16. Whether I live or die
Bothers me little,
Provided I remain
Poor, and wealthy in God.
Having nothing, etc.

17. Be rich in this world?
Lord, I would prefer death!
On you alone I depend
For I am all yours.
Having nothing, etc.

18. O precious pearl,
O divine poverty,
How happy the soul
That truly loves you!
Having nothing, etc.

19. My state makes me master
Of the whole world;
But to understand the world well
One must leave everything.
Having nothing, etc.

20. I am not in style
Except with the beggars,
I get along with them well
And I share their lot.
Having nothing, etc.

21. I am a clever lender,
For one, I gain a hundred;
For a creature,
I gain the living God.
Having nothing, etc.

22. My way to glory
Is the widow and orphan.
My weapon for victory:
Solidarity with them.
Having nothing, etc.

23. I neither plant nor sow
Except in childlike hearts
And so I harvest God himself
And all Paradise.
Having nothing, etc.

24. The rags the poor wear
Let me understand them
And show me their castles
And their kingdom in heaven.
Having nothing, etc.

25. With much indifference
I look at swanky people,
But with all reverence
At destitute beggars.
Having nothing, etc.

26. Without reasoning or caution,
With no will of my own,
Holy obedience
Keeps me safe and sound.
Having nothing, etc.

27. I am, when commanded,
Like a one year old child.
I would never ask

The why or the how.
Having nothing, etc.

28. To God himself I say:
I would prefer to die
And to die accursed
Than ever disobey.
Having nothing, etc.

29. I honor and respect
Every superior;
None is too harsh for me
Since I am a sinner.
Having nothing, etc.

30. In Paris as in Rome,
In the lawmaker
I no longer see man
But God alone, my creator.
Having nothing, etc.

31. If I am slandered,
I say: God be praised!
If someone hurts me
I tell him: *Merci!*
Having nothing, etc.

32. The cross is my treasure,
The cross is my pleasure,
The cross is my teacher:
Either suffer or die.
Having nothing, etc.

33. I proclaim everywhere:
Live Jesus forever,
Live Mary forever
In my heart, and naught else!
Having nothing ...
I possess everything
I love Jesus and Mary
And nothing else.

GOD ALONE

## 92
## GOOD SISTERS DIALOGUE OF THE THIRD ORDER

1. SISTER FRANCES:
Are you not the Sister devoted
To Saint Francis?
Your contemplative bearing reveals it
So often.

SISTER DOMINIC:
I am a Sister of Saint Dominic.
What do you think of that?
SISTER FRANCES:
Both of them are seraphic.
So let's be united.

2. SISTER DOMINIC:
Why would we be at odds,
My dear sister?
Our saints loved each other here on earth
So ardently.
They both now enjoy the same glory
In the Lord.
My dear Sister, we must be believed,
Let's be of one heart.

3. SISTER FRANCES:
Both are the great patriarchs
Of the same era.
Both are living arks
Of God's Covenant.
Francis and Dominic are both
True faithful servants
And the two are for all,
Sanctity's excellent models.

4. SISTER DOMINIC:
If one finds on Calvary
His element,
The other finds it in his Rosary
Equally.

One had his flesh pierced
Like his God;
By the same fire, the other had
His soul touched.

5. SISTER FRANCES:
They are both children of Mary,
Her most beloved,
She gives both of them life
In her dear Son.
One, at Our Lady of the Angels
Was enriched.
The other, by proclaiming her praises
Was exalted.

6. SISTER DOMINIC:
Our two Orders are very similar,
My dear sister,
Our habits only differ
In their color.
To encourage us even more
To purest love,
Let's now speak its holy language,
Each one in turn.

7. SISTER FRANCES:
My habit, ashen tinted, either
Gray or brown,
Does not indicate or denote something
The least bit common.
It signifies perseverance
By its length;
Poverty and penance
By its color.

8. SISTER DOMINIC:
My black cloak, from top to bottom,
Studied well,
Shows but contempt for the world,
Death to all things.
My hidden, all white tunic
Clearly tells that
Under the black cloak, my soul
Is truly risen.

9. SISTER FRANCES:
Our two habits, my dear friend,
Symbolize well
All the virtues of the life
Of good Christians:
Poverty, penance,
And purity,
Charity and patience,
Humility.

10. SISTER DOMINIC:
It is prayer that nourishes me
Every day
Although the flesh moans and grumbles,
Still I pray.
When I am dry or distracted
By Satan,
I persevere in prayer, in perfect peace
To the end.

11. SISTER FRANCES:
I obey in all things
Blindly.
I do not trust my prudence
At all.
My dear father, what should I do?
Tell me.
Eat, fast, speak, be quiet?
Guide me.

12. SISTER DOMINIC:
I preach through modesty
By silence,
My meek and simple manner edifies
Tacitly.
My countenance is so simple
And gentle,
Full of happiness and kindness
And meekness.

13. SISTER FRANCES:
I am neither harsh nor sarcastic
In reproving,
I am meek and compassionate
In punishing,

I offer to everyone
My service.
When I can give or forgive,
It's my pleasure.

14. SISTER DOMINIC:
Now in utmost confidence
I tell you:
On Mondays I abstain from meat
And Wednesdays.
I fast during Advent, Lent,
Ember days,
Vigils, and even all Saturdays,
Loyally.

15. SISTER FRANCES:
To satisfy God's justice
And his wrath,
I secretly wear a hair shirt
With fervor.
I take the discipline or belt despite
My feelings,
Sleeping on straw or on the floor,
Most always.

16. SISTER DOMINIC:
I go to confession and communion
Most frequently
In order to receive true life
And nourishment.
I usually say every day
My rosary,
Sometimes even fifteen decades,
To be perfect.

17. SISTER FRANCES:
My sister, I cannot tell you how much
My heart
Seeks, sighs and longs for my Savior,
My God.
Jesus Crucified is my wisdom,
My home.
He is my honor, He is my wealth,
My love.

18. SISTER DOMINIC:
    I go through Jesus to His Father,
    Fittingly.
    I go to Jesus through His Mother
    Most surely.
    My goal is to do everything in her
    And by her;
    To be always faithful to God, this is
    My secret.

19. SISTER FRANCES:
    The last shall be first has not our God
    Said.
    I take, being the least, the lowest
    Place,
    Without flattery, or vanity,
    Pride,
    I truly humble myself at everyone's
    Feet.

20. SISTER DOMINIC:
    Cursed be the world, cursed,
    My heart cries,
    For I have only extreme horror
    For this deceiver.
    Neither its threats nor its promises
    Nor its illusions,
    Nor its contempt nor its caresses
    Ever bother me.

21. SISTER FRANCES:
    We should never bicker about the graces
    Of the blessed,
    But think only of following their example
    Here on earth.
    Dominic and Francis live again
    In holiness,
    If the brothers and sisters follow them
    Dutifully.

22. SISTER DOMINIC:
    I want to become Dominic
    In charity.
    SISTER FRANCES:
    I want to become seraphic

In poverty.
SISTER DOMINIC:
I say and I preach the rosary.
Such is my choice.
SISTER FRANCES:
For me, I only know Jesus on Calvary,
Crucified.

23. SISTER DOMINIC:
Let's sing, sister, let's sing, brother,
Each in turn:
Long live Jesus! Long live his Mother!
Long live love!
Long live Mary in her delights,
Nothing is more lovely!
SISTER FRANCES:
Long live Jesus in His sufferings!
He is my Spouse.

24. PRAYER OF SISTERS FRANCES AND DOMINIC:
O Jesus, our loving brother,
Save us all!
O our most loving Mother,
Pray for us.
Great Saints Francis and Dominic,
We pray you
To help us put your deeds
Into practice.

25. A priest needs wisdom,
Grant it to him,
He wants no other riches,
No other support.
So by Jesus, and Mary
We urge you
To give him in this life
This gift of gifts.

GOD ALONE

## 93
## GOOD CHILDREN

1. THE CHILDREN:
You are our teacher,
Child Jesus!
We want to know you
And your virtues!
Oh, speak to us!
We are listening.
Teach us the way
To go to you.

2. JESUS:
So, you want to hear me,
My dear children?
I can not resist,
Yes, I consent.
Listen to Me,
Prepare your ears
To know the marvels
Of my divine law.

3. I greatly love your age
My dear little ones,
I took it for my own,
God that I am.
I am a child
And I love childhood too,
Provided that innocence
Is its only adornment.

4. Honor father and mother,
Do not grieve them;
Say your prayers
Without fail;
Love one another,
Refrain from cursing,
From doing or saying anything
That would harm anyone.

5. Each day, try to say
Five decades of the rosary.

I encourage you to do it.
It's a good thing to do.
Go to confession
At least once a month.
Hear Mass well
On my appointed days.

6. Behave yourselves in church,
Without chatting there,
Accept that some will scorn you,
Do not retaliate.
Say nothing
When they sing insulting ditties,
Without grumbling, suffer all things
Like a Christian child.

7. Never let an oath
Come from your lips.
He who lies hurts Me
Intimately.
Children, be chaste
In body and in soul.
Flee from man or woman
Of the opposite sex.

8. You must hate the world,
It is a deceiver.
You must flee it,
Though this sorcerer rumbles.
You honor Me,
By honoring my Mother.
You please God my Father,
For you imitate me.

9. The cross is necessary,
All must suffer;
Either go up to Calvary
Or perish.
If you wish
To have the reward,
Renounce yourself,
Practice mortification.

10. Proclaim my praises
And sing them,

Honor your guardian angels
And pray to them.
Without wearying,
Spend time in prayer.
The devil is angry,
He wants to devour you.

11. Don't go out on the streets
To play there,
For it is there the devil kills,
It is his turf.
Associate with those
Whose lives are orderly.
Use your time well
And don't be lazy.

12. In spite of your nature,
Obey these laws.
God that I am, I swear:
You will be kings;
You will reign
Forever in my glory.
You will be crowned
As a sign of victory.

13. THE CHILDREN:
O Jesus, many thanks
For your lessons.
We walk in your footsteps
And follow you.
Knowing well
How weak we are,
Love urges you
To be our support.

GOD ALONE

## 94
## LOVING PENITENT WOMAN

1. THE PENITENT WOMAN:
My tears are my food,
My sighs are my joy,
Awestruck is my heart,
I yield and surrender,
For in God are more charms
Than my heart can desire.

2. In God all is capable
Of ravishing and charming,
He is a most loving Spouse
And an adorable King.
How it bothers me still,
To have lived not loving Him.

3. In vain the world is adorned
With its most brilliant lures.
In vain it decks out its wealth;
For I, now leaving it,
Declare: A heart is too greedy
If God doesn't suffice.

4. In silence, in my solitude,
Alone with Jesus alone,
I possess Him in secret,
I know perfect peace,
I tell, I tell Him repeating:
My God, you alone, and naught else.

5. The Good Shepherd sought me
Wherever I wandered,
He saw me, He found me,
He carried me gently,
Saintly, He compelled me.
The time has come; I love Him.

6. I laugh at the ridicule
That my conversion causes.
I laugh at all my companions
Who accuse me of folly.

I would give a thousand lives
To love my God ardently.

7. Oh all you puny creatures,
My heart is not for you;
You are but refuse;
Let me, I beseech you,
Love my God, no limit,
And taste His meek goodness.

8. Penitent sinful woman,
Day and night, that is my name;
I am both joyful and sad,
I am captive and happy.
Do you find that surprising?
It's because love guides me.

9. Mary is my good Mother
To whom I always turn,
To support my misery,
To calm God my Father;
It is through her I do hope
To persevere to the end.

10. More sinful than Magdalene,
Jesus, your feet I embrace.
Comfort me in my troubles,
Break and shatter all my chains.
It is love that compels me.
Forgive me, if I love too much.

11. THE PHARISEE:
O awesome, vengeful Justice
Of my holy, mighty God!
Look at this sinful woman
Daring to approach so close.
O great God, what insolence!
Throw her out, no delay!

12. JESUS:
Pharisee, are you surprised
To see how I respond?
Do you see this woman?
I give her all my wealth,
I forgive all her sins,

For she has loved so much!

13. THE PENITENT WOMAN:
Yes, my Jesus, I love you
Although many others rant,
Your greatness is so supreme,
And your love we know extreme.
I love, and say anathema
To those who do not love you.

14. What would I not do
For you, Jesus, my Savior?
I wish that I were thunder
To proclaim to all the world,
One thing is necessary:
To love God with all one's heart.

GOD ALONE

## 95
## GOOD SOLDIER

1. A courageous soldier am I,
Serving the King of Heaven,
A monarch invincible.
Under the cross and the *fleur de lis*
I battle all my foes;
Everywhere I am both
Good Christian and French soldier,
This is why I am awesome.

2. No enemy do I fear;
Having the Lord as ally,
I am always victorious.
With Him, I yearn to conquer
The world and hell.
Here below but one monster I fear:
Sin, which is not feared.
This fear is my glory.

3. I flee both the sight and the company

Of those who don't live properly,
No matter what they say or protest;
If they ridicule my piety,
I say: "Things are going quite well, thank you."
Whoever wishes to live piously
Must necessarily suffer
The scorn of the world.

4. I abhor women and wine,
Both are a fatal poison
Putting me at risk.
I shun all idleness.
Working faithfully,
Avoiding dances, gambling,
Cabarets and evil places
Where the devils seduce us.

5. Although a soldier, I love peace,
And will never be seen
Starting a fight.
I am satisfied with my pay
Although I barely live on it.
I never swear in vain,
I do no wrong to my neighbor,
I am loyal everywhere.

6. I try to do nothing
Unseemly of a good Christian,
Even in my speech.
Nothing against truth,
Nothing against humility,
Nothing against charity,
Nothing against purity,
No frivolous conversations.

7. When I see someone offend God
I stand up for Him right away
In spite of ridicule;
I say: Jesus, help me!
Oh Mary, come to my aid!
With their support, I fight,
I strike and conquer
The proud and the ungodly.

8. One of my most important rules:

To go to confession every month
To remain in the state of grace.
I piously pray my rosary
Daily, or even more often.
I pray to God morning and evening,
And examine my conscience at night.
This is how my life is spent.

9. Soldiers, do you want to be happy
Both on earth and in heaven?
Imitate what I do.
Don't ever be a deserter, for
God forbids it; it angers Him
To fall back like cowards,
To let the demons win.
Everyone, now sing after me:

10. Behold the flag unfurled,
Behold Jesus Crucified.
May He be loved and obeyed.
Reign, reign, great King of kings,
Plant your cross everywhere.
The time has come, Lord, the time has come
To plant it above the Crescent.
May your kingdom come!

GOD ALONE

## 96
## GOOD PRISONER

1. I accept, Lord, despite my aversion,
The gentle punishments of your love.
I submit entirely to your Providence
My soul, my body and my freedom.

2. Now I see how kind you are to me
In punishing me with fleeting pain,
For I should, according to your justice,
Spend eternity in hell's dungeon.

3. Not letting me go from crime to crime,
Or punishing me like a severe judge,
You want to free me from the abyss
By punishing me as a most kind God.

4. You yearn to free my soul from slavery
By confining my body in captivity.
Agreed, Lord. Without further delay,
Break the chains of my iniquity.

5. You sought me like a good shepherd,
When I wandered in spite of you.
Clasp tightly this rebellious sheep
To guard it from the jaws of wolves.

6. I leave, my God, moans and grumbling
To those who are the devil's martyrs.
Now penitent, whatever pain I bear,
I endure with joy, abandoned to you.

7. I humbly kiss the hand that chastens me,
I wholly accept prison and my plight.
Finally, I bless the shackles binding me,
Begging the forgiveness of my God.

AFTER BEING SENTENCED TO DEATH

8. Innocent Jesus died for the guilty,
The Good Shepherd to save his sheep.
May I also die for our most loving God
To expiate the evil I have done.

## 97
## IMPORTANT LESSON OF CHILDREN WHOM WE MUST RESEMBLE TO ENTER HEAVEN

1. Whoever wishes to be
A most powerful king,
According to our Master,
Must become a child.

So let's go to heed
A baby, oh! so tiny;
Let's then go to learn
His kind and gentle lesson.

2. Jesus now is napping
In his little crib.
Believing everything,
Let's lift up the veil.
He wishes to be seen there
As a month-old child,
There he speaks as Teacher,
Let's listen to his voice.

3. See his face, so gentle,
Filled with tenderness.
Do you see the image
Of our blessed Savior?
He is a new infant,
Speaking without words,
His air so innocent
Preaches powerfully.

4. He is so charming
And so natural,
That he disarms
Even cruel people.
One cannot but love
All his childlike ways;
He bears within himself
A charm all divine.

5. How adorable he is
When he breaks into a smile!
He is so loveable
Even when he cries.
His crib, his swaddling cloths,
His little trinkets,
Form the praises
Of little Jesus.

6. He does, without rejoinder,
Everything he's told,
Believing without grumbling,
Never talking back,

Instructing us as Master
By his obedience,
Teaching us submission
Of our own ideas.

7. He has no malice,
He has no deceit,
In him there is no cunning,
Neither stubbornness.
He never thinks
Ill of his neighbor,
He bears no grudges,
He holds no rancor.

8. Far from here the ways
Of the deceitful world.
This crying little child
Weeps over its misfortunes.
Despising all its glory
And its vanity,
He proclaims victory,
Though snugly enrobed.

9. Here there are no insults,
Nor are there disputes,
Never any grumbling
Never any fighting.
We find no weapons
Among the little ones,
Only gentle tears
And their soft cries.

10. Listen, worldly people:
Do you yearn for heaven?
Leave aside, without regret,
Your haughty airs.
Become by grace
Like this child
And you will have a place
In heaven.

GOD ALONE

# 98
# CONVERTED SINNER

## DIALOGUE

GOD THE FATHER:

1. Listen to me, I am complaining like a good father,
For a long time I have been searching for a child;
Up to now, I have held back my anger,
Oh! must I use punishment?

2. My son, why do you so offend me?
What do you see in me that so upsets you?
Come home to me, Come home, repent;
Woe to you if you are not stirred.

THE FRIEND:

3. Come back, sinner, your God is calling you;
Come back quickly, submit to his rule
You have already been too defiant.
Come back to him, since he comes back to you.

4. In your wayward life, his voice is heard,
For he pursues you, never wearying.
He is a good and most tender father.
Prodigal son, He yearns to embrace you.

THE REPENTANT SINNER:

5. My God, here is your rebellious child
Whom you have deigned to seek for so long;
O love, O fatherly love!
Without delay, I'm coming back, I surrender.

6. I acknowledge my foolish behavior,
Against you alone, father, have I sinned;
Turn away your eyes and thoughts from my waywardness
And look only at my tear filled heart.

JESUS:

7. Ah! I have lost, I have lost that dear soul,
What a pity, I have let my sheep wander away.
How much it upsets me, my Sacred Heart swoons.

My sheep has been handed over to my worst foes.

8. I have given everything, even my own life
To win you over and unite myself to you,
Yet you cruelly flee from me and forget me
And in return, you arm yourself against me.

THE FRIEND:

9. Come back, sinner, your God is calling you;
Come back quickly, submit to his rule
You have already been too defiant.
Come back to him, since He comes back to you.

10. In your wayward life, His voice is heard,
For He pursues you, never wearying.
He is a good and most tender father.
Prodigal son, He yearns to embrace you.

THE REPENTANT SINNER:

11. O my Jesus, O my loving Master,
You alone can enthrall me,
How long a time without knowing you!
How long a time without loving you!

12. My cruel injustice I acknowledge,
Forgive me for having strayed from you so long!
I do regret it, it is now my torment,
And for that alone, how bitter are my tears.

THE HOLY SPIRIT

13. It is over and done with, O dear soul that I love,
You no longer want me as your spouse.
You trample the vows of your baptism,
Weep, angels ...! Stagger, O heavens!

14. If I am good, then why must you offend me?
Your wicked heart takes pride in it every day!
More severity would conquer your resistance;
You would love me, had I loved you less.

THE FRIEND

15. The Holy Spirit begs and exhorts us
To return to Him wholeheartedly;
He yearns to enter, He is knocking at our door.
Will we always be busy elsewhere?

16. In our wayward life, his voice is heard,
For he pursues us, never wearying.
He is a spouse, a most tender spouse.
Let him in, let's cease to offend him.

THE CONTRITE AND HUMBLED SINNER:

17. Ah! I have sinned against God Himself
I have despised my Creator.
Forgive, forgive, supreme Goodness,
I regret it with all my heart.

18. I have run away from you, good father
Trampling underfoot all your kindness.
Calm, calm your anger;
Weeping, I beg for peace.

19. Do not render blow for blow,
See my humble, contrite heart,
I have no fear of your thunder
When I am covered with the blood of Jesus Christ.

20. Drop, Lord, drop your arms,
For I am the price of your blood.
Forgive, forgive, see my tears;
From now on, I will sin no more.

21. Come, Holy Spirit, God aflame,
Espouse me once again.
Forgive, forgive, God of my soul,
May I again find grace with you.

22. Pray for me, divine Mother,
Sure refuge of sinners!
Forgive me, forgive; your prayer
Is all powerful with my Savior.

23. O INFINITE MERCY,
You can not refuse me.
O sweet Jesus, sweet Mary,
You can not rebuff me.

JESUS TRIUMPHANT

24. For your joyful return, I, glorious Savior,
Order that today there be feasting in heaven.

Sing, Angels, sing of my gentle conquest,
Celebrate, celebrate the power of my precious blood.

THE ANGELS:

25. Let us sing, angels, let us sing His gentle conquest,
Let us celebrate, let us celebrate the power of His precious blood.

THE ECHO OF PARADISE

26. May all the heavens rejoice.
The sinner has joined the rank of saints;
Divine Savior, we bless you
For this masterpiece you have wrought.
May everyone, may every angel
Repeat unceasingly:
The sinner is back in the fold! (*twice*)
Glory and praise to you alone! (*twice*)

GOD ALONE

# 99
# GOOD SHEPHERDESS

1. SYLVIE:

Good morning, dear shepherdess,
Servant of the Lord,
I've come over the meadow
To speak heart to heart.
*Laus Deo. Laus Deo Domino.*

2. Here, far from the crowds
Let's stay for awhile
In profound stillness;
May holy love be our theme.
*Laus Deo. Laus Deo Domino.*

3. GENEVIEVE:
Ah! how delighted am I
To chat with you here!
Let's speak, dear Sylvie,

Of our only Good.
*Laus Deo, Laus Deo Domino.*

4. These meadows are pure,
Everything here is holy,
All created things
Tell us of our God.
*Laus Deo, etc.*

5. These rocks, these sheds,
These sheep, these lambs,
These woods, this greenery,
Are choristers new.
*Laus Deo, etc.*

6. SYLVIE:
Are you truly happy?
Is anything lacking?
Are you not awaiting
A change for the better?
*Laus Deo, etc.*

7. GENEVIEVE:
Know, dearest friend,
My heart is well satisfied.
I may be poor and hidden
But my happiness is great.
*Laus Deo, etc.*

8. Seated here on the grass,
In the middle of the woods,
I prefer my shepherd's crook
To the scepters of kings.
*Laus Deo, etc.*

9. I find more glory
Watching over my flock
Than in winning victory
Over a new world.
*Laus Deo, etc.*

10. Whether windy or drizzly,
In winter, in summer,
I thread my distaff
Singing so cheerfully:

*Laus Deo, etc.*

11. SYLVIE:
Are you not attracted
To pleasures, to honors,
To this visible world
Which ravishes hearts?
*Laus Deo, etc.*

12. GENEVIEVE:
No harm do I afflict
On the proud miser,
I leave him the earth
And I choose the heavens.
*Laus Deo, etc.*

13. The world and its show
Have no attraction;
I am assured happiness
In heaven, forever.
*Laus Deo, etc.*

14. SYLVIE:
What! Nothing bothers you
In this lonely place?
Are you at your ease?
I don't think it's possible!
*Laus Deo, etc.*

15. No shelter, no blankets,
Dressed in those tatters,
You suffer the havoc
Of all the seasons.
*Laus Deo, etc.*

16. The world shoves you aside
With all your poverty;
Your master and mistress
Are really quite harsh.
*Laus Deo, etc.*

17. GENEVIEVE:
In spite of these hardships,
My heart, at all times,
Is happier than queens

In the midst of their court.
*Laus Deo, etc.*

18. I have Jesus and Mary
Etched in my heart;
My friend, could I have
More perfect joy?
*Laus Deo, etc.*

19. In this withdrawn place
I have pleasant talks,
Everything secretly
Speaks and supports me.
*Laus Deo, etc.*

20. Some things uphold me,
Others may nourish me,
This one may humble me,
The other instructs me.
*Laus Deo, etc.*

21. Looking at these plains,
I say to my Lover:
Your sovereign beauties
Are their decorations.
*Laus Deo, etc.*

22. The bird in its flight
And in its sweet chirping,
Blames me for laziness,
For all my sluggishness.
*Laus Deo, etc.*

23. The murmuring waters
Complain of my heart
And condemn the hurt
I afflict on the Lord.
*Laus Deo, etc.*

24. These immovable rocks
Have an air of innocence;
They condemn the towns
Where the air is so evil.
*Laus Deo, etc.*

25. Here in the deep silence,
Everything speaks truth,
Everything preaches innocence
And holy simplicity.
*Laus Deo, etc.*

26. My sheep are the model
Of all the virtues;
When I contemplate them
I believe I see Jesus.
*Laus Deo, etc.*

27. How innocent the lambs!
How loving they are!
How patient the sheep,
How humble they are!
*Laus Deo, etc.*

28. I take so much pleasure
In seeing this hamlet.
How more so is the Artist,
So lovely His work.
*Laus Deo, etc.*

29. The rustling of the leaves
And the sound of the birds,
Make me sing my own tune
To the sound of the pipes.
To the glory and praise
Of Jesus my Love.
We blend our voices,
We sing each in turn:
*Laus Deo, etc.*

30. My glory is so deep,
All my riches within.
Here on earth I don't crave
Anything I see.
*Laus Deo, etc.*

31. Shame on this passing world
And those who are foolish!
The world sullies, it hinders,
It makes them all perish.
*Laus Deo, etc.*

32. I prefer my small sheds
To the palaces of kings,
I prefer my greenery
To their vain decorations.
*Laus Deo, etc.*

33. Resound, countryside!
Leap, wee lambs!
Answer me, mountains
With echoing sound!
*Laus Deo, etc.*

34. Sing, dear pastures!
Sing, narrow streams!
Sing, tiny clearings!
Sing, little birds!
*Laus Deo, etc.*

35. Jesus is our Master,
Be gone, all you sinners.
All in this country place
Renders all honor to God.
*Laus Deo, etc.*

36. Reign, Virgin Mary
In the highest heavens!
And may you be blessed
Even here below.
*Laus Deo, etc.*

37. Dear Sylvie, let's sing:
I bless you, Jesus,
I bless you, Mary,
Grant us your virtues.
*Laus Deo, Laus Deo Domino.*

*The following lines can be added for the refrain:*

I desire nothing
But God alone for my good;
Long live Jesus
In my heart, and naught else.

## 100
## CONSOLATION OF THE AFFLICTED (2)

1. THE AFFLICTED ONE:
Someone's getting after me,
For no reason and no fault of mine.
Someone else has no use for me;
I'm having so much trouble!

2. THE DEVIL:
Get revenge for these insults,
You must save face,
Prove your innocence,
Restore your honor.

3. THE FRIEND OF GOD
Don't seek vengeance,
God will do it better.
The best reward
Awaits you in heaven!
Blessed cross of Calvary,
As long as it, as long as it,
Blessed cross of Calvary
As long as it endures.

4. This injury is malicious
But if you get even,
You're plunging yourself
Into eternal damnation.
Blessed cross, etc.

5. Dogs bite into rocks,
Fools bite each other;
The wise suffer on earth
And ever it shall be.
Blessed cross, etc.

6. THE AFFLICTED MAN
Someone insulted me
On such and such occasion
I'll pay him back, I swear,
Or my good name is ruined.

7. THE DEVIL
You have to get back at him
With all the might you have.
Show him how things are done,
Show him what he ought to do.

8. THE FRIEND OF GOD
God Himself commands you
To love your enemy
And, as he forgives you,
You must forgive in turn.
Blessed Cross,

9. Those humble and wise
Forgive quite easily.
The bloodiest outrage
Seems mild and acceptable.
Blessed cross, etc.

10. THE AFFLICTED MAN
Oh! What a horrible event
Oh! What a miserable thing!
I thought I was doing so well,
How despondent I am!

11. THE DEVIL
Someone through jealousy
Did this rotten thing to you;
Get even, cry, scream,
You're suffering a lot.

12. THE FRIEND OF GOD
The wise chuckle and forget it
When their goods are stolen;
They rarely go to court
To get back what they own.
Blessed Cross, etc.

13. Lawsuits are cruel flames
Which eat away at peace,
Property, health, soul,
And even heaven, forever.
Blessed Cross, etc.

14. THE AFFLICTED MAN

Hey there! You devil beast!
My God! What an animal!
He hit me on the head
And boy, does it hurt!

15. THE DEVIL
Take revenge right now
On this dirty creature!
Strike, storm and swear
For your injury is great.

16. FRIEND OF GOD
People get to know themselves
Through unfortunate incidents.
The good say to the Master:
O my God, we accept it.
Blessed Cross, etc.

17. But the evil, the ungodly
Who do not get what they want
Curse, grumble, scream
And swear, as much as they can.
Blessed Cross, etc.

18. To make a hurt amiable,
Say: Blessed be God!
These words chase away the devil,
And make the angels rejoice.
Blessed Cross, etc.

19. THE AFFLICTED MAN:
Here I am, absolutely miserable,
For I lost my case at court
And my arguments were the most logical
That I had ever made.

20. THE DEVIL:
Quibble about your case,
Appeal to the Parliament,
Let hate and jealousy
Secretly inspire you!

21. THE FRIEND OF God:
Suffer this disgrace,
Then you will have peace,

You will merit grace
And glory forever.
Blessed cross, etc.

22. But if by your greed
You scandalize your neighbor,
You are calling for justice
And you suffer all in vain.
Blessed cross, etc.

23. THE AFFLICTED MAN
To accept being bossed around
Like a dog's valet?
To tolerate that I'm despised?
Sorry, not for me!

24. THE DEVIL:
To suffer, what a humiliation!
My good man, uphold your position,
Honor your rank,
Respect your noble blood.

25. THE FRIEND OF GOD:
When someone debases us,
He raises us to heaven,
Provided we are shrewd enough
To suffer it quite joyfully.
Blessed cross, etc.

26. To give up is victory,
And suffering preserves it,
To be humble is glory,
To lose everything is triumph.
Blessed cross, etc.

27. The unfailing secret
Of achieving the first
And most well thought of place,
Is to be the last.
Blessed Cross, etc.

28. THE AFFLICTED MAN:
Zounds! They want me to be
A worthless man, a nothing.
O no! I'll not be quiet

And when I speak, I'll blow up!

29. THE DEVIL:
Arm yourself with greedy thoughts,
Let them be your secret weapons.
Drag down and slander
Anyone who harms you.

30. THE FRIEND OF GOD
Dust, dare you swell with pride
Though God chose to be lowly?
You want your name in lights
Though God eclipsed himself.
Blessed cross, etc.

31. Spare your brother,
His price is infinite;
Envy and anger
Harm you more than him.
Blessed cross, etc.

32. Accept that others cause you
Sorrow upon sorrow.
Do not harm anyone,
Love, love your neighbor.
Blessed cross, etc.

33. THE AFFLICTED MAN
Suffer because of this monkey face,
Because of this stupid idiot?
No, no! O the bloody outrage!
He will pay for it, by God!

34. THE DEVIL:
Strike with your sword,
Don't be a coward;
Hit him with a volley
Of good whacks with a club.

35. THE FRIEND OF GOD:
Behold God who tolerates you
Yet you can't tolerate others;
And there you are so close to a cliff,
Watch out! You're soon to perish.
Blessed cross, etc.

36. It is God who sends you
    This wolf, this wolf so wicked.
    Suffer him joyfully
    You will gain a great deal.
    Blessed cross, etc.

37. Angels have noticed it
    The heavens rejoice,
    All sing your praises
    And all hell runs away.
    Blessed cross, etc.

38. THE AFFLICTED ONE:
    See that evil woman
    Slapping my child!
    Go away, scram, beggar,
    Or better, come, I'm waiting for you.

39. THE DEVIL
    Run over this shrew,
    She's out of her mind.
    Stomp on her mane
    Be brave and hold fast.

40. THE FRIEND OF GOD
    By your screams so furious
    You condemn yourself, Alas!
    Suffer like a wise woman
    And don't react so fast!
    Blessed cross, etc.

41. You lose the victory
    Together with charity,
    You lose all your glory.
    Suffer, have pity!
    Blessed cross, etc.

42. God has lightning in hand
    Since you so anger him;
    He'll reduce you to dust
    Just as you deserve.
    Blessed cross, etc.

43. THE AFFLICTED ONE:

What! Suffer in silence
When I am struck!
Oh! what stupid extreme!
Let others act thus!

44. THE DEVIL
Fling a stone for a stone,
Whack a tooth for a tooth
Wage war for war:
Then you'll be prudent.

45. THE FRIEND OF GOD
Yes, suffer in silence
Is your glorious deed
Which God will reward
On earth and in heaven.
Blessed cross, etc.

46. When someone is humble
And suffers for Jesus,
Your angel records it
In the book of life.
Blessed cross, etc.

47. There is nothing stronger
Than a patient man;
Those who win wars
Are not as valiant.
Blessed cross, etc.

48. A roaring lion
Calms down if flattered.
The most arrogant spirit
Becomes meek by silence.
Blessed cross, etc.

49. An ounce of suffering
Accepted with calm
Works an immense weight
Of glory forever.
Blessed cross, etc.

## 101
## CONSOLATION OF THE AFFLICTED (3)

1. THE AFFLICTED SOUL:
My house has burned down,
Only misfortune befalls me!
I have just been robbed,
A plague on the thieves!

2. THE DEVIL:
Go to the police,
Consult a psychic,
You know who did it,
He's evil, that man!

3. THE FRIEND OF GOD
What evil befalls
God Himself permits.
With such lively faith
We gain infinitely.
Blessed cross, etc.

4. May we take for guide
Now and forever,
Whether winning or losing,
God's holy will.
Blessed Cross, etc.

5. Abominable strategy:
Having recourse to the devil!
Appalling insult
To God's holy name.
Blessed cross, etc.

6. THE AFFLICTED SOUL:
OK, topple everything, smash, break;
Clumsy blockhead, If I catch you!
Get out of here! Be more careful
When you pass through here again!

7. THE DEVIL:
Your threats are all worthless,
He mocks them, he scoffs them.

With a good hard whack, please,
Bring him back to his senses.

8. THE FRIEND OF GOD
Remember, a fault is slight
When there is no sin involved,
You must, like a good father,
Have pity on him.
Blessed cross, etc.

9. By your impatience
You add to the evil.
You cause great scandal,
And offenses galore.
Blessed cross, etc.

10. THE AFFLICTED PERSON:
You're trying to kill me!
Go away evil man,
Go far from me. I'd like
To leave everything, now!

11. THE DEVIL:
Hey, he wants you dead!
Get back at him, right to the end.
Give him all you've got
Or else, you will die of regret.

12. THE FRIEND OF GOD:
Wise woman, put up with
Your impatient husband
Or your marriage will be
No more than a living hell.
Blessed cross, etc.

13. A crime for a crime
Only makes things worse.
But sublime virtue
Stops crime and charms him.
Blessed cross, etc.

14. It's by your silence
That you will teach him,
It's by your patience
That you will sanctify him.

Blessed cross, etc.

15. THE AFFLICTED ONE:
What bothersome housework!
I'll enter a convent
Or go to a hermitage
Where I can live happily.

16. THE DEVIL:
You'll not be cranky,
You'll live in peace;
Your sisters and brothers
Make you do all the work.

17. THE FRIEND OF GOD:
It isn't your angel,
But often the devil
Whose words you hear
During your devotions.
Blessed cross, etc.

18. The problem lies in you,
You do not love the cross;
Your extreme anger
Always takes over.
Blessed cross, etc.

19. A large household always has
Many crosses and worries;
When they are well accepted
Their value is priceless.
Blessed cross, etc.

20. Except by obedience
Let nothing ever be done.
Acting through one's own wisdom
Spoils or corrupts any good.
Blessed cross, etc.

21. THE AFFLICTED ONE:
No matter what I do or say
I do all things the best I can;
I am a martyr here,
This place is so boring.

22. THE DEVIL
    Notice how they maltreat you!
    You can surely find elsewhere
    A peaceful, much better job
    And better masters.

23. THE FRIEND OF GOD
    Suffer, holy maid,
    Suffer, holy page,
    Thus you will overthrow
    The devil's temptations.
    Blessed cross, etc.

24. The fools, so they say,
    Suffer all things though guiltless
    And even to shedding
    Their blood until death.
    Blessed cross, etc.

25. We see our good Master
    Die although innocent;
    And then we want to be
    Guilty without suffering.
    Blessed cross, etc.

26. If we roam through the earth
    From Japan to Peru
    We will suffer hostility
    From either wise men or fools.
    Blessed cross, etc.

27. THE AFFLICTED ONE:
    What's going on! Cutbacks, tolls,
    Many heavy new taxes;
    This constant bad news
    Doubles my troubles.

28. THE DEVIL:
    Among those thieving companies
    Which so infuriate you,
    Find yourself some business
    To make up for your losses.

29. THE FRIEND OF GOD
    The wise patiently

Bear all their taxes;
Without any resistance
They pay them all promptly.
Blessed cross, etc.

30. With no ruse at all,
They conceal nothing;
Though they cry injustice,
They turn all things to good.
Blessed cross, etc.,

31. O atrocious slander
To speak ill of the king!
The most ferocious beast
Has far meeker instincts.
Blessed cross, etc,

32. It is Caesar who commands,
It is Caesar who protects;
To Caesar then we pay
The tribute he demands.
Blessed cross, etc.

33. THE AFFLICTED ONE:
Good God, I am so bored
During all my prayers!
I agonize so much
Over my distractions.

34. THE DEVIL:
You're doing nothing worthwhile,
You're just wasting your time;
You have much work to do,
Go! It's waiting for you.

35. THE FRIEND OF GOD
Jesus Christ persevered
In prayer though in darkness.
He then is your model,
Suffer then like him.
Blessed cross, etc.

36. Pray most patiently,
Despite body and soul.
The prayer of suffering

Is the prayer of the strong.
Blessed cross, etc.

37. God only works in the soul
When the soul knows how to suffer;
He enlightens, He sets it afire
Without making Himself felt.
Blessed cross, etc.

38. THE AFFLICTED MAN:
I am but a victim
During my prayer;
I see myself so sinful
And wholly abandoned.

39. THE DEVIL:
Go on! Blaspheme, despair,
God has abandoned you!
He is so full of wrath,
Too much have you hurt Him.

40. THE FRIEND OF GOD:
The Lord is testing you,
Hold firm, pray well;
Surely He finds in this
Your honor and His own.
Blessed cross, etc.

41. Turn to His grace;
Suffer this trial, suffer;
You will again see the face
Of your dear Spouse.
Blessed cross, etc.

42. This loving eclipse
Brims the heart with love,
Makes the soul luminous
And full of strength.
Blessed Cross, etc.

43. THE AFFLICTED ONE:
How miserable I am!
I have sinned enormously,
I am so depressed,
Ah! I am so annoyed!

44. THE DEVIL:
How disgusting your sin!
You have no virtue,
Cry and despair,
Alas! All is lost.

45. THE FRIEND OF GOD:
This evil sadness
This anxiety and depression
Are a very bad sign,
They are the work of the devil.
Blessed cross, etc.

46. When, by your weakness
You have just fallen,
Love urges you on
To be humble of heart.
Blessed cross, etc.

47. See God as a Father
Ask Him for forgiveness;
Suffer your misery,
Good will come of it.
Blessed cross, etc.

48. Everything profits
The just, even sin;
He draws good from it,
Though sin angers Him.
Blessed cross, etc.

49. THE AFFLICTED PERSON:
O Jesus, I embrace
And I kiss my cross,
But please do help me
Carry well its weight.
Blessed cross, etc.

50. I bless your punishment
And I adore your blows,
For considering my offenses
You punish me too lightly.
Blessed cross, etc.

51. A God who suffers!
Hell at the ready!
Only big fools think
They have suffered too much!
Blessed cross, etc.

52. Strike! That's fine!
Either suffer or die!
Whether I live or die
I want always to suffer.
Blessed cross, etc.

## 102
## TRIUMPH OF THE CROSS

1. The Cross is essential.
We must always suffer:
Either climb Calvary
Or perish forever.
Blessed cross of Calvary,
As long as it, as long as it,
Blessed cross of Calvary
As long as it endures.

2. The Cross is a mystery
Most secret here below,
Without abundant light
Its meaning is not known.
Blessed cross, etc.

3. Nature loathes the cross
Reason struggles against it
The learned man ignores it
And the demon cuts it down.
Blessed cross, etc.

4. Saint Augustine proclaims
We are among the cursed
If God does not chastise us
As His beloved children.
Blessed cross, etc.

5. The way to our Homeland
Is the way of the Cross.
It is the way of life,
It is the way of kings.
Blessed cross, etc.

6. Each stone the builders use
On Holy Zion's heights
Is cut and made to fit
Or thrown to the devil.
Blessed cross, etc.

7. What value has the triumph
Of the greatest conqueror
If he win not the glory
Of self-control through crosses?
Blessed cross, etc.

8. Despite sense and nature,
Politics and reason,
The truth does assure us:
The Cross is a great gift.
Blessed cross, etc.

9. The Cross is the princess
Where we truly find
All grace, all wisdom
And divinity.
Blessed cross, etc.

10. God could not resist
Her singular beauty;
The Cross made Him come down
To our humanity.
Blessed cross, etc.

11. Entering the world He said:
Yes, Father, I yearn for her.
O cross, I thrust you deeply
Into the center of my heart.
Blessed cross, etc.

12. He thought her so stunning
He made her His honor,

His eternal companion,
His heart's loving spouse.
Blessed cross, etc.

13. Even as a young child
His heart constantly longed
For the loving presence
Of the cross He so cherished.
Blessed cross, etc.

14. He has, from His youth,
Sought her eagerly.
He died in her arms
Of tenderness and love.
Blessed cross, etc.

15. I desire a baptism,
He proclaimed one day,
The dear Cross I so love,
The object of my love.
Blessed cross, etc.

16. He called Saint Peter
A scandalous Satan
When he wanted Him
To reject and deny it.
Blessed cross, etc.

17. Through the Cross, our great Master
Put all hell in fetters,
Crushed Satan the rebel
And won all creation.
Blessed cross, etc.

18. This Cross, now scattered
Wide upon this earth,
One day will rise whole
And be carried to heaven.
Blessed cross, etc.

19. The Cross, on a cloud
Of blinding beauty
Will judge, by its light,
The quick and the dead.
Blessed cross, etc.

20. It will cry vengeance
From all its foes,
Joy, peace and pardon
For all its faithful friends.
Blessed cross, etc.

21. God gives it as a weapon
To those who serve Him well.
It charms or it disarms
Hands, and hearts as well.
Blessed cross, etc.

22. "By this sign you shall conquer"
He proclaimed to Constantine.
Every outstanding conquest
Is hidden in its bosom.
Blessed cross, etc.

23. The cross is adorable,
But Mary is not.
O ineffable grandeur,
Unknown here below!
Blessed cross, etc.

24. With no cross, the soul is sluggish,
Soft, cowardly and dull!
But the Cross renders the soul
Fervent, full of strength.
Blessed cross, etc.

25. How ignorant we are
If we do not suffer!
How wise we shall become
If we suffer well.
Blessed cross, etc.

26. A soul for long untried
Would be of little worth,
A frail soul, untested,
With no learning whatsoever.
Blessed cross, etc.

27. O what sovereign sweetness
An afflicted soul does taste

Who in suffering finds peace
Without experiencing relief.
Blessed cross, etc.

28. During their life, the saints
Sought nothing but the Cross;
It was their great desire,
Their choice centered on it.
Blessed cross, etc.

29. Not satisfied with those
That God Himself did send,
They punished themselves with others
Of their own invention.
Blessed cross, etc.

30. The chains of Peter
Bring him more honor
Than being on earth
The vicar of the Savior.
Blessed cross, etc.

31. Notice, Paul forgets
His awesome rapture,
Finding his glory
Only in the Cross.
Blessed cross, etc.

32. He is more honorable
In his frightening dungeon
Than in his great ecstasy
Ravishing him to heaven.
Blessed cross, etc.

33. O holy cross, proclaims
The faithful Andrew;
So I may come alive
Let me die on you!
Blessed cross, etc.

34. O cross, our wisdom,
Our redemption
Our only hope
Our perfection.
Blessed cross, etc.

35. The cross is so precious!
The souls now in heaven
Would joyfully return
To suffer here on earth.
Blessed cross, etc.

## 103
## DESIRES OF INCARNATE WISDOM OR OF THE CHILD JESUS

1. Forgive, Divine Wisdom,
My ardor.
For you are the mistress
Of my heart.
Hasten to my assistance,
Give ear to my pleas.

2. Son of God, supreme beauty,
Come to me.
Without you I am accursed,
Come to me.
With you, I shall be king,
A king obedient to your law.

3. O Word, equal to the Father,
Come to me.
Light of light,
Come to me.
With you, I shall see clearly
And confront all hell.

4. Jesus, uncreated Wisdom,
Come to me.
Jesus, incarnate Wisdom,
Come to me,
What is sweeter than to be with you?
But what hell to be without you!

5. O Wisdom, God made man,
Come to me.

I acknowledge you, I call you,
Come to me.
With you and your cross,
I shall be happier than any king.

6. O my powerful princess!
Come to me.
O my charming mistress,
Come to me
To be with you bestows more pleasure
Than our heart could ever imagine.

7. O my immortal Spouse
Come to me.
My beautiful one, my faithful one,
Come to me.
With you I am stronger
Than hell and death.

8. People abandon you, my friend,
Come to me.
You are treated like a fool,
Come to me.
With you I shall be wise,
Without you, one of the fools.

8. (a) Wisdom, you are maligned,
Come to me.
You are rejected and rebuffed,
Come to me.
With you, we both consent,
I want to live until I die.

9. O my greatest riches!
Come to me.
O my sweetest tenderness,
Come to me.
With you, we are so joyful!
So rich and so happy!

10. Your glance makes the earth quake,
Come to me.
Your hands clap the thunder,
Come to me.
With you, we are never afraid

Of death or of evil.

11. I burn with your fire,
    Come to me.
    You are enthroned in my soul,
    Come to me.
    With you and with your love
    I am happy day and night.

12. I yearn for you desperately,
    Come to me.
    Without you, life is martyrdom,
    Come to me.
    With you, I shall have everything,
    Without fear of lacking anything.

13. Your folly is wisdom,
    Come to me.
    Your penury is plentiful,
    Come to me.
    With you, what treasures
    In our bodies and souls!

14. Your demands are delightful,
    Come to me.
    Your sorrows are sacrifices,
    Come to me.
    With you, we are happy
    Both on earth and in heaven.

15. Your contempt is full of glory,
    Come to me.
    But no one believes you,
    Come to me.
    With you, more grandeur
    Than all the emperors together.

16. You only dwell on Calvary,
    Come to me.
    The cross is your only pulpit,
    Come to me.
    With you, I shall suffer
    And then I shall reign.

17. You give crosses as rewards,

Come to me.
You only love suffering,
Come to me.
With you, what sweet pleasure
To suffer all, and to die.

18. Your friends flow tears,
Come to me.
Crosses are their only weapons,
Come to me.
But, forgive my sins,
Then cut, prune, sever.

19. You are seeking an abode,
Come to me.
Swiftly, without delay,
Come to me.
With you, how lovely!
May my heart be your home.

20. I tell you often fearlessly,
Come to me.
My soul will become holy,
Come to me.
With you come all the virtues,
And the wonders of Jesus.

21. All the virtues follow you,
Come to me.
With you they come,
Come to me.
With you are charity,
Purity, humility.

22. There is none like you,
Come to me.
Before you, gold is but sand,
Come to me.
With you, although penniless,
I am rich and satisfied.

23. O my life and my light,
Come to me.
O my Spouse and my Mother,
Come to me.

With you I shall have peace,
Grace and glory forever.

24. Wisdom, unknown to the world,
Come to me.
Whatever they say, whatever they do,
Come to me.
With you, contempt
Seems like treasure.

25. Farewell, mortal beauties,
Come to me.
Yours are eternal,
Come to me.
With you, truthfully,
I shall live eternally.

26. Wisdom, I want to win you over,
Come to me.
Bah to money! I want none of it,
Come to me.
With you, I want to play
To lose everything and win you.

27. We shall proclaim victory,
Come to me.
You alone will be glorified,
Come to me.
With you I shall speak,
In speaking I shall triumph.

28. I want to walk in your footsteps,
Come to me.
That is the grace of all graces,
Come to me.
With you, I shall advance joyfully
Straight to the cross and to heaven.

29. Jesus, Child of Mary,
Come to me.
It is she who begs you,
Come to me.
With you in this exile,
I shall have all good things. Amen.

## 104
## NEW CANTICLE FOR OUR LADY

1. If someone wants graces
From heaven with ease,
To Mary, first of all,
Let him come to find God,
Let him come (*three times*).

2. God is appeased by Mary,
As all sinners know!
So come with a contrite heart
To Jesus through Mary,
Let him come, etc.

3. Does some great sinner wish
To break his chains forever?
Mary can surely do it.
Let him come and see,
Let him come, etc.

4. Do you desire the heart of a David
Or that of a Madeleine?
You can obtain this heart
From the Savior's Mother,
Let him come, etc.

5. Do you want to overcome
The world which drags you down?
To Mary, then, without fail
Cling tightly,
Let him come, etc.

6. If you wish to defy hell
And scorn its hate,
Always come to Mary
To be armed with strength,
Let him come, etc.

7. Let every hardened sinner,
   Let every Christian soul
   Come present his greetings
   To Mary, Queen of Heaven,
   Let him come, etc.

8. Does someone seek virtue?
   Mary is its Queen.
   Let him come as did the saints,
   To receive virtue from her hands,
   Let him come, etc.

9. Who wishes to burn with love,
   Without scruple or constraint,
   Let him come to Mary, in God
   She is aflame with its fire.
   Let him come, etc.

10. Who wants fruit and grapes
    Or wheat from the fields,
    Let him entreat with assurance
    Her maternal goodness,
    Let him come, etc.

11. Who wants a cure for any hurt,
    Let each one always remember:
    Whoever has recourse to Mary
    Will find ample help.
    Let him come, etc.

12. Do you want to go to heaven?
    The Blessed Virgin leads you there.
    Let him come by this path
    To this final home.
    Let him come, etc.

13. God has filled us with blessings,
    Always keep them in mind,
    Glory to the Lord far and wide.
    Victory to Mary in heaven!
    Victory, etc.

14. She has conquered God
    Our invincible monarch;
    Through her He came down,

It is she who made Him
Visible, etc.

15. If our Judge is won over,
If He is the Savior of the world,
It is through her virginity,
It is through her humility
Profound, etc.

16. Alas! we would be lost
Without our good Mother,
She prayed God for us
And appeased His anger
Severe, etc.

17. She has routed the demon
That cruel beast,
She has put him in irons
To crush in hell
His head, etc.

18. The world and the demon
With all of their minions
In the name of Jesus her Son,
In the name of Mary, have taken
Flight, etc.

19. Without her, all were drowned
In the waters of the flood,
She has delivered us,
Becoming our assured
Refuge, etc.

20. She has conquered Lucifer,
Shackled all hell,
Removed sin from our hearts,
Opened the gate to happiness
Supreme, etc.

21. Through her Son she has given
Both grace and glory,
Life to the dead, hearing to the deaf,
And every help to the poor,
Victory, etc.

22. Let us all sing with joy
To our glorious Queen,
Always and everywhere,
On earth and in heaven:
Victory! Victory! Victory!

## 105
## JESUS CHRIST'S CALL TO THE SINNER TO PROFIT FROM THE MISSION

1. What graces surely
The good Lord gives here;
Don't make them useless,
O hardened sinner.
What! God who loves you so much
Has wasted His efforts?
What! God who loves you so much
Has wasted His time?

2. On this small island
God seeks for you now.
So be humble and docile
And truly repentant.
What! God, etc.

3. If His tremendous love
Touches you this blest day
Tell Him that you love Him.
Returning love for love.
What! God, etc.

4. He is a tender father,
Also a skilled physician;
Sinner, get to the mission
Or perish eternally.
What! God, etc.

5. To his pleading voice,
Harden not your heart,
Rebel not against
This powerful Lord.
What! God, etc.

6. Choose well, I beg you,
   Pick good or evil,
   Select death or life,
   God wants all or naught!
   What! God, etc.

7. Choose peace or warfare,
   Thunderbolt or cross,
   Choose heaven or earth,
   God gives you the choice.
   What! God, etc.

8. Great God, what vengeance
   Will follow such gifts,
   Unless by your penance
   You make your peace!
   What! God, etc.

9. Weep, weep many tears,
   Groan from your heart's depths,
   God is then disarmed,
   You will be the winner.
   What! God, etc.

10. At this propitious time,
    Make this mission your own,
    God gives the wickedest
    Remission of their sins.
    What! God who loves you so much
    Has wasted His efforts?
    What! God who loves you so much
    Has wasted His blood?

*RESPONSE:*
Oh! God who loves me so much
Has not wasted His efforts.
Oh! God who loves me so much
Has not wasted His blood.

GOD ALONE

# 106
# CONDEMNATION OF THE WORLD

## DIALOGUE

JESUS:

1. Christians, you must listen either to me or to the world.
Choose between the two.
Are you listening? Each one must answer.
I teach how to do good, always I do!
The world, how to do evil.

2. Christians, you must believe either me or the world.
Choose between the two.
Do you believe me? Each one must answer.
I never deceive, never I do!
But the world deceives.

3. Christians, you must follow either me or the world.
Choose between the two.
Are you following me? Each one must answer.
I never change, never I do.
But the world changes.

4. Christians, you must serve either me or the world;
Choose between the two.
Do you serve me? Each one must answer.
I never pass away, never I do!
But the world passes away.

5. If you follow this detestable world,
I swear it now,
I will make you miserable forever.
Will you follow the world or me?
Each one must answer.

*RESPONSE:*

6. 1. I want to listen to you, I do;
I want to listen to you.
2. I want to believe you totally, I do;
I want to believe you.
3. I want to follow you in everything, I do;
I want to follow you.

THE GROUP:

7. Together we say: Anathema!
 To this present world.
 We believe you, O supreme Truth!
 Oh! May you be heard,
 May you be heard.

8. We serve you, O Supreme Monarch;
 May you be heard, therefore.
 May you be heard.

9. You alone are Truth and Life,
 You alone, our Good Shepherd;
 Speak to us then, we beg you
 We each listen to you peacefully,
 We each listen to you.

10. Speak to us, good Master, speak to our hearts.
 Speak to us, good Master.

JESUS:

11. Discern well the cross which calls you.
 The world is a deceiver.
 It distorts my eternal word,
 It stings secretly! Really!
 It stings secretly.

THE WORLD:

12. Friends, let's drink, sing, be merry;
 No need at all to be bored,
 Our youth, everything, calls us.

THE ANGEL:

13. That is the voice of the world you hear.
 That is the voice of the world.

THE GROUP:

14. [Be still, be still, deceiving world]
 We all believe in the Lord.
 Woe to those who trust in you!
 Blessed those who live by faith!
 We condemn the laws of your realm,
 We detest what you have just said.

JESUS:

15. You must always mortify yourselves
To be my friends,
You must either perish or do penance.

THE ANGEL:

16. It is God who speaks to us, God speaks,
It is God who speaks to us.

THE CHRISTIAN:

17. I believe you, Jesus, my Master
And I respect your law.
The world is an evil traitor
Guard me then, increase my faith.

THE GROUP:

18. We all believe you, good Master,
We embrace your law.
The world is an evil traitor.
Help us then, increase our faith.

THE WORLD:

19. Dance, laugh, eat and drink,
God doesn't forbid it;
Scrupulous people, there's no need to believe you.

THE ANGEL:

That is the voice of the world you hear,
That is the voice of the world.

THE GROUP:

20. Be still, be still, deceitful world
We all believe you, etc.

JESUS:

21. If anyone claims to honor and love Me,
He must walk in My footsteps,
Carrying his cross, renouncing himself.

THE ANGEL:

It is God who speaks to us, God speaks.
It is God who speaks to us.

THE CHRISTIAN:

I believe you, Jesus, my Master,

We embrace your law, etc.

THE GROUP:
We all believe you, good Master,
We embrace your law, etc.

THE WORLD:
22. To be saved when we die,
A *peccavi* suffices.
No need to be morbid!

THE ANGEL:
That is the voice of the world, etc.

THE GROUP:
We all believe you, good Master, etc.

JESUS:
23. Do not delay to do penance,
Or you will die accursed,
Flattering yourself with vain hope.

THE ANGEL:
It is God who speaks to us, etc.

THE CHRISTIAN:
I believe you, etc.

THE GROUP:
We all believe, etc.

THE WORLD:
24. Without scruple, let's make merry, brother!
The Lord is so good!
He'll give us a plenary indulgence.

THE ANGEL:
That is the voice of the world, etc.

THE GROUP:
We all believe you, good Master, etc.

JESUS:
25. Because I am good, must you offend me?
Oh! What flawed logic!

I await, I await the day of my vengeance.

THE ANGEL:
It is God who speaks to us,
It is God who speaks.

THE CHRISTIAN:
I believe you, Jesus, good Master, etc.

THE GROUP:
We all believe you, good Master, etc.

THE WORLD:
26. Get wealthy and rise from the dust,
That's the main thing!
It's the way to enjoy life to the full.

THE ANGEL, etc.

JESUS:
27. Seek heaven, preserve your innocence.
That's the main thing!
For then you will have the rest in abundance.

THE ANGEL, etc.

THE WORLD:
28. Climb the ladder, be indispensable,
Now that's smart!
Only a great fool doesn't know how to do it.

THE ANGEL:
That is the voice of the world, etc.

JESUS:
29. Humble yourself to rise in my glory;
I exalt little ones,
I confound those who exalt themselves.

THE ANGEL:
It is God who speaks to us, etc.

THE WORLD:
30. Hang out with big shots and get rich,
Become like them.

What do you gain by an ordinary life?

THE ANGEL:
That is the voice of the world, etc.

JESUS:
31. If you want true friends
Who will lead you to heaven,
Win the hearts of the wretched poor.

THE ANGEL:
It is God who speaks to us, etc.

THE WORLD:
32. Be well-dressed, be stylish in everything,
Make a good impression,
To do otherwise makes you look silly.

THE ANGEL:
That is the voice of the world, etc.

JESUS:
33. Always preserve Christian simplicity,
It's a beautiful adornment;
Beware of worldly fashion.

THE ANGEL:
It is God who speaks to us, etc.

THE WORLD:
34. Devout and fanatic mean the same,
So avoid being known as "devout"
If you want the world to love you.

THE ANGEL:
That is the voice of the world, etc.

JESUS:
35. The truly devout always please me.
Deserve this title
By becoming meek, humble and kind.

THE ANGEL:
It is God who speaks to us, etc.

THE WORLD:

36. What! You are leaving this beautiful company?
What will people say of you?
They will laugh at your fanatic devotion.

THE ANGEL:
That is the voice of the world, etc.

JESUS:

37. Dear sheep, keep your distance
To avoid the wolves,
Listen and speak to me in secret.

THE ANGEL:
It is God who speaks to us, etc.

THE WORLD:

38. What makes you so uncivilized and uncouth?
It's because you are so devout!
Drop, drop this gloomy behavior.

THE ANGEL:
That is the voice of the world, etc.

JESUS:

39. Be devout but without hypocrisy.
Be prayerful;
Be joyful but with modesty.

THE ANGEL:
It is God who speaks to us, etc.

THE WORLD:

40. What! This scum makes you suffer?
Get revenge immediately.
Otherwise he'll hurt you again.

THE ANGEL:
That is the voice of the world, etc.

JESUS:

41. Bear with everyone, harm no one,
This I command you,
And forgive, as I forgive you.

THE ANGEL:
It is God who speaks to us, etc.

THE WORLD:
42. Avoid being bossed around
And treated like a baby.
Wise people will only laugh at you.

THE ANGEL:
That is the voice of the world, etc.

JESUS:
43. Imitate me and you'll be victorious
Through obedience;
Be childlike and you'll enter into my glory.

THE ANGEL:
It is God who speaks to us, etc.

THE WORLD:
44. Oh! you bother too much about trifles
In observing regulations.
These things are not essential.

THE ANGEL:
That is the voice of the world, etc.

JESUS:
45. Your rules, though they seem insignificant,
Are important to my eyes,
Observe them entirely.

THE ANGEL:
It is God who speaks to us, etc.

THE WORLD:
46. God forbids you to bury
Your gifts and talents.
Show how clever you are.

THE ANGEL:
That is the voice of the world, etc.

JESUS:
47. Practice my deep humility.

Prudently, lead a hidden life,
Flee the world's splendor and honor.

THE ANGEL:
It is God who speaks to us, etc.

THE WORLD:
48. Be attractive, well-spoken,
And remember your rank,
You are not a simple servant.

THE ANGEL:
That is the voice of the world, etc.

THE GROUP:
49. Be still, be still, deceiving world,
We all believe in the Lord.
Woe to those who trust you!
Blessed those who live the faith!

50. We condemn the laws of your realm,
We detest what you have just said.
Woe to the blasphemous world!
Praised be the God of truth!
Amen.

## 107
## FAREWELL TO THE FOOLISH WORLD

1. Farewell, deceitful world!
With God my Redeemer,
Whom I so love and serve,
I say to you, Be cursed!
Minister of Satan,
God has damned you, damned you on earth;
Imitating Him, I too
Declare war against you.

2. Satan teaches you
Your cunning and malice;
Against the Almighty

You make vice itself reign.
You resist Him in everything.
He yearns to heal, save our souls;
You seduce them, corrupt them,
You lead them to hell.

3. Bear with it, says Jesus Christ,
If you are persecuted,
If you are cursed,
Mistreated, abused.
You say, such people are fools.
O real cowards, get revenge;
As men of valor, as men of honor,
Avenge all insolence!

4. God repeats a hundred times:
Happy those who weep,
We must carry our cross
Conquering ourselves at all times.
Carry one's cross, you say,
Weep, suffer, mortify, what folly!
Laugh and dance, eat and drink,
Bon vivant, that's life!

5. Blessed the innocent
Suffering poverty.
Unhappy the wicked
Living in abundance.
Let us want for nothing, you say,
Let us be shrewd, let us rise from the dust.
Happiness consists in being rich
And living the good life.

6. For your neighbor, you have
Only a stony heart.
You have only contempt
For the dejected poor;
When he begs,
You reply: 'Go away, you rascal, get a job!
Who told you to bother me?
I have neither vest nor cloak.'

7. O world, tell me:
Do you think it's possible
That God is right and not you?

But alas! You're abhorrent!
Your illness is terminal;
The devil, who instructs and incites you,
Has made you blind and deaf,
And set in your crimes.

8. Your looks are pompous,
You put on a good show
For those that you intend
To reduce to slavery.
You make vain promises;
Cunning and shrewd, you seduce,
You kill, you damn
Those whom you caress.

9. Your smiles are deadly,
Your possessions an illusion,
Your delights coddle the body
And your joy impure.
Those who have best served you
Have only regret for reward,
And for eternity, and for eternity,
Hell as their legacy.

10. Money is your king,
The devil, your father,
Pleasure, your guide
And the flesh is your mother.
But what have you learned?
Nothing but vanity, wickedness, crime.
Those who commit them most cleverly
Are the greatest in your estimation.

11. You reckon sin
Nothing but valor,
You consider virtue
Nothing but zealotry.
According to you, meekness
Is cowardice; humility, servility;
Prayer, peasant behavior;
Fear of hell, weakness.

12. Your palace is named
Infamous Babylon,
Where you cleverly set

The Devil on the throne.
There, your human respect,
Your gourmet meals, false pleasures, your fame,
Your games, wine and your money,
Make you think you're a winner.

13. Arise! O great God, arise!
Take, take up arms
To combat with us
The world and its charms.
Trust, my son,
I have conquered it, you will too;
It has hated me; if it hates you,
What better sign that I love you.

14. Everyone, take my part
Against this detestable world,
It is Satan disguised
In pleasing looks;
Christian, be prudent,
I find horrendous the grandeur he boasts;
Love, seek just the opposite
Of all his temptations.

15. Ah! worldly people, until when
Will you love this world
Which passes in an instant?
Flee, no matter what,
Such a cunning serpent;
Flee, flee or you will die, my brother.
At first sight, it pleases, but sooner or later
Its sweet poison takes.

16. O Lord, we yearn
To walk under your banner
Against this sorcerer,
Although it growls and complains.
Oh! How glorious,
Oh! How great, oh! How great, good Master,
To have you for our leader
In combating this traitor!

17. Farewell, wretched world,
More evil than an atheist
Who has neither faith nor God;

Less stable than a Proteus
More cunning than a serpent;
Farewell, accursed! accursed, farewell!
We despise, we detest,
We condemn your life.

## 108
## TREASURES OF POVERTY

1. THE POOR:
O GOOD Jesus, teach us,
We want to believe only you,
Let the world be silent!
What gives happiness,
Riches or poverty?
Are the poor in heart worth more
Than the proud-hearted rich
Living so comfortably?

2. JESUS:
Come all you poor, listen to me,
I so enjoy talking to you
For you want to believe me.
Come, my chosen ones,
Elders of my house.
It is for you I have come,
You always give me
The most honor and glory.

3. I prize and deem great
All those considered
Desolate on earth,
Those thought to be last,
In my sight, are first.
Beggars, the lowly,
Are my closest friends
For they resemble me.

4. THE POOR:
Let's all cry aloud:
Wretched the wicked
Living in luxury!
Happy the blameless

Treated so harshly,
Living in penury!

5. JESUS:
I conceal myself from the rich and the wise
I reveal myself to the poor unlettered,
To the truly humble.
A good poor person is always satisfied,
The miser never is.
The more he has, the more he wants,
The more he knows, the more he has to know,
He is insatiable.

THE POOR:
Let's all cry aloud:
Wretched, etc.

6. JESUS:
I find in lady poverty
Such splendor and majesty,
That I have espoused her.
This deceitful world's wealth
Is horrendous to me.
I despise all its pomp,
Its false treasures, vain honors,
Its bewitching glory.

THE POOR:
Let's all cry aloud:
Wretched, etc.

7. JESUS:
Holy poverty of heart
Is the true joy
Of the children of the light;
It is the mark of the blessed,
The pledge, the key to heaven,
The spouse of the King of kings,
The companion of his cross
And his beloved daughter.

THE POOR:
Let's all cry aloud:
Wretched, etc.

8. THE POOR:
Lord, presently we deem
Poverty as torment,
As an extreme evil.
The world always chases
After fame and money,
It treats all poor beggars
As rakes and wretches,
Unworthy of love.

9. JESUS:
The world wholly opposes me.
It has always defied me
With all its maxims.
Those I curse, it blesses,
Those I bless, it curses.
Woe to all its followers
For it is a cheat which leads
Everything straight to hell.

THE POOR:
Let's all cry aloud:
Wretched, etc.

10. THE POOR:
My loving Savior, why do
Sinners and the ungodly
Get rich and prosper?
They always have pleasures,
They satisfy their whims
While the innocent suffer,
Starving, weeping, moaning,
Stuck in their misery.

11. JESUS:
Let evil-doers prosper,
Their riches are so fleeting,
And that is their reward.
I send the just many woes,
I leave them in distress
So that they may be purified,
Meriting then a great weight
Of immense glory.

THE POOR:

Let's all cry aloud:
Wretched, etc.

12. JESUS:
Poor, lowly friends, you will be
The great lords in Paradise
And truly kings forever;
I will transform your hovels
Into eternal castles,
Your rags into cloth of gold,
Your want into treasure
Of unspeakable splendor.

THE POOR:
Let's all cry aloud:
Wretched, etc.

13. You rich, wail your tragedy:
Mirth will be turned into tears,
Glory into flimsy smoke,
Stunning castles into pens,
Your good friends into devils,
Your new precious clothing
Into fiery garments.
What destiny awaits you!

THE POOR:
Let's all cry aloud:
Wretched, etc.

14. THE POOR:
Are all the poor saved
And all the rich damned?
Teach us, great Master.
Many poor suffer,
The patient poor are few;
Many rich are evil
But aren't there some
Living as Christians should?

15. JESUS:
I only adopt as my children
The joyful poor in spirit
Who suffer patiently.
The good rich will be saved,

The wicked poor will perish.
My Paradise is for all;
The great as well as the lowly
Receive their just reward.

THE POOR:
Let's all cry aloud:
Wretched, etc.

16. JESUS:
My dear friends, lovingly accept
The poor status I gave you,
And thank me for it.
Endure everything without grumbling,
Work without tiring,
Avoid sadness and boredom;
Never envy another's possessions
And you will walk in my footsteps.

17. THE POOR:
Our woes, Lord, are great gifts
For which we thank you
And bless you always.
How rich who possess you!
How great who resemble you!
Prune then, impoverish us;
We can do nothing without you,
So help us in our weakness.

Amen.

## 109
## PRINCIPAL MYSTERIES OF FAITH

1. ON THE UNITY OF GOD AND THE BLESSED TRINITY
Listen, Christian soul
To what faith teaches you.
To remember it,
Sing piously:
I believe in one God, Father most gracious,
Infinite Being, omnipresent,

The Almighty Creator
Of heaven and earth.

2. There are three persons in God:
Father, Son and Holy Spirit.
Three infinitely perfect,
I believe it, God has said it.
The three are only one God, for the three have only one [essence:
The Father is God, the Son is God,
And the Holy Spirit is God,
All equal in substance.

3. ON THE INCARNATION AND REDEMPTION
Adam, by his offense,
Has fouled us all;
But God, in His mercy
Has redeemed us all.
The Son became incarnate in Mary's womb
Taking there a body like ours,
To redeem us all
And to give us life.

4. This adorable Savior
Whom we call Jesus-Christ,
Was born in a stable
In the middle of the night.
He always lived for us in suffering,
He shed all his blood for us,
Dying on the cross in disgrace
Through immense love.

5. The Church commands us
To believe in Jesus Christ,
One person,
The person of the Son.
But she believes that in him are two natures,
That is: the divinity
Joined to our humanity,
Yet each nature unmixed.

6. He has no other father
Than the Eternal Father
And Mary is his Mother
Inasmuch as he is mortal man.

The Holy Spirit produced this without stain,
For, by an astonishing miracle,
Mary, after giving birth,
Remained a virgin pure.

7. ON THE SACRAMENTS
Like the Church itself
I believe there are seven sacraments:
They are: Baptism,
Always necessary;
Also, Penance, Holy Eucharist,
Holy Orders, Confirmation,
Matrimony and the Anointing
At the end of life.

8. ON BAPTISM
Baptism alone wipes out
Original sin,
It gives us grace,
It opens heaven for us.
It makes us children of God Himself and of the Church.
No one is justified,
No one will be saved
Unless he be baptized.

9. ON CONFIRMATION
The sacrament we call
Confirmation
Fills a man's heart
With strength and unction.
It bestows the Holy Spirit and finally, it strengthens us
To steadfastly profess
All that faith teaches us,
Even at the risk of dying.

10. ON PENANCE
Penance wipes out
Actual sins,
Giving, with grace,
Supernatural gifts.
There are three main parts of Penance:
Contrition, confession,
And the penance.
That is its essence.

11. ON THE EUCHARIST
The Holy Eucharist
Contains in truth
The Body, Blood, Soul
And Divinity
Of Jesus Christ, hidden under the species
Of bread and wine only.
This is what I firmly believe,
In spite of any reluctance.

12. ON EXTREME UNCTION
The Church comforts us
Through Extreme Unction,
When during our final passage
The devil tempts us.
It helps us to die well, or restores life,
Wiping out even the sins
That may be hidden to us.
The sacrament sanctifies us.

13. ON HOLY ORDERS
The order of priesthood
Makes mortal men
Ministers of the Church,
Ministers of the altar.
The priest has power over the body of the Savior
He alone opens and closes heaven
- - - - - - - - - - -- - [*line missing in manuscript*]
In the sacrament of Penance.

14. ON MATRIMONY
The goal of matrimony
And its spirit too,
Is to unite inseparably
Wife and husband
To bring forth children and to raise them
To love and serve Jesus Christ.
That is its goal and its spirit
Which are indispensable.

15. ON THE SACRAMENTS IN GENERAL
They are visible signs
That each sacrament
Bestows invisible grace
On those who receive it.

Jesus Christ instituted them to give us grace,
In order to make us holy,
To nourish us and to help us
Walk in His footsteps.

16. ON ORIGINAL AND ACTUAL SIN
From birth itself
This sin rules within us;
Adam, through his sin
Has infected us all.
We freely commit, of our own free will,
The sin called actual,
Either mortal or venial,
After holy baptism.

17. ON MORTAL AND VENIAL SIN
We always lose grace
By a mortal sin,
We incur the disgrace
Of a just, immortal God.
We also become worthy of eternal punishment.
As for venial sin, it cools
The love of the Holy Spirit,
Its punishment is temporary.

18. ON THE FOUR LAST ENDS,
ON DEATH AND JUDGMENT
Experience by itself
Teaches me that I will die,
The hour is coming,
But when? I do not know.
The soul, leaving the body, presented before God
Will receive from Him his sentence,
Forever to be punished
Or forever rewarded.

19. ON PARADISE
It is a place of delights,
Holy Paradise,
That the most just God
Grants to his friends.
He welcomes there those who die in grace
And there they will forever dwell,
Praising Him, seeing Him,
God Himself, face to face.

20. ON HELL
It is a place of torments,
This hell so cruel,
To punish the malice
Of the wretched sinner.
Those who die unrepentant go there
And there they will forever dwell,
Burning and suffering,
With no hope whatsoever.

21. ON OUR FINAL END
God has given me being
By His good pleasure,
To know Him,
To love Him and to serve Him.
That is my only goal, all else is trivia.
If I serve God well now,
I will rejoice over it
In eternal glory.

22. ON THE NAME AND CHARACTER OF CHRISTIAN
I praise and glorify
God who made me Christian
And I thank Him for it,
As for a great gift.
Whoever has received baptism in the Church
And carries out and believes what she teaches,
Is, unquestionably, a Christian
And a child of God Himself.

23. ON THE SIGN OF A CHRISTIAN
The cross, adorable sign,
When well done,
Is the sure mark
Of a faithful Christian.
This all-powerful sign makes the devil flee,
Forms and enlivens us,
Protects and leads us.
It is of great merit.

24. THE ACT OF FAITH
I believe, as one of the faithful,
What the Church proclaims,
For God Himself, through her,

Speaks to us and teaches.
God can not deceive us, and the same for the Church;
Following her, we walk righteously.
We lose our way if we abandon her
By a horrible mistake.

25. THE ACT OF HOPE
I hope in my weakness
To find in you, Lord,
As you have promised,
Grace and favor.
I firmly hope, my gentle Savior,
To find help in you
And to possess you yourself
In recompense, forever.

26. THE ACT OF CONTRITION
Forgive me, Supreme Goodness,
Forgive me for I have sinned.
For love of you,
Lord, I am distressed.
Forgive me; through your Son and by your tenderness
By your grace, henceforth
I shall never sin again.
I shall keep my promise.

27. THE ACT OF LOVE
O my God, I love you
From the bottom of my heart,
For love of you
And as my happiness.
I also love my neighbor for he is my dear brother
He is the temple of the Holy Spirit
- - - - - - - - - - - - - - - - - - -
And God Himself is his Father.

28. ON THE SEVEN CAPITAL SINS
We recognize and name
Seven capital sins
Which cause man
All kind of evil.
They are: Envy, pride, gluttony, greed
Anger, sloth, lust.
God, for all eternity
Will punish their malice.

29. REQUISITES FOR RECEIVING PENANCE
I examine my conscience
I regret all my sins
I confess them, even the most hidden ones,
And I perform my penance,
Making a firm promise
To amend my life or rather die.

30. THE APOSTLES' CREED
I believe, as faith teaches
In God, Creator almighty.
I believe in God the Father.
I believe in His Son, Jesus Christ,
True God, conceived by the Holy Spirit,
Born of a Virgin Mother,
Died on the Cross for love of us,
Buried on the same day,
Then brought to the netherworld
Joy and light.

31. After three days, this mighty God
Rose from the dead
Achieving victory.
He ascended into heaven,
Next to his eternal Father,
He has the same glory.
From there, this loving Savior
Will come, as a powerful conqueror,
To judge the living and the dead.
This is what I will to believe.

32. I also believe in the Holy Spirit,
The Church, which everywhere is called
The Universal Church.
I believe in the communion of goods
Among saints and Christians,
Among each of the faithful.
The remission of sins
Detested and confessed,
The resurrection of the body
And life everlasting. Amen.

33. THE COMMANDMENTS OF GOD
Adore one God Almighty,

Love Him perfectly
For He is your good father.
Do not take His name in vain.
Do no wrong to your neighbor.
Honor father and mother.
Keep the Lord's day holy.
Be chaste in body and heart.
Neither lie nor steal,
Nor seek to do evil.

34. THE COMMANDMENTS OF THE CHURCH
Hear Mass and keep holy
Feasts and Sundays, entirely.
Go to confession and communion
At least at Eastertide, piously.
On Ember days and during Lent,
And on vigils, you will fast,
On Fridays and also Saturdays
You will abstain from meat.

35. THE PATER
Our Father, who in heaven
Reign in light,
Reign also here below,
May everything revere you;
As it is in heaven, may you be obeyed
Here below on earth.
Give us all this day
Our necessary bread.

36. As we forgive from the heart,
In the same way, forgive us;
Keep us from offending, Lord,
Your Supreme Goodness;
So that we do not succumb
To the devil who tempts us,
Deign to help us everywhere
With your powerful grace.

37. THE PATER
Our Father, who in heaven
Reign powerful and glorious,
May you be loved and blessed.
Make us, like your friends,
Sharers of your Paradise,

And be gracious to us.
Reign over us in this world
So we may reign with you in the next.
As in heaven, may your will
Be done here below.

38. As a father to his child
Give to us this present day
Our necessary bread.
Lord, forgive us
As we forgive our enemies
As a most loving God,
Do not let the devil
Conquer us in temptation,
But keep us from evil
Like a good guardian.

39. THE AVE MARIA
I salute you, Mary,
Mirror of purity,
Virgin brimming over
With grace and beauty.
The Lord is in you among all women,
Your name is holy and blessed
As is Jesus, your Son
Who alone reigns in our souls.

40. You are our mother,
Worthy Mother of God,
Help us in our misery
Always, everywhere.
Pray for us sinners, hide us under your wing,
Be our buttress here below,
Grant us a holy death
And eternal glory.

## 110
## PRAYER TO THE HOLY GUARDIAN ANGEL

1. Holy Angel, all my thanks
For your care and for your help.

Maintain your love for me, please,
For the rest of all my days.

2. Offer my prayers to the Lord,
Lead me in all my ways,
Uphold me in my troubles,
Sustain me in my struggles.

3. Always be my companion,
Overcome my enemies.
Then, one day, in the life to come,
We will be forever one.

## 111
## TO JESUS LIVING IN MARY

1. O Jesus, alive in Mary's womb
Come, dwell in us and reign,
Pour out your life within us,
Now to live for you alone.

2. Form in us your noble virtues,
Your Spirit and His holiness,
The purity of your teachings,
The passion of your charity.

3. Make us sharers in your mysteries
So we may mirror you on earth;
Instill in us your shining wisdom
To lead us at our every step.

4. To the glory of your Father,
In the power of your Name,
Reign in us through your Mother
Over nature and demon's sway.

Amen.

## 112
## DESIRES FOR COMMUNION

1. My heart ardently longs for you,
   O my Jesus, ah! when will you come?
   To be without you is martyrdom
   Come then, O my dear Spouse, Come!

2. I am extremely weak,
   Love, without you, I languish night and day.
   Do you not want me to love you?
   Come then, come, set me afire with love.

3. I am the wayward sheep,
   O Good Shepherd, guard me from the wolves.
   Without you, I would be devoured.
   Come then, let me abide with you, Come!

4. I crave you, O bread of life,
   Today, not waiting for tomorrow
   I want to eat; I die of hunger,
   I am famished, give me bread, I am famished.

5. I come to you, panting
   To become intoxicated at this banquet new,
   For the water of the Samaritan woman
   I thirst, give me water, I thirst.

6. My poor heart is frozen,
   O fire of heaven, come upon me now;
   May my soul be set aflame.
   I am so cold, give me fire, I am so cold.

7. I am a blind man crying:
   Lord Jesus, have pity on me.
   Son of David, Son of Mary,
   Let me see, increase my faith, let me see.

8. I suffer an incurable illness,
   You can heal me by only one word.
   Without you, loving physician
   It's over, I am going to die, it's over.

9. Lord, I knock at your door,
I am in great need, I am dying of poverty
I ask with a strong, tender voice
Give me alms, alms, give me alms.

10. I am, Lord, I am unworthy
To receive Holy Communion,
Say the word, I will be worthy
And come to my dwelling, Come!

11. Come, my true friend,
My dear treasure, my only joy.
Without you, how miserable I am!
Come then, *(twice)* enter into my heart, Come!

GOD ALONE

12. My soul is aflame
I carry my Lord
Deep in my heart.
Thanks, thanks, thanks to Love
Victorious in my heart today.

## 113
## CALVARY OF PONTCHATEAU

Oh, What marvels we will see in this place,
What conversions,
What cures and unique graces!
Let us build, etc.

Oh! what crowds will come here on pilgrimage!
What processions!

# 114
# MISERIES OF THIS LIFE AND TRUST IN GOD

1. My God, when I ponder my weakness,
The power of my enemies,
Their number, strength, and cunning,
I tremble and I truly shudder.

2. I sail on a stormy sea
Where a thousand dangers threaten me.
The tempest is so violent and so furious,
Few there are who pull safely into port.

3. This sea is full of crags,
False friends and many thieves
Offering to help me;
They plan to run me aground.

4. The demon comes, disguising his rage,
Enticing me with earthly pleasures
So that I fall into his slavery
And in the end, into his eternal flames.

5. The world, with its wily fashions,
Its 'point of honor' and 'what-will-they-say,'
Takes my part, smiles, obliges,
Dragging me to its damnation.

6. Under a beautiful appearance
It declares "I am your humble servant,"
Pretending to come to my defense,
So to plunge a dagger to my heart.

7. I sense death on my trail, stalking
Softly, in unfamiliar guise;
Each second it slinks closer,
Ready to seize me by surprise.

8. Yet I have nothing that protects me
From its attacks and dreadful laws;
Even the barriers at the Louvre
Do not shield our kings from their demise.

9. At every moment, eternity approaches
With stinging fire or river of peace,
Not knowing where I shall dwell
Forever, alas! forever.

10. But the enemy most fearsome
Which I nourish, carry everywhere,
Is myself, the sinner, the abominable sinner,
Who wrestles with me to the very end.

11. My soul is full of ignorance,
Weakness and iniquity;
In my heart, only concupiscence,
Sickness or poverty.

12. I feel in myself this rebellious flesh
Struggling with me everyday,
My poor soul is almost overcome
To the point of ceding to its whims.

13. Ah! What would this poor worm do
Who is, of himself, wicked, nothing,
If he had not in this dreadful struggle,
O my Jesus, your all powerful support.

14. Would I not have sunk a thousand times
If you had not been my rudder
And my pilot, dodging storms
Which threaten my labor every day?

15. After Jesus, Holy Virgin Mary,
You are my strong and firm support.
O truth I tell far and wide: Without Mary
I would have long since perished in the sea.

16. In you I place all my hope,
My help and consolation,
Under your wings I am safe,
No matter the flesh, the world and devil.

17. With both of you, I shall be faithful
In the combats of this stormy exile
And gain the eternal crown
Given only to the brave.

GOD ALONE

## 115
## OPENING OF THE PARISH MISSION

1. The Mission has begun!
Drop everything to make it,
For to miss it is a loss,
And it cannot be retrieved.
Profit from this holy time
For it passes, passes, passes,
Profit from this holy time
For it quickly passes.

2. Men and women, are you wise?
Forget your daily chores,
Your family and your home,
For your eternal salvation.
I wish it with all my heart,
Mercy, mercy, mercy, mercy
I wish it with all my heart
Thanks to Jesus, my Savior.

3. Nothing will you lose, I pledge;
For one, you gain a hundred
And for a piece of filthy trash,
The grace of the Living God.
Profit from this holy time,
For it passes, passes, passes,
Profit from this holy time
For it quickly passes.

4. God Himself is the preacher
Through a man like us;
What he teaches, so must we do
Or we will all perish.
It is Jesus our Savior
Speaking, speaking, speaking,
It is Jesus our Savior
Speaking to our heart.

5. We must listen, faithful friends,
And guard within our hearts
This eternal word God speaks
And forever we'll know joy.
Profit, etc.
*or* I wish it, etc.

6. Away with that nagging spirit
So lacking in charity;
Away with those in heresy
Who contradict the truth.
Profit, etc.

7. Penance then is called for,
We must beg for contrite hearts;
Our conscience must be probed
Then all our sins confessed.
I wish it, etc.

8. Accursed mortal sin
Should stir in us great horror;
We must fear even the appearance
Of the slightest venial sin.
Profit, etc.
*or* I wish it, etc.

9. Let us adore God, our Father
Let us love Him perfectly;
Let us offer Him our prayer
Morning, night, and piously.
Profit, etc.
*or* I wish it, etc.

10. Let us calm Him in His anger
By fasting and meditation
And merit his gift of light
By assisting at the sermon.
Profit, etc.

11. Have a horror of blasphemy
And of the smallest oath;
Let's not even say, "By Jove!"
Or "swear to God!" either.
Profit, etc.

*or* I wish it, etc.

12. How well we should assist at Mass,
Shun gambling and dancing.
Often should we confess our sins
And offer unceasing prayers to God.
Profit, etc.

13. The rosary is admirable,
It gives help to us all,
It heals the sin-sick soul,
So let's pray it everyday.
Profit, etc.
*or* I wish it, etc.

14. There is but one thing necessary:
To serve God well, to be saved.
This is our sole concern,
It must be our essential task.
Profit, etc.
*or* I wish it, etc.

15. So let's despise all passing things
As unworthy of our hearts,
Grace alone must we seek,
For only grace can make us better.
Profit, etc.
*or* I wish it, etc.

16. Rising high above our nature,
Let's always live by faith.
In loving God so faultlessly,
His entire law is filled.
Profit, etc.
*or* I wish it, etc.

## 116
## JOYS OF PARADISE

1. Raising my eyes on high
Right up to our home above,

How miserable I feel
That I am still on earth.
Take me away, my God I beg you,
From this distressing exile.

2. Your beauties, O Paradise,
Are completely ravishing,
Your pleasures, never dull,
Your sweetness, innocent.
Your lovely days will never set,
Your splendors are beguiling.

3. Paradise knows no misfortune,
No boredom or grief.
The blessed seem to float in joy,
They delight in all their works.
The pleasures there are always new
Although never changing, endlessly.

4. What tongue can then express
This glory so colossal?
For it flows from the hands
Of God the All Powerful
Who gives Himself as reward
In amazing mystery.

5. O my God, what delight
To have for companions,
The martyrs, confessors,
And the gentle Mary,
To see, without a speck of envy,
The saints decked out in glory.

6. The saints brim over
With admirable joy,
With torrents of pleasures,
With inexpressible peace;
In God alone they are plunged.
O delectable abyss!

7. They see God clearly
As he is in himself.
They praise him unceasingly
At his glorious throne,
Holy, holy, holy, our all-powerful God,

May all love and adore Him!

8. O most lovely abode,
O pleasant springtime,
O reign of pure love,
O desirable dwelling!
Away from you I languish
In a miserable body.

9. If only I could take flight!
Ah! Would that I had wings
To go contemplate
These eternal beauties!
O my God, come free me
From my mortal languor.

10. What! Would I wish forever,
For nothing but a trifle,
To lose this peaceful abode,
This eternal glory?
No, my God, I pledge from now on
Greater fidelity to you.

GOD ALONE

## 117
## PSALM LAUDATE PUERI
## or THE HYMN OF THE PREDESTINED SOUL YEARNING FOR HEAVEN

1. My soul, let us often sing
A delightful canticle,
Praising the Almighty God
And his unutterable name.
May everyone forever praise
This most adorable name.

2. His name is worthy of all honor
On earth and on the sea,
For its majesty surpasses
All the nations here below,

It extends high above the heavens
Its glory, without peer.

3. Nothing can be found equal
To this great God, our Father.
He reigns above the heavens
In grandeur, clothed with light,
Yet with eye so sharp, he sees
Each speck of dust on earth.

4. Oh! How good he always is
Toward each one of his creatures!
From the middle of dung heaps
He rescues the destitute
Setting them on princes' mighty thrones.
O goodness without measure!

5. This great God of majesty
Watches over orphans,
Grants the gift of fruitfulness
To the barren woman,
He supports in infirmity
The weak and the feeble.

6. All of us, with mutual accord,
Let us love this supreme God.
Glory be to the eternal Father
Glory also to the Son,
All honor to the immortal Spirit
Whom we adore and love.

GOD ALONE

7. We offer you, gentle Savior,
Our heart in homage,
But guard well this heart
For it is very fickle.
We will never take it back
In any way. So we may sing:
Live forever Jesus!
Live his Holy Mother!

## 118
## SIGHS OF THE DAMNED

1. Wretched damned soul,
Who has consigned you to these flames?
Who has put you, wretched soul,
In these dismal dungeons?

2. THE DAMNED SOUL:
Ah! It is my unadulterated wickedness
That has plunged me into this fire,
Here I feel the justice
And the punishment of God.

3. THE DAMNED SOUL:
My loss is total:
God lost, all is lost.
God lost, cruel loss!
Who has understood these words?

*4.* *Lesson:*
Mortal man, be wise
And do so at his expense;
If you do not understand his words
You will undergo his torment.

*5.* *Response:*
Oh! What a misfortune, what words!
I shudder, I am stirred.
Yes, I want to become wise
By avoiding sin.

6. THE DAMNED SOUL:
Ah! How miserable I am!
For I can not love God.
Oh! unbearable misfortune,
Only understood here.

*Lesson*:
Mortal man, etc.

7. THE DAMNED SOUL:
I no longer have God for father,

He is my angry judge
Punishing my guilt
In His great wrath.

*Lesson*:
Mortal man, etc.

8. As I am completely opposed
To this holy and powerful God,
He returns blow for blow,
Overwhelming me constantly.

*Lesson*:
Mortal man, etc.

9. I have, for a trifle,
For a moment's pleasure,
Lost eternal life;
I am constantly infuriated.

*Lesson*:
Mortal man, etc.

10. Alas! My life is over,
Oh most cruel memory!
I feel my soul devoured
By undying regret.

*Lesson*:
Mortal man, etc.

11. I moan without repentance
I burn without consuming
I suffer without hope,
I regret without loving.

*Lesson*:
Mortal man, etc.

12. I breathe only flames
Both within and without
The fire penetrates my soul,
I am a burning coal.

*Lesson*:

Mortal man, etc.

13. In everything that surrounds me
I find new agony;
I suffer without receiving
The tiniest relief.

*Lesson*:
Mortal man, etc.

14. All the demons vex me
The demons are my butchers;
These cruel tyrants invent
Ever new tortures.

*Lesson*:
Mortal man, etc.

15. Despair, rage
And the grinding of teeth
Are my only language
In the midst of my torments.

*Lesson*:
Mortal man, etc.

16. I am torn and consumed,
Vexed and cursed
For my wretchedness is strange,
My hardships are endless.

*Lesson*:
Mortal man, etc.

17. Suffering overwhelming:
The long eternity.
Oh! dreadful "forever"
Oh! terrible truth!

*Lesson*:
Mortal man, etc.

18. Forever with the demons,
The damned and the snakes,
In unbearable fires,

In these stinking dungeons.

*Lesson:*
Mortal man, etc.

19. Forever this abode!
Forever damned!
Miserable and damned hour
When I was born!

*Lesson:*
Mortal man, etc.

20. Rage, despair, blasphemy,
Since one must always suffer,
Since one must stay the same
Without ever dying!

*Lesson:*
Mortal man, etc.

21. I await you, O accursed father,
Who made me offend God
*Or* I await you, O accursed brother
Who made me offend God.
*Or* I await you, O accursed mother
Who made me offend God.
Come, I will battle you
Forever in this place.

*22. Response:*
Oh! What a misfortune, what words!
I shudder, I am stirred.
Yes, I want to become wise
By avoiding sin.

GOD ALONE

## 119
## LAMENTATIONS OF THE SOULS IN PURGATORY

1. Mortals, heed us, listen,
   Listen to us, dear brothers!
   We send up our sighs to you
   From the depths of misery.
   Alas! how we do suffer!
   Who could ever understand it?
   We weep, we cry out, we moan
   And no one wants to listen.

2. We are your relatives,
   Your fathers and mothers,
   Dear friends, dear children,
   Kindly hear our prayers!
   If bonds of love or blood
   Make you have pity,
   Please, please comfort now
   Our terrible pain.

3. You have your pleasures,
   You live at your ease,
   And you leave us all
   Here in this furnace.
   You spend your money
   On frivolous goods,
   Being able by far
   To relieve our pain.

4. And you, most gentle Lord,
   You wage war upon us.
   Ah! when will you finish
   Being against us?
   How your great goodness
   Makes you appear kind!
   How our iniquity
   Makes you so dreadful!

5. Friends, this relentless God
   Shapes all our torments;
   We feel the rigor

Of all his justice.
Yes, we do love him
As our good Father
But we now do feel
He is a stern judge.

6. He gives us a glimpse
Of His supreme beauties,
It is in this mirror
That our pain increases;
To see for a second
His infinite beauties,
Justice would demand
Living a thousand lives.

7. Beware of sinning,
Beware of believing
That it's not much to go
Burn in purgatory!
There is no little sin,
There is no tiny fault,
Since God punishes it
With so much anger.

8. Alas! a searing fire
Is devouring our soul,
Piercing it, making it
Only a blazing coal.
These fires are so fierce,
They are sheer flames;
Your most violent fires
Image them so faintly.

9. Here there is no way
For us to help ourselves,
We merit nothing
In our extreme torment.
Mortals, if you wish,
It would be so easy,
The least you would do
Would be most helpful to us.

10. Pull us out from these flames,
God himself requests it,
To bring us to heaven,

Building up his kingdom.
You will glorify Him
With glory all anew
If you obtain for us
Eternal glory.

11. If you rescue
Or assist us,
You will surely glimpse us
Full of gratitude;
For, winning through you
Full victory,
We will exploit all means
To bring you to glory.

12. If even very small actions,
A glass of water given,
Have before God their reward,
Their glory and their crown,
Oh! what great reward, Good God,
Will your alms receive,
If, for a bed of fire,
You give us a throne!

13. If you do not answer
Our most just request,
The Lord, here below,
Will do the same to you.
You will be measured
With the same measure;
You will then be left
In this place of torment.

14. Get us out of prison
By your righteousness;
Please pay our ransom
By holy penitence.
Do you hear our cries?
We shout to all: Help!
Please be kind to us,
Help! Help! Help!

15. PRAYER TO JESUS AND MARY:
Lord, be merciful
To these poor victims.

Let your anger fall on us
For their enormous crimes.
Deliver them from the flames,
Bring them all to glory!
You will then have, far and wide,
Total victory.

16. Pray for our relatives,
O Holy Virgin Mary.
They are your dear children
Be then merciful to them.
Show them at this moment
That you are their mother.
Calm the All-Powerful
In his just anger.

GOD ALONE

## 120
## DESPAIR OF THE SINNER AT DEATH

1. What! must I then die,
Leaving all I own?
O cruel, accursed hour
Robbing me of all I hold!

2. O bitter, dreadful death,
I must part from all things!
Grant mercy to my moan,
O please delay your blow.

3. I am caught in the snares
Satan hid so well from me,
I'm aware of all my blasphemies,
I perceive all my sins.

4. How many graces scorned!
How much advice disdained!
How many hours wasted!
How many gifts trampled!

5. My Jesus have mercy
On this wretched sinner;
Mother of all mercy
Beg my Savior for me.

6. JESUS:
You, now so wretched, scorned
All my loving calls;
It is just and fitting
I scorn you in turn.

7. I laugh at your alarm,
At your false repentance,
I ridicule your tears,
You must die and perish.

8. MARY:
During life you should have
Prayed to me and changed;
It's too late to beg me,
I no longer wish to help.

9. THE DYING PERSON:
Woe to me! No longer Father,
He is my angry judge.
Woe to me! No longer Mother,
I am by all forsaken.

10. My enemies surround me,
My body still grows weak,
And yet there is no one
To come and help me out.

11. Alas! must I die
To be damned forever?
Wretched, cursed hour
When I first saw the day.

12. I see too late, sinful world,
Your so deadly blindness:
I now perceive all your scams,
But alas! There is no time.

13. Farewell, damned carcass,
Farewell, food for worms,

I will wait for you in the cell
Reserved for you in hell.

14. Ah! If I had subdued you,
Death would be my pleasure.
Alas! since I flattered you,
Death is my cruel regret.

15. I see you, wretched devil,
Lingering near my bed.
Carry me off, loathsome monster,
For you have seduced me.

16. I am flayed alive, torn apart,
Since I die in spite of myself.
Alas! must I then expire
In my sins now clearly seen?

17. I breathe my last, impenitent
For having, until death
Deferred my penitence.
Sinner, do not copy me.

18. They alone are wise
Who prepare for many years
The journey through this dreadful passage.
Judge for yourself, at my expense.

19. Live better than I did, I beg,
Then you'll have a better fate.
For as your life is spent,
So also will be your death.

GOD ALONE

## HYMNS IN HONOR OF SOME SAINTS

### 121
### IN HONOR OF THE HOLY GUARDIAN ANGEL

1. How blessed I am *(twice)*
   To have ever at my side
   A angel as my guardian.
   He is a prince of Paradise,
   A favorite of God,
   The terror of his enemies,
   One of the pure spirits
   Not of this earth.

2. His power is enormous, *(twice)*
   He can alone, by his strength,
   Overturn the whole world.
   He has a ravishing appearance,
   And is a spirit most perceptive,
   Subtle and active.
   In an instant he can even
   Cross the earth and sea.

3. Being so perfect, he chooses *(twice)*
   To be himself my guardian,
   To strengthen my weakness,
   For he forms me, leads me,
   Admonishes and warns me,
   Protecting me silently,
   As the enemy who beguiles me,
   Loses all his cunning.

4. He keeps me constantly *(twice)*
   From so many adverse occasions,
   Many find it difficult to believe.
   It is through his inspiration
   That I am devout.
   He makes me conquer the devil,
   Overcome temptation,
   And win the victory.

5. But of whom does he take such care? *(twice)*
   Imagine! He helps in need

A poor worm of the earth,
A poor sinner, a nothing
Who, for all the good done to him,
Refuses to give thanks,
And knowing that the angel is near,
Makes no effort to please him.

6. My holy guardian angel, I want *(twice)*
To entrust to you
My happiness.
I thank you for the honor
Of being in your care.
I will overcome the tempter,
With you as my protector,
Against his impudence.

GOD ALONE

## 122
## IN HONOR OF JOSEPH SPOUSE OF MARY

1. Let's sing a hymn in honor
Of Saint Joseph, the protector
And humble spouse of Mary.
Lowly Joseph is little known,
No one on earth appreciates him,
But he ravishes the blessed.
May earth unite with heaven
And all proclaim his praises! *(twice)*

2. Great saint, you alone God found
To be the worthy spouse
Of his admirable Mother.
Spouse of the Queen of heaven,
This privilege is marvelous;
The witness of her holiness,
The guardian of her purity,
O incomparable glory!

3. The Eternal Father chose you

To nourish his Son on earth,
In fact, to be His vicar.
You have carried in your arms
The Child holding all things in His hand;
By a most special vocation
You have been the nurturer
Of your own Father.

4. Who would have seen Him caress you,
Smile at you, embrace you
With extraordinary love!
His smiles pierced your heart
Filling it with meekness.
All aflame by His love,
You told Him, in your turn:
My dear Son, I love you.

5. If a word of Mary was able
To sanctify, by its power,
Saint John with his mother,
What must have wrought in you
His words so meek and holy!
His talk surely ravished you,
And his presence filled you
With graces and with light.

6. How great your humility!
Humility prompted you
To keep silence,
To take the lowest place,
To live as a poor carpenter,
To appear ignorant,
Incapable, without talent,
Simple and unwise.

7. The more you humbled yourself
The more God has exalted you
Close to Him in glory.
Your merits are astounding,
Your privileges are great,
Heaven admires your splendor,
The world is full of your favors
Even in Purgatory.

8. No one ever prays to you in vain,

Your intercession is supreme
As Teresa herself confirms.
Your Son is the glorious God
Your Spouse, the Queen of heaven.
Praying, you command them;
If you ask, nothing is refused.
O power without measure!

9. SAINT JOSEPH:
Try to be the last in all things,
To hide yourself, and grow in love
Of Jesus and Mary!
Seek what the world rejects
And flee from what it pursues.
Let faith alone govern you,
In order to be happy with me
By imitating my life.

10. PRAYER:
Saint Joseph, be my patron
To obtain for me a great gift:
Divine Wisdom!
To glorify my Savior,
To convert sinners,
To help poor little ones,
To crush my enemies.
Love impels you.

GOD ALONE

## 123
## TREASURES OF THE CROSS

DIALOGUE OF OUR LORD WITH THE FAITHFUL SOUL

THE SOUL:
1. O Jesus, my adorable Master,
Show me the way to heaven,
Show me which is better:
To be rich or poor,
To rule or serve,
To be at ease or suffer greatly.

JESUS:

2. Learn, dear faithful soul:
Great God that I am,
I so strongly loved contempt,
And the cross appeared so stunning,
I came down from heaven and took flesh
To adorn myself with them.

3. In my wisdom I find
Treasures in poverty,
Splendor in humility,
Greatness in lowliness!
With great scorn I look upon
Wealth, pomp, all worldly honor.

4. I lived in obedience,
Humbled myself to serve,
Chose to be born and to die
In want and suffering.
Would you reign with me?
My example must be your guide.

THE SOUL:

5. But Lord, my dear model,
The world seeks grandeur,
Pleasures, wealth, honors;
You do the exact opposite.
Its pleasure is to dominate,
It knows nothing of obedience.

JESUS:

6. Know that I esteem
What the world shuns.
Unhappy whoever follows it,
For it leads straight to the abyss.
I curse those the world deems happy
But bless those it considers mad.

7. With kindness, I regard
The afflicted, the poor and the despised,
Those suffering without cause,
If they bear it patiently;
My favors are theirs,
Wonders await them in heaven.

8. Would you offer God my Father
Great, perfect honor?
Suffer well, esteem the pain,
Embrace the cross,
Be the servant of every one;
Then my spirit will rest upon you.

9. For the crosses I send you,
Offer me thanksgiving
As for my greatest gifts;
For the cross begets joy,
Virtue, grace and peace,
And in heaven, happiness forever.

10. Is your life hidden,
Are you overlooked?
Is your status vile and lowly?
Be consoled, my well beloved,
Your plight, so like mine, is a sign
That I love you dearly.

11. Have you been slandered?
Are you bearing bodily pain,
Within or on the outside?
Is someone envious of you?
Fine! I am delighted.
My close friends are all treated in this way.

THE SOUL:

12. O Mary, O afflicted Mother,
Let me partake of your sorrows,
Share your flowing tears with me
So that my soul be cleansed.
No cross without you and Jesus;
Neither of you, if the cross is no more.

MARY:

13. The cross is my tree of life,
I am the Mother of the living,
All my good children share the cross,
Do you not desire some?
I have crosses of great price
But they are only for my favorites.

THE SOUL:

14. Willingly, O afflicted Mother,
I shall share your grief
If, with your sweetness, my cross will be
Sweetened and well blended.
No cross without you and Jesus;
Neither of you, if there is no cross.

15. O Jesus, thank you a thousand times
For your lesson all divine!
How I beg you for forgiveness,
So poorly have I followed you.
I set forever my true joy
In modeling you, my Savior.

16. If your gentle Providence
Grants me a share in your cross,
It is far too much an honor.
But strengthen me in my weakness,
Humble, sever and strike
And I'll still be happy, if you help.

GOD ALONE.

## 124
## DESIRES FOR WISDOM

1. O Wisdom, come, a poor soul begs you
By the blood of my gentle Jesus,
By Mary's womb.
We shall not be disappointed! *(twice)*

2. Why do you so prolong my martyrdom?
I seek you night and day!
Come, my soul longs for you,
Come, for I am languishing of love. *(twice)*

3. My beloved, open, I knock at your door,
Ah! It is no stranger,
It is a heart, by love transported
Who has no dwelling place but you! *(twice)*

4. If you do not want me to be yours,
Then let me pester you.
Leave me always in the anguish
Of seeking and never finding you. *(twice)*

5. I cast myself in spirit at your throne.
If you want nothing to do with me,
At least give me some alms
For the faith-filled poor. *(twice)*

6. Wisdom, how I fear that misfortune befall me:
To be fainthearted and negligent,
Lacking lively faith
To love you passionately! *(twice)*

7. Worthy Mother of God, Virgin pure and faithful,
Share with me your faith.
Through it, I shall have Wisdom
And all good will come to me. *(twice)*

8. Wisdom, come then, through Mary's faith,
You could not resist her.
She gave you life,
In her, incarnate you became. *(twice)*

9. I believe, without hesitating: nothing is impossible for me.
Wisdom will come to me.
God has said it, He is infallible!
Who prays with faith will receive, *(twice)*
Who knocks with faith will enter,
Who seeks with faith will find.

GOD ALONE

## 125
## PURSUIT OF WISDOM

1. Let us not ape the worldly,
Nor this deceiving world;
Impoverished though we be,
True happiness we seek;

In spite of trickery,
In spite of derision,
In spite of vanity,
Let us seek the truth. *(twice)*

2. Then let us all seek Wisdom,
She is a hidden treasure;
We must seek her constantly,
Nothing should restrain us.
Let us roam around the world,
The heavens, the earth and seas,
Suffering, sparing nothing,
So this wealth may be found. *(twice)*

3. Let us pursue Wisdom,
One day we will find her.
Always pursuing her,
At the end we will have her.
Let us climb the mountains,
Roam the countryside,
Penetrating forests
And most secret places. *(twice)*

4. This path we must follow,
Wisdom has passed by it;
Believing fully, we will
Surely one day find her.
We must spare no effort;
Her sovereign loveliness
Deserves from us far more.
Let us delay no longer! *(twice)*

5. Let us then leap for joy,
Believe, without falter;
We will possess Wisdom,
We must never doubt it.
A faith-filled heart
In one fell swoop arrives
Within Wisdom's dwelling.
Let us firmly believe it. *(twice)*

6. Let us knock at the door
Of a Most Gracious God
He himself exhorts us
To fear not pester Him.

We must repeat our needs,
Increase our offerings,
And in holy rapture
Shout even the louder. *(twice)*

7. O Divine Mary,
You alone have found
Infinite Wisdom
In the Word enfleshed.
Being His great Mistress,
Love now impels you
To send Him to us
To teach us all,
To help us all,
To help us all.

8. O Divine Wisdom,
Source of truth itself,
The world forsakes you,
Following vanity.
We will all seek you
With most lively faith
And no matter what,
Yourself, we beg, reveal. (twice)

9. O Wisdom, assistant
Of the Divinity!
We eagerly await
Your beauty to behold.
Having deigned this promise,
Why then delay so long
This gift so glorious?
O Come, O come at last! (twice)

GOD ALONE

## 126
## PRAYERS TO WISDOM

1. O Divine Wisdom,
I love you ardently!
You are my mistress,
I am your lover!
On earth you alone
I seek and I love,
You are so attractive,
I am just about delirious!

2. Tell me who you are
I see you so vaguely.
You are a mystery
To your poor friend.
I love you so purely,
My pure beloved,
Reveal yourself fully,
Now, to my sick soul.

3. Where is your dwelling?
Wisdom, let me know.
I will fly there right now,
Love orders me to do so.
Must I traverse the seas
And roam through the world?
Must I soar through the air?
Anything to find you!

4. You are, great queen,
Wounding my heart;
I love such pain deeply,
It is my great bliss.
O how glorious
To suffer your wounds;
How aggravating
To suffer those of creatures.

5. You are so beautiful
In Jesus, my love!
I will be true to you
Both by night and by day!

Our love most pure
Is miraculous,
Stronger than ramparts,
Death can not quench it.

6. Know that when I love you
I love Jesus in you.
He is wholly in you,
He alone is your rule.
Let no one accuse me
Of loving a creature.
I know your many charms,
Spells of a pure virgin.

7. World, I detest you
And your deceiving loves;
Mine is most heavenly,
Full of wonders sublime!
You love, now and then,
Only stinking carrions.
I love devoutly and always,
Wisdom's splendors so charming.

8. May we both have one soul
In two different bodies!
We will be but one flame
With the same raptures.
Let us both have for goal
Only Jesus and His glory.
Routing the evil one,
Together, we shall sing victory!

9. O Eternal Wisdom,
Without you, all is lost.
Earth cries out to you,
Come, come and help us!
To extend everywhere
Your wonderful realm
Come, come to us as God
Otherwise, everything will perish.

GOD ALONE.

10. Justice, you are allowed
To strike, it is time!

But, O mercy,
Forgive the repentant;
Strike the proud
Who will not believe,
But pity for those
Who believe and praise you.

11. O Victory, victory
To Jesus Crucified!
Honor, praise and glory
To this great King of kings.
It is time, it is time
That His kingdom take over,
That His Cross overpower the Crescent;
I believe it with lively faith.
Let those who believe follow me now!

GOD ALONE.

# 127
# ABANDONED SOUL
# FREED FROM PURGATORY BY THE PRAYERS OF THE POOR AND OF CHILDREN

## A DIALOGUE HYMN

NOTICE

In order to sing this dialogue in a way pleasing to God, edifying to neighbor and useful to the souls in purgatory, the following points must be observed:

1st Begin by the *Veni, Creator Spiritus, Accende lumen sensibus,* followed by *Ave, maris Stella, Monstra te esse Matrem.*

2nd Twenty persons are needed:

| | |
|---|---|
| God the Father, | The abandoned soul, |
| God the Son, | 4 suffering souls, |
| God the Holy Spirit, | 4 living souls, |
| The Blessed Virgin, | Genevieve, Catherine, |
| The Guardian Angel, | Agnes, Frances, |
| The Devil, | Armelle |

This does not include the Angels who surround the throne of God, or the poor, who will all pray as one voice.

3rd Each person must learn her hymns by heart, sing them calmly, and practice in the sections in which they take part. Five chairs will be prepared, the one in the center higher than the others and the actors arranged something like this:

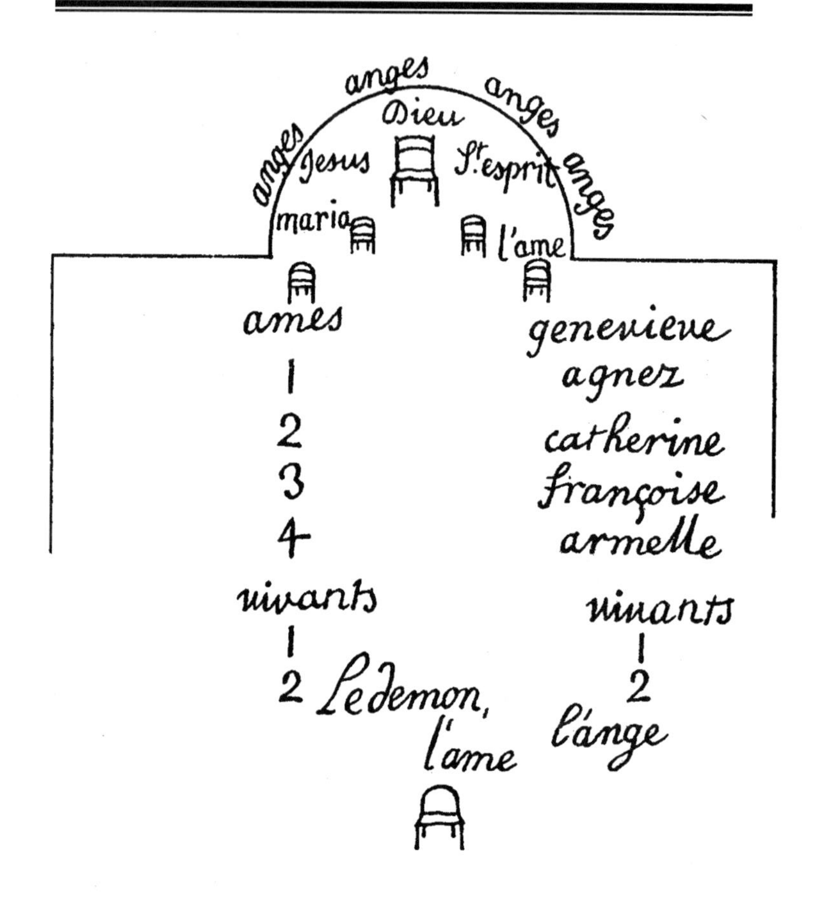


*A copy of the drawing by St. Louis Marie de Montfort*

THE SOULS:

*The four souls begin together, Singing with longing and calmly, hidden and at a little distance:*

1. Mortals, listen to us,
Listen to us dear brothers,
We sigh to you
From the depths of our miseries.
Alas! how we suffer!
Who could understand it?
We weep, we cry,
But no one to hear us.

| | Dialogue | Stage direction |
|---|---|---|
| | GENEVIEVE: | |
| 2. | Oh! the pitiful cries!<br>My heart is touched<br>Who are these miserable ones<br>Who suffer nearby?<br>Beloved companions,<br>Whence come these sighs,<br>These broken voices?<br>Are they not martyrs? | Genevieve leaves her place and turning toward her companions while making fitting gestures, says to them: |
| | AGNES: | |
| 3. | These cries, you must believe,<br>Are those of our relatives<br>In Purgatory,<br>Suffering cruel torments.<br>Let us listen to their pleas<br>From the depths of their dungeons;<br>Let us feel their sufferings<br>And hearken to their sobs. | Agnes takes one step forward toward Genevieve and says to her: |
| | CATHERINE: | |
| 4. | Is it not a trick?<br>I want to uncover it.<br>Let me, I beg you,<br>Leave for a moment! | Catherine leaves her place and turning toward the living says to them: |
| | THE LIVING: | |
| 5. | Go, right away!<br>You would make us happy.<br>Show us where they dwell<br>Or make them come here! | The living respond to her: |
| | CATHERINE: | |
| 6. | Souls, tell us who you are,<br>Where do you dwell? What do you suffer?<br>Leave your secret dwellings.<br>Speak to us, show us,<br>Ask, ask and you shall receive! | Catherine goes over to the side where the souls are and cries out as much as she can: |
| | THE SOULS: | |
| 7. | We are your relatives<br>Your fathers and mothers,<br>Your friends, your children,<br>Your own sisters and brothers.<br>If love or blood | |

Do not make you unfeeling
Comfort, now
Our terrible sufferings.

CATHERINE:

8. Ah! I am inconsolable
I recognize a voice:
It is my loving father,
I have sinned, I know it.
Alas! I was compassionate
When I saw him die
Then I became distracted
While he was suffering!

Catherine, turning toward her companions says to them as she strikes her breast and with a languishing tone:

THE LIVING:

9. (First) That is my father's voice,
My heart is touched!
(Second) That is my mother's voice,
I recognize her cry!
(Third) It's my sister or my brother!
(Fourth) It's my dead husband!
(Fifth) Alas! It's the prayer
Of my old friend!

The living speak slowly, one after the other:

THE ABANDONED SOUL:

10. I am burning in the fire
For more than a year.
By men and by God
I am abandoned.
Ah! I can not die
In my bitter miseries,
Deign to help me
By your holy prayers.

The abandoned soul cries out from her place:

GENEVIEVE:

11. See, O sweet Savior,
Your conquest in chains!
See, O good Shepherd
Your sheep in trouble.
Sweet Jesus, snatch them from the fires
And place them in heaven!

Genevieve leaves her place and goes before Jesus; kneeling before Him, she says:

ALL TOGETHER:

12. Sweet Jesus, snatch them from the fires
And place them in heaven!

Agnes, standing at the center of the stage, cries very loudly:

AGNES:
13. What is your martyrdom?
Souls, describe it to us.
Appear, to tell it
And we will pray for you.

The four souls leave slowly from their hidden place and once arrived, with veiled faces, they say:

THE SOULS:
14. From a deep abyss
We leave right away
To seek in the world
Some comfort.

The souls, after a moment or two, continue to cry without raising their head:

THE SOULS:
15. We are in a place
Filthy and dark
We grovel in the fire
Of a most angry God.
The devils, our executioners,
Burn us, exhaust us
And torture us in a thousand ways
Which can not be described.

The poor kneel with hands joined and head bowed:

THE POOR:
A GROUP OF CHILDREN:
16. Lord, have pity
On these poor victims!
Rather, punish us
For their great crimes!
Snatch them from the fire,
Take them to heaven,
You will have everywhere
Full victory.

The abandoned soul without appearing, cries out:

THE ABANDONED SOUL:
17. You amuse yourselves,
You live at your ease
And you leave me
In this furnace.
You spend my money
On foolish purchases,
When you could easily
Alleviate my sufferings.

AGNES:

18. O Good God, cast your eyes
On this unfortunate soul.
Pierce this dark place
With a loving light.
Sweet Jesus, snatch them from the fire
And take them to heaven! (twice)

Agnes, kneeling before God the Father, humbly says to Him:

A GROUP OF CHILDREN:

19. See, O King of Glory,
Your child in chains.
He burns in Purgatory,
He is abandoned.
Good Father, You must grant
Forgiveness for his sin,
Your heart is too tender
Not be touched.

Several children kneeling before God the Father.

GOD THE FATHER:

20. I am Beauty without blemish,
The Sovereign Sanctity,
This soul is not pure enough
She offends my majesty.

God, without getting up, says in a serious tone:

GUARDIAN ANGEL:

21. Be consoled, my beloved,
People are praying for you.
You will soon be freed,
You will soon be with us!

The Guardian Angel says to the abandoned soul:

22. O Good Jesus, be appeased
With this poor suffering soul;
You are her dear Spouse,
She is your dear lover.
Sweet Jesus, etc.

Genevieve kneeling before Jesus, says:

THE POOR:

23. Pardon, our good Master,
For your poor friends,
Deign, deign to bring them
To your Paradise.
By our holy sacrifices,
Our alms, our promises,
Plus all our good deeds,
Bring them to heaven!

GOD THE SON:
24. I am pleased with your requests,
Knock, and it will be opened to you:
I readily accept your offerings;
Give, and you will receive.

THE SOULS:
25. The fires are very fierce
In this place of torture,
Your fires, the most keen
Are but an image of them.
It is a devouring fire
Which penetrates your soul
Devouring it and making it
A coal all aflame.

AGNES:
Agnes, on her knees before the Holy Spirit says:
26. Holy Spirit, Comforter,
Behold your creature.
Be her liberator
In the torments she endures.
Holy Spirit, snatch her from the fire (twice)
And take her to heaven.

A GROUP OF CHILDREN:
27. Hear us, O Father of lights
Be touched by your children's sufferings.
Lend your ear to our humble prayers,
By helping our friends and relatives!

THE HOLY SPIRIT:
28. If I allow these souls to suffer
It is because they resisted me too much;
They despised my ardor,
My meekness and my love.

THE SOULS:
29. How evil to offend God,
And what an error to believe
That it's a trifling matter to go
Burn in Purgatory!
There is no slight fault,
There is no light fault
Since God punishes them

With such anger.

THE ABANDONED SOUL:
30. My soul, in this place,
Constantly casts itself toward God,
And constantly, God
Rejects it and humbles it.
No mortal man
Has ever felt this sorrow;
My martyrdom is cruel,
My discomfort extreme.

GENEVIEVE, *on her knees*
31. Show yourself, O dear friend,
To this soul who loves you;
At this moment, show her
That your love is unending.
Sweet Jesus, etc.

THE POOR, *on their knees before Mary:*
32. Pray for our relatives,
Holy Virgin Mary.
They are your dear children,
Be merciful to them.
Show them now
That you are their mother.
Calm the All-Powerful
In his just anger.

GUARDIAN ANGEL:
33. Be consoled, my beloved,
Mary is interceding for you.
You will soon be freed,
You will soon be with us.

THE SOULS:
34. A powerful and holy God
Forms our torments.
We feel the weight
Of all his justice.
It is true, we love Him
As our good Father,
But we experience Him
As a severe judge.

AGNES:

35. O good Jesus, be appeased
Toward so many poor victims.
Avenge yourself rather on us.
Punish us for their crimes.
Sweet Jesus, etc.

THE POOR:

36. O God of love, O sovereign Goodness
You fill both heaven and hell.
Reveal yourself in this terrible place
To sweeten it, to break its chains.

THE ABANDONED SOUL:

37. God makes me see
His sovereign beauties
And it is in this mirror
That my sufferings grow.
For, to see for a moment,
These infinite beauties,
I would justifiably
Live a thousand lives.

The four souls kneel before God the Father and say:

THE SOULS:

38. Alas! Most sweet Lord,
You are against us.
Ah! when shall we see you
Our God, our Father!
You who in your beauty
Seem so loving to us!
You, whom our iniquity
Renders so awesome!

39. Father, you love us
As your true children,
And you forget us
As now we are pitiful.
O God of love,
Pardon, mercy!
O God, full of goodness,
Have mercy!

GOD THE FATHER:

40. No mercy,
For its time has passed.

I do not want to be approached
Until everything has been well paid.

41. I am the God of vengeance,
This is my own dwelling.
It is in this place of suffering
That I rule at my turn.

42. Suffer, poor creature,
I have no pity on you.
For you are not yet pure enough
To be worthy of me.

43. I love you, it is true, I love you
As my own image
But your tepidity is extreme,
Your sin has defeated you.

THE SOULS:

*The four souls go before Jesus and say:*

44. Most amiable Jesus,
Calm your Father.
Do you no longer love us
In this place of wrath?
We cost you so dearly,
Love your heritage,
Come, free us,
Crown your own work!

JESUS:

*Jesus, without getting up, says to them:*

45. I love you without limit,
But nothing impure enters heaven.
When you will be completely pure
I will take you from the fires.

THE SOULS:

*The four souls kneel before the Blessed Virgin.*

46. O our good Mother,
Can you look upon us
And not be touched
By our misery?
We sigh to you our plea,
In our cruel sorrows.
Calm your angry Son
By your womb that bore him,
By your sweet breasts!

MARY:

*Mary, without getting up, says to them:*

47. My children, I am touched.
Loving you so tenderly
As your Mother, my prayers
Calm the All-Powerful.

THE SOULS:

*The four souls go before the living and say:*

48. Do you also wish,
Dwellers of the earth,
To forget us here
And wage war against us?
Have pity on us,
Dear charitable souls,
We all beg you
By our pitiful cries.

THE ABANDONED SOUL:

49. Come, help me,
Even God desires it;
It gives him pleasure,
It builds his kingdom.
You will glorify him
With new glory
If you procure for me
Eternal glory.

FRANCES:

*Frances, kneeling before Jesus:*

50. O Jesus, gentle lamb
Free our relatives from the flames,
They cost your Precious Blood!
Alas! Alas! You wage war against them,
They cost you your Precious Blood!
Alas! Alas! Take them to heaven.

51. Sweet Jesus, these souls love you,
Sweet Jesus, give them peace,
As your greatest gift, forgive them.
Alas! Alas! Their sorrows are extreme.
Ah! give them, as the greatest gift,
Eternal rest in heaven!

THE POOR, *kneeling:*

52. You help the ravens that beg you
And you give to all abundantly;

Do you forget the poor souls crying to you?
They have cost you your blood.
No, your heart is too compassionate.

THE SOULS:

53. If you free us — As before.
Or give help
You will see us
Full of gratitude,
For, having had through you
Complete victory,
We will do everything
To glorify you.

THE ABANDONED SOUL:

54. Here, there is no longer any way
To help myself,
I merit nothing
In my extreme anguish;
Friend, if you wish,
It would be easy for you.
The little that you will do
Will be very useful for me.

FRANCES:

55. Help, o Virgin Mary, — As before.
Your children and your servants.
See them suffering so much pain,
Alas! Alas! be moved.
See them suffering so much pain,
Calm a rigorous God.

MARY:

56. My child, I am moved, — As before.
For my heart is full of love,
I am praying and speaking to my Son
For you all, night and day.

THE POOR:

57. O most gentle Jesus, rise, — As before.
For the poor beg you,
With your Mother, Mary.
By her womb which bore you,
By her sweet breasts,
Show your beauty in heaven

To these faithful souls.

GUARDIAN ANGEL:

*The angel goes in front of the soul and says:*

58. Be consoled, my beloved,
The poor are urging God for you.
You will soon come with us.

THE ABANDONED SOUL:

*Kneeling, the soul says:*

59. O my faithful guardian,
How you console me!
Oh! The good news
That you bring me!
I will enter into glory
I will possess God!
I will sing victory
Even in this lowly place!

THE SOULS:

*As before.*

60. If very small good acts,
A glass of water given,
Have before God their reward,
Their glory and their crown,
What a great prize, O Good God,
Your alms will receive
If, for a bed of flames
You give us a throne.

THE SOULS:

*As before.*

61. If you do not listen
To our just plea,
The Lord, on this earth,
Will treat you the same.
You will be dealt
The same measure,
You will be left
In this place of torment.

THE ABANDONED SOUL:

*As before.*

62. Free me from prison
By your good deeds,
And pay my ransom
By your holy penances.
Do you hear my pleas?
I am asking for help
Be moved by my cries

Help! Help! Help!

ARMELLE:

Armelle, kneeling before Jesus, says:

63. I am a weak creature,
Prostrate here before you,
Lord, I beg you
To have mercy on them all.
Let these souls redeemed
By such precious blood
Be forever adorned
With glory in heaven!

64. I am a servant,
Have pity on me;
For this suffering soul,
Love obliges me.
Although I am not worthy
To ask you for anything,
As a great grace
Grant me this favor.

65. My Spouse, you must set
This soul in liberty
And give him your Being
For all eternity.
Grant my prayer,
By your gracious heart
By your holy Mother
By the poor orphan.

MARY:

Mary kneels before Jesus:

66. Behold your Mother,
O Jesus, my child;
I pray to you
For a poor suffering soul.
Give him the grace
By his poor little ones,
O heavens, make room for him,
He is your friend.

JESUS TO HIS MOTHER:

Jesus gazes at His Mother and then standing, says:

67. You wish it, my mother,
Then it's done. It is enough.
You do not need to ask,
Command, command.

JESUS TO HIS FATHER:

68. My Father, I beg you
To hear now
Both my Mother Mary
And the price of my blood.

Then turning towards his Father, he says:

THE POOR:

69. Lord, you must listen to
Your true Son,
You cannot resist
His adorable Blood,
You cannot rebuff
An admirable mother,
You cannot reject
A miserable sinner.

The poor before the Father:

GOD THE FATHER:

70. Yes, I am obliged to hear,
For He is my true Son
No, I cannot resist
His adorable Blood.
No, I cannot rebuff
An admirable mother.
No I cannot reject
A miserable sinner.

Without getting up:

71. Angel, descend quickly
To Purgatory,
To lead now
This soul to my glory
I want him like me
To wear a crown,
Powerful and rich as a king;
It is I who command you.

An angel comes. God says to the angel:

THE ANGEL TO THE SOUL:

72. Rise promptly,
Ascend to heaven.
The Lord is calling you.
To reward you
And to crown you
With eternal glory.

THE ANGEL TO SATAN:

73. Satan, withdraw,
Obey the great King,
Fly to the abyss
And go burn in hell.
This soul is going to heaven
In splendor supreme!

THE DEVIL:

The devil, slinking away and striking himself, says to the same melody of the damned souls:

74. I am outraged, I am furious
I cast myself into the flames
For this soul has inherited
What I have lost in heaven.
Miserable, miserable,
I will burn in the flames.

THE FREED SOUL:

The Angel, leading the soul by the hand, moves toward the throne of God and says:

75. Let us fly like a turtledove,
We are given wings,
To the throne of the Lamb
To the eternal splendors.
I enter in you to love you,
O Supreme Monarch!
To see you and to rest
Forever in you.

GOD:

God speaks lovingly to the soul and places the soul on a throne:

76. I ardently desire
To possess you, my beloved,
Approach boldly then,
All fear is past.

77. I give myself entirely to you
In all my glory
Enter then forever in me.
Sing victory forever.

ALL THE ANGELS:

When the soul is enthroned, all the Angels sing together:

78. Let the heavens rejoice
A soul joins the ranks of the saints
O God, Most High, may you be blessed
For this masterpiece of your hands!
Let all men, let all angels
Sing joyfully:
Our brother is in heaven (twice)
To God alone glory and praise!

THE POOR:

79. Let us forever bless
The Lord in his goodness
An abandoned soul
Who suffered in the fires
Is in heaven,
She is crowned.
Let us forever bless
The Lord in his goodness.

Together:

## 128
## BLESSED SACRAMENT: FOR SUNDAY

1. How overwhelmed am I,
Seeing the lowliness
Of the Supreme Majesty
In the Blessed Sacrament.
I see there our True God, the King of Glory
Hidden in obscurity
Without splendor, without majesty.
Oh! who could believe it?

2. This gentle Lamb
Assumes this state
To stand before His Father
As our advocate.
There He remains night and day in His presence,
Holding back God's avenging arm
Ready to punish the sinner
Who angers and offends Him.

3. There He offers Himself as victim
To calm the Father's wrath,
Unceasingly pleading with Him
To have pity on us.
There He offers to God all honor and homage,
Making Himself our complement,
Infinitely loving Him in our stead.
What more could He do?

4. In His Father's presence, He is
   In adoration,
   Full of reverence
   And of love for His name.
   There at every moment His Sacred Heart desires
   That God be exalted everywhere,
   And that everything be truly
   Subjected to His reign.

5. Through Him the angels
   And all the blessed
   Give unending praise
   To God in heaven.
   What they do in heaven, we also can do
   Since Jesus is with us there
   To become all things to all
   As our model.

6. Since Jesus lowers himself
   Through an excess of love,
   His love urges us
   To make a like return.
   Let us visit Him often in this great mystery;
   *Amen* to all He says there,
   To all he does there day and night
   To honor his Father.

7. O most amiable Jesus
   We give ourselves to you.
   How reasonable that is
   Since you give everything to us.
   Come, reign in us as in your temple,
   To adore the Father profoundly
   And to love him perfectly;
   We follow your example.

8. Render, as you do
   For us on this altar,
   Perfect praise
   To the Eternal Being.
   Sacred Heart, intone the awesome hymn
   That you alone can truly sing.
   All heaven, on hearing it, experiences
   Great joy.

## 129
## BLESSED SACRAMENT: FOR MONDAY

1. He whose beauty ravishes
All the saints in glory,
Dwells on our altars day and night,
Hidden in the tabernacle.
The All-Powerful, in His grandeur
One with God His Father,
Is present in this mystery
To ravish our hearts.

2. Truly Jesus possesses
In the Eucharist
Fullness of love,
Fullness of life.
He is the infinite treasure
Since He is Wisdom;
His splendor is not tarnished
By lowering Himself to us.

3. In the Eucharist, He spares nothing,
Giving Himself completely,
All things to all and to such an extent
That He can do no more.
Without becoming less, He gifts everyone,
Excluding none.
To give is His greatest pleasure,
He is happy when giving.

4. Oh! who could describe
The eternal sweetness
This Spouse lets his faithful lovers
Taste in this Sacrament?
He is a delicious wine
That has no equal,
He is a precious perfume,
A delightful nectar.

5. There He is all things to all,
So charitable is He;
There He is our dear Spouse,
Our true God,

Our gentle master and physician,
Our friend, our brother,
Our way and our path,
Our gentle light.

6. In His Heart reside His treasures,
It is their dwelling place,
To bestow them with kindness
Provided we place no obstacle;
This Sacred Heart ardently desires
To give, to pour Himself out,
He calls us incessantly;
But who really wants to hear Him?

7. "Come, dear friends, come everyone,"
This most kind Master says,
"Come see how sweet it is
To know me and to love me.
I give you my flesh as food,
Eat, for I love you,
Drink my Blood in long drafts,
Even to inebriation."

8. Jesus loves us, let us love in turn;
Doesn't that make sense?
Let us approach Him without fear,
For He is all lovable.
Do we wish to love Him ardently
As we will in Heaven?
Let us go to the Blessed Sacrament,
It is the raging fire of such desire.

9. Bestow, O divine Jesus,
Your grace into our souls,
For we will resist no longer
Your sweet flames.
Through your love, make
Our souls courageous,
Cast on our poverty
A loving glance. Amen.

## 130
## BLESSED SACRAMENT: FOR TUESDAY

1. Oh! the Blessed Sacrament
Is a wonderful school
To learn in a short time
Without expertise or words
The science of the virtues,
Divine wisdom!
The professor is most sweet Jesus,
He preaches there constantly.

2. He is a teacher without peer,
He enlightens the soul
And like a divine sun,
Warms it, setting it afire;
In this mystery, He is
Our holy model,
Living day and night in secret
What He constantly preaches.

3. When He descends to the altar
It is through obedience,
The voice of a mortal man
Brings Him there willingly.
It is there His Sacred Heart
Burns with the greatest zeal;
He comes to save sinners,
He calls and enlivens them.

4. The love of humility
Draws Him from glory,
To hide his majesty
In a simple ciborium;
It is there that he teaches
His customary lesson:
Learn I am humble, gentle,
And a most loving lamb.

5. Although often the sinner
By his behavior
Insults His dignity
In the Eucharist,

No one can imagine
How patient He is,
His Heart suffers everything,
Not seeking vengeance.

6. It is there that he is always
Dead to worldly things,
Without use of his senses,
In profound peace.
His heart is so meek,
(His favorite virtue!)
Supporting sinners sweetly,
Without any wrath.

7. This mystery is all about love,
Rather, is love itself.
Jesus is there day and night
To show that He loves us.
Like a very faithful friend
He constantly begs us
To love Him, to seek in Him
Authentic life.

8. How much does he love God the Father?
There is no limit,
Since He loves Him here
As much as He should.
Finally, all the virtues
Have for their sole source
The Heart of most loving Jesus:
He alone bestows them.

9. Dear friends, let us all visit
This supreme monarch
Since He wishes to remain with us,
To show that He loves us.
We will learn the secrets
Of obtaining victory,
Of becoming perfect
And of acquiring glory.

10. O Jesus, enlighten us,
O infinite Light!
Only in you can be found
The words of Life.

Form in us your virtues
And your living image,
Our hearts will no longer resist
This labor all divine.

## 131
## BLESSED SACRAMENT: FOR WEDNESDAY

1. May my tongue everywhere proclaim,
All the days of my life
The grandeur of the Blessed Sacrament.
Come, see the Savior of our souls,
Come, see his Sacred Heart
Aflame with ardor divine,
It is but fire *(twice),* it is but flame.

2. This Heart is always open
To make itself our home,
Our sure refuge,
For everyone a mighty fortress
Never pierced by any foe.
It is the kingdom of peace,
Where we become *(twice)* invincible.

3. In this Heart, God the Father
Never vents his just anger
Against the sinner staying there.
The Sacred Heart hides him under his wing
Covering him with His love,
Calming His wrathful Father.
O love *(twice)* most paternal!

4. O Christians, flee far from the world
Into this Heart where all good abounds;
This Heart is found in the Blessed Sacrament.
Come, taste within this faithful Heart
More sweetness, more delight
Than your own could desire.
Fear nothing, *(twice)* this Heart calls us.

5. Come, sinner, find true life

And all kinds of wealth
In the Holy Eucharist;
Come, hide, rest in safety
Within my Sacred Heart;
You will find there the sorrow,
The forgiveness *(twice)* for your sin.

6. Fervent souls, why delay
Tasting the delightful sweetness
Which always fills my Heart?
Rest there, learning in silence
The language of holy Love,
To speak there, at your turn,
With love *(twice)* and reverence.

7. My Sacred Heart becomes all things
To every soul resting there;
It gives without diminishing,
Enriching, helping, encouraging,
Protecting, instructing constantly.
It loves, caressing and guiding.
It is for all *(twice)* everything, fully.

8. During the worst upheavals,
When despised and insulted,
Come there to be consoled.
Do your foes look to destroy you?
Let my Heart be your tryst.
You will crush them all,
Doing nothing *(twice)* but laughing at it all.

9. Soul all pure, come, visit me,
Leaving behind finite things;
I await you in the Blessed Sacrament.
Enter my Heart, remain hidden there,
Fearing nothing, for it is your home.
Savor my goodness there
Forever, *(twice)* my beloved.

10. O Jesus, then I must go there,
Your love too strong, too tender.
Shelter me in your Heart
To win victory over myself
And over my other enemies.
May your Heart alone be my Paradise,

Where forever *(twice)* mine loves you!

## 132
## BLESSED SACRAMENT: FOR THURSDAY

1. Truly, the Good Jesus
 Strikes me as so lovingly
 Generous of Himself.
 Not satisfied with thirty-three years
 In work and torment,
 Through extreme love
 He yearns to abide with us,
 To become all blessings for all.
 PRAISED BE THE BLESSED SACRAMENT,
 MAY IT BE ADORED AND LOVED!

2. He loves us to excess,
 Giving us free access
 To His holy presence,
 Hiding His divinity,
 His splendor and majesty,
 Under lowly appearance.
 He seems forgetful of grandeur,
 So to ravish our hearts.
 Praised be the Blessed Sacrament,
 Its love is immense!

3. God loves us here tenderly,
 Pouring himself out fully,
 Ah! who could believe it?
 He gives Himself totally,
 Giving His flesh to eat,
 His own blood to drink,
 His soul and infinite Being,
 So to change us into Himself.
 Praised be the Blessed Sacrament,
 So worthy of glory!

4. Though his power here always
 Performs great prodigies
 By changing nature,

His love is even more surprising
Since He unites it forever
With us, His creature.
Jesus and the soul form but one.
Everything between them is in common.
Praised be the Blessed Sacrament,
He loves without limit!

5. Come to me, come, sinners,
This loving Savior tells you,
Come, men and women,
My name is "consuming fire"
And my heart ardently desires
To set your souls aflame.
I have come down from heaven
Only to light fires everywhere.
Praised be the Blessed Sacrament,
His Heart is all afire!

6. If you wish to share this fire
Come to my Heart, where it is found;
There this fire dwells,
There the saints were inflamed,
Come to be enkindled.
I share this fire lavishly,
You only have to ask,
Since I want to grant you everything.
Praised be the Blessed Sacrament,
His love spurs us on!

7. I became your Savior,
I carry you written in my heart
With a divine character.
My Heart has emptied itself for you
So that you all may become
The children of my Father.
It is open so you may dwell there,
So I may protect you and console you.
Praised be the Blessed Sacrament,
A dazzling mystery!

8. Christians, let's make a holy exchange,
Returning love for love,
Our God deserves it.
The flood of our iniquities

Could not impose on His bounty
Either end or limit.
Woe, anathema to the sinner
Who does not love this gentle Savior.
Praised be the Blessed Sacrament,
Now and forever!

9. Let us say gently and tenderly:
O Sacred Heart, set us on fire!
O Divine Flame,
Here are our hearts, consume them,
Making them, upon your altar,
An acceptable sacrifice,
So we may sing night and day
This sweet song of love:
Praised be the Blessed Sacrament,
He alone is our life!

AMEN.

## 133
## BLESSED SACRAMENT: FOR FRIDAY

1. Listen to my just complaint,
Lovers of my Savior.
I shall tell you fearlessly
The sentiments of my heart:
We forget, we abandon
JESUS IN THE BLESSED SACRAMENT.
Hardly anyone is seen there.
Sighing deeply, I say it.

2. The mansions of the mighty
Fill with numerous people
Who often, for their troubles,
Have only their wasted time.
But the church is neglected,
"It is boring to spend time there,
An hour seems like a year."
Oh weep, Oh weep, my eyes!

3. Do you see the king of glory
Abandoned on our altars
And banished from the mind
By the majority of mortals?
He who ravishes the angels
By His divine splendors
Is treated with strange contempt.
Oh flow, Oh flow, my tears!

4. The All Adorable
Often lodged so poorly,
The church seems a stable,
Dirty, without adornment!
Yet the world's esteemed
Dwell in homes well adorned,
Nothing lacking, in all things abounding,
All shines, everything is gilded.

5. Everything is in hushed silence
Within the royal chambers,
We respect the king's presence,
His words are laws;
While we see ungodly men
With no respect before God
And by their behavior
Dishonor His holy place.

6. The best of all masters,
After having surrendered everything
Is, by thousands of traitors,
Betrayed, mocked, profaned.
He is given for His dwelling
Even the devil's place,
Where His Heart suffers constantly
So bitter a passion.

7. We have seen heretics
Topple the sacred places
And in spite of Catholics,
Trample the host underfoot.
This is how men offend
Their loving Benefactor.
How I shudder just to think of it!
What cruel disaster!

8. What! Can we be indifferent
To this contempt, this abuse?
No, no, that would be impossible.
Let us weep then over gentle Jesus!
Let us visit Him often,
Taking the place of so many Christians;
His Heart entreats us,
He wants to shower us with gifts.

9. To make amends for these outrages,
Let us love Him deeply,
Let us render Him homage,
Let us pay court to Him.
Let us make an act of reparation
To His Heart so despised,
Since this most loving Heart
Has emptied itself for us.

10. Reign everywhere, powerful Master,
Even in the Blessed Sacrament.
Great God, reveal yourself,
For is it not, at last, time to do so?
Prevent anyone from approaching you
To cover you with contempt,
And be merciful
To our truly contrite hearts.

11. Since our possessions are yours,
Having received them from you,
May your contempt be ours
And may it fall on us
To make reparation for all these crimes.
Here are our hearts, take them
To make them victims
At the foot of your holy altar. Amen.

## 134
## BLESSED SACRAMENT: FOR SATURDAY

1. Jesus could not leave Mary,
So strong the love which bound them;

That is why, just before his death,
He established the Eucharist,
So that after the Ascension,
He could be her consolation here below.

2. Having taken so much pleasure
In her pure womb for nine months,
He again often wishes
To rest there in silence.
And to offer himself to the eternal Father
On the altar of her heart.

3. Banished from the heart of ungodly man
Jesus comes into His Mother's Sacred Heart
To receive perfect honor;
He praises and glorifies her Heart
With such a gentle and heavenly song
Which He alone can sing fittingly.

4. He reposes comfortably
On the bed of her purity;
In the fire of her charity
He takes inexpressible joy.
But above all, her humility
Draws her to Him and enthralls His majesty.

5. Jesus, full of gratitude,
Shares with her all His treasures,
Nourishes her with His own Body
That she nourished in His infancy.
For the milk of her most pure breast,
He feeds her with His divine blood.

6. What pleasures and what caresses
She receives in that sweet moment
When she holds her Son, her beloved,
The only object of her tenderness!
It is then that her Sacred Heart
Thrills for joy in Jesus her Savior.

7. Her holy Heart is a fire,
A burning bush all aflame
Which finds only in her God
Being, support and life.
It burns but is not consumed

For it can never love enough.

8. Love seems, in this great mystery,
Of their two hearts, to form but one;
Between them, everything is shared,
For the Son is completely in his Mother.
In the Mother, one can only perceive
Her dear Son, her love: Jesus.

9. It is then by her prayer
She obtains from our Savior
Pardon for the poor sinner.
He is her Son, she is His Mother.
Her holy Heart and most chaste breast
Make Him meek and mild.

10. O Christian, the faithful Virgin
Gives us in her communions
Holy examples.
Let us imitate this perfect model
To render perfectly
All our duties to the Most Blessed Sacrament.

11. It is from you, O Virgin Mary
That His body and blood come to us,
Raising us to such a high rank
That even angels envy us.
May you be blessed far and wide
For having given us this precious gift.

12. Lavish, o admirable Mother
All your virtues in our hearts
So the most sweet Jesus
May enjoy being in us.
Lavish your love in us
So we may love your dear Son through you.

13. O Jesus, your Holy Mother
Is our perfect supplement,
So come to us promptly
To unite us to your Father
Or, rather, come into her Heart;
She will provide for our lack of fervor.
Amen.

## 135
## HYMN ON THE LOVE OF GOD

1. How sweet to sing both night and day
The canticle of fair love!
O my Jesus, my love, I love you,
I want to love nothing but you,
No one really knows what joy
It is to love you, my Savior.
Christians, I love Jesus, say the same,
Taste how sweet is love. *(twice)*

2. Tell the truth. Am I not right
In loving so good a Lord?
He alone is infinitely loveable,
Beauty itself, without blemish
Rich and generous,
All good without trace of evil.
What could be sweeter, what then could be more sound
Than to love Him with all one's heart? *(twice)*

3. If I do not love this charming Lord
My heart cannot be content;
For it is captive, knowing only anguish,
And finally turns so bitter.
Love can set it free
And make it say, in truth:
O my Savior, your yoke is not a burden.
O! How sweet it is to love you! *(twice)*

4. What! The good God for loving us
Would receive nothing in return?
Will it be in vain that He loves us without end
And fills us up with his kindness?
No, No, anathema to sinners
Who do not give their hearts to Him!
Christians, let us love, His love propels us on,
Let us love Him forever. *(twice)*

5. O God of love, consuming fire,
Be our gentle conqueror,
Set us afire with your divine flames.
Let our hearts be your dwelling.

Forgive us, divine love,
For having so withstood you.
Reign henceforth in our souls,
And we will say both night and day:
Love, love, love, love (twice)
Amen.

*Jesus Maria*
AD MAJOREM DEI GLORIAM

# 136
# REPARATION TO THE BLESSED SACRAMENT

1. Let us sigh, moan, weep bitter tears:[38]
   Jesus is abandoned in the Most Blessed Sacrament!
   He is forgotten, His deep love abused,
   He is attacked, so insulted, and in His own house.

2. Everything gleams in Monsieur's well-furnished house.
   Yet the Church is ignored, the altar stripped,
   The pavement cracked, the roof unfinished,
   The walls are crumbling, covered with grime.

3. A broken crucifix, dusty paintings,
   Rotting linens, filthy vestments,
   Books are torn, the lamp unlit,
   Everything chaotic, thrown about in the dust.

4. The ciborium broken, the chalice tarnished,
   The monstrance nothing but tin or moldy brass,
   From the holy water fonts up to the sacristy,
   Everything is in a contemptible and disgraceful mess.

5. We dare not spit in pagan temples,
   But ours are filled with packs of dogs
   Running about, barking, covering everything with filth,
   And no one even cares about all this abuse.

[38] For the context of this hymn, see "Benefices" in the Introduction on page xi.

6. If anything is clean in the house of God,
It is the pew for the Lady or the Lord of the town.
On the filthy walls his coat of arms is boldly painted.
If you have faith, come, join me in my tears.

7. Instead of the name of the immortal Lord,
Monsieur's coat of arms at the center of the altar!
Both the priest and the mule wear Monsieur's coat of arms,
One honors him at the altar, the other in his stable.

8. How many people pay court to the famous,
And at Mademoiselle's place, night and day!
Altars are deserted, the church abandoned,
A very short Mass seems like a year.

9. Look at this elegant Abbé, look at the libertine!
He enters the church with a haughty air;
One knee on the bench, he looks around, waves hello,
Strolls about, chatting as though walking the streets.

10. But, how dreadful! He pinches snuff,
Either giving or taking it, *ab hoc* and *ab hac*;
All puffed up with himself and his elegance,
He wiggles, gets settled, as he prays twisting his face.

11. Often, he does not come to adore Jesus,
But to revere the goddess Venus.
His desires, his looks, his speech, his posture
Are all devoted to some creature.

12. Look, while you weep, look around:
A brazen woman in her brocade billowing out,
On dainty shoes, with a crest three layers high,
Entering our holy place just to show off!

13. Watch as this big windbag strolls
To the foot of the altar, close to the living God
Or at least to a pew where she can be seen
And with her eyes shoot arrows into men's hearts.

14. This devil's lackey challenges the honor
And the divinity of the Sovereign Lord!
Next to her finery, Jesus is not noticed,
The altar cannot shine next to her jewelry.

15. Her dog, her fan, her gloves, her adornments,
And often her Adonis amuse themselves there;
She reads a little then she primps,
Looking around to check who's noticing.

16. Strike, great God, strike the arrogant, the ungrateful!
At least then they will fear you, for they do not love you.
Join your justice to your patience,
And then arrogance will fade into fear.

17. Your glory is ravished, and your name tarnished,
You are derided, what infinite evil!
Hold back, nonetheless, your bolts of justice,
For your goodness outweighs their malice.

18. Pardon, my gentle Jesus, both for them and for us,
Have pity on us; have pity on yourself.
Ah, if only we could make amends for these insults
By your own blood and our weak praises.

19. Behold! We lie prostrate at the foot of your altar
You can strike us, we are guilty;
But if you consider your Heart and our tears,
You must graciously hear us for we are justly alarmed.

## 137
## NEW HYMN IN HONOR OF CALVARY (1)

1. DEAR friends, let us quiver with joy,
We have Mount Calvary here;
Let's hurry, love impels us,
To see Jesus Christ, dead for us.

2. For the believer, this Calvary suffices,
Here we see what was seen of old:
A God dies to calm God his Father,
A God dead for us on a cross.

3. Here we see God who loses his life
At the hands of ungrateful traitors,
Here, we see His glory overwhelmed

And crushed between two thieves.

4. We see a darkened sun,
Rocks splitting open with sorrow,
Tombs revealing their dust,
The universe trembling with fear.

5. This slain God makes us aware
Of the sins of criminal man,
Of the grandeur of the offended Lord
And of the miseries of eternal hell.

6. It is here that we see obedience
Triumph, giving us peace;
It is here that we are born
To die and to live forever.

7. It is here that a dying God enchains
Both death and hell to his cross,
It is here that his love draws
Heaven and the entire universe.

8. Here is the summary of the miracles
And the excess of the Savior's love,
The summary of the oracles
His mouth drew from his heart.

9. Here is the unfailing remedy
That puts an end to evil,
Here is the foolproof argument
Resolving all our problems.

10. Are you suffering a cruel sorrow?
Look, take the crucifix,
You will see in this faithful mirror
That your woes are small indeed.

11. It is from here that repentance springs,
It is from here that peace flows,
It is here that happiness begins,
It is here that it never ends.

12. Let us then love this kind Savior,
So pierced, all torn by blows,
Let us adore his adorable cross

And kiss his feet and the nails.

13. Let us be holy! This Calvary is dreadful
To those whose choice is sin;
Here, we must feel the sorrow
And let our hearts be touched.

14. Everything cries out in its own way:
Ah! sinner, God dies of love for you!
It is time to weep for your deeds,
It is time that you love him in turn.

15. Away from here worldly man!
Away from here carnal man!
Away from here warring people!
Away from here all lackeys of hell!

16. Afflicted soul, here is your refuge;
Penitents, this is your proper place;
Poor people, this is your home;
Here one becomes rich in God.

17. Let us leave our hearts and offerings here,
Let us embrace the cross joyfully,
To reap the benefit of our pleas,
To rise from this Calvary to heaven.
Amen.

GOD ALONE

## 138
## NEW HYMN IN HONOR OF CALVARY (2)

1. My God, I yearn to love you. *(twice)*
Love impels me,
I begin to be enflamed
And you begin to beguile me.
May everyone allow me to love.
May everyone allow me.

2. Entirely submissive to your law *(twice)*

From Paris right to Rome,
I choose you for my King,
I pledge fealty to you,
In spite of anyone, even myself,
In spite of anyone.

3. I want to love you, my God, *(twice)*
With an heroic love,
Although I am ridiculed everywhere,
Although all say farewell,
Although all vex me at my tasks,
Although all vex me.

4. Hell is all enraged *(twice)*
Shaking heaven and earth,
But, my God, in spite of wolves,
If you help me,
I will battle everyone.
I will battle.

5. Brave, not spineless, Christians, *(twice)*
Let us love with courage,
Let even our songs battle
The world and its monsters,
Even hell and the devils.
Let us love more, let us love,
Let us love more.

6. Let us love God with joyful heart, *(twice)*
Fearing no one.
If we suffer here below
Some blows of the envious,
Consider the crown in heaven,
Consider the crown.

Amen.

# 139
# PLAN OF LIFE
# OF A MAN CONVERTED DURING THE MISSION

1. Great God, Adorable Lord,
Would you permit a sinner
To hold the honorable title
"Your humble servant"?
May your mercy confer
And bestow it upon me,
So I may tell the whole universe
I love and serve you.

2. EXCELLENCE AND QUALITY OF THE SERVICE OF GOD
To serve God: what illustrious grandeur,
Greater than an emperor's!
Lord, I am not worthy
To be your servant,
But you will it, great Master.
I will then try to be one,
Telling the whole universe
I love you and serve you.

3. I received your light,
Your grace and my pardon
During the last mission
While listening to the sermon.
I have undertaken some holy practices,
Putting them to song;
I serve God with my whole heart,
It is my glory and my joy.

4. I serve God when I adore Him
"In spirit and in truth;"
To do so, I beg
The help of His goodness
For his grace is necessary
Both to will and to do it.
I serve God with my whole heart,
It is my glory and my joy.

5. “In spirit,” means total,
Without any contriving;
Whoever picks and chooses,
Does not serve God in holiness.
Fervently, not sluggishly,
Joyfully, not sadly,
I serve God with my whole heart,
It is my glory and my joy.

6. “In truth,” means without sham,
Without deceit or flattery,
With neither fear nor constraint,
Willingly, sincerely,
Without worldly human respect.
Whether they flatter or scold me,
I serve God with my whole heart
It is my glory and my joy.

7. DAILY SCHEDULE
As soon as I awake
I raise my heart to God.
Sleeping or waking,
Lord, I am all yours;
Here I am, ready to do
Everything to please you.
I serve God, etc.

8. Praying to God, I get dressed
After a sign of the Cross;
Without useless thoughts,
Without raising my voice,
Without any immodesty
Which would shock sight or hearing.
I serve God, etc.

9. I get dressed; I ready myself
So that I am clean,
But without affectation,
With neither sensuality nor vanity,
With respect and decency
Without wasting time and money.
I serve God, etc.

10. Then, I say my prayers

On my knees, piously,
Quietly, without distractions
Of my own volition,
Devoutly, not sluggishly
Joyfully, not sadly.
I serve God, etc.

11. I meditate in His presence
On death and final judgment,
Heaven and its rewards,
Hell and its punishments,
The eternity of delights,
The eternity of torments.
I serve God, etc.

12. I put my room in order,
After praying to God;
Or I do some other work
Depending on time and place,
For God alone, in His presence,
And without being self-centered.
I serve God, etc.

13. Every hour of my days
Is regulated as by a compass.
I have designated times
For everything, even my meals:
A time for this spiritual exercise,
A time for that mortification.
I serve God, etc.

14. From time to time, and at each hour
I look toward heaven
And I say: There is my dwelling
And my eternal home.
O my soul, keep vigil,
All things are passing, God watches you.
I serve God, etc.

15. I read, I write or pray,
I work steadily,
Spending my life for God
Without wasting a single moment.
Time is so precious
And cannot be reclaimed!

I serve God, etc.

16. Before sitting down at table
    I say *Benedicite.*
    While eating, I am pleasant,
    Moderate and courteous,
    Modest in my bearing
    And silently joyful.
    I servc God, etc.

17. I devoutly give thanks
    At the end of my meals.
    The world may do it with a smirk
    Or not even at all.
    Long meal, short prayer.
    As for me, I do just the opposite.
    I serve God, etc.

18. If I can, I hear Mass
    Every day, devoutly;
    In order to do so, I leave
    Everything aside, promptly.
    After Mass, all other tasks
    Usually turn out better.
    I serve God, etc.

19. I give time to mental prayer
    Faithfully, every day,
    Without neglecting vocal prayer;
    Both are a great help
    In serving God completely
    And in loving Him even more.
    I serve God, etc.

20. Every day I pray the Rosary
    Or at least five decades;
    A voluntary practice
    But a perfect secret
    Which makes our life joyful
    And our death so precious.
    I serve God, etc.

21. To be righteous and faithful,
    I live all things by faith,
    I am guided by it in all things;

It is my torch, my law.
What faith decrees,
I observe without quarrel.
I serve God, etc.

22. Every month, usually,
I receive the sacraments
And more often, if necessary,
Depending on times and places;
The more often I receive Communion
The more Life I share.
I serve God, etc.

23. I never excuse myself
From making, at least every night,
An examination of conscience
On my principal duties.
Then, as punishment for my offenses,
I perform some penance.
I serve God, etc.

24. After saying my prayers,
I go to bed modestly,
With no imprudent chatter,
Or any delay,
In a spirit of obedience,
In a spirit of penance.
I serve God, etc.

25. When I lie down I take
The position of a corpse;
This posture truly affects me.
Thinking of God, I fall asleep;
Lord, for you I slumber
As my heart beats and keeps watch.
I serve God, etc.

26. RULES REGARDING TEMPORAL GOODS
Not having been made for this earth,
But for an immortal good,
I plan neither lawsuits nor fights
For gaining temporal goods.
I obtain them justly,
Possessing them with no greed.
I serve God, etc.

27. I would prefer to be stripped
    Of my vest and coat,
    Than to keep my clothes
    By quibbling in court.
    A servant of God yields;
    God does not want him to sue.
    I serve God, etc.

28. For the Church and its interests
    One can rightly wrangle;
    Also, through zeal, for the good of another.
    But beware of being damned
    If such charity is not impartial,
    With no bitterness, no insults.
    I serve God, etc.

29. As soon as I can, I pay my debts
    Willingly, joyfully,
    Without inventing excuses
    To avoid their payment;
    No need for police intervention,
    No detours, no trickery.
    I serve God, etc.

30. I give alms for God alone,
    In order to make friends,
    To gain a scepter, a throne,
    A kingdom in Paradise;
    But my almsgiving is secret,
    Prompt, cheerful and faultless.
    I serve God, etc.

31. With prudence and wisdom
    I manage my estate.
    If I make a generous gift,
    I do it as a Christian,
    No ostentation, no fanfare,
    No foolish outlays.
    I serve God, etc.

32. No showiness in my belongings,
    No luxury in my clothing,
    Nothing sumptuous in my home,
    No extravagance in its furnishings,

For, at my baptism, I have said
Anathema to the world.
I serve God, etc.

33. In the town, in the countryside,
At home, or in the field,
Whether I lose or win
My heart is always satisfied:
No argument, no anger,
No flamboyant joy.
I serve God, etc.

34. REGARDING HONOR AND PRAISE
I never aim for
Praise or honors;
But if granted to me,
I refer them to the Lord.
Nothing a person says of us
Makes us foolish or wise.
I serve God, etc.

35. At other times, in silence,
I consider my place in hell,
Taking no satisfaction
In human praise;
For, speaking ill of oneself
Is often supreme pride.
I serve God, etc.

36. Content with my lot in life
I have no ambition to climb higher.
Although my condition is quite ordinary,
I have all that I need.
My only glory and the highest one,
Truly lies within me.

37. Bah! to the sage in his wisdom,
If he is not wise in the Lord.
Bah! to the noble in his nobility
If he is not noble of heart,
If he does not forgive an injury
Without getting even or complaining.
I serve God, etc.

38. I find my greatest glory

By humbling myself in suffering;
I find my full victory
By conquering myself in forgiving,
In honor without self-satisfaction,
In insults without getting even.
I serve God, etc.

39. At the most inexplicable insults,
I say, "May God be praised!"
Without seeking revenge
Or punishment for the troublemaker.
I forgive him willingly,
Complaining to no one.
I serve God, etc.

40. REGARDING PLEASURE
I condemn and detest
All forbidden pleasures,
Knowing that by this plague
Great saints have been lost.
I am also moderate
In necessary pleasures.
I serve God, etc.

41. We must crucify ourselves
To belong to Jesus Christ.
Constantly mortifying ourselves
Both in mind and body,
Whether eating or drinking,
Never attracting attention.
I serve God, etc.

42. The finest dish on the table,
The choicest, the imported,
The most exotic,
I forgo, as a sacrifice to God,
To maintain in my soul
The purity of its flame.
I serve God, etc.

43. At times, I hold back a word,
Or perhaps stifle a wish,
Sometimes, a frivolous giggle,
Or some other vain pleasure:
A clever remark, a glance,

A simple quip.
I serve God, etc.

44. I don't discuss hairshirts,
Or iron belts
Or any voluntary penances
We may inflict on our flesh;
I prefer the penance
Performed by obedience.
I serve God, etc.

45. REGARDING WHAT MUST BE AVOIDED
I hate with extreme hate
All sin - even venial -
Because it attacks God Himself,
Closing heaven to us.
I flee even its appearances
In the slightest occasions.
I serve God, etc.

46. I battle sin
To save the sinner.
I fear nothing on earth
Except this terrible misfortune.
As dreadful as it is, hell
Without sin seems even pleasant!
I serve God, etc.

47. I flee from fancy, high society,
For it is deadly.
If it screams and scolds me for this,
I am even happier.
If it considers me uncouth,
I become that much wiser.
I serve God, etc.

48. God forbid that I be found
In gambling dens, in nightclubs.
I prefer the haunts of a mother-wolf,
Or even the wolves of the forest.
Those places are abominable
Because of their horrifying scandals.
I serve God, etc.

49. On urgent business,

When we travel
And must stay at an inn
We can eat and drink there
But not like the impious,
Who guzzle until they're rambunctious.
I serve God, etc.

50. Farewell, balls and dances
Whose inventor is the demon.
Oh! in these stupid beats
How we offend the Lord!
They are but cunning training
For even greater debauchery.
I serve God, etc.

51. Farewell to degrading games,
And to all games of chance,
Profaning so many festivals
Where the demon alone takes part;
They hide so much malice
Beneath the pleasure and the tricks.
I serve God, etc.

52. Far from me those assemblies
And those patron saint festivals;
Through abuse, how often changed
Into festivals of the devil!
I condemn those night-long parties
Which stain so many souls.
I serve God, etc.

53. I condemn and detest
Frivolous tales, novels,
That spread like the plague:
The downfall of so many!
Far from reading them
I burn them or scrap them.
I serve God, etc.

54. Far from my eyes these statues
Where the demon lurks,
Those nudes, those paintings
Fools believe priceless!
I'd rather shatter them, topple them,
Deface them and break them.

I serve God, etc.

55. Far from me, heretics
Whom the Church has condemned
With all their fancy practices
And their sophisticated books;
Far from me, Calvinism!
Far from me, Jansenism!
I serve God, etc.

56. After Scripture, I read
Pious books
Whose doctrine is orthodox
And full of charity;
Not to enjoy their style
But to become wiser.
I serve God, etc.

57. The sword and the gown
Entail such pernicious tasks!
What sins, what deceptions
Done cleverly, with brilliance,
But make souls fall
Into eternal flames.

58. When the world offers me
Some gain, some position,
I find out, among other things:
Does God want this for me?
Can I perform this office
And still remain in his service?
I serve God, etc.

59. Finally, I avoid and abhor
All occasions of sin;
Still, I scarcely am able
To avoid them or stop them
For evil is so widespread,
The flesh so corrupt.
I serve God, etc.

60. REGARDING SEVERAL DEVOTIONS
My primary devotion
Is to the Blessed Sacrament.
I adore the Lord a whole hour

Every month, regularly.
It is the sun of my soul
Which enlightens and enkindles it.
I serve God, etc.

61. I am devoted to Mary
She is my help and support,
She is the glory of my life,
She is, after God, my entire fortune.
To be faithful to God
I depend on her in everything.
I serve God, etc.

62. She is my Queen and Princess
And I am her servant.
She is my Mother and Mistress,
I am the child of her heart.
I truly am her follower
For I honor and imitate her.
I serve God, etc.

63. I have great trust
In the archangel Michael
Whose zeal and prudence
Chased Lucifer from Heaven,
Who weighs all souls
For heaven or hell.

64. I am grateful also
To my Guardian Angel.
With confidence I beg
His light and support.
I honor his presence
And imitate his innocence.
I serve God, etc.

65. I always have compassion
On the souls in purgatory,
Remembering them at Lauds,
Giving them help.
To render them service
Is my kindest practice.
I serve God, etc.

66. I am modest in church

Without ever chatting,
Filled with docile faith
And great recollection,
With loving trust,
And reverential fear.
I serve God, etc.

67. I reprimand prudently
Those who swear by God's name,
Those who are irreverent
Without respect in His holy place;
If they do not do penance for their wrong
I do it for them in their presence.
I serve God, etc.

68. To be assured,
I have chosen a good director.
In all trust,
I open my heart to him;
I listen to him and follow his counsels:
These are my greatest miracles.
I serve God, etc.

69. A perfect practice
From which I draw great help
Is to make a retreat
Every year on certain days;
God, speaking to my soul,
Purifies it and sets it aflame.
I serve God, etc.

70. I despise what's going on
As unworthy of my heart;
I only esteem grace
And the love of my Savior.
Let the world dance and sing,
Nothing about it satisfies me.
I serve God, etc.

71. What I most want in the world
Are the costliest crosses:
Someone who mocks or scolds me,
Treating me with contempt,
Who maliciously attacks me
Who humiliates and ruins me.

I serve God, etc.

## 140
## CONVERTED SINNER

1. I have lost God by my sin.
   Oh! how troubled my heart!
   True, it has been stained
   But even more, it is distressed.

2. To betray one's king, how ungrateful!
   To fight one's own defender,
   To offend God, what an assault!
   Angels, weep, weep over my state.

3. Could I immolate a hundred hearts?
   Would I had a spring of tears
   To deplore all my evil deeds!
   Alas! It overwhelms me! Alas! It's killing me!

4. Great God, neither hell nor demon
   Make me beg for forgiveness;
   You alone are the reason for it,
   It is because you are so good.

5. I detest from my heart and soul
   Every reason for your displeasure.
   But have pity on a contrite heart
   Bathed in the blood of Jesus Christ.

6. All centuries have never seen
   Nor has it ever been heard
   That close to this shed blood
   A contrite heart was lost.

7. Behold, Great God, Great King, behold
   Your Son between you and me.
   If His blood does not command you,
   I lose all faith and hope.

8. How true that I deserve
   Hell for all eternity;

But I know your goodness
Exceeds all my iniquity.

9. Forgive me, then, my Lord, forgive
Such a miserable sinner,
By the Mother of the Savior,
By her blood and by her heart.

10. My heart soaked with remorse,
Lord, I beg for peace,
I declare and promise
Never shall I offend you again. *(unfinished)*

## 141
## INVOCATION OF THE HOLY SPIRIT

1. Come, Father of Lights,
Come, God of Love,
Fashion in me (us) my (our) prayers.
Show me (us) the truth,
Send into my (our) soul(s)
An ember of your fire
To penetrate it with flame
And fill it with God.

2. Come, Holy Spirit, you create
Martyrs, confessors,
Apostles, prophets,
Great heroes, valiant hearts.
You are the only guide
My Savior has followed;
So that I may imitate Him,
Lead me as you led Him.

3. You who work miracles
Through powerless mortals,
You who utter oracles
Through poor ignorant humans,
By the power of your grace
Strengthen my languor;
To melt my coldness

Speak to the depths of my heart.

4. Distance me from the fads,
The well-traveled road,
The delusions, so convenient
Yet so full of evil.
Teach me the path,
Unknown to almost everyone,
Which leads with certainty
Straight to heaven and to you.

5. I beg you, open my ears
To the words of faith,
To practice the marvels
Of your divine law,
To listen only to God Himself
In every preacher;
And to cry anathema
Against this deceitful world.

6. Speak, your words are
What I seek night and day.
Speak, destroy the idols
That attack your love.
Speak, proclaim victory
Over all my enemies.
Speak, receive the glory
Of having yielded them to us.

7. Speak, Holy Spirit, create
A fountain in my heart,
Whose pure, healthful water
Saves the greatest sinner,
Heals the most incurable
By opening his eyes,
And pardons the most guilty
By gushing up to heaven.

8. More than Magdalene,
Than Lazarus in the tomb
More than the Samaritan woman,
I beg you for this water;
I thirst for it, I beg you!
I know it is a precious gift;
The greater this favor is,

The more you will be glorified.

9. Support my weakness,
   I am a fragile reed.
   Steady my faltering,
   I change more than the breeze.
   Dissipate my darkness,
   I am as one born blind.
   Calm my concupiscence,
   Otherwise I'm damned.

10. Without you my soul is barren,
    Empty of any good,
    Without you I hasten to my doom
    And I fall for a trifle.
    I can neither think nor speak,
    Nor do any good deed for God,
    Unless to accomplish it,
    You sustain me at all times.

11. Give me your wisdom,
    This taste for truth,
    This charity which impels
    Without forcing the will,
    This grace so fruitful,
    This lure so ravishing,
    This peace profound and blessed,
    This aid all-powerful.

12. If you wish me to shed tears
    And that my heart be moved,
    Let me see now
    How loathsome my sin!
    Let me know you well
    And then I shall love you.
    Convert me, dear Master,
    And I will be converted.

13. You do not wish to compel
    My evil will,
    That is why I have everything to fear
    From my own liberty.
    The lure of your grace
    I have too often resisted.
    I surrender. Take over

With full authority.

14. Great God, make yourself the Master
Of my whole heart so I may love,
Of my mind so I may know,
Of my tongue so I may charm,
Of my senses and powers
So I may act and suffer,
Of my possessions, of my pains
And of all, so I may serve you.

15. Make a temple of my heart,
Of my tongue, an instrument
To speak to all by example,
To speak eloquently
Through Jesus and Mary,
Reign powerfully in me
So that I may then glorify
God alone forever.

GOD ALONE

16. O holy and faithful Virgin
Spouse of the Holy Spirit,
Change my rebellious heart
Into a heart humble and contrite.
Give me a docile heart
Truly faithful to his voice,
So I may live the Gospel
According to its counsels and laws.

# 142
# RESOLUTIONS OF A CONVERTED SINNER DURING THE MISSION

**To abandon the world and the occasions of sin**

1. Finally, your grace, Lord,
Has conquered my heart.
I am aware of my sin and misfortune.
Let us leave the world

Which tricks and snarls,
Let us leave the world, it is a liar.

2. I begin to see clearly
The world and its blindness.
Alas! I weep over it bitterly.
Let us leave the world
Which tricks and snarls,
Let us leave the world joyfully.

3. The power of truth
Has shown me my iniquity
And has set me free.
Farewell world
Which sullies and snarls,
Farewell world which flattered me.

4. Farewell gambling and partying
Farewell immoral friends,
Farewell all human respect.
Farewell world
Which flatters and snarls,
Farewell world and all the worldly.

5. Farewell pleasures, Farewell fame,
Farewell all enchanting goods
Enticing almost all hearts.
Farewell world
Which charms and snarls,
Farewell world and its fans.

6. Farewell world and its din,
Farewell home, Farewell worries,
So I may prepare myself for death.
Let us leave the world
Which quarrels and snarls,
Let us leave the burdensome world.

7. Farewell news of the royal court,
And of the army and of love,
Farewell city and its goings-on.
Let us leave the world
Which sullies and snarls,
Let us leave the world and not return.

8. They will think me a fanatic,
A savage and of fake piety;
They will call me "fool."
Let us leave the world
For it rants and snarls,
Let us leave the world as soon as we can.

9. Farewell world, Farewell earthly things,
My heart is an immortal heart
Created only for the Eternal.
Let us leave the world
Which passes and snarls,
Let us leave the world and seek heaven.

10. Oh! So many vain amusements,
So many foolish pastimes,
So many unfortunate changes!
Let us leave the world
Which changes and snarls,
Let us leave the world for it is time.

11. Our most obedient servants
Will be our enemies tomorrow,
In spite of all promises.
Farewell world
Which changes and snarls,
Farewell world, Farewell its friends.

12. What! I would love gold and silver,
This bothersome clod of earth,
Subject to robbers, to sergeants?
Let us leave the world
Which changes and snarls,
Let us leave the world disloyal and changing.

13. In spite of fire, in spite of chains
In spite of complaints of the flesh
In spite of hell's rage,
Farewell world
Which charms and snarls,
Farewell world, I must be victorious.

14. Let the world pass by,
Let the worldly tire of it,
Let fools threaten us.

Let us leave the world
Which passes and snarls,
Farewell world, we must hurry.

15. Lord, since I now serve you,
I can see almost the whole universe
Plunging into hell.
Let us leave the world
Which damns and snarls,
Let us leave the world for the desert.

16. I prefer the song of the birds
And all the cries of the animals
To the worldly new tunes.
Let us leave the world
Which sings and snarls
Let us leave the world full of evil.

17. Everything in the world leads to sin.
It's decided: I will seek
The woods or a hole in the rock.
Farewell world
Which sins and snarls,
Farewell world, I must hide.

18. Here are woods and hills,
A spring and brooks,
A thatched cottage and hamlets.
Leave me, world
Which troubles and snarls
Leave me, world, so I may live in peace.

19. Oh! what mysterious contentment,
Oh! what sweet and holy peace
My heart tastes in these forests!
Leave me, world
Which sins and snarls.
Leave me, world, and forever.

20. Alone with you, O my good Jesus,
I want only you and nothing more.
Farewell world and its abuses.
Leave me, world
Which passes and snarls.
Leave me, world, so I may live for Jesus.

21. Be gone, world, seek me no longer,
    I am a lone hermit,
    With Mary, with Jesus.
    Cursed be the world
    Which deceives and snarls
    Cursed be the world! Live Jesus forever!

    GOD ALONE

## 143
## CONVERSION OF A WORLDLY SINNER

### And her entrance into the Poor Clares after 25 years of worldliness

1. Glory be to God![39]
   The world loses you, my Benigne,
   Glory be to God!
   Despite its charming ways.
   This is the fruit of a marvelous grace;
   You must deem yourself unworthy.
   Glory be to God!

2. What struggles
   To be victorious!
   What struggles
   Of grace against your feminine charms!
   You alone remember the clash,
   To God alone the glory.
   What struggles!

3. I have a glimpse
   Of fickle lovers angry with you now!
   I have a glimpse
   Of fools who wanted to be kings!
   But we have seen you push aside everything:
   The idol and her worshippers.

[39] For an explanation of this hymn, see footnote 27 in the Introduction on page xviii

I have a glimpse!

4. Let us not count
What your head has sacrificed;
Let us not count,
Although it is fantastic:
Off with the three-crested hat,
The veil has won over it.
Let us not count.

5. Where are your eyes
With their alluring brilliance?
Where are your eyes
With their winning looks?
Alas! They have traded weapons:
Their allure has changed to tears.
Where are your eyes?

6. Where are those airs,
Those games, that wit, that grace?
Where are those airs
Admired by all?
Religious airs have replaced
Vanity so base.
Where are those airs?

7. We no longer see
Those flirtatious twirls,
We no longer see
Those baubles and ornaments.
Goodbye galas, goodbye plays,
Your modesty has conquered!
We no longer see.

8. You were seen
As a show, sad and joyful;
You were seen,
One stalked you, the other took flight.
Now, despite every obstacle,
Seeing you everyone shouts: Miracle!
You were seen!

9. What a transformation!
Garlands to hairshirts;
What a transformation

In a weak character!
Wealth, glory and pleasures
Now are only suffering.
What a transformation!

10. Leave all behind!
Relatives, the most faithful friend.
Leave all behind,
Pleasures and highly sought wealth!
The fool believes you mad or cruel
But heaven finds you beautiful!
Leave all behind!

11. Immortal heart,
How disastrous this world is for you,
Immortal heart!
No mortal man suffices,
Love only your heavenly Spouse,
Be indifferent to everything else.
Immortal heart!

12. Bemoan forever
O illustrious penitent,
Bemoan forever
Your vanities, your loves!
Be a strong and fervent woman
And one day you will triumph.
Bemoan forever!

13. All or nothing!
One must be either worldly or a Clare,
All or nothing!
A generous heart chooses the best:
Of convents, the most austere
Of victories, the most complete.
All or nothing!

14. Coarse habit,
What brilliance in ashen color!
Coarse habit,
You are worth more than the whole world.
But who could truly understand
That such courage could overpower you?
Coarse habit!

15. Be vigilant!
    I both admire you and fear for you.
    Be vigilant!
    The world is full of swindlers
    Making even rocks tremble.
    May they not deceive you; I shudder with fear.
    Be vigilant!

16. If you look back,
    What fatal blow, what treason!
    If you look back,
    You commit yourself to such evil!
    God underfoot; the world, master.
    Will you do it? Alas! perhaps,
    If you look back!

17. You are mature,
    You are no longer a child
    You are mature,
    You play the game for keeps
    But your great self-confidence
    Flows from your humble distrust.
    You are mature.

18. Hidden in God,
    Flee the poison of the grill,
    Hidden in God,
    The world revives its fire there;
    Dead to your parents, dead to the city,
    Belonging totally to God, totally to the Gospel,
    Hidden in God.

19. In prayer,
    Go melt your coldness.
    In prayer,
    Arm yourself like a porcupine.
    Be consoled in your misery
    Enrich yourself with grace,
    In prayer.

20. What will they say?
    Always despise such attitude.
    What will they say?
    Crush this wily devil.
    Leave completely behind the world and man;

Before God everything is but a speck.
What will they say?

21. To protect yourself
Imitate the faithful Virgin;
To protect yourself
Take care to gaze at her.
Entrust everything to her care.
Always go to God through her
To protect yourself.

22. Always obey
The rule and its least details.
Always obey
To the end of your life!
For the whole rule is important,
Even the rule of silence,
Always obey.

23. Blindly,
Obey like a child!
Blindly,
Without asking why or how!
With no preference,
No wheedled exceptions.
Blindly!

24. Poverty,
The deepest humility.
Poverty
In all its severity,
The most fertile charity:
Your only possession in this world.
Poverty!

25. No more pride!
Humble yourself, dust and ashes,
No more pride
Under a poor habit!
With humble Francis for father,
Near a God dead on Calvary.
No more pride!

26. Taste, taste
Poverty in its richness,

Taste, taste
The sweetness of austerities,
Taste Jesus in his tenderness,
Taste love in his caresses.
Taste, taste!

27. Lured by these perfumes,
Hasten, hasten worldly ladies,
Lured by these perfumes,
Truly so extraordinary!
Leave, flee, break your chains
And transform into Magdalenes,
Lured by these perfumes.

28. If you only knew
The sweetness of solitude,
If you only knew!
You would seek it immediately;
But no, fashionable custom
Holds you under a rough yoke.
If you only knew!

29. Ah! until when
Will you search after lies?
Ah! until when
Will you remain blind?
Your wealth is empty, but a dream
Which leaves only a gnawing worm.
Ah! until when!

30. The Crucifix
Has shattered everything, even ice.
The Crucifix,
Victorious over the world's rubbish.
Goodbye to fleeting vanity,
The Creator has taken its place.
The Crucifix!

31. Glory to the Shepherd!
The sheep was a runaway,
Glory to the Shepherd!
Now she is lodged in His heart;
Ah! His grace overflows there,
So that another may follow her.
Glory to the Shepherd!

32. Persevere,
Strong woman, wise servant,
Persevere!
Watch, pray, sing and suffer,
Be brave, Benigne, be brave,
Paradise is worth much more.
Persevere!

33. Long live Jesus!
Always be his loving victim.
Long live Jesus!
Love only Him and naught else;
Sing to God, completely enraptured:
Long live Francis! Long live Mary!
Long live Jesus!

34. Please forgive me
If I praise you in this song,
Please forgive me!
Humility governs us.
For God alone I explained my thoughts
To make you seraphic.
Please forgive me! (*twice*)
Pray for me!

HER ANSWER:
*Inveni portum, spes et fortuna, valete,*
*Nil mihi molestum, ludite nunc alias*

35. I have entered the harbor.
Farewell, parents; farewell, wealth;
I have entered the harbor.
Nothing disturbs me in my rapture.
Go play, you other brunettes,
Unfortunately too numerous;
I have entered the harbor.

GOD ALONE

## 144
## POOR IN SPIRIT

1. When I go forth through the fields,
   My walking-stick in hand,
   No shoes, no baggage,
   No care,
   I stride with great pomp
   Like a king in his court.
   To the sound of the trumpet, trum, trum, trum, trum trumpet,
   The day long I ring out:
   Hurrah for Holy Love!

2. You greedy landowners,
   You are my landlords!
   Neither lawsuit nor battle
   Will get you your rent.
   You greedy, I trick you, for
   The best portion I take,
   To the sound etc.
   Without being a thief.

3. I travel the world
   Like a lost child.
   A vagabond am I,
   My possessions are sold.
   You greedy, I trick you, for
   The best portion I take,
   To the sound etc.
   And without being a thief.

4. Yes, much have I sold,
   And made quite a profit,
   For I have my ticket
   For Paradise.
   You greedy, etc.

5. Gather well, my brothers,
   The manure here below,
   Take care of my affairs,
   Don't burden me so!

You greedy, etc.

6. Make my land show a profit,
   I want revenue!
   Resolve all my conflicts,
   Let me hear no complaints.
   You greedy, etc.

7. You have done quite well
   To treat us like fools:
   Despite you we possess all we need
   And from your own store!
   You greedy, etc.

8. From here or there, I find,
   Without searching far,
   Just like the apostles,
   Enough bread for the day.
   You greedy, etc.

9. My foresight is shrewd,
   I lack nothing at all;
   Without kitchen or cellar,
   I have fine food and drink.
   You greedy, etc.

10. No lease, no farms,
    No burdensome taxes,
    No payments are due
    So no bill-collectors.
    You greedy, etc.

11. In God, I feel like a lord,
    The universe is mine.
    Whoever seeks to know me
    Must leave all behind.
    You greedy, etc.

12. Through grace, God has given me,
    A king's heart and soul;
    I trample on fleeting things,
    I'm worth more than they!
    You greedy, etc.

13. I utilize, without earnings,

No worry about tomorrow,
The bounty of Providence
That falls into my hands.
You greedy, etc.

14. I flit from branch to branch
Like a small bird,
My heart is never heavy,
For no burden I carry.
You greedy, etc.

15. My treasure is astounding.
Don't you envy it?
My belongings hop with me;
Everything's in my pocket.
You greedy, etc.

16. Do you think that I esteem
The famous, portly rich men
Who, fearing no sin,
Are renowned everywhere?
You greedy, etc.

17. I heartily despise
The brilliant put-on of a fool,
Of a captive in chains,
And of a toad in his hole.
You greedy, etc.

18. Fathers and mothers in the hundreds I have,
In place of those left behind;
Hundreds of sisters and brothers are mine,
And all are filled with love.
You greedy, etc.

19. No violence,
No bother to anyone,
I use with all innocence
Whatever freely is given.
You greedy, etc.

20. My retinue, my glory,
These poor beggars compose;
Whatever I eat or drink,
All with them is shared.

You greedy, etc.

21. If someone wants to follow me,
Most welcome is he!
But he must agree to live like me,
No belongings, no income;
Let him follow me without show!
So let us sing merrily,
To the sound etc.
Hurrah for Poverty! (*twice*)

GOD ALONE

## 145
## OUR LADY OF PATIENCE

1. Come to my help,
O gentle and divine Mary,
Come to my help!
I suffer and groan every day.
Show compassion on my plight.
Free me from my troubles, I beg you.
Come to my help!

2. Help me,
You are most merciful,
Help me!
Everything is under your rule.
Provide me then with some comfort
Or at least, the gift of patience.
Help me!

3. Say the word, say the word,
You can do everything, powerful Queen,
Say the word, say the word!
If you will it, I shall be healed.
With one word you will break my chains
And all my suffering will end.
Say the word, say the word!

4. Through love,

Console me in my misery.
Through love,
Be it patience or be it health.
In you alone I place my hope,
Show me that you are my Mother.
Through love!

5. Are you no longer
The cure of incurables?
Are you no longer
The health of all the disabled?
The strong refuge of the guilty,
The sole help of the destitute?
Are you no longer?

6. Strike, strike,
The enemy shoves me and tempts me.
Strike, strike,
Crush him, trample him underfoot.
Under your invincible hand,
All hell will be stricken with terror.
Strike, strike.

7. What! As you watch
Shall I die in my misery?
What! As you watch,
Shall I perish, Queen of heaven?
No, no, I have placed my hope
In your most bountiful name.
What! As you watch?

## 146
## CHRISTIAN WEDDINGS

1. Sing! Let your voice resound:
At the Wedding Feast of Cana
The Lord in person
Was present long ago.
To today's holy festival
Let us beg Him come,
At the sound of the trum, trum, trum trumpet (*twice*)

To bless us. (*twice*)

2. Beautiful and divine banquet!
Happy married couple,
Where Jesus and His Mother
Were the honored guests!
To today's holy celebration,
Let us then invite them both
At the sound of the trum, trum, etc.
So we may know true happiness. (*twice*)

3. Their holy company
Tolerates no evil.
No immodesty
Of dance or ball.
Let us drive from this celebration
The pleasures of Bacchus
At the sound of the trum, etc.
And the games of Venus. (*twice*)

4. In their sacred presence
What sobriety!
What chaste innocence!
What holy joy!
To this holy celebration
Let us invite these virtues,
At the sound of the trum, etc.
To keep Jesus with us. (*twice*)

5. Mary, so attentive
To the needs of the feast
Prayed with lively faith:
My dear Son, they're out of wine!
Let us cry out at this celebration,
And cry out everyday:
At the sound of the trum, etc.
Mary, help me! (*twice*)

6. O miracle! O wonder!
Water changed to wine!
Since then no bottle
Contained wine so divine.
Miracle at this celebration!
We beg you Lord,
At the sound of the trum, etc.

To change our heart. (*twice*)

7. Farewell, carnal wedding feasts
Of the Turks and heathens!
May ours resemble
Those of yesteryear!
Their vows at the celebration,
Their innocent meal
At the sound of the trum, etc.
Made God Himself present. (*twice*)

8. Far from here the malice
Of the world and Satan!
All the guests rejoice here
Like Abraham's descendants.
God reigns in this celebration!
Let evil be excluded!
At the sound of the trum, etc.
The Lord, and nothing else. (*twice*)

9. Great God, by your grace,
Of these two make but one.
May the two accomplish
Their salvation together.
Join our hearts at this celebration
In such a sturdy bond,
At the sound of the trum, etc.
That no one will trouble us ever . (*twice*)

10. In our marriage,
Grant us children;
Protect us from shipwreck
And from all disasters.
Everything shouts in this celebration,
With the bride and groom:
At the sound of the trum, etc.
Lord, bless us! (*twice*)

GOD ALONE.

## 147
## IN HONOR OF SAINT PIUS (POPE, FIFTH OF THIS NAME, NEWLY CANONIZED)

1. May earth unite with heaven,
   May all the earth canonize
   The virtues of great Pius.
   Nothing's small where all is great,
   Where everything astounds, surprises.
   Do you understand what I say?
   The Church is my guarantee
   And his very holy life.

2. Great in birth and lineage,
   Greater the gifts God granted
   Than those received from creatures.
   Great he was during his life,
   And no great man his equal.
   All at his feet did fall,
   For they all knew who he was:
   A Bishop of Rome.

3. A vicar of Jesus Christ,
   The Spirit's pure instrument
   Whence divine oracles flow.
   A burning and brilliant torch
   Enkindling all in the West,
   Shining even to the East.
   His powerful radiance
   Made all cry: miracle!

4. With rosary in hand,
   He fought Turks and Selim
   From his private chapel.
   This Moses so marvelous,
   Was on earth and in the sky
   Shooting brutal arrows,
   Which struck down the proud foe,
   Winning us the victory.

5. Look! The shattered vessels,
The Turks drowned and destroyed
At the Gulf of Lepanto.
Look! other ships are captured.
Fifteen thousand slaves freed,
Turks in thousands surrender!
This decisive rout was wrought
By the ardent prayer of Saint Pius.

6. Oh! Man of iron all aflame
With fire of pure love for God,
With iron against himself!
A burning fire in prayer,
In speech and in action,
Iron in suffering
And mortifications.
In everything, supremely great.

7. He is the general model
For bishops and cardinals,
Even for the Holy Father.
All princes and all religious,
The small and great, the young and old,
Need only cast an eye on him
To know the way to heaven.
What a phenomenon!

8. Religious see in him
Such total detachment,
Humble obedience;
Sovereigns, humility;
Bishops, deep charity;
Cardinals, firm loyalty;
Popes, great fidelity,
And everyone, prudence.

9. Holy penitents, behold
Penance and all its power:
A pope immersed in tears
Prostrate before his Savior,
His heart broken with sorrow,
To give his people victory,
So God's wrath may be calmed,
And his anger appeased.

10. O fear not, poor orphans,
He is your buttress, your bread
Though he is grandeur sublime;
Blind men, here is your staff;
Prisoners, your ransom;
Destitute, your shelter;
Penitents, your pardon,
If you wail your crimes.

11. At his palace, what order,
And what dedication
For the good of the Church!
To reform morals,
How many errors he shattered!
How many abuses, horrors,
He drove from Rome and all hearts!
History is stunned.

12. More than his dignity,
I esteem his humility
At the summit of glory.
Glory he fled but it followed;
Elected pope, he trembled and fled,
Burst in tears day and night.
What a burning and shining torch!
He alone cannot believe it.

13. If his heart could be opened,
This kingdom of the Savior,
This rich sanctuary,
We would see these great secrets:
Gentle repose, the peace
God shares with the perfect.
Above all, we would see the features
Of Jesus and his Mother.

14. Great Shepherd, led by the Lord
From grandeur on to grandeur,
.................................................
Keep your sheep from all the wolves,
Finely disguised among us.
Pray, intercede for us all!
Then draw us to yourself
Into the glory where you dwell.

GOD ALONE

# 148
# HYMN ON CHARITY

1. I must love, I must love,
God hidden in my neighbor
And God hidden in oneself;
Both dwell deep within me.
I love and also curse
The heart not full of both.
I must love, I must love
God hidden in my neighbor.

2. With love, we can do everything,
Without love, we do nothing.
Love is the one thing necessary,
The summary of all good,
The divine imprint,
The essence of a Christian.
I must love, I must love, etc.

3. When this love is visible,
Sincere, and from heart's depth,
It is the infallible sign
Of the love of the Creator.
One is impossible without the other;
Who denies this is a liar.
I must love, I must love, etc.

4. No one should be astonished
If I love my neighbor so,
Everything about him is great:
His redemption is divine
The Lord is his crown,
His beginning and his end.
I must love, I must love, etc.

5. My neighbor has God for Father,
He resembles Him in everything.

He has Jesus Christ for brother,
He has all His charm
For he is the fruit of Calvary,
The object of His gifts.
I must love, I must love, etc.

6. Though my neighbor offends me
Or plays dirty tricks,
Although he shows no concern for me
And never thanks me
I love him patiently,
I intensify my love.
I must love, I must love, etc.

7. Be he saint, or sinner,
Be he lowly or a king
Be he rude or gracious
Be he for or against me
He is no less lovable
When I look at him with faith.
I must love, I must love, etc.

8. To love because of emotion
Is to love as a dog.
By reasoning and emotion
Is to love as a pagan;
By faith, in spite of all hurts,
Is to love as a Christian.
I must love, I must love, etc.

9. To love, for God alone,
A man deserving hell's fire,
Who from Paris to Rome
Hounds me everywhere,
Who assaults and wants to kill me,
Is to be a child of God.
I must love, I must love, etc.

10. This charity draws me
To be all things to all people.
When one loves, nothing is difficult,
Harshness is delight.
What glory in its chains
What pleasure in its blows.
I must love, I must love, etc.

11. When Queen Charity commands
    I obey on the spot
    In small things or great
    I obey like a child.
    Even superman must submit
    To her winning charms.
    I must love, I must love, etc.

12. The merchant, all year long,
    Is on the byways and highways.
    The laborer, each day
    Works for a pittance
    But the soul is neglected;
    That is what causes me grief.
    I must love, I must love, etc.

13. This noble, immortal soul
    Which cost my God so dearly,
    This beautiful light
    Will be lost, will sin!
    Ah! what then, will he perish
    When I can prevent it?
    I must love, I must love, etc.

14. I would suffer a thousand pains
    I would endure a thousand hardships
    I would bear a thousand chains
    I would sacrifice a thousand hearts
    And all the blood in my veins
    To save a single sinner.
    I must love, I must love, etc.

15. Let us love, let us love then our brothers
    After the example of the Savior
    Despite all their miseries
    Despite their bad moods
    And let us try by our prayers
    To win their heart to God.
    I must love, I must love, etc.

16. Let us comfort the afflicted,
    Protect the orphans,
    Convert the sinners,
    Rebuke the evildoers,

Console the incurable,
And lend a hand to all.
I must love, I must love, etc.

17. But above all, let us help the souls
Who are falling into hell
Let us try to extinguish their flames
And break all their chains
In spite of all the rebukes
And despite entire creation.
I must love, I must love, etc.

18. Listen to Jesus crying out:
Let the little children come.
By my life-giving words
Instruct the ignorant!
Forget not, I beg you,
Poor convalescents!
I must love, I must love, etc.

19. Great God! Who can dispense himself
From the laws of charity,
Since it made you descend
Into our humanity?
From now on, I want to submit
To its gentle authority.
I must love, I must love
God hidden in my neighbor.

GOD ALONE.

## 149
## TO THE DAUGHTERS OF WISDOM

1. O Daughters of Wisdom,
Succor poor invalids,
Those overwhelmed by sorrow,
The disabled, the outcasts.
Those whom the world rejects
Ought to touch you the most.

I must love, I must love
God hidden in my neighbor.

2. Rely on Providence,
No thought for tomorrow.
Scorn that prudence
Seeking stable support.
Do not put your hope
In what someone puts in your hand.
I must love, etc.

3. How clever the Lord!
He draws all things from nothing.
So, my daughter, have no concern
For the key of gold and silver
Which, so contrary to the Gospel,
Opens the door to the Convent.
I must love, etc.

4. Is this poor young woman
Docile, poor in spirit?
Leave aside the young lady
Rich and well-known,
If, besides, she is not the type
Whom Jesus Christ seeks.
I must love, etc.

5. Be the servant of everyone,
Giving all without dissimulation.
That is both your capital and income
Which you'll find inexhaustible.
They are your legal certification
So no one can refuse you.
I must love, etc.

6. Love, with an immense love,
Love has no limit.
But, by obedience
Govern your charity.
Otherwise, an imprudence
Would tarnish its beauty.
I must love, etc.

7. To be fully victorious
To shine like the sun,

In God choose a father-director
For your mind and your senses.
Consult him in everything
And follow well his advice.
I must love, etc.

## 150
## DISSOLUTENESS OF RENNES

1. Farewell, Rennes, Rennes, Rennes,
Dreadful is your fate,
Your troubles we foretell,
You'll perish in the end
If you break not the chains
You hide in your bosom.
Farewell, Rennes, Rennes, Rennes.

2. It is true that you rule
And here are the reasons,
Without fearing your revenge:
Not because of your dwellings,
Nor because of your furs,
But because of your lethal poisons.
Farewell, Rennes, Rennes, Rennes.

3. Fools believe you're brilliant
And you spend your time well.
In town, all is laughter, all is play
And filled with so much fun.
But sages of the Gospel,
Weep bitterly about it.
Farewell, Rennes, Rennes, Rennes.

4. The place is one big party:
Monsieur in the cabaret,
Mademoiselle at the ball,
And Madame playing cards;
All carousing with different toys,
Believing that they do no wrong.
Farewell, Rennes, Rennes, Rennes.

5. Everyone's character is formed
By wealth or by pleasure.
The elderly at home
Think only of getting rich,
And the young man, in his youth,
Seeks nothing but amusement.
Farewell, Rennes, Rennes, Rennes.

6. It is normal there to see
Double-dealing hearts;
Each one has his own secret;
Even the devout servant,
Who seems the most sincere
Is often the most perfidious.
Farewell,, Rennes, Rennes, Rennes.

7. So many unhappy women
Beneath their joyful air!
So many scandalous girls
Beneath a pious air!
So many proud people
Beneath borrowed clothes!
Farewell Rennes, Rennes, Rennes.

8. So many flagrant wrongs
Covered over with pity!
So many sharp words
Under the guise of charity.
So many disgusting demands
Considered "de rigueur."
Farewell, Rennes, Rennes, Rennes.

9. See how many hussies
In clownish, form-fitting dress
In colors of green or yellow,
Parading in their high boots,
Preaching their sermons both night and day,
Seducing worldly men.
Farewell, Rennes, Rennes, Rennes.

10. The day is spent
On the streets or gambling.
The church is abandoned,
Time there is boring,
An hour there seems like a year.

Oh, weep, weep, my eyes.
Farewell, Rennes, Rennes, Rennes.

11. The torrents of all the crimes
That always overflow,
Drag along to the abyss
Almost all the inhabitants,
Making them victims
Of all excesses.
Farewell, Rennes, Rennes, Rennes.

12. By your infinite malice
Even the just are tainted
Or they must flee
To some community
Which has not been tarnished
By your foul air.
Farewell, Rennes, Rennes, Rennes.

13. If someone full of courage
Wants to confront you on your turf
Your henchmen, full of rage,
Cruelly attack him.
And use every device
To cleverly trick him.
Farewell, Rennes, Rennes, Rennes.

14. The poor man cries at your door,
While the rich enter with honor;
It's a nuisance to bring him
The leftovers of a servant.
You mistreat in that way
The dear members of the Savior.
Farewell, Rennes, Rennes, Rennes.

15. Who goes into your churches?
Often, fools, dogs,
Well dressed gossips,
Libertines, pagans,
Who meet there
Among very few Christians.
Farewell, Rennes, Rennes, Rennes.

16. In your strange misery
You sleep along with your friends;

No one fears anything, everyone hopes
That all sins are forgiven.
Oh! who will shed light
On these poor deluded people?
Farewell, Rennes, Rennes, Rennes.

17. You answer those who confront you
To show you your errors:
"God will have mercy,
He is good, do not be afraid
When a person wants it, He grants it."
And after all, "Everyone's a sinner."
Farewell, Rennes, Rennes, Rennes.

## 151
## OUR LADY OF GIFTS
## AT SAINT-SAUVEUR-DE-NUAILLÉ, in L'AUNIS

1. Whoever yearns to be faithful,
Should come to the Mother of Gifts.
In these cantons, everything calls us
To her throne,
So that all may be renewed
In these times.

2. Through her hands, God gives
His divine gifts and treasures.
His mercy forgives
Through her mediation
And crowns in heaven
All the saints.

3. Mary possesses in her domain,
The fullness of all good.
At her side, everything becomes easy.
Let's go, Christians,
She is lavishly generous
To her own.

4. She is the Mother of Grace,

She is its wonderful channel,
It is through her that everything good
Comes to pass on earth,
That everything ascends and descends
In the heavens.

5. We find everything in her:
Riches, pleasures, honor, health;
For God alone, she bestows them
With kindness.
The universe rests in her care,
In all truth.

6. Vinedresser, do you want your vine
Loaded with grapes,
Producing good tasting,
Quality wine?
Mary has this remarkable grace
In her hand.

7. Do you want an abundant crop
In your fields, poor workers,
And protection from the boldness
Of thieves?
Know that she has in her power
These favors.

8. She is your sweet hope,
You who are worried, unhappy.
You will receive help
Through your pleas
Or the gift of patience,
One or the other.

9. Poor sinner, if you approach her
The greatest gifts will be given:
Grace, clemency
And forgiveness.
Know that heaven grants them
Only in her name.

10. Children, come to her breasts,
Suck milk filled with tenderness;
Faithful people, come and rest
On her heart.

Come everyone, shelter your fervor
Under her wings.

11. To obtain your request,
Give, it shall be given you;
Let each one offer
What he has.
If it is his heart, the offering is great;
He will be heard.

12. Let us all approach Mary
To share in her bounty,
To find grace in this life,
Peace as well,
And to see God in our true home
Forever.

13. O Blessed Virgin, O Good Mother,
Share your gifts with us.
Be sensitive to the misery
Of sinners
By granting the humble prayer
Of our hearts.

GOD ALONE

## 152
## ROAD TO PARADISE

1. THE FERVENT SOUL:
Let's go, my dear friends,
Let's get on the road to Paradise; (*twice*)
How necessary this is!
Let's force ourselves to do it.(*twice*)
There is nothing that we cannot do
With divine grace.(*twice*)

[Let's go, my dear friends,
Let's get on the road to Paradise;
Whatever may be gained on earth,
Paradise is worth far more.]

2. THE LAZY SOUL:
What violence must be done
For this reward!
It is necessary
But so difficult to do.
I just can't do it.

3. THE FERVENT SOUL:
No matter the cost
Let's get on the road to Paradise.
For such trivial sufferings,
We gain infinite joys.
It is so necessary,
Let's force ourselves to do it.
There is nothing that we cannot do
With divine grace.

4. THE LAZY SOUL:
What! Blind oneself to believe?
Surrender to gain the victory?
It is necessary
But so difficult to do.
I just can't do it.

THE FERVENT SOUL:
*(Unfinished)*

## 153
## SERVICE OF GOD IN SPIRIT AND TRUTH

1. Let us serve God and without reserve,
For a divided heart is lost.
All or nothing is God's language.
Any little bit is fine with me, says Satan.

2. Give all, God urgently implores:
I am the supreme Lord of all.
The whole heart, the whole mind, the whole soul,
Give all or give me naught.

3. A divided heart wounds me deeply,
I cannot stand a crippled heart;
My mouth vomits the lukewarm
And I shall never take them back.

4. Give God half a sacrifice,
Divide in two a puny heart?
What theft, what ghastly wrong,
What scorn for the mighty Lord!

5. What? This heart, so weak in itself,
A bird would not be happy with it,
Is too great for the mighty God who loves it?
What contempt for a monarch supreme!

6. Our good God, through immense love,
Gives all, promises all that He is.
Let us give all, it's gratitude
That he requests, and for our own sake.

7. A divine oracle: one cannot
Serve two masters at the same time,
Because each will hinder the other
For they have different regulations.

8. We're lost if we attempt
To mix God with gold and silver,
To ally Gospel with what's in style.
Let's get out of this deadly situation.

9. So often God imitates us:
He is holy with the holy.
Halfhearted? God also holds back.
Surrender all? He gives lavishly.

10. Keep watch? He sleeps not, He guards.
Love God? He burns, He is aflame.
Asleep? He is cold, He slumbers.
Our little bit compels him to give little.

11. Whoever commits a serious sin
Breaks all the commandments,
Forfeits heaven and stands guilty
Of hell and all its pains.

12. When the fault is not grave,
    Alas! You don't make much of it;
    From there a transformation starts:
    Saint turns into scoundrel.

13. To rebel against God for something petty,
    To compromise Him for something trivial,
    To compare Him with something puny,
    Is to be His friend no longer.

14. No one turns to crime suddenly,
    Nor do the good turn evil suddenly,
    But one abyss calls up another
    When leanings are followed too closely.

15. Unfaithful in little things,
    Neglectful in small rules,
    Then come betrayal and revolt;
    The result, a hardened heart.

16. A small item, a point of practice
    Neglected, fought, rejected,
    Forms the impious, the heretic,
    And leads to all iniquity.

17. Attachment to a favored fault
    Often trips up the greatest saints.
    Their salvation and His greatest plans
    Often hinge right on this point.

18. Away with waffling souls
    Party to both sides,
    Away with those slack souls,
    Cursed be their betrayal!

19. Fight these wicked passions,
    This mood and dominant fault,
    Destroy such vineyard foxes
    Causing untold harm.

20. Let us set the whole mind to know,
    The whole heart to love,
    The whole body to serve this great Lord,
    Unceasingly, unsparingly.

21. Be strong, O faithful servant:
Having been faithful in small things
You will be, in eternal life,
Set over all the goods of God.

22. I take you, O faithful Mary,
After God, for my exemplar.
May I copy, throughout my life,
Your faithful, generous heart!

23. Never again, great God, any conflict,
I shall obey your least wish,
I shall submit to your will
My whole heart, undivided, always.

GOD ALONE

## 154
## TRUE CHRISTIAN

1. A good Christian is holy says the Apostle,
And he is not like others.
Worldly Christian, you are not one of us.
You, a Christian? To others, to others, you belong.

2. A true Christian is not of this life,
His heart is already in heaven.
Worldly Christian, etc.

3. A true Christian is humble and meek,
Chaste, fervent, loving and sincere.
Worldly Christian, etc.

4. Can you really tell God that you love him
When you offend him, and even outrage him?
You love God? You lie, says the Apostle.
You a Christian?, etc.

5. Has anyone seen, from Paris to Rome,
Someone so foul? You're not even human.
Worldly Christian, etc.

6. Like pagans, you love only the world,
   And you love like a filthy beast.
   Worldly Christian, etc.

7. Like a fox, you cleverly pillage,
   Like a dog, you never stop barking.
   Worldly Christian, etc.

8. You quibble over a trifle
   And mimic a grasshopper's dance.
   Worldly Christian, etc.

9. You proud peacock, you only love glory;
   Greedy pig, you always look for a drink.
   Worldly Christian, etc.

10. You speak evil, you bite like a viper;
    You become like an angry lion.
    Worldly Christian, etc.

11. Like a toad you love only dirt;
    Like a dragon, you only love war.
    Worldly Christian, etc.

12. Like a snake, you sting your own brother,
    And you close your ear to his misery.
    Worldly Christian, etc.

13. Does God speak? You walk like a tortoise.
    Is it money? You run through the streets!
    Worldly Christian, etc.

14. Slow for good, feeble for justice,
    Prompt for evil and zealous for vice.
    Worldly Christian, etc.

15. What do you follow? Custom and style.
    What do you seek? In all things, the easiest.
    Worldly Christian, etc.

16. Conform your life to the Gospel,
    Become humble, meek and docile,
    Then we will say that you are one of us
    But otherwise, to others, to others, you belong.

## 155
## IN HONOR OF OUR LADY OF SHADOWS

1. It is through Mary
   That heaven allures us.
   To be happy, we must love her,
   Everything invites us
   To love her in this life.
   How lovely, how lovely!
   In her shadow let us hide.

2. Under her wings
   In the shade of her mercy
   Sinners are safe.
   Even the most hostile
   Become most faithful.
   How lovely, how lovely!
   In her shadow let us hide.

3. May all find hope
   In the shade of her holy name,
   Hidden under her protection!
   At her prayer
   God calms His anger.
   How lovely, how lovely!
   In her shadow let us hide.

4. May all admire
   The radiance of her holiness
   Under the shade of her humility.
   Who can fathom
   The mystery of her reign?
   How lovely, how lovely!
   In her shadow let us hide.

5. What a great mystery!
   The Holy Spirit's shadow alone
   Formed Jesus Christ in her,

Made her His mother,
Without becoming His father.
How lovely, how lovely!
In her shadow let us hide.

6. Her shining faith
In its obscure splendor
Surpasses the starry sky.
All heaven sings,
Even her shadow is powerful.
How lovely, how lovely!
In her shadow let us hide.

7. Although darker
Than the tents of Kedar,
All the canopies of Caesar
Have less glory
Than this ivory tower.
How lovely, how lovely!
In her shadow let us hide.

8. Her holy shadow
Makes demons tremble more
Than battalions in thousands.
Hell screaming in fear
Cannot weather its attack.
How lovely, how lovely!
In her shadow let us hide.

9. Close to her
We rest from our labors,
Sheltered from all evil;
There the faithful
Taste everlasting joy.
How lovely, how lovely!
In her shadow let us hide.

10. All hope is found
Under the shade of her mantle!
Never hell, fire, or flood,
Never any power
Harms us in this fortress.
How lovely, how lovely!
In her shadow let us hide.

11. All must run
To this sure refuge,
Even the hopeless sinner.
No place so loving.
So let's run there quickly.
How lovely, how lovely!
In her shadow let us hide.

12. In this clearing,
In these peaceful hideaways,
In the shade of these forests,
What a godsend.
What silence! Yet what conversation!
How lovely, how lovely!
In her shadow let us hide.

13. What tenderness,
What sweet refreshment,
What rest, what charming bliss!
What intense joy
Close to this Princess!
How lovely, how lovely!
In her shadow let us hide.

14. In silence,
In shade and shadow,
Mary has hidden her beauty.
Yet Heaven is firm
In making it evident.
How lovely, how lovely!
In her shadow let us hide.

15. Divine Mother,
Reign within me
In the shadows of your faith,
So I may believe and do
The will of my Father.
How lovely, how lovely!
In her shadow let us hide.

16. Full of grace,
By the shadow of the Holy Spirit,
Form Jesus Christ in my heart.
Melt my frozen heart
So I may follow in your steps.

How lovely, how lovely!
In her shadow let us hide.

17. My trust
Lies in you, Queen of heaven,
To live happily under your shade,
In the hope
Of having God for reward.
How lovely, how lovely!
In her shadow let us hide.

GOD ALONE

## 156
## VANITY OF THE WORLD

1. Vanity of worldly goods,
Vanity of vanities!
On your truths,
O my God, my heart is set.
Vanity of worldly goods,
Vanity of vanities!

2. What are all creatures?
As it is written, nothing
But misery of spirit,
Vain illusions full of filth.
Vanity etc.

3. What vanity, man and his life!
All flesh is but a bit of hay
Needed by no one here on earth.
Why then do we crave it so?
Vanity, etc.

4. Its pleasures are a rubbish pile
Its treasures, a bit of tin,
Its rest, hard work;
Its glory, grimy smoke.
Vanity, etc

5. Far from me, these worldly men,
These men of gold and silver,
Whom this changing metal
Ensnares in war and troubles.
Vanity, etc,

6. Far from me, high living crowd,
You love only pleasures,
Satisfying all your whims;
Your only joy, to laugh and please.
Vanity, etc.

7. Far from us, those worldly ladies,
Those idols of good looks;
Their vanity enchants
Even more than sirens.
Vanity, etc.

8. A fragile thing, decrepit
And mortal, cannot suffice
My immortal heart.
It craves something lasting.
Vanity etc.

9. You alone, sovereign Good,
Can satisfy my heart;
You are its happiness,
What torment without you.
Vanity, etc.

10. Were you even greater than
An Alexander, a Samson,
Cresus and Solomon,
The human heart seeks more.
Vanity, etc.

11. Let the whole world be moved
Into my heart to fill it;
This heart, in its desire,
Will always cry: More! More!
Vanity, etc.

## 157
## ON SOLITUDE

1. FAR from the world, at this hermitage,
Let's go into hiding to serve God.
Can a place be found
Where grace is more likely?
Far from the world, at this hermitage,
Let's go into hiding to serve God.

2. LOCATION OF THE PLACE
This deserted place has for approach
A league or more of woods,
Luxuriant shrubbery,
Rocks as far as the eye can see.
Far from the world, etc.

3. Three paths lead to this hideaway
The wide path for wagons,
One, through the woods,
Another along the hidden streams.
Far from the world, etc.

4. The hermitage, a deep cave
In a rock, facing north,
Offers shelter for
The fawn and the weary doe.
Far from the world, etc.

5. BEAUTY OF THE PLACE
In the summer, its chill is pleasant,
Offsetting the great heat.
In winter, at the top, one finds
A nice flow of air from the south.
Far from the world, etc.

6. At the top, the eye spies a plain,
Churches and castles,
Meadows and streams,
Charming the view and also one's troubles.
Far from the world, etc.

7. At the bottom flows a river,
The Kedron stream,
Abundant in fish,
Delightful in every way.
Far from the world, etc.

8. It extends its clear waters
Over flourishing fields,
And then, exuberantly
Rushes between the hills.
Far from the world, etc.

9. On the sides, three clear springs,
Where the never failing water
Gushes from above and below,
Watering the plains.
Far from the world, etc.

10. On the plains, everything thrives
Without any laborer's work.
By the hand of God
This land is virgin and fertile.
Far from the world, etc.

11. In the lovely groves, no sound
Of squabbles among neighbors,
No chatting among the worldly,
No battles or shipwrecks.
Far from the world, etc.

12. The groves ring with sweet harmony
Of the birds and the echoes,
The cries of animals;
Not those of ungodly men.
Far from the world, etc.

13. The eloquent silence
Of rocks and forests
Only preach peace,
Breathe only innocence.
Far from the world, etc.

14. Notice the town's madness?
Or those floods of iniquity,
Those frivolous melodies?

No, not here, all is fresh and calm.
Far from the world, etc.

15. The countryside holds
None of those dangers.
The woods and the rocks
Are the holy, wise masters.
Far from the world, etc.

16. The rocks preach fidelity,
The woods, fruitfulness,
The streams, purity,
All things, love and obedience.
Far from the world, etc.

17. You can see, flying overhead,
Birds in their season,
At your feet, all sorts of fish,
And alongside, all kinds of animals.
Far from the world, etc.

18. The Creator's mighty hand
Which formed this universe,
Shines in these remote sites
Of innocent nature.
Far from the world, etc.

19. These glories of nature
Have God for their creator.
Never has sinful man
Laid his criminal hands.
Far from the world, etc.

20. But, if nature is so beautiful
Grace is even more so,
Forming a Paradise
For a soul steadfast and pure.
Far from the world, etc.

21. What happiness, even in this life,
And what marvelous rapture
We experience in these places
As the soul is recollected.
Far from the world, etc.

22. To taste these chaste delights
You must be a wise Christian;
Fools cannot understand this.
The desert would be their torture.
Far from the world, etc.

23. It is truly in solitude,
Providing that it's spiritual,
That one finds Jesus Christ,
The only beatitude.
Far from the world, etc.

24. Solitude is the wise book
Which all the saints have read,
Drawing from it stunning secrets
On how to live this life well.
Far from the world, etc.

25. Solitude is the great school
Where the saints were formed,
Where their hearts, all afire,
Received the gift of the word.
Far from the world, etc.

26. It is the shelter from the tempest,
A perfect resting place,
A dwelling so attractive,
Every day is a Feast.
Far from the world, etc.

27. A thousand times happy the souls
The Spirit leads into the desert!
For one who is lost there, thousands
Fall into the flames elsewhere.
Far from the world, etc.

28. I am the One, says God, who leads
A sinner to the wilderness,
To speak to his heart,
And submit it to my reign.
Far from the world, etc.

29. Let us then flee, like the Pacomes,
The Pauls, the Hilarys,
The many temptations

Which in the world conquer us.
Far from the world, etc.

30. In this solitary place we attend
To our salvation;
We have no other goal,
For it is the only one needed.
Far from the world, etc.

31. Sheltered from the world's concerns
Let us savor recollection,
Praying continually,
Tasting profound peace.
Far from the world, etc.

32. Martha, Martha with Magdalene,
Go aside into retreat.
It is the better part
Without trouble or sorrow.
Far from the world, etc.

33. Zealous folk, Jesus calls you
To rest awhile,
To fill yourself with God
And His words of life.
Far from the world, etc.

34. Oh! let us leave the cares of earth
To the infinite number of fools.
Let us take heaven for ourselves,
Fleeing to the niches in the rock.
Far from the world, etc.

35. Brave all things with courage,
Assuring eternity,
In spite of our poverty
And of our livid foes.
Far from the world, etc.

36. Dead to all, hidden within,
Distracted by nothing
Possessing the true Good,
We contemplate Supreme Beauty.
Far from the world, etc.

37. Dear soul, chaste turtledove,
Let us moan in this desert,
Let us sigh together,
Toward the God of eternal life.
Far from the world at this hermitage
Let us go into hiding to serve God.

GOD ALONE

## 158
## MOST BLESSED SACRAMENT

1. The Most High, the Incomprehensible
Is here enclosed in one dot.
Christians, let us not ask:
Is it possible? *(twice)*
Be quiet then my senses, be quiet, heretic,
You are mistaken,
You are lost;
God told us so.
No contradicting.
God told us so,
That is enough for us.
Let us believe, without explanation.

2. What miracles of power!
Bread and wine which are no more,
Accidents suspended
Without their substance; *(twice)*
The body, the blood of a God full of life and glory,
Without change
In all times,
In all places,
On earth, in the heavens,
In all places
As glorious.
Truth from God which must be believed!

3. O marvel of obedience!
At the voice of a mortal man,
God descends on the altar

Willingly; *(twice)*
He is dead and alive, docile and awesome.
He is child,
And triumphant,
Let us submit to one another,
Let us be all to all,
Let us submit to one another
Even at the feet of everyone,
Since God is so obliging.

4. Behold glory annihilated,
The sun of truth
Hidden in the obscurity
Of this host. *(twice)*
Under a simple exterior He hides His light,
He shows
Neither his power,
Nor His beauty,
Nor His holiness,
Nor His beauty,
Nor majesty,
Hide, O dust and ashes!

5. We see how much God loves us,
How passionately He loves
In this divine sacrament,
It is excess itself. *(twice)*
In giving all to us, He addresses us:
Take, eat me,
I am yours,
In my ecstasy,
Take all my treasures
In my ecstasy,
My body and blood.
Could He love us more?

AT MASS

6. Here is the perfect sacrifice,
Which contains all those of the Law
And which alone encloses
All righteousness. *(twice)*
A God immolates Himself to God as priest and victim
To appease Him,
To urge Him
To be gracious to us,

To pardon us,
To be gracious to us,
To crown us
And to render Him sublime honor.

AT THE SANCTUS

7. Three times holy the King of Glory!
Glory to our God three times holy,
To our God three times holy
Glory and victory!
Everything is full of the grandeurs of the great God of armies.
How great He is!
How powerful he is!
O Holiness!
O Immensity!
O Majesty!
O Eternity!
Adore, crowned heads!

AT THE AGNUS DEI

8. Lamb of God, mercy!
Lamb of God, Lord most kind!
Mercy and pardon,
Mercy! *(twice)*
Since you alone take away the sins of the world,
Take away, Lord
Those of my heart.
Pardon us
Pardon everyone,
Answer us;
For love of you,
Grant us profound peace!

BEFORE COMMUNION

9. The just man who receives communion
Becomes another Jesus Christ,
Filled with His spirit
And His life. *(twice)*
Let us eat this living bread, let us drink this wine of angels,
Frequently,
Piously.
Let us eat, let us drink,
And we will be filled.
Let us eat, let us drink

And we shall be inebriated,
And let us praise God.

10. I languish for love, I sigh
For you, my loving Savior,
Rush into my heart,
Or else I die *(twice)*
To be one minute without you is a hell most harsh.
O powerful King,
Reign in me;
O chaste spouse,
I hear only you
O dear spouse,
Come, hasten,
And be my happiness.

ACT OF REPARATION

11. Great God, how holy is this church,
Since it is your own house
And the house of prayer!
Let us tremble in awe. *(twice)*
This place saves the believer and condemns the ungodly.
Let us adore God
In this holy place;
We damn ourselves
If we chatter here,
We save ourselves
If we pray here,
Let us choose either death or life.

12. Let us make sincere reparation
To Jesus Christ dishonored
Even in this sacred place
So awesome. *(twice)*
To oppose the supreme Monarch in his palace,
What a crime
By ungrateful man!
Angels, weep,
Mortals, sigh,
Angels weep,
Weep, make amends for
This excess, this supreme insult.

BEFORE BENEDICTION

13. Praise, love, honor and glory

To Jesus in the most Blessed Sacrament
The more one sees His lowliness
The more one must believe; *(twice)*
If He loves us to excess, let us also love Him likewise.
Let us pay love
With a prompt return
Let us love and praise,
Let us praise and honor,
Let us love and praise,
Let us praise and adore
The majesty of a God who so loves us.

14. Suffer, great God that we approach you
And that poor criminals
Say to you by the altar:
Mercy! *(twice)*
Bless us, Lord, remove all the obstacles,
You can do it
If you wish.
It is a sinner
Weeping in his heart;
It is a sinner,
Forgive, Lord,
Forgive us, bless us, we will cry miracle.

GOD ALONE

## 159
## OUR LADY OF CONSOLATION

1. Vouvant, bless the Lord,
The Father of Light,
Who grants you a favor
Most spectacular:
The Queen of Heaven has set
Her throne among you.
She wills to defeat your enemies
And grant you her favors.

2. Pray, penitent sinners,
To your Mediatrix.

Invoke, little children,
Your nursing Mother.
Honor, good servants,
Your kind Mistress.
Let's all go to receive her favors,
She impels us to do so.

3. All consolation
For body and soul
Through my intercession,
Provided one asks for it.
I am, for the greatest ills,
An unfailing remedy;
In storm and in toil,
A welcome rest.

4. I am the all-powerful support
Of poor miserable souls,
And the ready remedy
Of incurable ills.
I am the sure refuge,
The salvation and life
Of the most desperate sinner,
As soon as he prays to me.

5. Implore, suffering souls,
My maternal kindness,
And you will be consoled
Here in my chapel.
Pray to me in your struggles
And you will be victorious.
Pray to me when you are laid low
And I will raise you up in glory.

6. Pray, poor people, consumed
By excessive taxes.
You will be unburdened
Without lawsuit.
Come, poor laborers
You will have a rich harvest.
But above all, come, poor sinners,
You will be treated with leniency.

7. Do you fear that the devil
Will deprive you of grace?

Have recourse to my holy name,
And I will destroy him.
When you are in his chains
You will be set free.
I have over him, even in hell,
All power.

8. TO THE VIRGINS:
Wise virgins, follow me.
Follow me into the temple.
Come receive the law,
The law of my example.
It is there that the Holy Spirit
Speaks to faithful virgins,
To form Jesus Christ in their hearts,
In the shadow of His wings.

9. Flee iniquity
And the world's lures
Which sully the purity
Of a fruitful virgin.
Stay away from the perils
And the sources of wrongdoing
To taste my Son's meekness
And accept His teaching.

10. Are you of very high rank?
Then do nothing base.
Your Spouse is bloodied,
Do not be weak.
Mortify your flesh,
Spend time in prayer,
Choose either hell's fire
Or Calvary's blood.

11. Courage, little flock,
Your Spouse prepares for you
A kingdom, totally new,
Extraordinary glory,
A magnificent robe,
A wondrous halo.
It will be yours, fight bravely,
Count on my word.

12. Virgins, I am here

Your perfect model,
My hand is molding you in God
And protecting you.
My womb brought you into light,
I have given you birth.
My heart fills you with love,
With love the most tender.

13. Whoever wishes to be mine
And receive my graces
Must take me for guide
And walk in my steps.
To love me, but not follow me,
Not leaving sin aside,
Is to perish, casting oneself
Into the depths of the abyss.

14. At the proper time, praise
And say my rosary,
Take my chain, wear
The habit of the scapular
But have no other intention
Than to imitate my life.
Otherwise, it is an evil trap,
Nothing but hypocrisy.

15. Not to be rejected
But to obtain help,
Pray humbly,
Perseveringly.
Knock, seek, ask for
Your basic needs.
Sooner or later you will be heard
Through your sincere prayers.

16. PRAYER:
Hasten, Queen of heaven,
Come to our assistance.
Look upon us tenderly,
Bestow healing on our ills,
You have the power to do so,
You are the Queen,
You have only to wish it,
And our sorrow disappears.

17. Above all, remember well,
O divine Mary,
There is nothing you refuse
To those who pray to you;
All generations
Have so proclaimed.
Permit, then, that on your goodness
Each one of us may rest.

GOD ALONE

18. It is I who form kings
It is I who crown them,
It is I who make their laws,
It is I who command them.
I make certain that my true followers
Have grace as their lot,
Treasures, pleasures and repose,
With glory as their heritage.

*(When this hymn was sung at Villiers, the following stanza was used)*
Dear people of Villiers,
Proclaim your glory!
Cry out unceasingly
Cry out: Victory
To Our Lady of Hearts
To your august Queen!
Let all proclaim today, all honor
Throughout this plain.

## 160
## LAUDATE DOMINUM OMNES, etc.

1. Christians, pagans and barbarians,
Praise the Lord, give praise to Him.
Sing in many different tongues
Of His mercy upon us.
He assures us of his tenderness
By filling us with his blessings.
He is faithful to his promises,

His truth reigns forevermore!

2. Glory to Jesus Christ through his Mother
On earth and in heaven,
At the right of God His Father,
And in the Blessed Sacrament of the Altar.
Honor, love, glory and praise
To the Father, Son and Holy Spirit,
By all the saints, by all the angels,
Through Jesus Christ, forevermore!

GOD ALONE.

## 161
## SPECIFIC REMEDY FOR LUKEWARMNESS

1. The discipline
Is medicinal.
Let each one strike his back
To the bone, *(twice)*
Let each one strike, strike, strike
To the bone, *(twice)*
It's therapy for all ills.

2. To this remedy
Hell surrenders.
When you strike your flesh, you strike
All hell, *(twice)*
Strike, strike, strike, strike
All hell. *(twice)*
Strike, that you may triumph.

3. Your insolent flesh
Likes to tempt you.
Strike it with all your strength
And you will overcome. *(twice)*
Strike, strike, strike, strike
And you will overcome. *(twice)*
Strike, do not hold back.

4. If you grow drowsy

Your flesh wakes up,
Strike and you'll not sleep.
Doublet lowered, *(twice)*
Strike, strike, strike, strike.
Doublet lowered, *(twice)*
Strike and you'll wake up.

5. Do you want fame
And victory?
Strike your body vigorously,
Strike hard *(twice)*
Strike, strike, etc.
Strike hard, *(twice)*
Strike this body of death.

6. All illnesses
Are cured by it.
Strike, it dispels moods
And also pain. *(twice)*
Strike, strike, etc.
And also pain, *(twice)*
For all yields to its rigor.

7. You flatter yourself,
Delicate flesh.
Satan strikes the lazy
In the fires. *(twice)*
Satan strikes, strikes, strikes
In the fires, *(twice)*
Those never striking their backs.

8. Soul, carnal
And criminal,
Strike to put out the fire.
So little to ask. *(twice)*
Strike, strike, etc.
So little to ask. *(twice)*
Strike and God is disarmed.

9. Innocent soul,
Strike and sing
The *Miserere* on your back,
To the bone. *(twice)*
Strike, strike, etc.
To the bone, *(twice)*

Strike up to *vitulos.*

GOD ALONE

## 162
## HOLY JOURNEY

1. DEAR company
Marching cheerfully *(twice)*
And so piously,
Tell us, I beg you,
The goal you seek,
Giving you such joy. *(twice)*

*2.* *RESPONSE:*
We seek life,
Glory and peace *(twice)*
Which lasts for ever.
Aren't you jealous?
Come along with us,
And we'll all possess it. *(twice)*

3. Choose then war for yourself,
Soldier and sergeant *(twice)*
Choose money for yourself,
Men glued to mud and dirt.
As for us, most joyfully
We are winning Heaven. *(twice)*

4. Worldly man at the dance,
Drunkard with great wine, *(twice)*
Gourmand at the feast,
At pleasure, at revelry;
As for us, most joyfully
We are going to Heaven. *(twice)*

5. Merchant, at the market,
Trying to make money
Without sparing yourself,
So you'll get rich and drink well.
As for us, very joyfully,

We are winning heaven.

6. Go to the army,
Men of high rank
Shed your blood
For an illusion of glory.
As for us, very joyfully,
We are going to heaven.

7. Seek, filthy beast,
As much as you desire,
Goods and pleasures,
And worldly honors.
As for us, very joyfully,
We are seeking heaven.

8. Seek a mirage,
A dream in the night
A fleeting shadow,
A dot, a speck.
For us, very joyfully,
We are seeking heaven.

9. We are seeking grace,
The rest is nothing,
Not even a good,
Since it hoodwinks then fades.
As for us, etc.
We are seeking heaven

10. Hoard, you miser,
Laugh, you bons vivants,
Climb higher, upper-class.
Such fools are common.
As for us, etc.

11. The earth is covered
With numerous fools
Who do as you do,
Rushing only to their doom.
As for us, etc.

12. Pursue illusions,
Store up manure,
Gain the entire world.

What gain, if the soul is damned!
As for us, etc.

13. Universal loss:
To lose one's Savior,
To lose one's happiness
To lose eternal life.
As for us, etc.

14. Our immortal soul
Is made for God,
Earth is too little;
For others this trinket!
As for us, etc.

15. Our only task
Is our salvation,
That is our goal,
Our only business.
As for us, etc.

16. We are seeking Mary,
We are seeking Jesus,
Jesus and nothing else.
That is glory and life.
Come along with us,
And we'll all possess it.

17. No other good
But humility.
Our poverty
Is our abundance.
As for us, etc.

18. Glory is had
By humbling ourselves.
Through obedience,
Total victory is ours.
As for us, etc.

19. Our savoir-faire
Is all in the Cross.
We are kings,
But only on Calvary.

# 163
# FERVOR'S GOAD or ALARM CLOCK OF THE MISSION

DEAR INHABITANTS OF SAINT POMPAIN

1. My dear family, my dear neighbor
   Let's all get up very early
   God calls us to his banquet;
   Let's seek grace,
   Let it snow, let it freeze,
   Let's seek grace and love divine.

2. Despite the fire, despite the impasse,
   Despite the cold, despite the frost,
   Despite the moaning of the flesh,
   Let's seek grace,
   Let it storm, let it freeze,
   Let's seek grace, and spite hell.

3. The whole household is against it,
   The devil howls and the flesh advises:
   Stay by the fire, stay in bed!
   Let us seek grace,
   Let it ice, let it freeze,
   Let's seek the grace of Jesus Christ.

4. Leave Martha to her fussing,
   Leave the frail in bed,
   Let's march, heaven counts our steps.
   Let's seek grace,
   Let it drizzle, let it freeze,
   Let's seek grace, faithful soldiers.

5. Quit your work, plowman,
   Settle your case, plaintiff.
   Renounce your sins, sinner,
   Seek my grace,
   Let it drizzle let it freeze,
   Seek my grace, thus says the Lord.

6. Ask, says God, you will receive,

Seek and you will find,
Knock and you will enter.
Seek my grace,
Let it snow, let it freeze,
Seek my grace and you'll find it.

7. Carpenter, for a while, leave your wood,
Locksmith, quit your anvil,
Laborer, put aside your work.
Let us seek grace,
Let it thunder, let it freeze,
Let's seek grace, give no quarter.

8. Let's go, let's go, great and small,
And let's not be sluggish.
We seek infinite goods.
Let us seek grace,
Let it rain, let it freeze,
Let's seek grace and Paradise.

9. It's heaven we must bargain for,
The port where we must dock,
The blessing we must beg.
Let us seek grace,
Let it ice, Let it freeze,
Let's seek grace without delay.

10. To arrive at this port,
Let's battle well and fear no toil.
Let's sail on, rowing hard.
Let's seek grace,
Let it snow, let it freeze,
Let's seek grace until we die.

11. Let's get moving, lazy people,
Even though the church be far,
Let's seek grace the best we can.
Let's seek grace,
Let it drizzle, let it freeze,
Let's seek grace, let's buy heaven.

12. Wake up, sleepy people,
Let's seek, in spite of foes,
Forgiveness for our sins.
Let's seek grace,

Let it drizzle, let it freeze,
Let's seek grace, my dear friends.

13. Let's go listen to the Savior,
He's speaking through a preacher
And yearns to touch our heart.
Let's seek grace,
Which speaks and passes,
Let's seek grace and true joy.

14. Let's go to the mission
To obtain remission,
Despite the world and hell.
Let's seek grace
Which speaks and passes
Let's seek grace, to the sermon we go.

15. If it's hard to get there,
Paradise is well worth it;
Let's cheer each other on.
Let's seek grace
Which speaks and passes,
Let's seek grace, God will bless us.

16. Let's then seek heaven with all our might,
Let's seek only its glory,
Rising to heaven, to the skies,
Right up to the Crown.
Let it storm, let it thunder,
Up to the Crown, eternally!

## 164
## CALVARY OF PONTCHATEAU

1. Alas! The Turk still holds Blessed Calvary
Where Jesus Christ has died.
Christians, we must erect one here.
Let's build a Calvary here,
Let's build a Calvary.

2. Let us possess this holy hill,

By a divine rapture,
In our heart and in our countryside.
Let's build a Calvary here,
Let's build a Calvary.

3. Great people have done all they could
To recover that holy place.
Let us have it here with no crusade or war.
Let's build a Calvary here,
Let's build a Calvary.

4. Shall Our Lord and God,
Be left in disgrace
Who through love gave us His life?
Let's build a Calvary here,
Let's build a Calvary.

5. Shall we leave Jesus in the dust?
No, No, fervent Christians,
Let us go to great lengths to place him in light.
Let's build a Calvary here,
Let's build a Calvary.

6. He is mocked by Jews and heretics,
The Turks and all the pagans,
Above all by bad Catholics.
Let's build a Calvary here,
Let's build a Calvary.

7. *(THERE IS NO STANZA 7)*

8. Let us recapture the holy places,
Not by violence but by copying them;
Despite the weather, the trouble and expense,
Let's build a Calvary here,
Let's build a Calvary.

9. O! What marvels we shall see in this place!
What conversions,
Healings, graces without compare.
Let's build a Calvary here,
Let's build a Calvary.

10. O! how many people will journey here,
How many processions

To see Jesus and offer Him worship,
Let's build a Calvary here,
Let's build a Calvary.

11. Let us set Him on the cross to remind us
Of His passion and His death;
For our good and His greatest glory,
Let's build a Calvary here,
Let's build a Calvary.

12. On this cross He will calm His Father,
Vanquish the demon
And receive our hopes and prayers.
Let's build a Calvary here,
Let's build a Calvary.

13. Let us plant the Cross, it is the faithful Spouse,
It is the royal throne
Of the King of kings, the eternal Wisdom.
Let's build a Calvary here,
Let's build a Calvary.

14. For the gentiles, it is folly
And for the Jews, scandal
But for Christians, wisdom and life.
Let's build a Calvary here,
Let's build a Calvary.

15. This mystery is our only model,
The cure for all ills,
The treasure of heaven and earth.
Let's build a Calvary here,
Let's build a Calvary.

16. For a long time, Jesus, I have wanted
To raise you on high,
To attract all hearts to your empire.
Let's build a Calvary here,
Let's build a Calvary.

17. Jesus on the cross, may your kingdom come,
It's time, it's time.
That all may adore and follow you
Let's build a Calvary here,
Let's build a Calvary.

18. Mount the cross, raise yourself on high,
For we are powerless,
We shall sing of your supreme power.
Let's build a Calvary here,
Let's build a Calvary.

19. JESUS:
Yes, I will it, it glorifies me,
And from the height of the cross
I shall proclaim victory in this holy place.
Build my Calvary here,
Build my Calvary.

20. I will attract the most rebellious hearts,
Everyone will obey my law.
I shall heal the most deadly wounds.
Let's build a Calvary here,
Let's build a Calvary.

21. Work, everyone, my power is immense,
I am working with you.
And I shall be most grateful.
Let's build, etc.

22. (ALL SHOUT TOGETHER):
Let us all work on this divine project,
God will bless us all,
Great and small, men and women of all ages,
Let's build a Calvary to God,
Let's build a Calvary.

# *GENERAL ANALYTICAL TABLE*

*The numbers refer to the number of the hymn*